Protean Power

Exploring the Uncertain and Unexpect

Mainstream international relations continues to assume that the world is governed by calculable risk based on estimates of power, despite repeatedly being surprised by unexpected change. This groundbreaking work departs from existing definitions of power that focus on the actors' evolving ability to exercise control in situations of calculable risk. It introduces the concept of "protean power," which focuses on the actors' agility as they adapt to situations of uncertainty. *Protean Power* uses twelve real-world case studies to examine how the dynamics of protean and control power can be tracked in the relations among different state and non-state actors, operating in diverse sites, stretching from local to global, in both times of relative normalcy and moments of crisis. Katzenstein and Seybert argue for a new approach to international relations, where the inclusion of protean power in our analytical models helps in accounting for unforeseen changes in world politics.

Peter J. Katzenstein has served as President of the American Political Science Association and is a member of the American Academy of Arts and Science, the American Philosophical Society, and the British Academy. He has been the recipient of the Helen Dwight Reid Award, the Woodrow Wilson prize for the best book published in the United States on international affairs, and the Masayoshi Ohira Memorial Prize as well as five honorary degrees of European and Chinese universities. He has taught at Cornell for over forty years.

Lucia A. Seybert is a Professorial Lecturer at American University, School of International Service. She is a former Title VIII Research Scholar at the Woodrow Wilson Center and a recipient of a number of research grants and fellowships, including from the American Council of Learned Societies.

Cambridge Studies in International Relations: 146

Cambridge Studies in International Relations is a joint initiative of Cambridge University Press and the British International Studies Association (BISA). The series aims to publish the best new scholarship in international studies, irrespective of subject matter, methodological approach or theoretical perspective. The series seeks to bring the latest theoretical work in International Relations to bear on the most important problems and issues in global politics.

Cambridge Studies in International Relations

Series list continues after index.

Protean Power

Exploring the Uncertain and Unexpected in World Politics

Edited by

Peter J. Katzenstein
Cornell University, New York

Lucia A. Seybert
American University, Washington DC

CAMBRIDGE
UNIVERSITY PRESS

CAMBRIDGE
UNIVERSITY PRESS

University Printing House, Cambridge CB2 8BS, United Kingdom

One Liberty Plaza, 20th Floor, New York, NY 10006, USA

477 Williamstown Road, Port Melbourne, VIC 3207, Australia

314–321, 3rd Floor, Plot 3, Splendor Forum, Jasola District Centre, New Delhi – 110025, India

79 Anson Road, #06–04/06, Singapore 079906

Cambridge University Press is part of the University of Cambridge.

It furthers the University's mission by disseminating knowledge in the pursuit of education, learning, and research at the highest international levels of excellence.

www.cambridge.org
Information on this title: www.cambridge.org/9781108425179
DOI: 10.1017/9781108597456

First published 2018

Printed in the United Kingdom by Clays, St Ives plc

A catalogue record for this publication is available from the British Library.

ISBN 978-1-108-42517-9 Hardback
ISBN 978-1-108-44125-4 Paperback

For

Lucia

and

Livia, Michal, Darian, and Leon

Contents

Figures and Tables

Figures

Tables

Contributors

RAWI ABDELAL, Herbert F. Johnson Professor of International Management, Harvard Business School.

PETER ANDREAS, John Hay Professor of International Studies and Political Science, Political Science and Watson Institute, Brown University, Providence, RI.

PHILLIP M. AYOUB, Assistant Professor, Political Science, Drexel University, Philadelphia, PA.

NOELLE K. BRIGDEN, Assistant Professor, Political Science, Marquette University, Milwaukee, WI.

JENNIFER L. ERICKSON, Associate Professor of Political Science and International Studies, Boston College.

JESSICA F. GREEN, Assistant Professor, Environmental Studies, New York University.

PETER J. KATZENSTEIN, Walter S. Carpenter, Jr. Professor of International Studies, Government Department, Cornell University, Ithaca, NY.

ERIN LOCKWOOD, Assistant Professor, Political Science, University of California, Irvine, CA.

BARAK MENDELSOHN, Associate Professor, Political Science, Haverford College, Haverford, PA.

STEPHEN NELSON, Associate Professor, Political Science, Northwestern University, Evanston, IL.

CHRISTIAN REUS-SMIT, Professor, School of Political Science and International Studies, University of Queensland.

LUCIA A. SEYBERT, Professorial Lecturer, School of International Service, American University, Washington DC.

Preface

In large lecture halls and small seminars, students ask the hard questions. Why do big changes so often catch their teachers unprepared? Why did the Cold War end (peacefully)? Why did the world economy come so close to falling off the cliff in 2008? Why did the Arab Spring of 2011 represent such surprise, hope, and disappointment? Policymakers have strong intuitions but no clear answers. For example, Roger Altman, former Deputy Secretary of Treasury under President Bill Clinton, writes that on all major economic questions "unpredictability may be the new normal."[1] The US National Defense University posted an opening for a new job in 2016. It aims at training leaders who can "operate and creatively think in an unpredictable and complex world." In writing this book we seek to provide better answers for our students. We follow Stanley Hoffmann, always a teacher's teacher, who studied power "so as to understand the enemy, not so as better to be able to exert it."[2]

Confronted with the probing questions of their students and the strong intuitions of policy practitioners, scholars of world politics offer unsatisfactory answers, typically issued with the benefit of 20/20 hindsight. When pressed, they sound unconvincing, perhaps even to themselves, while claiming that momentous changes are just small data points in a very large universe of events. Alternatively, they concede that the causes of unexpected, large-scale change are exogenous to their theories of world politics, a fancy acknowledgment of the obvious: they are often blindsided by the unexpected.

Greek mythology offers a way out. The first-born of Poseidon, legend has it, Proteus, was able to tell the future, once captured. Preferring freedom, Proteus changed his shape as soon as he was seen. Inconstant with his affections in Shakespeare's *The Two Gentlemen of Verona*, Proteus entered the world of English letters half a century before Hobbes wrote his masterful analysis of the all-powerful *Leviathan*. This book's cover

---

[1] Altman 2016.   [2] Grimes 2015.

summarizes its central point: Proteus and Leviathan, together, help us understand better the unexpected in world politics.

This book extends an invitation to scholars and practitioners of power in domestic and world politics to incorporate uncertainty into a more complex analysis of power dynamics. This change in perspective does not enhance our predictive accuracy. But it adds depth of understanding and a fuller explication of how power arises, operates, and dissipates in situations that are both risky and uncertain.

Protean power is the name we give to the results of actions by agile actors who are coping with the uncertainty that bedevils and frustrates a multitude of Leviathans exercising control under assumed conditions of risk. In contrast to relatively predictable control power, protean power stems from processes that are "versatile" or "tending and able to change frequently and easily."[3] Protean power emerges in uncertain contexts often experienced as such, when previous performance does not provide a reliable foundation for future moves. Although protean power follows from intentional actions, the outcomes of those actions are unforeseen and unforeseeable at the outset. Rather than emerging as a competing force, protean power is often closely related to and co-evolves with control power.

Power has causal impact in world politics. But power is also an outcome that needs to be explained. Protean power responds to and deepens unanticipated change, and is often a response to crises that catch everyone by surprise. Creative moves and their power effects can alter basic rules of the game and leap over or circumvent deeply grooved pathways of control power. Protean power stops us from assuming away the unknown. Instead, it makes us focus on how actors handle the unexpected with improvisation and innovation, deepening uncertainty as they go along. "Viral" manifestations of protean power invite attentive actors to adopt and normalize emergent innovations, converting what was once a novelty into best practice, and eventually an attribute of control power. Often, control and protean power processes unfold in variegated and complex relationships that are difficult to disentangle empirically. Nothing about protean power is inevitable; all of it is unpredictable. Its signature in world politics is real. Scholars of world politics have missed it largely because they have not looked.[4] The blinders limiting the analysis of power are both individual and institutional. When we presented our work at the 2016 Annual Meetings of the American Political Science Association,

---

[3] *Oxford Advanced Learner's Dictionary.*

[4] The same general answer, but without explicit mention of power, was suggested by Ted Hopf in his exchange with John Gaddis about the Cold War's peaceful end. Hopf and Gaddis 1993.

the menu of available keywords to characterize our paper included an entry for "risk"; "uncertainty" was not an option.

The dynamics of protean and control power can be tracked in the relations among different state and non-state actors, operating in diverse sites, stretching from local to global, both in times of relative normalcy and moments of crisis. Since crises offer compelling illustrations for the relevance of protean power, we use them here in two brief sketches to elaborate on our central point in different empirical domains and across different levels of analysis.

The ongoing instability in eastern Ukraine serves as background for a first thought experiment. Risk-based, control-power arguments focus on causal stories showing what actors set out to accomplish and whether they succeeded as well as how and why. They seek to answer questions such as: who sparked the conflict and what were these actors trying to achieve? How effective was the two sides' framing of their respective claims to legitimacy? What was the extent of Russia's involvement at various points in time? But they also ask questions about the diffusion of control power in Europe. What is the impact on the security of states along the European Union's periphery? How is Russia's position in the former Soviet Union and its satellites affected? Implicitly or explicitly, such questions emphasize control power's operation through compulsion and the constraints of institutions, structures, and discourses.[5]

Plausible though they are, all these lines of inquiry are incomplete in disregarding how actors improvise as they face unknown unknowns and how improvised approaches actualize power potentialities and create new ones that we label protean. In fact, there is as much guessing as there is prediction, including worst-case scenario thinking that can drive actors away from experimentation and into war. Introducing uncertainty as a relevant context and experience and incorporating protean power dynamics suggests different questions. What specific actions or behaviors changed the rules of the game and produced unexpected outcomes? How did they coincide with broader processes enabling power potentialities that escalated into uncontrollable crisis? To what extent were actors aware of the underlying uncertainty, and did they abandon established ways of coping as a result? In post-transition, post-Orange Revolution Ukrainian politics, the rules governing order and defining power hierarchies became extraordinarily fluid. Prisoners became prime ministers, prime ministers prisoners. Improvisation and innovation, but also affirmation and refusal by Ukrainian residents of annexed Crimea, became the new normal. In the midst of the turmoil surrounding suspected

[5] Barnett and Duvall 2005.

Russian troop presence in the contested eastern region of Ukraine, commanders of separatist militias justified their reason for existence by means that brought down a civilian jetliner flying at high altitude changing everyone's exposure to uncertainty.[6] On the ground, an elderly woman carrying a hen from Ukraine to newly separate Crimea over the heavily guarded border left a customs officer speechless when she declared the bird her pet, not poultry violating an export restriction.[7] Protean power allows agile actors to handle the uncertain.

Our second sketch examines power dynamics operating across different levels of analysis. For decades the Mediterranean has been a path for migrants to Europe. The issue gained sudden urgency when in 2015 refugees from the Syrian civil war began streaming in unprecedented numbers across EU borders. The control power differential between the countries receiving them and the individuals flooding in could not have been greater. One side possessed economic wealth, relative stability, and political clout in the form of immigration regulations, border police and, later, barbed wire fences. These tools and institutions of control were met by refugees of all ages and backgrounds who often lacked travel documentation and personal belongings. Their actual capabilities to *power over* the hurdles they were meeting was non-existent. And yet the relentlessness with which they progressed, their determination in walking, for example, from Budapest to the Austrian border when train connections were severed, reveals potential capacities and a *power to* do something. The radical uncertainty this created led to still further improvisation by other actors. Lacking control power themselves, many ordinary Europeans not only facilitated the improvising moves by Syrian migrants but devised innovative strategies of their own, like developing useful smartphone apps or shuttling stranded refugees across state borders, bypassing state-imposed obstacles and avaricious smugglers.[8]

In terms of power relations it is next to impossible to draw a clear distinction between improvising and innovative refugees and their supporters, on the one hand, and governments seeking to enforce rules and exercising control, on the other. In fact, when faced with uncertainty governments also generate protean power effects at all levels of policymaking and implementation. We refer to this process as the circulation of protean power – *a priori* no specific actor is more likely to wield it or claim to have it. Extraordinary situations can require extraordinary measures. In taking a moral stance and a leap of faith when welcoming a torrent of

---

[6] Harding and Luhn 2016.   [7] Interview with Tetyana Sydorenko, April 2016.
[8] Dewast and Chaturvedi 2015.

refugees, the German chancellor and the Canadian prime minister were not acting on any expectation of probable gain. Numbers simply could not be known when refugees were still getting off boats, trains and planes. And reactions of the public added another element of uncertainty. Ultimately, any agile actor can produce outcomes that rearrange the playing field in ways that no one could have imagined. Traditional accounts of control power say little about such decentralized, uncoordinated, but highly impactful dynamics.

Ever since James Scott named them, it has become intuitively plausible to highlight the weapons of the weak when tracing how decentralized improvisation and innovation generates protean power.[9] The core of protean power lies in agility and the circulation of power potentialities rather than specific attributes, like social position or material capabilities and systems of rules so central to the exercise of control power. It may not be their default reaction in predictable environments when the capability to dominate weaker actors is routine business. But despite their large bureaucratic apparatus, governments and international organizations, too, have the capacity to adjust to uncertainty, and on occasion even to embrace it. What matters, we argue, is not only the asymmetric distribution of control power but also the navigational agility and mobilization of power potentials that go hand in hand with protean power effects. Equal in importance to Hobbes, the power theorist of those effects is Machiavelli. As a scientist and rigorous theorist, Hobbes focuses on what power is and what it can cause. As an astute observer of practice, Machiavelli highlights what power does and how it creates effects. Both insights are indispensable for an understanding of the profound interrelation, co-evolution, even co-constitution of control and protean power in the domains of risk and uncertainty.

For Peter Katzenstein this project started at Cornell University, Ithaca, in spring 2008 when the financial crisis became evident to all who cared to look. Since he remembered that the last financial crisis had led to disastrous consequences for his native Germany, Europe and the world, he sensed that this one, too, would have momentous consequences. A series of co-authored papers (with Stephen Nelson) helped him to grapple with the normalcy of crisis in the world of finance and the concept of Knightian uncertainty – learning to his delight that Frank Knight developed this important idea in his 1916 Cornell dissertation. Following a vague hunch, PK also started research on the American film industry – aware that in the early twentieth century Ithaca was an important production center of America's movie industry. As in finance, in film America looms very

[9] Scott 1985.

large while lacking any sense of exercising control over unpredictable markets. Furthermore, since Hobbesian control power is of little help in making sense of the dynamics of popular culture, he saw an opening for learning more about technologies of constraint and mobility operating in fluid cultural fields.[10] Stephen Nelson's initial bibliography provided an excellent start. A colleague and leading scholar of the film industry, Aida Hozic, became a source of inspiration, advice and support. PK published his preliminary ideas on power as an epilogue in a book that some of his former students had put together.[11]

The initial draft paper on the movie industry grew as it went through many iterations. Lucia Seybert became its second author and, eventually, this book's second editor and co-author of five chapters. Her earliest political memories were formed during the surprisingly non-violent dis-solution of Czechoslovakia. Later, in studying the less-than-uniform spread of international norms, many of them in the context of the enlar-gement of the European Union in 2004, she learned not to take even the most likely of outcomes for granted. A separate course of unexpected events drove her to appreciate uncertainty not necessarily as an obstacle and not inevitably as an opportunity but as a fact of life. At one stage, PK teased her for noticing protean power even when pouring a glass of milk.

With such a wide-angle lens, the initial draft paper soon became ever more unwieldy. It eventually dawned on us that we were writing not one paper but two – an empirical one on film and a theoretical one on power. Sensing that we were onto something, a few years later we decided to reconceive these two papers as the nucleus of a book. In book format we could elaborate and deepen our theoretical argument beyond what a journal article could accommodate. And with the help of others we could extend the empirical reach of our argument into a substantial number of important political domains. After innumerable drafts, this book has temporarily found its final shape. Since social science disci-plines are partly defined by unending disagreements about their core constructs – capital in economics, status in sociology, and value in anthropology come to mind – this inquiry into the nature of power is only one chapter of a never-ending story in the analysis of politics that is bound to be superseded soon by other and hopefully better ones.

We could not have completed this project successfully without our collaborators, friends and colleagues – many of them with close connec-tions to Cornell. In three workshops they constantly pushed us to rethink our half-baked ideas. The collaborative process of joint discovery and

---

[10] Greenblatt 1990: 225.   [11] Katzenstein 2014.

clarification was scholarship at its very best, exhilarating, illuminating, and joyful – we hope not just for the two of us.

We received useful suggestions, criticisms, encouragements, and careful comments from many colleagues. Most of our readers were letting us know that versions of the initial paper were, at best, producing smoke (in the form of hot air); they concluded that there was no fire. Many asked why we were introducing still another concept of power. The conventional one after all had served pretty well for centuries. And many recent ones were faddish diversions that added heat rather than light to scholarly discussions. We recall, then with consternation, now with amusement, the time when one sympathetic critic and close friend made liberal use of the track-change function to help us clear an early draft paper of its underbrush and, with the best of intentions, trimmed away everything we wanted to say about protean power. Several years later we took comfort, when another colleague, a specialist on Aristotle no less, having listened to the core argument, reacted by simply nodding her head and saying "of course." We knew then that the finish line was in sight.

We have no interest in starting a school of thought or articulating a unifying theory of power. Instead, we are locating with this book a vantage point that permits us to recognize connections previously concealed by deeply engrained habits of thought that leave too many of us simply dumbfounded and speechless when the unexpected happens.

We are deeply in debt to Stefano Guzzini for his lengthy and penetrating comments on several drafts of Chapters 2 and 3; Aida Hozic and Stephen Nelson for their never-ending, important pointers and encouragement, offered from very different vantage points; and David Lake for his sympathetically critical commentaries and generous tutoring on some of the finer details of an approach to international political economy that he favors and we criticize in Chapter 2.

For their critical comments and helpful suggestions on earlier drafts of Chapters 1 and 2 we also thank Rawi Abdelal, Yuen Yuen Ang, David Baldwin, Michael Barnett, Felix Berenskoetter, Jacqueline Best, Benjamin Jerry Cohen, Mark Dallas, James Davis, Matthew Evangelista, Jill Frank, Peter Gourevitch, Victoria de Grazia, Linus Hagström, Roger Haydon, John Ikenberry, Jeffrey Isaac, P. T. Jackson, Miles Kahler, Robert Keohane, Jonathan Kirshner, Stephen D. Krasner, David Laitin, David Lake, Lukas Linsi, Kathleen McNamara, Barak Mendelsohn, Toby Miller, Henry Nau, Stephen Nelson, Daniel Nexon, Joseph Nye, Benoît Pelopidas, Galia Press-Barnathan, Christian Reus-Smit, Leonard Seabrooke, Rudra Sil, Etel Solingen, Sidney Tarrow, Daniel Thomas, Alexander Wendt, Anna Wojciuk, Cornelia Woll, David

Yoffie, and the participants of panels at the Annual Meetings of the International Studies Association (2013, 2016) and the American Political Science Association (2014–2016), the Foresight Lecture Fireside Chat at the University of Potsdam, and seminars hosted by the BGIE unit of the Harvard Business School, the International Relations section of the Science Center Berlin, the London School of Economics, the Max-Planck Institute in Cologne, the Cornell Government Department IR Faculty Seminar, Columbia University, the University of Queensland and Leiden University.

We received a careful reading of our full-throated criticism of international relations scholarship on questions of security and political economy in Chapter 2 from Judith Kelley, Sarah Kreps, David Lake, Andrew Little, Tom Pepinsky, Barbara Walters, Jessica Weeks, and members of the Cornell IR Faculty Seminar. The section on political theory in Chapter 13 benefitted enormously from PK's co-teaching, in a manner of speaking, a seminar on power in political theory and international relations with his colleague Professor Jill Frank in fall 2016. We received insightful comments and suggestions on a draft of that section of Chapter 13 from Jill Frank, Stefano Guzzini, Jason Frank, Alexander Livingston, and Anna Wojciuk who, in addition, debriefed and tutored PK in weekly, post-seminar sessions over hot chocolate and the occasional cookie.

We thank Jacqueline Larson for her first-rate editing of our prose in an early version of parts of Chapters 1 and 2; Sarah Tarrow for her once again supreme skill at preparing a book manuscript for submission; and, at Cambridge University Press, John Haslam for his consistent interest and unfailing support, Robert Judkins for his efficient management, and Lyn Flight for her care and attention. PK also thanks Emma Clarke, Akhilesh Issur, Rachel Mitnick, Julia Saltzman, and Kirat Singh for their excellent research assistance.

PK dedicates this book to Lucia who has met the unfathomable uncertainties of her life with incomparable courage and grace. LS dedicates this book to Livia Antalova and Michal Daniel, who have her back in all uncertainty, and to Darian and Leon, who it is all for.

Peter Katzenstein
Ithaca, August 2017

Lucia Seybert
Washington DC, August 2017

Part 1

Theory

1   Protean Power and Control Power: Conceptual Analysis

Lucia A. Seybert and Peter J. Katzenstein

In 2016, the Director of National Intelligence told the Senate Armed Service Committee that "unpredictable instability" is the new normal.[1] But is this a *new* normal? After all, surprises have been far from rare in world politics. Mere weeks before the outbreak of the Bolshevik Revolution in February 1917, Lenin predicted that the Russian revolution would come only after his death. Unexpected peoples' revolutions toppled regimes in Asia in the 1980s; ended the Cold War in 1989; led to the breakup of the Soviet Union in 1991; and convulsed the Middle East during the Arab Spring of 2010–12. In 2016, voters in Britain and the United States handed the incumbent parties and their neoliberal programs stingingly unexpected defeats. And we were similarly unprepared in recent years for the financial crises of 1997 and 2008; Al Qaeda's and ISIS's entry onto the international security landscape; tidal waves of migrants heading for developed regions' southern borders; and the social changes brought about by radical innovations in science and technology. How do we make sense of the unexpected in world politics?

In answering this question, scholars scramble to recalculate power configurations and alignments, point to distinct forms of control, such as soft power[2] and discursive framing,[3] or simply invoke exogenous change as the source of puzzling surprise.[4] Steadfastly, they hold on to the assumption that the world is dominated by calculable risk. If only we could accurately map and measure all of the different components of power, we would know the probabilities of outcomes, at least in principle. Unexpected change is typically thought of as part of the diffusion of the power to control events and peoples. This is an old trope of international relations scholarship. Harvard professor and power theorist Joseph Nye restates the insights of liberals and realists like Ray Vernon and Susan Strange from decades past: power is diffusing away from states to a kaleidoscope of non-state actors.[5] Repeating Henry Kissinger's arguments

---

[1] Garamone 2016.   [2] Nye 2011.   [3] Haas 2002; Price 1998.
[4] Krasner 1984; Streeck and Thelen 2005.   [5] Nye 2011: 118–22.

3

from the late 1960s, a former head of Policy Planning under President George W. Bush and the current President of the Council on Foreign Relations, Richard Haass, concurs: "Power is more distributed in more hands than at any time in history."[6] Although the diffusion of power is often not aligned with the interests of political actors accustomed to exercising control, it is a relatively orderly and predictable process that lends itself to social scientific analysis.[7] Rationality points to the feasibility of controlling legible, linear history. And this model of a "general linear reality" writes Andrew Abbott, "has come to influence our actual construing of social reality."[8] We put the unexpected aside at the cost of being tripped up by it time and time again.

This failing, we argue, has two roots. An exclusive focus on existing control power capabilities overlooks the actualization of potential capacities that mark what we call here protean power.[9] We define protean power as the effect of improvisational and innovative responses to uncertainty that arise from actors' creativity and agility in response to uncertainty. Furthermore, the assumption that the world is governed only by risk overlooks the pervasiveness of uncertainties not amenable to probability calculations. The result is to underline the efficacy of control power and slight the importance of protean power. Unexpected changes or shocks are not exogenous to how power relations unfold, but to how our theories depict them. The actualization of potential power capacities in conditions of uncertainty always loom. Machiavelli is not alone in reminding us of the importance of chance in the affairs of states. Actors at the front lines of financial, humanitarian, energy, environmental, and other political crises routinely acknowledge the pervasive intermingling of the known and unknown, and direct our sight to potentialities in the shaping of power dynamics.[10] The fluidity of those dynamics is what prompted former President Obama to echo Thucydides by invoking "hope in the face of uncertainty."[11]

Our argument embraces the usefulness of risk-based power calculations in many situations. At the same time, we must take account of the

---

[6] Haass 2017: 11.

[7] It is, therefore, understandable that diffusion has become an important subject of study in international relations, political science, and the social sciences. See Graham, Shipan, and Volden 2014.

[8] Abbott 1988: 169.

[9] "Protean" derives from the sea god Proteus in Greek mythology who had shape-changing capacities. We thank Lukas Linsi who pushed us to adopt a term that, according to Google Books, is quite common in many fields of scholarship though not in the analysis of world politics.

[10] Rumsfeld 2011.

[11] Obama 2016. In the Melian Dialogue the Athenians call "hope danger's comforter." Strauss 2008: 353 (5.103).

existence of uncertainty that is experienced as familiar by most international actors. The power to control thus must always be viewed in its relation to protean power, which is not a mere appendage of control power. Instead, it can pass from potentiality to actuality in a flash, changing power's terrain, often dramatically. Effects of actions in contexts of risks, experienced as such, can be understood in terms of control power; effects of actions in contexts of uncertainty, experienced as such, in terms of protean power. The two kinds of power co-exist and co-evolve.

How, for example, was it possible for the Berlin Wall to fall? The answer to this question encapsulates our central point: the confluence of two different kinds of power. Mary Sarotte focuses on the accidental nature of the Wall's opening. Her analysis stresses the agency of local actors and historical contingency such as the misreading of a list of government instructions that was handed to a government spokesman named Günter Schabowski during a press conference on the evening of November 9, 1989.[12] That mistake permitted people to stream across a border that had been hermetically sealed for a generation. This constituted a heartening, though rare, event of citizens disarming peacefully a repressive regime. People power as the actualization of protean potentialities was one part of the story. Diplomatic and financial control power was the other. During the 1980s, economic power drained away from East Berlin as the GDR leadership became dependent on Western capital. Lacking sufficient productivity gains in manufacturing to serve the escalating cost of its debts, the unforeseen collapse of the price of oil in 1985 sharply reduced earnings from the GDR's most important export product, mineral oil refined from Soviet crude.[13] Gorbachev's reform program in the Soviet Union put additional pressure on the East German government. East Germany's leadership faced only unappealing options: sharp reductions in living standards or blood on the streets. Permitting emigration in the hope of further West German loans with lenient conditions thus became the preferred policy that the government planned to adopt before the end of 1989. While the specific details of what happened on the night of November 9, 1989 were contingent, the diffusion of control power away from East Berlin was central for matters to evolve as they did. Significantly, the GDR's financial and political straits produced consequences that Western actors did not foresee.[14]

To help us better understand the unexpected in world politics, our argument in this chapter takes three steps. First, we begin the analysis by reviewing the discussion of the different faces of power, ending with the notion of power demarcating fields of political possibilities. Second, we

[12] Sarotte 2014.   [13] Hertle 1999.   [14] Bartel 2017: 395–465.

distinguish between two kinds of power. Control power seeks to dominate; operating in a world of risk, it penetrates and diffuses. Protean power results from the improvisations and innovations of agile actors and processes of the actualization of potentialities; coping with uncertainty, it creates and circulates among actors and sites. Control power operates most clearly, and reliably, in situations marked by calculable risk that actors experience as such; protean power arises in situations of deep-seated uncertainty that actors often experience as a crisis. Because they can create room for each other, the two types of power are not mutually exclusive. As hopes of deliberately controlling outcomes diminish, protean power potentials loom large. The balance between them follows from an interaction of two dimensions affecting actor practices: the degree to which such actors experience the world to be risky or uncertain and whether it is, in fact, so. Third, in contrast to conventional international relations scholarship, we show that control and protean power analysis requires us to conceive of world politics as an open rather than a closed system.

Power

One of the many paradoxes of power is this. It is an explanatory construct practitioners and scholars of international relations cannot do without. It is also a concept that needs to be explained, rather than do the explaining. The prevailing understanding that power is a thing we "have" or "lack" in order to create a desirable effect is a starting point of our political experience and analysis.[15] In the study of international politics, for example, power is widely understood to be about capabilities typically measured by indicators such as military spending, the size of the economy, or technological advancement; articles and books proceeding in this manner fill libraries. Such capabilities are then used to explain or predict specific effects or outcomes.

Yet what remains normal in the analysis of international relations, theorists of power have dismissed as inadequate long ago. Unfortunately, their writings have had little discernible effects on the field of international relations, which treats the concept of power as a synonym for more or less narrowly construed actor capabilities. While not denying the importance of the base and means of power, theorists of power insist that power is grounded in the relationships among actors rather than in their attributes.[16] Along with David Baldwin, we thus view "the elements of

[15] Hayward 1998.
[16] Guzzini 2016a: 3–6. See also Baldwin 2013: 288; 2016: 50, 77, 128.

national power" approach with its exclusive focus on national capability as profoundly misleading.[17]

A relational view of power has been the shared premise of a vigorous and prolonged debate about the different faces of power, here understood as different forms of control. Ultimately, the debate has centered on where and how to draw a distinction between "free action and action shaped by the action of others."[18] Generally speaking, over time scholars have broadened substantially the empirical context where we should look for the effects of power.

For Lasswell and Kaplan "political science, as an empirical discipline, is the study of the shaping and sharing of power."[19] Building on what he called Lasswell's seminal contribution, Robert Dahl started the modern debate with his definition of power as the ability to get others to do what they otherwise would not.[20] Dahl drew a distinction between the base of an actor's power and the means of employing the base, on the one hand, and differences in the scope of responses elicited and the number of comparable respondents, on the other. For the purpose of comparing the power of actors, Dahl insisted, we need to focus primarily not on the actions of A but on the responses of B;[21] power base and means, though important, do not provide us with a comparison of the power of actors.

In an important critique of Dahl, Bachrach, and Baratz broadened the context of the effects of power by drawing a different distinction between free and constrained action. They focused on political dynamics that Dahl's analysis of bilateral power relations, revealed in concrete decisions about key issues, blended out. Two in particular: power exercised to limit the scope of the political process to safe issues; and power exercised to avoid taking a decision. Non-participation and non-decisions are effects of power that can stop a conflict from arising and from being acted upon. Unobservable processes and issues thus can be the effects of power and help to maintain the status quo in the absence of overt conflict.[22]

Steven Lukes broadened further the context where we should track free and constrained action. He pointed to a basic agreement between Dahl and Bachrach and Baratz. All three assumed that power was exercised by actors. Lukes focused also on the effects of structures that can shape the wants, needs, and desires through the impersonal workings of socio-cultural arrangements and practices.[23] To have effects, power does not

---

[17] Baldwin 1989: 166.   [18] Hayward 1998: 3; 2000: 1–39.
[19] Lasswell and Kaplan 1950: xiv.   [20] Dahl 1957: 202–3.   [21] Ibid.: 206.
[22] Bachrach and Baratz 1962; 1963.
[23] Lukes 2006a; 2005: 485–91; 2006b. For an empirical application of this perspective, see Gaventa 1982. Despite its greater emphasis on political agency than structure, and

need to be intentional or active.[24] Lukes argued that power should neither be reduced to its exercise nor its means, and that it operates within and upon structures.[25] His theory highlighted structural features of society that make actors powerful without having to exert control directly. Yet, like Dahl, Lukes insisted that we need to study both the agents and the subjects of power. Power is about an agent's potential capacity and specifically the scope for personal reasoning and self-definition. "Power identifies a capacity: power is a potentiality, not an actuality – indeed a potentiality that may never be actualized."[26] Lukes' theory is thus both subject- and agent-centered.[27]

Building on and adapting different aspects of the writings of Michel Foucault, theorists of power, including in the field of international relations, have broadened still further the context of tracking the effects of power.[28] Foucault's analysis is subject- rather than actor-centric. Power both controls and generates through every-day mechanisms of discipline. It creates the characters of actors and streamlines, among others, their sexual, health and mental practices so that they fit existing social and political arrangements. Disciplinary power molds souls and inscribes bodies.[29]

Informed by Lukes and Foucault in particular, Clarissa Hayward's subsequent analysis proves especially fruitful for our purposes. Hayward argues that power's mechanisms are best conceived not as instruments that powerful actors use but as social boundaries. "Power defines fields of possibility."[30] Laws, rules, norms, customs, identities, and social standards are such boundaries. They enable and constrain all forms of action, including for the most powerful. Actors can change the shape and

---

despite its lack of specificity about different modes of persuasion, "soft power" has considerable affinity with Lukes' third face of power. See Nye 2011; Lukes 2005: 485–91.

[24] Lukes 2005: 479.   [25] Hayward and Lukes 2008: 6–7, 11–12.

[26] Lukes 2005: 478. See also ibid.: 479, 484, 492–93.

[27] This is in contrast to Foucault and Nye, with the first refusing to draw this important distinction and the second failing to do so. Ibid.: 492.

[28] Barnett and Duvall 2005; Reed 2013; Digeser 1992; Neumann and Sending 2010; Krasner 2013. See also a further discussion of Foucault in Chapter 13. It is worth noting that in the field of American politics power has ceased to be a topic of intense discussion as attention has shifted toward the concept of information. See Moe 2005; Pierson 2015.

[29] In recent decades critical security and political economy studies have produced a substantial body of scholarship that analyzes power dynamics in world politics from this perspective. For some examples, see Bially-Mattern (2005) and Solomon (2014) on soft power; Diez (2013) and Manners (2013) on Europe's normative power; Epstein(2011), Hagström (2005) and Krebs (2015) on discursive and narrative power; Seabrooke (2010) and Hopf (2010) on everyday and habitual power; and Sending and Neumann (2006) and Guzzini (2012) on governmentality and dispersed power. For two reviews of recent writings on "relationalism" and the "practice turn" and historical institutionalism, see, respectively, McCourt 2016 and Fioretos 2011.

[30] Hayward and Lukes 2008: 10,14,16; Hayward 1998: 12; 2000.

direction of power through practices that result from both structured fields of possibility and actor endowments. Conceived as social boundaries and endowments, power defines what is possible for self and other. Contrary to Dahl's strong rejection, "action at a distance" for Hayward is an identifiable and important site for tracking power effects.[31] In global politics, the possible can be constrained or enabled at long distance without the existence of any discernible connection between the source and the target of power. To inquire into the workings of power we should not ask "how is power distributed" as we seek to distinguish between conditions of power and powerlessness. We should ask instead "how do power's mechanisms define the (im)possible, the (im)probable, the natural, the normal"?[32] What matters is the mutability of asymmetries in power that define the field of what is possible.[33]

Control and Protean Power

Power is an elusive concept. Hence, no single framework can "claim to have found the essence of power."[34] Instead, each partial conceptualization can provide some important insights about key aspects of power.[35] Typically, analysis focuses exclusively on the shifts in the dynamics of control power operating under conditions of risk. The concept of protean power broadens the analysis by acknowledging the existence and explanatory potential of power dynamics operating under conditions of uncertainty. Including both types of power promises more analytical breadth and a richer explication of unexpected change in world politics.[36] As a first step we distinguish between two ideal typical situations. When the context and the experience of power are marked either by risk or by uncertainty control and protean power form an ideal typical distinction (Table 1.1).

[31] Dahl 1957: 204. Dahl argues that a necessary condition for the exercise of power is that "there is no action at a distance." Although he leaves the term "connection" undefined, Dahl argues that "unless there is some 'connection' between A and α, then no power relation can be said to exist . . . One must always find out whether there is a connection, or an opportunity for a connection, and if there is not, then one need proceed no further." Protean power operates in the space that Dahl acknowledges opaquely by leaving the terms "connection" and "opportunity for a connection" undefined. Also see Hayward 1998: 17–18.
[32] Hayward 1998: 16.   [33] Ibid.: 20–21.   [34] Haugaard 2010: 420.
[35] Berenskoetter (2007: 2, 13–14) insists that international relations and the social sciences are lacking a fully articulated, general theory of power that integrates analysis across all existing power concepts and theoretical as well as meta-theoretical domains. We agree and do not believe that such a general theory is possible since the concept of power depends on the theoretical context in which it is deployed. See also Guzzini 2012.
[36] Hagström and Jerdén 2014: 350; Guzzini 2016b; Haugaard 2010.

Table 1.1 *Control and Protean Power: Basic Comparison*

	Control power	Protean power
Actor experience and underlying context	Calculable risk	Incalculable uncertainty
Mode of operation	Direct and indirect	Indirect and direct
Agency	Capabilities deployed by *ex ante* identifiable agents lead to probabilistic outcomes	Potential capacities of agile actors improvise to find solutions to local problems with *ex ante* unknown effects on others and the system at large
Primary focus	Actuality	Potentiality
Power operating through	Direction and diffusion	Creation and circulation

Of all the theorists of power Robert Dahl has been most explicit about the close affinity between control power and risk. Probabilities of an event with and without the exercise of power is for Dahl an indispensable way of comparing the power of different actors.[37] Observations of the two different conditions may be difficult but are "not inherently impossible: they don't defy the laws of nature as we understand them."[38] Many decades after the quantum revolution in physics, Dahl's appeal to the laws of nature remained Newtonian and was expressed in classical notions of probability. Half a century later there is no indication that conventional views of international politics have changed – even though it is time for international relations scholarship to wake up from its "deep Newtonian slumber."[39] Arguably, today quantum physics and quantum probabilities define the laws of nature "as we understand them." They resonate with the concepts of possibility and potentiality that are central to protean power dynamics.[40]

The incalculable provides the context and experience of what we call protean power. It arises either through direct relations between actors or indirectly in the follow-on effects that reconfigure complex systems. Protean power is the effect of actors' improvised and innovative responses to an incalculable environment or their experience of the world as equally uncertain. This type of power cannot be harnessed consciously. It is a creatively generated shift in accepted problem-solving that circulates across different sites of political life. It emerges in specific moments. It is an inextricable part of variable combinations of risk and uncertainty

[37] Dahl 1957: 206–7, 210.   [38] Ibid.: 214.   [39] Kavalski 2012.   [40] Wendt 2015.

that encompass affirmation and refusal as well as improvisation and innovation.

Protean power has generative effects on the broader context. These can be entirely unanticipated and as such bypass all attempts to exert control. While the processes underlying the two power types may co-occur, and converge, their relation to actor experiences of the world are diametrically opposed. From the perspective of those amassing control capabilities, the effects of protean power in settings of uncertainty enhance the unpredictable and result in frustration.

In our understanding, the unexpected is an integral part of power dynamics. This means that we should add the concept of what is possible to what is probable and what is natural. The mutability of the world goes beyond the predictable effects that constitute control power. It includes convention-defying uncertainties that destabilize the world. Admittedly, in common language risk and uncertainty are often used as synonyms. The confusion between the two concepts is both perfectly understandable and intellectually damaging. The *Merriam Webster* dictionary, for example, defines risk in terms of uncertainty, as "the possibility that something bad or unpleasant (such as an injury or a loss) will happen."[41] Despite this confusion, we should distinguish clearly between the concepts of risk and uncertainty. Both are relevant for an analysis of power and unexpected change.

Terminological confusion has been deepened by a questionable translation of Max Weber's analysis into English. A widely accepted view holds that Weber's definition of power is operating only in the world of risk – power as the likelihood of achieving one's will while overcoming the resistance of others. The conventional view is based on a problematic and theoretically constricting translation of the capacious German concept of *Chance*. That term has two valid translations: one probabilistic risk (*Wahrscheinlichkeit*), the other possibilistic uncertainty (*Möglichkeit*).[42] Following Weber, we hold that power operates in the world of risk *and* uncertainty. Actors accomplish their objectives *over* others in dominating relations (*potestas*), as well as *with* others in enabling relations (*potentia*). Weber's conceptualization of power thus invites us to look

---

[41] See at: www.merriam-webster.com/dictionary/risk, last accessed April 22, 2016. See also O'Malley 2004.

[42] Weber 1925: 28. Although we develop it in a different direction than he does, we are indebted on this point to Felix Berenskoetter's important observation (Berenskoetter 2007: 21, fn.4). Talcott Parsons insisted in his translation of the German concept of *Chance* that the concept should be stripped of all mathematical or statistical connotations, suggesting that "chance" could be measured numerically, a caution that has been conspicuously absent in the quantitative and behavioralist tradition of American political science and international relations research. See Guzzini 2016a: 7, fn. 8.

simultaneously at control power in terms of processes that connect capabilities with effects in relations that penetrate and diffuse, and at protean power in terms of agilities that create and circulate.

How do actors facing risk and uncertainty choose their practices? Risk-based models of power-as-control assume that they are playing the odds. Eager to apply statistical techniques he had learned on Wall Street to professional sports, after three disappointing seasons, the general manager of the Philadelphia 76ers basketball team, Sam Hinkie, observed ruefully in his resignation letter that "the illusion of control is an opiate ... It is annoyingly necessary to get comfortable with many grades of may be."[43] Confronting uncertainty, actors can turn to prior beliefs (priors over priors in the language of economics) in order to make reasoned decisions based on implicit probabilities. Unfortunately, no plausible answers exist to the question of which prior beliefs are chosen and why. Actors can also turn to imagined futures of the possible and impossible, something international relations scholarship tends to overlook.[44] Hence, most actors cope and muddle through, typically informed by standards of reasonableness rather than rationality. The assumption of rational decision-making may, of course, be correct for some individuals and situations, for example, American traders on Wall Street or American defense officials in the Pentagon. But what about Japanese traders in Tokyo or Japanese defense officials in the Self-Defense Forces? They do not differ from Americans because they adhere to inherently irrational beliefs. Instead, differences in institutional and intellectual settings suggest distinctive engagements with the theory and practice of arbitrage and coercion. They underline how much conceptual redefinition, extension, and ambiguity can occur in different settings.[45] To insist that the mix of risk and uncertainty will always and everywhere yield the same probability calculation does not help us understand better power dynamics in the domain of the unexpected. It seems more sensible to let go of the notion of invariant, omnipresent, rational probability calculations and to acknowledge the existence of variable standards of reasonableness under conditions of risk and uncertainty. Control and protean power thus are brought into one analytical perspective as they make crises normal and endogenous to world politics rather than abnormal and exogenous.[46]

---

[43] Silverman 2016.   [44] We explore this issue further in Chapter 13.
[45] Katzenstein 1996; Miyazaki 2013.
[46] Our insistence on the importance of the relationship between protean and control power resembles that of Digeser's (1992: 991) characterization of the relationship between existing approaches to power's three faces and its fourth Foucauldian one. It "does not displace the other faces of power, but provides a different level of analysis." It also resonates with Dell's (1986) view of the compatibility between circular causality at the level of family system and of linear control systems in particular family subsystems. Dell 1986; Digeser 1992.

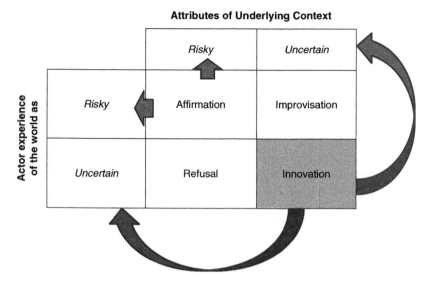

Figure 1.1 Context, Experience, and Power

The theoretical shift in perspective that is needed to explain the surprises assumed away by risk-only views is that power is not only a cause of empirical patterns but also their effect. Figure 1.1 captures the connection between practices and power outcomes by depicting two dimensions: attributes of the underlying context and actor experiences.[47] The coexistence and co-evolution of control and protean power do not occur along a simple continuum. Instead, the four cells in Figure 1.1, populated by characteristic political practices, are produced by the interaction of the two dimensions. As such, they reflect both the degree to which complete knowledge or ignorance of probabilities prevails and the degree to which actors seek it in the first place. We acknowledge that empirically, in the depth of a crisis, for example, the effect of actor experience and context attributes on political practices, and therefore power, may not be readily distinguishable. This can, however, be done in principle and certainly in retrospect. Both dimensions thus have their place in the framework.

Each of the political practices captured in the four cells generates power dynamics that feed back on uncertainty and risk depicted along the two dimensions. The context- and experience-altering impact captured by the arrows in Figure 1.1 thus makes control or protean power the effects of diverse political practices. Affirmation, in the top left cell, is the

[47] We thank Stefano Guzzini and Anna Wojciuk for pushing us to clarify this point.

recognition by actors that capabilities can be amassed and deliberately deployed to exercise power. From the perspective of those subject to such power, affirmation may take the form of acquiescence or compliance in the context of predictable risks. In the end, as the short arrows show, it enhances the utility of probability calculations concerning future outcomes; reliance on established power templates reinforces the risk-based nature of the world and is experience by actors as such. This is the domain of control power. The discipline of international relations is replete with examples of authors assuming, mistakenly, that this is the only world in which politics unfolds.

Our analysis highlights the existence of two other worlds captured by the other three cells in Figure 1.1. Depicted in the bottom right cell, for example, innovation is a response to a second, fundamentally uncertain world. It generates protean power, shifting the goal post for exercising control in the process and necessitating still more agility in the future. Protean power, then, is the effect of innovation that generates further uncertainty and at the same time underscores the futility of control power. Finally, we can also find ourselves in a third world that mixes risk and uncertainty. During an emergent crisis, actors operate in the top right cell: uncertainty has made probability calculations impossible, though actors do not realize it. This is the root of the disorienting nature of most crises. Actors assume "old ways" still apply when the ground has already shifted to make possible unexpected outcomes. When they discover that familiar solutions no longer work, they are compelled to improvise to stay afloat in increasingly unstable and uncertain contexts. Conversely, as previously earth-shattering solutions evolve into best practices and uncertainty is replaced by risk, actors' assumptions of pervasive uncertainty may persist. They continue to make decisions affecting their immediate environment only, refusing attempts at risk-based decision-making, without any desire to control others directly. The shortcomings of control power experienced by actors generate room for surprising solutions, while success transforms protean power into control power. This is captured by the bottom left cell.

The four cells in Figure 1.1 exemplify but do not exhaust the range of practices available. In our labeling we focus on particular practices that relate actor experience and context attributes to power manifestations, and the degree to which the latter reinforce or undermine the different constellations of risk and uncertainty. Power as either cause *or* effect is not coterminous with political practice, a common mistake that invites the spinning of tautologies. It is instead analytically separate from practice as it affects the experience and context of risk and uncertainty. Illustrated by the two large arrows, innovation, the response to immediate experience of uncertainty in an uncertain world, generates protean power and so exacerbates further the uncertain conditions from which it arose. It is for this reason that we find it impossible to link protean power to specific attributes or capabilities and instead highlight its agile nature that jettisons any semblance of regularity.

Each cell in the figure can be populated by empirical illustrations, some of which we present in this volume. For example, Jennifer Erickson's discussion of arms control during the Cold War in Chapter 11 approximates the situation of a risky world that actors experience as such (top left cell). The analysis of science and technology in Chapter 6 discusses the opposite case of an uncertain world that is experienced as uncertain (bottom right cell). The awareness and acknowledgment of pervasive uncertainty at all levels shapes how actors engage in innovation and how protean power is generated. In Chapter 8, Erin Lockwood and Stephen Nelson offer an analysis of a mixed case of risk and uncertainty (top right cell), evidenced particularly well by the growing instability of mismatched responses to financial crises. They show how market players, operating in the domain of both risk and uncertainty, have relied on modeling conventions and contractual clauses that illusorily seek to transform uncertainty into manageable risk. In Chapter 5, Noelle Brigden and Peter Andreas analyze protean power effects of migrant improvisations and innovations as well as the anticipated, yet unintended, escalatory dynamic between more police control and more migrant evasion. And in Chapter 7, Rawi Abdelal addresses the relations surrounding hydrocarbon flows in Europe that also mixes risk and uncertainty (bottom left cell). He offers an excellent illustration of actor experiences that generate protean power under crisis conditions. Such innovative solutions may briefly settle into control mode, leaving a landscape of (rerouted) pipelines behind. But in the interaction of the two power types, actors will find control disrupted further down the line. In short, conventionally deduced behavioral implications of different power constellations conceal important variations in the degree of uncertainty, and thus can easily mislead us. Specifically, they make us overestimate the importance of control power in world politics.

In its relationship to uncertainty and risk, control power can be compared with a game of billiards with its discrete movements. There is room for strategy, but there is no question about the rules, which are closely linked to laws of motion in physics that govern a player's decisions and constrain their execution. By contrast, protean power resembles a game of interactive fluidity, like tennis. It is about "being in the right place, at the right time" that extends well beyond coincidence. For the world's leading physicist of tennis, Howard Brody, there was nothing flighty about the game. Yet he would have acknowledged that individual ball control, motivation, mutual weakness recognition, and interaction with the spectators produce enough uncertainty to make the exact score unpredictable.[48] Such is the world of protean power, moving past simplified equations of force.

Even though an actor may be too weak to exercise "power over" (understood here as actual capability) the human or non-human world, she or he may nonetheless be sufficiently empowered to have "power to" or "power with" (understood here as the capacity to actualize potentialities, without or with others) to be able to navigate in that world successfully.[49] One way of illustrating the operation of protean power is to focus on the effects of human action without design. Under conditions of uncertainty it is not necessarily strategic actions but their emerging byproducts that create the most consequential effects.[50] It is clear that actors *want* to do something in response to the uncertainty that surrounds them. What *should* be done, however, is typically unknown. Actors do their best, guessing and coping, uninformed by calculable probabilities and unknown determinants of success or failure. Once their actions have resulted in outcomes, ascribed power effects are linked to specific actors who are seen as having caused the outcomes. Who wins is therefore determined through traceable (*ex post*) but not predictable (*ex ante*) assessments. We thus gain a deeper understanding of the fragility and limits of control power, not a handbook of how to beat *fortuna* at her game. Figure 1.1 is a useful reminder that the two kinds of power are analytically separate. Drawing on the empirical case studies in this book, Chapters 2 and 13 argue that they are also deeply interrelated. Uncertainty makes control power fragile, tugs our conceptualization toward protean power dynamics, and sets the stage for the co-evolution of both power types.

Complexity and Power

How was it possible for China to transform itself within a generation, lifting hundreds of millions out of abject poverty? Nobody inside or outside China foresaw this revolutionary change in 1979 when Chairman Deng announced his reform package. Now almost everybody assumes that it happened because of one or several well-known factors, such as less state supervision, smart technocrats, unleashed entrepreneurship, better access to world markets, or more secure property rights. Reminiscent of

---

[48] *The Economist* 2015b.   [49] Pansardi 2011; Göhler 2009; Slaughter 2017: 161–82.
[50] Dallas 2014.

the story of migration (Chapter 5), Yuen Yuen Ang offers a very different answer: the inherent unpredictability of the reform journey and the co-evolution of control and protean power.[51] The guiding tenet of that journey was to "cross the river by touching the stones," toes gripping hard but with an unknown destination on the other side of the river. Central leaders were at times alarmed about the unanticipated consequences of their decisions. The reforms empowered local state and party officials and market actors to pursue adaptive development strategies that permitted improvisation and innumerable specific solutions to ever-changing problems. Chairman Deng, for example, was totally surprised at the proliferation of township and village enterprises, the centerpiece of the early reforms. "This result was not anything I or any of the other comrades had foreseen; it just came out of the blue."[52]

In answering "how was it possible?" Ang turns to complexity theory.[53] It highlights the adaptive character of open systems and their unpredictable, emergent properties.[54] Complicated systems are predictable. Complex systems are not. They produce "outcomes that cannot be precisely controlled."[55] Sharing hidden, communal lives, trees are complex and resilient. Solitary toasters with no secrets to hide are complicated and lack resilience.[56] Complexity demands incessant improvisation and successive approximation, innovation by recombination, local knowledge, and accumulated experience. It acknowledges the inescapability of uncertainty that control power cannot conquer.[57] But even if it could in particular instances, Robert Jervis reminds us that "local predictability, if not simplicity, produces a high degree of complexity and unpredictability."[58] Often that complexity reflects a momentary indeterminacy in the cross-balancing of control and protean power.

The circulation of protean power comes into play in situations of uncertainty, fueled by the effects of improvisation and innovation. The fit between improvising solutions and particular aspects of an uncertain context matter, even though it becomes apparent only in retrospect. By contrast, control power operates in situations of calculable risk. In relatively stable and predictable environments, the effects of control power emerge directly. Implicitly, our understandings of control power tend to assume that its predicted effects occur in closed systems, such as laboratory settings, which invite partial equilibrium analysis that holds constant all variables that might confound the stipulated power effect. This is not

---

[51] Ang 2016: 73, 84, 86, 240.   [52] Ibid.: 80.   [53] Byrne and Callaghan 2013.
[54] Axelrod and Cohen 1999; Bookstaber 2017.   [55] Ang 2016: 10.
[56] Ibid.; Wohlleben 2017. Scott (1998: 11–22) discusses the contrary, legibility approach as exemplified by German forestry (*Forstwirtschaft*).
[57] Scott 1998: 311–28; Dequech 2003.   [58] Jervis 1997: 16.

so in open systems. Although large numbers yield predictable averages in the aggregate, individual behavior is typically unpredictable and seemingly erratic. Furthermore, in open systems the interaction of a sizable number of factors form wholes that may not be readily captured by linear models of the world.[59] In a linear world, small things follow from large ones. In a non-linear world, large things can follow from small ones.[60]

The worlds of risk and uncertainty and control and protean power resemble the well-known difference between clocks and clouds.[61] The French astronomer and mathematician Pierre-Simon Laplace was convinced that the world is a big, complicated clock. As science developed, more and better knowledge about the clock's inner workings would enable us to predict the future with deterministic or probabilistic equations. All that is needed is work and patience. The present state of the world is the effect of its past and the cause of its future. In the world of clocks, there is, at least in principle, no uncertainty. Like the past, the future is fully knowable to an omniscient present. Various insurance markets are clocklike in their predictability. And our experience confirms daily many of our predictions. We could not function in a world in which everything was possible. This is the risk-based world of control power.

Protean power operates in the world of clouds. Modern meteorology knows vastly more than in the past about the conditions under which clouds form, and its predictive power of general weather patterns has improved greatly. Yet it is much less confident in its ability to make specific predictions about the shape of particular clouds. Historical probabilities summarize the possible ways the future could unfold. And the curve summarizing those possibilities looks nothing like a normal bell-shaped curve that is necessary for the calculation of risks. It has fat tails that describe a much more volatile world than risk models lead us to believe. Historians are the first to understand intuitively and acknowledge explicitly that the world we experience as the only real one is the result of statistical distributions of possible worlds that emerged from once-possible worlds. So are playwrights such as Nick Payne.[62] "The past did not have to unfold as it did, the present did not have to be what it is, and the future is wide open."[63] The indeterminacy that inheres in the field of power points to almost infinite alternative pasts and futures – the field of protean power possibilities.

[59] Weaver 1948: 539.
[60] Abbott 1988: 173; McCloskey 1991: 26, 32–33. There is no reason to believe that either type of power operates only in a linear world.
[61] Almond and Genco 1977; McCloskey 1991; Tetlock and Gardner 2015: 8–10.
[62] Payne 2012.   [63] Tetlock and Gardner 2015: 248.

Complexity thus brings into one perspective risk and uncertainty and control and protean power. "Risk," Mary Douglas writes, "is not a thing, it's a way of thinking."[64] The same is true of uncertainty. Searching for a combination of both, Karl Popper settled for something "intermediate in character, between perfect chance and perfect determinism."[65] Popper's solution points to a kind of freedom that is not mere chance. He contrasts his preferred "plastic-control" to "cast-iron control."[66] Following Popper, Almond and Genco argue that we are living in an open system with emergent, creative properties, regularities with a short half-life, human inventiveness, and low-probability conjunctions. Plastic control endows the exercise of power with a looseness of fit that undercuts planning.[67] This is an apt description of a complex world marked by risk and uncertainty and the operation of protean and control power.

The evolution of the universe, biology, geological patterning, climate, hurricanes, and other processes in the natural world are often modeled as a set of complex, open systems, governed not by universal laws and equilibrium but by pervasive chaos and disequilibrium. Within and across such systems volatility sets free a "protean capacity of self-organization" ... containing "the potential for creative evolution."[68] System trajectories can be made intelligible *ex post* but are not predictable *ex ante*. For the analysis of control and protean power this is the ontological foundation of analysis. It is at odds with the control power logic of international relations scholarship based on the assumption of closed systems. The experimental method that seeks to uncover general laws is inadequate to come to terms with the emergent properties of open systems. For practical reasons, linear causality does not capture such properties. It is, of course, entirely possible that open systems contain simple rules that we should be able to decipher. But in the social world predictive capacity is systematically limited by the the time it takes the system to run through enough iterations to watch how things map out. Stephen Wolfram calls this "computational irreducibility."[69]

Open system analyses of control and protean power differ in how they make sense of the world. The reason is simple. Causality is understood and works differently in the domains of capability and of the capacity to actualize potentialities, of control and of protean power. When mapping causal configurations, current convention draws the causal influence in an unbroken line from actor A to actor B; when modeling two-way causation a broken arrow is typically drawn to connect actor B to actor A. This does not mean that the first arrow is in some ways stronger or more

---

[64] Douglas 1994: 44. For a good survey of risk analysis, see Kammen and Hassenzahl 1999.
[65] Popper 1972: 228.   [66] Ibid.: 232; Almond and Genco 1977: 490–91.
[67] Almond and Genco 1977: 492, 494, 496–97, 503; Popper 1972: 503.
[68] Connolly 2005: 83.   [69] Ibid.: 84–85.

important than the second. To the contrary, for Dahl and many other theorists of power the main action is in and from B, not in and from A.[70] In the language of contemporary discussions of causality, the first account of causality can, in principle, overcome the problem of endogeneity. Because it focuses on more than efficient causation, the second cannot. Less or more capacious views of the social scientific enterprise make scholars choose differently at this juncture. Less capacious conceptions treat world politics as a closed system that should, at least in principle, be investigated through controlled experiments. More capacious conceptions conceive of world politics as an open system, not amenable even to quasi-experiments. This book views the world as an open system.

Explication provides a method to operate at the intersection of these two conceptions of science. Explication differs from both "mere" description and "law-like" explanations.[71] This style of analysis combines "how" questions, understanding, descriptive inference, and constitutive analysis, on the one hand, with "why" questions, explanation, causal inference, and causal analysis, on the other.[72] Constitutive effects are productive or generative, and in practice are difficult to distinguish from causal effects.[73] "Constitutive relations *are* causal, albeit not causal in the neopositivist sense ... [Constitutive explanation] is not a rival to causal explanation, but simply an alternative to the neopositivist focus on cross-case covariation."[74] The analysis of control and protean power politics thus benefits from, indeed requires, a broad notion of causality and an eclectic approach that suits the analysis of open systems.[75] On this point we thus follow Lévi-Strauss for whom a "mind in its untamed state is distinct from a mind cultivated or domesticated for the purpose of yielding a return ... it is possible for the two to co-exist and interpenetrate."[76]

Complex, open systems undercut the efficacy of using past trends and performance as a predictor of future outcomes. If control power worked in the past, it is often assumed that it must do so also in the future.

---

[70] Dahl 1957: 206.

[71] Finnemore 2004: 14–15; Tannenwald 2005: 33–40; Gerring 2012. Dray argues that explication addresses "how-possibly" questions that require explanations and that specify only necessary (rather than necessary and sufficient) conditions to rebut the presumption of impossibility. Such explanations differ from standard covering law explanations. "Explanations how-possibly are no more to be assimilated to how-probablies than to why-necessarilies." Dray 1968: 392.

[72] Wendt 1998: 101–3; Ylikoski 2013: 278.   [73] Laffey and Weldes 1997: 204–5.

[74] Jackson 2011: 107–8.

[75] Parsons 2015: 6–20; Sil and Katzenstein 2010. Counterfactual analysis is part of that approach.

[76] Lévi-Strauss 1968: 219. We thank David Laitin for alerting us to Lévi-Strauss' distinction.

Disregarding fluctuations in interactive, entangled, competitive, complementary, parallel, or nested co-evolving factors that mark complex systems can easily lead astray any analysis of power dynamics. Although the underlying uncertainty can be the result of exogenous shocks, it typically arises endogenously through a combination of inefficacious control power and an amplification of uncertainty through the circulation of protean power. Complexity thus necessitates an "inherently humble approach that is conscious of the limitations to predictability and control."[77]

This is a point that resonates deeply with the writings of both Friedrich Hayek and Elinor Ostrom. Their arguments for decentralization and polycentrism rest on the existence of control frameworks of ideology and institutions in which market exchanges can occur and subsidiary choices can be exercised. But despite the existence of constitutive and regulatory opportunities and constraints such frameworks provide, Hayek and Ostrom both stress the importance of the unpredictable and the advantages of decentralization.

Hayek's analysis emphasizes spontaneity, although in a market system that he sees as existing largely in isolation from rather than closely related to and imbricated in other self-organizing and open systems. Hayek directs our attention to the market context in which control and protean power are interrelated. The complexity and unpredictability inhering in social and economic life means that all hierarchical orders, important as they are in guaranteeing property rights, have distinct limits. Scholars must accept that actors need to "adapt to the unforeseeable."[78]

Hayek alerts us to the tensions and contradictions between the desirability of utilizing all actors' dispersed knowledge and attempts to improve underlying orders through direct commands.[79] The division of knowledge stands at the center of socio-economic and political life.[80] Knowledge revolves around an infinitely complex and profoundly political process of communication. Imperfect communication produces distorting rather than self-organizing knowledge systems. The errors of centralized control are rooted in the pretentious ignorance and utter disregard of pre-scientific knowledge on which most of the theories of social scientists and political engineers rest.[81] The price system does not connect demand and supply in the abstract. It connects innumerable actors, situated in distinctive locales, acting at specific times, and with

---

[77] Bousquet and Geyer 2011: 1.   [78] Hayek 1973: 54.
[79] Ibid.: 51; Connolly 2013: 54–63.   [80] Hayek 1945: 519–28.
[81] Ibid.: 521; Kessler 2012: 286–88.

unique understandings of themselves and the expectations of others. Hayek deploys a vocabulary that applies well to the analysis of protean power and allows us "to capture the continuous reproduction and fluidity of economic processes."[82]

Abstract orders, of course, require institutions that make social and economic life possible in the first place and a vibrant ideology that supports those institutions.[83] Rational designs of allocative institutions that are focused on top-down control, however, are suboptimal. They are beholden to inaccurate abstractions that fail to engage the uncertainties of practical life.[84] And when uncertainty engulfs actors, they rely on micro-level repertoires of knowledge and action to get by. In doing so, such actors add new factors to an already complex environment and exacerbate both normal, operational, and radical, crisis-induced uncertainty.

Hayek views markets as devices that coordinate activities without an omniscient center exercising control.[85] Markets disperse knowledge and thus power.[86] Except for their self-perpetuation, they are instances of social orders that evolve without predetermined ends. Although the power effects they produce are clearly identifiable with hindsight, these practices are inherently unpredictable, a distinct characteristic of protean power.

Stressing, like Hayek, the virtues of decentralization Elinor Ostrom's probing treatment of environmental resource management captures the need for linking all types of speech, knowledge, and practices, working through "mechanisms of mutual monitoring, learning and adaptation of better strategies over time."[87] Actors dealing with a profoundly complex environment are faced with the challenge of seeking to improve, without being able to fully control. They respond with innovative solutions and continuous adjustments that thrive in decentralized, polycentric systems and create conditions for the emergence of protean power.

In her Nobel Prize acceptance lecture, Ostrom challenged the presumption that governments and centralized authority-wielding organizations more broadly do a better job than other actors who are more immersed in local contexts.[88] Actors are placed in networks and wield power by virtue of defining and redefining webs of connection rather than by claims to their official positions. Ostrom questions the belief that we cannot do without abundant external resources to govern effectively.

---

[82] Kessler 2012: 292.   [83] Hayek 1973: 43; Boykin 2010: 21; Hayek 1984a; 1984b.
[84] Hayek 1973: 54; Fox 2009.   [85] Hayek 1960: 159.
[86] Hayek's views on law and social change are consistent with legal theorists such as Lon Fuller and the importance of decentralized judge-made law that adjudicates specific conflicts between individual litigants.
[87] Ostrom 2010b: 552.   [88] Ostrom 2010a; 2010b.

Rather, actors traditionally viewed as weak have a unique ability to produce governance systems. Too often we underestimate their efficacy.[89] Reaching beyond the obstacles of collective action, she suggests that problems that span multiple levels (of action and analysis) should be addressed at the appropriate scale.[90] Citing the original definition of polycentric systems,[91] Ostrom highlights the role of formally independent decision centers in producing often innovative and effective policy solutions in legal contexts that can operate beyond the local level.

One-size-fits-all approaches that are externally imposed and dominance-backed do not work well in polycentric systems.[92] For example, we may be facing the consequences of our collective failure to respond to climate change. Although, or because, the specific manifestations of the resulting environmental pressures vary, actors and societies can be compared on their ability to deal with such unknown and, in their specifics, unknowable challenges. Ostrom, with her co-authors, labels this quality "adaptedness."[93] The reflexivity in such socio-ecological systems underpins the fundamental uncertainty about what collective action outcomes will follow and what the cumulative effect of innovative steps at all scales will be. At its base, Ostrom's account is about turning threats into opportunities,[94] recognizing that the most pressing threats are rarely, if ever, visible looking down from the top.

Hayek and Ostrom alert us to the fact that the simplifications of scholars tend to reduce complexity to complication. And in that process of simplification, research can easily lose sight of crucial aspects of protean power dynamics. What distinguishes protean power from control power is the unknown outcomes it produces. Protean power operates in networks that are extensive, loosely coupled and self-directed rather than intensive, tightly-coupled, and authoritative.[95] Although protean power is not readily aggregated, its effects are real and unfold in uncertain conditions that often evoke refusal or resistance and derive from improvisation or innovation. Viewed as agility in response to uncertainty, in a world that often defies control, actors cannot know what exact effects it will produce. They generate protean power through their creativity and local awareness and the creation of future potentialities as a result of new actualities, without claiming to seek or to cause specific outcomes.

---

[89] Ostrom 2009.   [90] Ostrom 2006.   [91] Ostrom 1961.
[92] For the Ostroms the extent to which complex relations connect independent actors or constitute interconnected systems remains an empirical question. Ostrom 2010b; 1961.
[93] Young et al. 2006. Adaptedness seems to refer to something like Morriss' concept of "ableness." Morriss 1987: 80–85.
[94] Ostrom 2006.   [95] Mann 1986: 27.

Expressing widely shared sentiments, Randall Schweller writes that "we are entering a jumbled world run by and for no one, in which the nature of power itself is changing, an ungovernable place ... a chaotic realm of unknowable complexity."[96] Yet a complex world is not necessarily chaotic and is not necessarily slipping out of control. Two compelling advocates of complexity theory, Axelrod and Cohen, for example, argue that "while complex systems may be hard to predict, they may also have a good deal of structure and permit improvement by thoughtful intervention."[97] In politics "governments not only 'power' ... they also puzzle."[98] Forecasting is more than a statistically informed extension of past trends into the future.[99] It requires a mind that is open to both intuition and science. Good forecasters are Isaiah Berlin's foxes who embrace the complexity of the world, not hedgehogs whetted on one big idea or trend.[100] Tetlock's research has established that, beyond the frame of three to five years, the accuracy of the predictions of the average expert is no better than random.[101] And it takes skill and hard work to be a successful forecaster of possible scenarios.[102] While some uncertainties are altogether unknowable, others are not, at least in principle. This does not mean denying the importance of control power and risk. It does mean, however, that we must incorporate protean power at the micro-level that can yield unanticipated consequences.[103]

Scholars and policymakers occasionally compare international politics to a game of chess.[104] That game has fixed rules and calculates probability in a complex environment. Yet it also illustrates the limits of control. The current world chess champion is a young Norwegian, Magnus Carlsen, the most highly ranked champion in the game's history.[105] In one of the most lop-sided matches in recent decades, he dethroned the defending world champion Viswanathan Anand in November 2013. This changing of the guard illustrated a broader trend. A handful of Russian grandmasters no longer dominate the sport; today more than 1,200 grandmasters of chess play the game, compared with eighty-eight in 1972. The collapsing chess order shows a dialectical relation between high levels of conformity instilled by risk-based, computerized chess training manuals and the continued relevance of improvisation and innovation. Carlsen's genius lies in his unorthodox and surprising strategies that rely on his prodigious memory rather than the conventions of computer chess. Carlsen has an aptitude for playing many different styles of chess, adapting readily rather than

---

[96] Schweller 2014: 16, 27.   [97] Axelrod and Cohen 1999: xv.   [98] Heclo 1974: 305–6.
[99] Tetlock and Gardner 2015: 191–92, 244–50.   [100] Herrmann and Choi 2007.
[101] Tetlock 2005.   [102] Bernstein et al. 2000.   [103] Susen 2014: 7–8.
[104] Haass 2014; Nye 2011: xv.
[105] Naíim 2013: 1–2; Tetlock and Gardner 2015: 43–44.

searching like a scientist for the best solution to a given problem.[106] His playing style confirms Adam Smith's insight: "in the great chess-board of human society, every single piece has a principle of motion of its own."[107] In the terminology of this book, Carlsen's huge success shows that chess is a game where risk and uncertainty and control and protean power meet.

Conclusion

Uncertainty breeds protean power and protean power intensifies uncertainty. The world is well stocked with low-probability events such as the sudden appearance of terrorist organizations operating on a global scale and waves of large-scale human migration. Typically, these events are available for risk-based political analysis only after they have happened. We have argued here that an adequate understanding of disruptive events and processes requires going beyond an analysis that focuses only on direction by and diffusion of control. It must incorporate also the analysis of the creation and circulation of protean power.

   As an analytical construct and policy tool, control power operates in "normal" situations where calculable probabilities of outcomes make it, at least in principle, measurable and deployable. Protean power, by contrast, emerges typically in situations of uncertainty. This form of power thrives on actors' agility. They can be innovative in reinterpreting the meaning of rules, and they can play without rules, relying on identity and other mechanisms for managing uncertainty.[108] As such, protean power creates political dynamics that alert us to the presence of endogenous uncertainty rather than merely responding to it as an exogenous force.[109] It allows actors to position themselves to derive relative advantage from unexpected challenges, while adding to the overall uncertainty everyone faces. The concept of protean power invites us to analyze refusal from the perspective of the targets of control power and to inquire into creative practices furthering mobility, ambiguity, and disorder and the improvisations and innovations that come in their wake – all markers of the circulation of protean power in contemporary world politics.[110]

---

[106] Max 2011.   [107] Smith 1853: 342–43.   [108] Hopf 1998: 188.
[109] Critical juncture and path dependency theory, for example, deal with the problem of unexpected change by making it exogenous. This creates a lack of interest in the endogenous effects of power dynamics and indifference to political agency and accountability in the exercise of all forms of power. See Seabrooke 2006: 11; Streeck and Thelen 2005; Krasner 1984.
[110] Darby 2004: 26; Ringmar 2007: 197.

In a disorderly and at times chaotic world predictive accuracy is unobtainable. This is old news. It recapitulates for our times a long-standing connection between two types of power embedded in the known and unknown. A widespread view holds that control power is diffusing and that regional and global orders are being undermined as the world is heading from predictable order to randomness. In a world where risk and uncertainty overlap and intermingle the case studies in this book point to a more complex world. To focus exclusively on risk and control power overlooks the fact that explanations of crises and far-reaching surprises require the analytical lens of protean power thriving in uncertainty.

The political world is more unfathomable than notions of control power permit us to recognize. It is filled with more potential for improvisation and innovation than false convictions and traditional practices concede.[111] Protean power can be creative – as in the case of Silicon Valley and innovative start-ups. And it can be destructive – as in some of the novel products and practices that made the financial industry fall off the cliff in 2008 and in the surge in terrorist violence in recent years. Smart forecasts, prudence, and resilience offer some measure of protection in a world open to a statistically staggering range of possibilities that the human mind meets with a psychological craving for often unobtainable predictability. That craving leaves many political actors and scholars of international relations, in the words of legendary investor Charlie Munger, in the position of "a one-legged man in an ass-kicking contest."[112] A broader concept of power provides needed protection and improved vision. The 9/11 attack on the United States and what some have called the "assault" of America by tens of thousands of children migrating illegally in the summer of 2014 serve as two simple reminders of one basic fact. Until we stop focusing only on control power and begin to recognize also the role of protean power, unfolding events in world politics will continue to outpace our ability to understand and cope with them.

---

[111] Davidson 2015a: 23.
[112] Tetlock and Gardner 2015: 146. See also Best 2008: 358–59.

2 Uncertainty, Risk, Power and the Limits of International Relations Theory

Peter J. Katzenstein and Lucia A. Seybert

Power is not ending, as the public intellectual and former editor of the journal *Foreign Policy*, Moisés Naím, argues.[1] But it is true that in different political arenas big players are challenged by small ones who are using new playbooks that make power both more available and more evanescent. Naíim's description of power dynamics is often on target; his exclusive focus on the erosion of control power is not. Otto von Bismarck, Germany's "Iron Chancellor," knew better. He did not aspire to "control the current of events, only occasionally to deflect them."[2] In a world of risk mixed with uncertainty it is the relations between protean and control power that shape the security of states, the competitiveness of economies, and the resilience of societies.

This is not how international relations scholarship typically views the world. In the consensus view, power is normally measured by material military, economic, or political capabilities – presumptive causes of change in international politics, such as the putative decline of the United States and the rise of China. Power, however, is not a property. It is a relationship. Drawing on some of the main writings on power, David Baldwin has reminded us that it is a mistake to equate the resource base and instruments of power with power itself.[3] Different indicators, for example, of military capability – the size of the armed forces, military budgets, preparedness for cyber-warfare, nuclear weapons – cannot be aggregated into one measure of military power. And different kinds of military, economic, diplomatic, and social power are not fungible. Problems of aggregation and conversion make pointless efforts to construct general power indices. Power is always context-specific. It matters when assessing the power of an architect whether she or he plans "to build a birdhouse or a cathedral," and whether she or he has good or bad relations with clients, zoning boards, and investors.[4] Baldwin's careful engagement with international relations scholarship is forcefully insisting that power must be understood relationally and situationally, and

---

[1] Naím 2013. Also see Owen 2015: 3–4, 9, 19.   [2] Davies 1996: 760.   [3] Baldwin 2016.
[4] Baldwin 2013: 277.

should highlight both the causes and the effects of power.[5] For the most part, and especially in America, international relations scholarship has not heeded Baldwin's call.

This book is built around the distinction between control and protean power. Control is exercised through coercion, institutions and structures of domination. Wielders of power everywhere can manipulate their relations with others, steer institutional agendas, and shape their structural positions to gain direct and indirect advantages. Furthermore, they derive advantages from controlling options external to the power relation between the parties in question.[6] Susan Strange, for example, applies this style of analysis to states operating in four domains of power: security, production, finance, and knowledge.[7] International structures, Strange argues, generate social power that give priority to some values over others and yield patterns of domination with or without intentional rule.[8] Unfortunately, Strange's realist analysis stops at this point. Her reticence is shared by Nye's liberal style of inquiry. His careful discussion of the relations between structural and soft power refers in a lengthy footnote to "unconventional" theories.[9] But he refrains from engaging them – since doing so would, he writes, "be purchased at too high a price in terms of conceptual complexity and clarity."[10] Both Strange and Nye thus disregard important strands of theorizing that point beyond the concept of control power.

The concepts of control and protean power are both about the causal force of agency; in addition, protean power focuses attention on the effects of power. In recent years the shift from state to non-state actors and from government to governance points to power dynamics that require us to understand both the causes and the effects of power. Power is reconfigured and augmented as it reaches all corners of global and domestic politics.[11] This change resonates with the arrival of disruptive technological innovations in recent years.[12] Yet there is no reason to believe that protean power is a late arrival on the stage of world politics. The history of the human rights revolution, LGBT movements,

---

[5] Ibid.: 288. Baldwin 2016: 3, 32, 43–44, 45–47, 69. See also Goddard and Nexon 2016.
[6] Culpepper and Reinke 2014: 429–32; Fairfield 2015: 3–15; Paster 2015; Guzzini 2012: 7–8; Kremer and Pustovitovskij 2012.
[7] Strange 1988: 45, 62–63, 71–72, 88, 115. See also May 2000.
[8] Strange 1996: 23–27; Guzzini 2012. Baldwin dismisses Strange's contribution because it incorporates unintended effects. Baldwin 2016: 81.
[9] Going beyond realism, liberalism, and constructivism as the three main paradigms of international relations, critical security scholarship has offered fresh insights, drawing, broadly speaking, on the fourth face of power. See Seybert and Katzenstein (Chapter 1, fn. 28), Guzzini 1993; Barnett and Duvall 2005.
[10] Nye 2011: 16, 242, fn. 37.   [11] Guzzini 2012: 2–3.   [12] Owen 2015.

migration, and jihad (Chapters 3, 4, 5, and 9), among others, offer many examples of protean power, stretching back decades and centuries. The argument of this book is not dealing with possibly ephemeral recent technological change.

Power dynamics unfold in the interplay of experience and context. Actors experience the world as anywhere from mostly risky to deeply uncertain, thus triggering control and protean power dynamics. Underlying contexts of risk and uncertainty also affect these dynamics. The congruence (or lack thereof) between experience and context matters greatly. Drawing on some of the evidence in the case studies this chapter addresses these issues in the first section. In the second section, we show that on questions of security and political economy scholars of international relations view the world in terms of risk only, and commonly focus only on control power. Thus, they ignore protean power dynamics operating under conditions of uncertainty and fail to grapple with the unexpected in world politics.

Power Practices, Risk, and Uncertainty

Uncertainty permeates the life of individuals everywhere. Yet it cuts against the grain of institutional and organized life in the twenty-first century. International relations scholarship reacts strongly to the second fact while all but disregarding the first. Our risk-based thinking expresses a deep desire for and faith in control.[13] This may explain why in the analysis of international relations "uncertainty" is often either conflated with "risk" or neglected altogether. To make matters even more confusing, some of the main research traditions in international relations define these terms differently.[14] The misleading affinity between the two concepts is even more problematic when a neglect of uncertainty turns risk calculations into "fictional expectations" and "visions" of a future that is unforeseeable.[15] Resting on assumptions about regular and incremental change we are prone to rely on accounts that are partial to the direction by and diffusion of control power even though they are often derailed by actor agility and unexpected creative effects in the circulation of protean power.

Focusing on risk and uncertainty, however, should not blind us to the fact that many actors are experiencing politics in terms of certainties, misplaced and otherwise. Actors may be overly confident that they know their adversaries' capabilities and intentions or both when, actually, they

[13] Eidinow 2011: 158; Scott 1998: 321–22.   [14] Rathbun 2007.
[15] Beckert 2016; Berenskoetter 2011: 648.

do not. Between states this can lead to security dilemmas and spirals toward war. In the world of known unknowns, or operational uncertainty, standard risk models apply. In the world of unknown unknowns, or radical uncertainty, emotions can create misplaced certainty and instill overconfidence.[16] Religious believers also perceive central aspects of their lives to be certain. They draw on deep reservoirs of convictions that give them the courage to cope, often creatively. Religion, for example, provides the certainty that ISIS fighters need while planning and committing atrocities (Chapter 9). Terrorism is all about the creation of fear and uncertainty; yet suicide bombers yearn for a certainty that affirms the value of their criminal self-sacrifice. The unfailing courage of many migrants who face forbidding odds is also often grounded in strong religious beliefs (Chapter 5). Their faith is a perfectly logical response to uncertainty.[17] Religion offers a confidence-inspiring language that, interspersed with everyday speech, provides a normative orientation to a migrant's unpredictable journey.[18]

Mastery of risk defines an important boundary between tradition and modernity. That the future can serve the present and that the chance of loss is also an opportunity for gain was once a revolutionary idea.[19] In modern, secular societies actors typically experience life as variable mixtures of risk and uncertainty. For example, migrants experience the unpredictable every hour along their shifting Odyssey (Chapter 5). When they play the odds – encountering border guards, gangs, relief workers, fellow migrants – they do so based on their experience, reasonable guesswork, and intuition while operating in the domain of uncertainty. Making mistakes can be costly, even fatal. In finance, uncertainty both exists as an objective fact and is also experienced subjectively as an indelible part of financial markets (Chapter 8). In contrast to migrants, bankers do not die when they make big mistakes in investing other peoples' money; often they emerge scot-free. They rely on sophisticated risk models to place their bets, informed by what they think are rational expectations. Yet, in the volatile world of finance, such expectations can easily be proven wrong and morph into panics. What is true of migrants and bankers is true more generally: subjective experiences of uncertainty meet objectively uncertain features of a given context. There exist, then, two ways to encounter uncertainty: through subjective experience and as objective reality. The two influence one another and blend together; whichever way the dial may shift in particular settings, the

---

[16] Mitzen and Schweller 2011.   [17] Brigden 2015: 254–55.   [18] Brigden 2013: 218–23.
[19] Bernstein 1996: 1, 337.

resulting effects cannot readily be explicated without invoking the concept of protean power.

To the extent that actors convince themselves that they live in a world marked only by risk they "may have become slaves of a new religion, a creed that is just as implacable, confining, and arbitrary as the old."[20] We are not products only of an inevitable or probable future. Uncertainty creates a kind of freedom.[21] When probability fails us in the domain of uncertainty we find, in the words of Kenneth Arrow, "the tentative, creative nature of the human mind in the face of the unknown" – illustrated among migrants just as much as among bankers.[22] Generally speaking, though, those controlling power rely on risk analysis as a political idiom that unlocks homogenizing social conventions as a preferred method to stabilize a world filled with unpredictable possibilities. Conventions emanate from knowledge, laws, rules, norms, and practices. They reflect and often reinforce asymmetries of control power. Peoples living in precarious circumstances can and do resist control.[23] They live in uncertain contexts experienced as such, and must cope the best they can with the unpredictable. Uncertainty and protean power thus exert a permanent pull on efforts to establish or perpetuate control.

In such a fluid world, choices are often contingent and respond to, reinforce, or create diverse power relations. Rather than thinking at the micro-level only in terms of the diffusion of control power as the sum of individual calculations, we should think also of interactive processes of translation viewed from the perspective of protean power.[24] Whenever power unfolds in "assemblages, distributed networks and circuits," rather than in homogeneous populations that share common knowledge, "translation becomes essential ... things never unfold quite as planned."[25] Assemblages are heterogeneous, not reducible to a single logic, yield unexpected relationships, and locate agency both in state and non-state actors, but also in "agentic swarms."[26] Assemblages can be found in deep structural or social contexts, often viewed exclusively as settings of purportedly stability-inducing control power. But they operate also in fluid conditions of improvisation and innovation with their effects on protean power dynamics.[27] In the "diffusion model," commands are obeyed and

---

[20] Ibid.: 7.   [21] Ibid.: 229.   [22] Ibid.: 220.   [23] Douglas 1990: 3.
[24] Latour 1986; Callon 1986.   [25] Best and Walters 2013: 232.
[26] McKeen-Edwards and Porter 2013: 24–27, 31–33.
[27] Itçaina, Roger, and Smith 2016: 22–31. Because actor-network theory denies the existence of a social context external to action, in contrast to sociological institutionalism, it does not focus on socially embedded action. See also Munro 2009. Recent applications of principal–agent, rational choice theory are beginning to examine the importance of stakeholders that influence indirectly what traditionally has been modeled strictly as a direct relationship among actors. See Johnson 2014: vi–vii.

disseminated because of an impetus from their original source. It assumes that for the most part actors share in the same knowledge of the world and rely only on "information updating." The "translation model" works differently. Agents observe would-be commands, following their own specific reasons as they translate, or are enrolled into, the projects of those who wield control power.[28] Translation into their own life experience and meaning thus becomes an important first step by which actors respond. That response often amounts to improvisation, a kind of Everyman's muddling through.[29]

Models of decision-making typically focus on choice that aligns means to ends under conditions of risk. Translation processes reveal a different kind of choice that bring into play both calculative and non-calculative practices under conditions of uncertainty. In a world of risk, choice is control-oriented and aims at the best tactics and strategy. Under conditions of uncertainty, choice is situationally adaptive to immediate circumstances and is indeterminate with respect to the specific and general outcomes it creates. James Scott has coined the term "infrapolitics" to describe the unobtrusive realm of discursive political struggle revealed in "hidden transcripts."[30] That struggle prepares the ground for organized political action, which may eventually produce control, as the last rather than the first stage.[31] Yet prior to that point, when agility truly matters, infrapolitics exemplifies the circulation of protean power. The pull that the world of uncertainty and protean power exerts on the world of control and risk is strong. It inheres in the fields of power potentialities that encompass and often undermine power probabilities.

This is illustrated by the political translations of local LGBT actors of the social and legal norms that emanate from international, non-governmental actors as well as the European Union (EU) (Chapter 4). The process can move in both directions. Actors translate norms and practices flowing downward in the initial stage of the propagation and partial adoption of LGBT rights as part of EU enlargement. And they can also translate norms and practices flowing upward during periods of backlash. This happened also in the case of individual rights after the Second World War. Newly independent, post-colonial states were able to use new forums, such as the United Nations, to universalize human rights, redefine the right to self-determination, and delegitimize the institution of empire (Chapter 3). Similarly, terrorists trafficking in the production of fears that are grounded

---

[28] Chabot 2002. The delegation of power or authority from principal to agent differs in that it proceeds by rules and the discretion such rules may confer. This results in negotiation in established orders rather than innovation and the attempt to create new ones. Between these two ideal types, empirical reality is likely to produce different mixtures.
[29] Lindblom 1959.   [30] Scott 1990: 183–201.   [31] Scott 1985: 28–47.

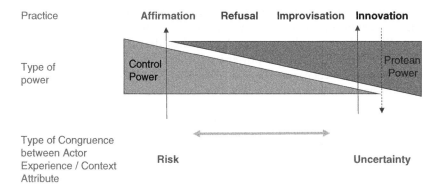

Figure 2.1 Risk and Uncertainty, Power Type, and Political Practice*

* The horizontal arrow captures different constellations of risk and uncertainty that create various relations between protean and control power. In the interest of simplicity of presentation, the figure does not capture in further detail mismatches between context and experience depicted in Seybert and Katzenstein, in Chapter 1, Figure 1.1, p. 13.

in uncertainty try to reveal to everybody the shallowness of the state's coercive controls and the high costs they may entail for life and liberty (Chapter 9). They do so with the hope that states will come to understand the futility of counterterrorism policies and accede to the demands of terrorist groups. Finally, private actors serving as regulators of a voluntary carbon offset market leveraged their power through translation when states were ready to shift to the policy position that NGOs had advocated all along (Chapter 12).

Figure 2.1 identifies affirmation, refusal, improvisation, and innovation as illustrations of four practices that arise from the interaction between the two dimensions introduced previously in Figure 1.1: attributes of the underlying context (as risky or uncertain) and actor experience of the surrounding context (as risky or uncertain). The two endpoints of the spectrum linking affirmation to control and innovation to protean power characterize situations where the experiences of actors and the context in which they operate coincide to create contrasting worlds of unambiguous risk and radical uncertainty. In the first case, affirmation generates risk-based control power, in the second, innovation uncertainty-inflected protean power. In-between, refusal and improvisation are shaped by a mismatch between experience and context. This results in different types of interaction between protean and control power that are illustrated abundantly in the empirical chapters of this book.

Figure 2.1 shares the premise of virtually all power theories: power relations cannot be analyzed by assuming the existence of actors in isolation. Since the control power wedge reaches deep into the domain of uncertainty, and the protean power wedge deep into the domain of risk, characteristic practices are not tightly wedded to the two kinds of power. Control-producing practices are a possible response in the domain of uncertainty where they lead to indeterminacy. Through disregard of new variables that occur outside established probability calculations, such practices can affect future power potentialities; we label them as refusal. Conversely, innovation is a possible response in the domain of risk, leading perhaps to anticipated gains or shocking reversals. There exists, however, an important difference here. Affirmation facilitating the diffusion of control power operates more often than not directly. In less direct ways, refusal, improvisation, and innovation can trigger with increasing intensity a circulation of protean power. Rather than focusing on narrow power effects in dyadic relations, this conceptualization highlights the broader context and actors' experiences. Depending on the balance between protean and control power, knowledge can dismantle or build up social conformity by freeing or disciplining multitudes of individuals or organizations at the micro-level and entire populations at the macro-level. In short, this conceptualization and the empirical studies in this book highlight fluid power relations that can show up in unexpected places.[32]

Reading Figure 2.1 from left to right traces different configurations of control and protean power. Despite the figure's simplified one-dimensional depiction of the categories, it seeks to convey the fluidity of real-life situations that oscillate between risk and uncertainty as a result of particular actions taken by actors, whose immediate experiences of context matter a great deal. On one end, affirmation is a response associated primarily with control power. We know control power worked if "actor B" gives in to "actor A," regardless of the reasons for such behavior: pluralist competition (Dahl), limited alternatives (Bachrach and Baratz), the structural shaping of what is considered desirable or normal (Lukes, Foucault), or persuasive and admirable traits or practices (Nye).[33] In principle, one can access probabilities of outcomes surrounding control and develop expectations about the behavior and likelihood of success by those who exercise power and those who submit to it.

[32] Control and protean power analysis differ in their understanding of causation. While efficient causes are linked to clear effects of control power, protean power analysis relies, in addition, on constitutive causation, indicated in Figure 2.1 by two vertical arrows, representing a response to uncertainty that innovation deepens further. See also Seybert and Katzenstein, Chapter 1, pp. 19–20, above.

[33] Dahl 1957; Bachrach and Baratz 1962; Lukes 2006a; Foucault 1982; Nye 2011.

For the present argument, *affirmation* characterizes situations in which experience and context meet in the domain of risk. The empirical contributions in this book frequently acknowledge an element of giving-in to authority. But they also consider instances where practices travel along the continuum. Migrants retain agency even when they experience a loss of freedom, exploitation, and degradation by the predatory exercise of protean power by individual smugglers and criminal organizations. Though affirmation takes the outward form of submission, at times migrants conspire quietly to regain their freedom (Chapter 5). There is nothing quiet about the change from affirmation to refusal as Poland, once it had been granted EU membership, developed a backlash against the international and transnational propagation of LGBT norms (Chapter 4). Similarly, while not seeking to compete with Hollywood head on, localized, niche, and diaspora-driven film industries manage to co-exist with the dominant channels of commercial distribution and cultural production, and still thrive through improvising or innovative practices that can sideline Hollywood's dominance (Chapter 10). Similarly, gas supply crises and near-crises trace the reinvented market relations and technological innovations to serve as unexpected improvisations, even for actors lacking resource endowments (Chapter 7).

It is therefore inaccurate to quip that "where control power stops, protean power begins." For experience and context often are not congruent. This opens an expansive analytical space between the two ends of the spectrum depicted in Figure 2.1. The evidence in this volume shows that it is a mistake to focus only either on the affirmation of evolving control power arrangements or on creative innovation in the domain of protean power. The zone demarcating "uncertainty about probability" most closely approximates the environment most actors face or assume they are facing in international politics. Figure 2.1 depicts this analytical space as a mixture of risk and uncertainty. It produces the practices of refusal on one side of this intermediate range and more disruptive improvisation on the other. The tension between and co-existence of risk and uncertainty in this context matters greatly. While many risk-accessible variables exist, there is much room for alternative approaches. Like skiing in fog, limited visibility and gravity remain important factors but may matter less than sudden icy patches, panicked fellow skiers, or diminished confidence. Refusal of the known is insufficient, even irrelevant; instead, resorting to trial and error, and continuous improvisation characterize such worlds. As the fog of uncertainty descends, obscuring the sight of previous paths, new ones need to be uncovered, possibly changing the course altogether.

In more direct contact with the world of risk than uncertainty, *refusal* does not so much dismiss as challenge underlying probabilities. It can take the form of outright resistance captured by images of heroic street action. Often, however, it takes more mundane forms. James Scott, for example, gives a rich account of the hidden transcripts that help to constitute refusal practices of power relations. He argues that hidden transcripts are "a condition of practical resistance, rather than a substitute for it . . . Under the appropriate conditions the accumulation of petty acts can, rather like snowflakes on a steep mountainside, set off an avalanche."[34] Similarly, Hayek's concept of spontaneous ordering entails refusal and creative circumvention by individual or collective actors endowed with tacit knowledge.[35] This can recreate or fundamentally change the exercise of control power. For Hayek "reliance on spontaneous order both extends and limits our powers of control."[36] Although they do not agree on much else, Foucault concurs with Hayek on the importance of refusal. For Foucault, "there is no power without potential refusal or revolt."[37] Power begets refusal that focuses on the immediate enemy and small zones of autonomy more than long-term and perhaps utopian dreams.[38] Explication of such fluid situations depends on the particular position occupied by each actor,[39] and is reflected in the sense-making practices that test the limits of control. Such practices can lead to refusal through diversion and the choice of alternatives.

For example, the refusal of skeptical, large states shifted the arms control negotiation strategies of NGOs and small states, intent on accommodating them, on both the Cluster Munition Convention (2008) and the Conventional Arms Trade Treaty (2013) (Chapter 11). Similarly, NGOs updating the terms of the climate change conversation found ways to creatively navigate a world where basic rules were firmly set by state actors, but the uncertainty surrounding the issue left ample room for maneuver (Chapter 12). The case of migration, too, supports the idea that protean power is better suited for creative refusal than for controlling the direction of state policy (Chapter 5). That said, it would be infinitely better for the migrants to have a revolution in US migration policy than to have to rely on the "weapons of the weak."[40]

Brought about through *improvisation and innovation* in an uncertain world, protean power dynamics make it impossible to anticipate which choices and practices will lead to which outcomes. Nor is that the objective. The fog of uncertainty clears only with hindsight, when we look back

---

[34] Scott 1990: 191–92.   [35] Hayek 1973: 46.   [36] Ibid.: 41.   [37] Foucault 1981: 253.
[38] Foucault 1982; 2007: 357; Lipschutz 2007: 239–41; Neumann and Sending 2010: 24–25, 159–60.
[39] Fligstein and McAdam 2012: 11.   [40] Scott 1985.

to identify how actors, deemed successful, navigated the fluid environment surrounding them. Knowledge is not only expressed in individual actors' calculated intentions and ensuing practices, it is also embodied in networks that react to acts of individual or social creativity and imagination and bottom-up, unexpected effects.

The case studies in this book provide many instances of improvisation and innovation when protean power is in play: smugglers discovering the useful deception of migrants singing religious hymns to conceal the group's true identity while passing the road blocks set up by crime cartels; US border guards profiling as they seek to identify illegal immigrants (Chapter 5); scientists and engineers improvising in their quest for new ideas and products (Chapter 6); Canada proposing a meeting of states favoring the Anti-Personnel Landmine Treaty outside the UN framework, beyond the reach of opposing states such as the United States (Chapter 11); firms developing negotiation strategies that exploit long-term trust and technological innovation in hydrocarbons (Chapter 7); ISIS developing tactics of attack and strategies of state-building in the case of terrorism (Chapter 9); Polish activists appealing to EU norms and subsequently translating these norms for different use in changed circumstances (Chapter 4); human rights advocates exploiting norm indeterminacy, cross-fertilization, and localization in their struggles for civil and political rights (Chapter 3); NGOs establishing parallel markets for carbon sinks and agile states subsequently appropriating approaches developed by NGOs (Chapter 12); financial firms developing over-the-counter derivatives and novel legal strategies in sovereign debt markets (Chapter 8); and, finally, Nollywood and other foreign movie industries both feeding off and bypassing Hollywood (Chapter 10).

Charles Tilly offers a helpful musical metaphor for our understanding of improvisation and innovation. We can appreciate musical practices better through focusing on the effects they have on the transformative potential of the relations they activate than their substantive content which, by definition, is case-specific and fleeting. In jazz, Tilly stresses "individual dexterity, knowledge, and disciplined preparation" without concrete knowledge of what the final result will be. Fundamentally innovative practices take the form of "improvised interaction, surprise, incessant error and error-correction, alternation between solo and ensemble action, and repeated responses to understandings shared by at least pairs of players."[41] In jazz, as in political life, "improvisation on a theme" and "free improvisation" illustrate the

---

[41] Tilly 2000: 723. We thank Dan Nexon for bringing this analogy to our attention.

range of practices covering conditions of risk and uncertainty. In deeply uncertain contexts, the potential for exercising power is not eliminated. On the contrary, Patrick Jackson reminds us that contingency breeds agency.[42] And nothing is more contingent than an uncertain world. The circulation of protean power operates through improvisation and innovation by actors that can engage and transform those involved. In the words of Emmanuel Adler, power lies in offering previously unavailable modes of consciousness that "break new social ground."[43]

Actors find themselves improvising, rather than innovating, when the uncertainty they encounter takes the form of inaccessible knowledge about where previously established strategies may lead. The kind of crisis that this produces is an emergency. In a risk-based world, the recommended course of action is often the taking of cognitive shortcuts. The misguidedness of that approach, however, is well documented in Kurt Weyland's account of the surprising failure of both the 1848 revolutions in Europe and the Arab Spring of 2011.[44] Such crises necessitate improvisation both as a strategy of political change and mere survival. By contrast, uncertainty invites innovation as the means to plant new stakes in continuously shifting grounds. This characterizes the world of unknown unknowns that scientific and technological innovation explores through processes of knowledge creation (Chapter 6).

As we move to uncertainty, it becomes clear that improvisation and innovation are not simply responses to external promptings. They are often endogenously created, a manifestation of protean power, as in Hayward's formulation of power as a field of possibilities.[45] Albert Hirschman's "principle of the hiding hand," for example, underlines the paradox that creative resources can come fully into play because of a prior misjudgment of the nature of the task at hand – of thinking of it as more routine and undemanding of creativity than it turned out to be.[46] The hiding hand principle commits risk-averters to change course and become venture-seekers. If the problem of misjudging the task at hand is one of "falling into error," the creativity it engenders is its opposite, "falling into truth." Normal language conspires to conceal falling into truth, just as control power conspires to conceal protean power. Under conditions of uncertainty, improvisation and innovation unfold largely beyond the reach of relations of control; it is what actors do to respond to uncertainty. One of its effects is to enhance creativity and the circulation of protean power.

---

[42] Jackson 2006: 33.   [43] Adler 2008: 203.   [44] Weyland 2012.
[45] Hayward 1998: 9–18; Latour 1986.   [46] Hirschman 1967: 13, 20.

Reading Figure 2.1 from top to bottom connects practices to power effects and underlying constellations of context and experience. Protean power starts with individual agents reacting to uncertainty but then multiplies the unknowns not only for specific individual experiences but also for the broader context and future potentialities. For example, in the case of migration viewing power dynamics through the lenses of individuals or organizations brings different phenomena into view (Chapter 5). Scholarship on hydrocarbons that focuses on states and corporations blends out the unceasing, variable renegotiations among firms, an important mechanism for coping with uncertainty in markets (Chapter 7). Most case studies in this book thus report and analyze power dynamics that cut across different levels of analysis connecting individuals to states, markets, corporations, movements, and regional organizations. The "level of analysis problem" in international relations turns out to be not a problem but a defining characteristic of protean power dynamics. Standing in for many other chapters, the case study on LGBT rights (Chapter 4) shows clearly how individuals are enmeshed with and connected to various levels: national movements, states, and regional organizations such as the EU.

Though opposed conceptually, the two ends of the axis depicted in Figure 2.1 are in reality inextricably connected. "The issue of power," writes Ulrich Beck, "is ignited especially by the knowledge that consequences cannot be predicted in advance ... The very power and characteristics that are supposed to create a new quality of security and certainty simultaneously determine the extent of absolute uncontrollability that exists ... All attempts at minimizing or eliminating risk technologically simply multiply the uncertainty into which we are plunging the world."[47] Variations in the diffusion of control power can mask deep-seated uncertainties that complicate probabilistic reasoning and open up possibilities for the circulation of protean power. This reworking of social relations through control and protean power dynamics is what Charles Tilly must have had in mind when he suggested that the "history of a social relation transform[s] that relation."[48]

Relying on their repertoire of coercive, institutional, and structural tools or positions, dominant actors are not masters of the universe, endowed with a special knack for controlling the main forms of social knowledge and political practices. If they were, we would be living in a world of risk only, accessible entirely to the power of calculation and prediction. However, we also encounter uncertainty, rapid change, and sudden shocks when established heuristics no longer work.[49] History does not only

[47] Beck 2005: 101–2.   [48] Tilly 2000. One could readily substitute "power" for "social."
[49] Ostrom 2010a: 20.

crawl; it also jumps.[50] Living with the expectation of the unexpected creates a systemic lack of organizational capacities, inherent limitations to knowledge, a weakening of control power, and an increasing relevance of protean power.[51] Intent as they are on exercising control, leaders cannot avoid but dealing with what Copeland calls "the pernicious problem of uncertainty."[52] More generally, uncertainty can create conditions ripe for improvisation. It can also incite unexpected innovations as political actors try to make the future meaningful by linking the self to something bigger than its singular, present existence.[53]

The distinction between control and protean power rests on underlying assumptions about the knowability of the world. The boundary between what is known and unknown is clear only in the abstract. "Social interactions are by definition indeterminate. They are inexhaustible sources of uncertainty ... While we can never eliminate social uncertainty, we can strive to contain it ... The core technology for managing social uncertainty, though, are institutions."[54] But institutions can also harbor politically possible worlds, not only constraining but also enlarging the realm of uncertainty. Chris Reus-Smit (Chapter 3) argues that institutions contain many control-resisting nooks and crannies. Furthermore, institutional norms are sites of uncertainty, as their meanings are inherently indeterminate. Both conditions create opportunities for control-defying innovations. The boundary between uncertainty and risk, control and protean power is unavoidably porous and is often difficult to discern empirically. While reflecting on his life in finance as head of Goldman Sachs and in politics as Secretary of the Treasury under President Clinton, Robert Rubin mused. "Luck or skill? We'll never know ... it seemed indispensable to be lucky, but it wasn't so bad to be smart either, if you could arrange both."[55] Rubin echoes a theme that has been prominent throughout the ages.[56] It agrees with the strong note of caution with which Tetlock and Gardner conclude their study of forecasting. "We frequently pass through phases of history riddled with irreducible uncertainty – phases in which luck trumps skill."[57] In those times we should have the humility to accept that the dynamics of power can easily produce unpredictable practices and outcomes.[58] Put differently, we should be prepared to accept a world in which protean power plays an important part.

---

[50] Tetlock and Gardner 2015: 240.   [51] Gordon 1991: 16–22; Walters 2012: 37–38.
[52] Copeland 2000: 206.   [53] Berenskoetter 2011: 652–54.   [54] Schedler 2013: 23.
[55] Weisberg 1998; Tetlock and Gardner 2015: 142–43.   [56] Eidinow 2011; Frank 2016.
[57] Tetlock and Gardner 2015: 272.   [58] McCloskey 1991: 35–36.

International Relations Scholarship's Exclusive Focus on Risk and Control

Important strands of international relations scholarship have followed the intellectual ascendance of economics and focus attention largely on the putatively controllable world of risk, while largely neglecting the uncontrollable world of uncertainty. By doing so, they train our sight only on control power, sideline protean power, and are unable to analyze the unpredictable. For example, in her authoritative and sophisticated analysis of risk-taking in international politics Rose McDermott writes that risk inheres in any situation where there exists uncertainty.[59] She combines both risk and uncertainty as she identifies underlying mechanisms of risk propensity that occur under conditions of "high" uncertainty. While it is impossible to scale the magnitude of uncertainty, it is possible to distinguish between two different kinds of uncertainty. Known unknowns create operational uncertainty, which, given more or better knowledge and information, may transform into calculable risk. Far from being a panacea, however, in situations of operational uncertainty more or better knowledge or information, as in the squeezing of a balloon, simply pushes radical uncertainty into some other, unrecognized part of the political context. Unknown unknowns are unknowable and cannot be converted to risk. Although she does not make the distinction between the two kinds of unknowns, McDermott acknowledges the importance of operational unknowns. She writes "most complex choices fall under the framework of judgment under uncertainty and decision-making under risk because it is impossible to predict the characteristics of many different variables simultaneously in advance, especially when they may have unknown interaction effects. Even the nature of many of the critical variables may be unknown beforehand."[60] Yet, in line with current practice of international relations scholarship, as she further develops and applies prospect theory, McDermott puts aside the problem of uncertainty. She thus makes invisible the practice-driven, protean power-generating actor responses to such uncertainty. The present framework insists on the need for completeness, rather than narrow selectiveness, in studying world politics and offers means of considering approaches focusing on risk-based control power alongside those tracing protean power practices in the face of uncertainty.[61]

---

[59] McDermott 1998: 3–5, 30. We would like to thank Professor McDermott for reading and agreeing with the substance of an earlier draft of this paragraph.

[60] Ibid.: 5. See also Gartzke 1999: 567.

[61] Some readers of this section have insisted that point estimates can be given with different confidence intervals. But it is difficult to see how confidence intervals could be specified in the realm of unknown unknowns. Furthermore, as a matter of research practice scholars of international relations treat confidence intervals strictly as a methodological

Security Studies

The invention and the destructiveness of nuclear weapons epitomizes the quest for control. The core idea of nuclear deterrence is "the threat that leaves something to chance." Based on the previously noted mistranslation of Weber, "chance" here is understood to describe risk rather than risk and uncertainty. Possible protean power effects are thus rendered invisible. Articulated and developed by Thomas Schelling in the 1950s and 1960s, a risk-based understanding of chance has had a pervasive influence on the theory and practice of nuclear deterrence for the last half century.[62] The idea is based on Schelling's highly creative conceptual move that reduces uncontrollable uncertainty to manageable risk and thus from a problem to a solution for the issuing of credible nuclear threats. For Schelling, uncontrollable, accidental factors feed seamlessly into an escalation of controlled, competitive risk-taking. Accidents, in this theory, are drawn from a known probability distribution that is said to increase as each party draws closer to the brink. In Schelling's theory nuclear accidents do not exist. For accidents do not cause nuclear war; decisions do. Accidents are reduced to decisions to manage risk in a particular manner. They are no more than appendices of rational decisions. And decisions are constrained by the logic that deterrence theory articulates. Schelling does not allow the theoretical possibility of accidental nuclear use or nuclear accidents to impose any limits on risk-based deterrence models. In this reading, "the threat that leaves something to chance" is so only in terms of probabilities transforming nuclear weapons into means of control, wielded by actors with select attributes, rather than creating room for unanticipated challenges to existing rules of interaction. It squeezes out of the model unacknowledged, unfathomable unknowns, contingencies and indeterminacies. Establishing the power of full control over "the ultimate weapon" upholds the claim that the theory explains the uncontrollable. Probabilistic and possibilistic thinking are not interactive and co-evolving but fuse into a double mask. By transforming, in one theoretical move, uncontrollable uncertainty into manageable risk Schelling offers a compelling theory of control power.[63] With the

---

issue. If there are instances in which the political content of confidence intervals has been probed, they must be very few in numbers. We do not know of any.

[62] This discussion of Schelling draws on the important papers by Pelopidas 2015, 2016.

[63] The term "luck" appears once in Schelling's *Strategy of Conflict* (1963); "uncertain" or "uncertainty" ten times; "risk" 102 times. "Chance" is mentioned seventy-five times, but for Schelling is coterminous with risk rather than uncertainty. Pelopidas personal communication, March 9, 2016. Pelopidas 2015: 14, fn. 28. Also see our discussion of the meaning of the German term *Chance* for Weber, Seybert, and Katzenstein in Chapter 1, pp. 11–12, fn. 41, above, and for Clausewitz in Katzenstein and Seybert, Chapter 13, p. 287, fn. 57, below. Schelling 1963.

elaboration of the concept of an organizational doomsday machine subsequent scholarship on nuclear deterrence has taken this approach to its (il)logical extreme.[64]

Schelling's work has had large consequences not only for the study of nuclear deterrence but for the study of war. In the last two decades, students of security studies have developed and tested extensively what is now known as the bargaining model of war. It offers a risk-based view of war that highlights control power and mostly disregards uncertainty and protean power dynamics.[65] This is made possible by the bargaining model's first core assumption: the parties to a conflict subscribe to the same understanding of how the world works.[66] This is vital for the model to work. Yet it is often wildly implausible to believe that parties locked in possibly deadly conflict share the same understanding.[67] Imagination and potentiality of how the world might work, central to protean power analysis, thus escape the attention of the bargaining model. Uncertainty is key in allowing competing models of the world to be sustained. It leads to irreducible and consequential deviations away from expectations created or implied by risk-based models. Convergence of views around one model thus does not occur. Based on the implausible assumption of convergence, rationalist models proceed to think about actors with different preferences. If they decide to fight, each side will pay a cost while fighting. These costs open up a range of bargained solutions that both sides should prefer to war. For the bargaining model, the puzzle of war is why the two parties fail to settle within the range of bargained solutions before war breaks out, knowing that war is always inefficient after its outbreak. The answer to the puzzle lies in the existence of imperfections in information and the incentive to misrepresent, on the one hand, and the inability to credibly commit to an agreement that prevents war, on the other.

The model introduces a second core assumption: updating of information will select out inferior models of the world. But in security affairs, misperceptions, the fog of war, and a host of other factors

---

[64] Rhodes 1989: 156.

[65] A number of colleagues have contested this point and suggested that we talk to game theorists who are developing sophisticated models. This misses the point. For the most part game theorists are not interested in offering political insights. Scholars of international relations are and should be; by adopting a risk-only bargaining model of the world, they have imposed serious limits on their analysis of power in world politics.

[66] We thank Jonathan Kirshner for clarifying conversations on this point.

[67] The issue is not whether game theory can account for actors playing different games, holding different preferences, or having different tastes for risk; it is about their causal models of the world. Models of the world can be explanatory, constitutive, or a mixture of both. The bargaining model's core assumption is restrictive in focusing only on explanatory models. See also Kirshner 2015.

prevent the emergence of a succession of probability-based, improved models. There exists no urn from which to pull red or white balls; players are color-blind; and there is no way of updating expectations based on the number of balls left in the urn. Instead, there is a lot of bluffing and interpretation. Crises are generators of uncertainty rather than risks with associated probabilities that are known or knowable.[68] In short, on issues of war and peace world politics simply does not offer, as the bargaining model assumes, a sufficiently large number of trials to select out inferior causal models. Even if all actors shared the same model of the world, which they do not, these models would fail. By making strong but implausible assumptions, the bargaining model of war focuses on the calculable directionality of control power and overlooks the creative imagination, or even improvised coping that generates protean power and transforms the surrounding uncertainty further still.

The bargaining model holds that different conclusions about future outcomes are possible, but only because of differences in information not because of differences in worldviews about the salience of risk and uncertainty. The probability of victory in any conflict and the cost of fighting are assumed to be calculable and subject to known or knowable probabilities by all parties to the conflict. However, disagreements are unavoidable when actors put the same information to work in different worldviews. As is true elsewhere, in world politics rationality takes the form of many situationally specific kinds of reasonableness. And standards of reasonableness differ in worldviews populated by different cosmologies, different historical memories, different conspiracy theories, different emotions, and different moral prescriptions.

For example, during the Cold War many American analysts and decision-makers believed that they had reached an understanding with the Soviet Union about the stability-inducing effects of a robust arms control regime. Russian archives opened after the end of the Cold War revealed a starkly different picture. In the mid-1980s, the Soviet Union had deployed a near-automatic nuclear strike force, which had been decades in the making. Because it was kept totally secret, this doomsday machine lacked the rationality of nuclear deterrence that makes contingent irrationality look rational.[69] "The Soviet Union," writes David Hoffman, "was looking through an entirely different prism than the United States."[70] It is a stroke of luck that today we are in

---

[68] We thank James Davis who helped to clarify our thinking on this point.
[69] Rhodes 1989: 155–202.
[70] Hoffman 2009: 18. Note that this is not an issue of asymmetric information, of the United States not knowing about the doomsday machine, as the bargaining model holds.

a position to study this near-calamity. Conversely, the period of détente in the 1970s rested on a bedrock of illusions that US and Soviet decision-makers shared about each other. "The super-powers," writes Eric Grynaviski, "were simply wrong; they did not understand each other as well as they thought."[71] Misunderstanding in this instance secured cooperation that accurate information would have stymied. Filtered through different worldviews, shared information can be destructive or constructive. It is not the infor-mation but the worldview that drives actors toward war or peace. Worldviews that incorporate constitutive elements of risk/uncer-tainty and actor experiences can capture protean power dynamics; information models that exclude those elements cannot.

Furthermore, many bargaining models typically suffer from the problem of multiple equilibria – solutions a rational player would not depart from voluntarily. The folk theorem establishes that the existence of multiple equilibria is unavoidable in repeated games with incomplete information and an appropriate discount for future payoffs. More complicated models that include uncertainty do exist. But the practical challenge of building models that can handle non-Gaussian distributions is formidable. In Lance Taylor's words, "reliably estimating parameters that specify the form of distributions with fat tails is difficult if not impossible – one reason why this approach has not been widely pursued."[72] Put simply, because models that incorporate uncertainty are messy and technically intractable most scholars of international relations who have adopted the bargaining model do not work with them and thus make us overlook the relevance of uncertainty in shaping actor responses in world politics.

Because of these shortcomings, scholars relying on the bargaining model of war systematically bias political analysis toward the manage-ment of risk through control power. One of the original proponents of the bargaining model of war, James Fearon, conflates risk and uncertainty when he writes "given identical information, truly rational agents should reason to the same conclusion about the probability of one uncertain outcome or another."[73] This conflation of the two concepts has become

In building and concealing the machine, as Hoffman argues correctly, the Soviet Union showed that it was holding to a radically different worldview.

[71] Grynaviski 2014: 13.
[72] Taylor 2010: 120. In the future, rigorous modeling efforts may help to broaden the restricted risk-only-no-uncertainty setting in which information-based models have oper-ated so confidently during the last two decades. To date, however, judging by the publications in leading journals of international relations, existing research has not ventured into that territory.
[73] Fearon 1995: 392; Kirshner 2000. Assuming that it is not serving as an escape hatch, the concept of "true rationality" begs the question of the meaning of "rationality."

deeply engrained in many theoretical extensions and empirical applications of the bargaining model. Andrew Kydd and Barbara Walter, for example, build their analysis of different strategies of terrorist violence on the bargaining model of war.[74] In doing so, they implausibly assume that terrorists are impelled by the same signaling and commitment logic as are states. Trafficking in uncertainty, they are not. Matthew Kroenig's analysis of nuclear bargaining implicitly equates risk with uncertainty.[75] He argues that coercive nuclear bargaining and nuclear brinkmanship rest on the manipulation of risk through "anguished" calculations of probabilities in situations of uncertainty and incomplete information. Page Fortna's analysis of ceasefire agreements is similarly inattentive to the difference between risk and uncertainty.[76] Fortna argues that war is risky since there is always a chance of losing rather than winning; uncertainty can undermine cooperation even when perfect information should yield cooperation automatically. Her empirical analysis relies on statistical models and significance tests that operate entirely in the world of risk.[77] Finally, relying on the language of the bargaining model of war, Debs and Monteiro argue that power shifts can be explained by information problems. Their model "provides specific probabilities for each event. The fact that the deterrer and target are uncertain about each other's actions is realistic."[78] In sum, important analyses of nuclear deterrence, terrorist violence, nuclear brinkmanship, ceasefires in civil conflicts, and power shifts are either reducing uncertainty to risk or treating the terms as synonyms.[79] This is odd in light of the models' focus on bargaining which is conducted by specific actors with specific experiences and balancing unique, locally anchored but broadly influential understandings of reality. Hunches and intuitions may be hard to measure and cannot, by definition, be systematized into a single model; nevertheless, they can play important roles in shaping bargaining outcomes. In their inattentiveness to such dynamics the authors of existing models differ from Napoleon who, acknowledging risk *and* uncertainty, had strong feelings about his generals. Although many of them were smart, he was partial to the lucky ones.

The problem lies in the realm of theory rather than its application to questions of security. Hedley Bull noticed long ago that the central ideas in Thomas Schelling's work were not derived solely from formal game theory operating in the world of risk; they also represented "an

---

[74] Kydd and Walter 2006: 56–59.   [75] Kroenig 2013: 144–45, 150.
[76] Fortna 2003: 340–41.   [77] Ziliak and McCloskey 2008.
[78] Debs and Monteiro 2014: 8 fn. 23.
[79] The difficulty of distinguishing risk from uncertainty can also be found in the European security literature. See Hammerstad and Boas 2015; Petersen 2011.

imaginative conceptual exercise" dealing with the problem of uncertainty.[80] In contrast to Schelling himself, scholars applying the bargaining model of war have overlooked the centrality of imagination. "In the final analysis," Schelling writes, "we are dealing with imagination as much as with logic . . . poets may do better than logicians at this game . . . Logic helps . . . but usually not until imagination has selected some clue to work on."[81] Bypassing the technical virtuosity of formal models of war, Jonathan Mercer similarly stresses the importance of creativity. Neglecting the importance of creativity political scientists risk "turning sophisticated political actors into lab rats . . . They have done so because predicting creativity is difficult and perhaps impossible – if one can predict creativity it cannot be very creative."[82] In short, imagination and creativity are integral to and constitutive of a world that mixes risk with uncertainty and control with protean power.

Political Economy[83]

The analysis of power dynamics is similarly imbalanced in the field of political economy and for the same reason: uncertainty no longer exists as a category worthy of analysis. In the 1920s, Heisenberg developed the uncertainty principle in physics at the very moment when Knight and Keynes drew a conceptual distinction between risk and uncertainty in economics. Knight argued that successful entrepreneurs are willing to make investments with uncertain payoffs in the future, for which they can charge a premium. For Keynes, probability is confidence in a conclusion given the evidence in support of that conclusion. Although he did not deny the existence of measurable probabilities in choice situations, for the most part Keynes argued that our tools or evidence are "too limited to make probability calculations: there may be no way of calculating, and/or there is no common unit to measure magnitudes . . . the degree of our rational belief in one conclusion is either equal to, greater than, or less than the degree of our belief in another."[84] Practical men and women, in Keynes' view, have no choice but to rely on conventions and similar mechanisms in deciding how to act.[85] Keynes did not see rational agents maximizing their utility; "rather, he emphasized the role of 'animal spirits' – of daring and ambitious entrepreneurs taking risks and placing bets in an environment characterized by uncertainty: that is, by de facto unknowns and epistemic unknowables."[86] For better and for

---

[80] Linklater 2000: 66.   [81] Schelling 1963: 58.   [82] Mercer 2013: 225.
[83] Some of the material in this section draws on Katzenstein and Nelson 2013a; Katzenstein and Nelson 2013b; Nelson and Katzenstein 2014.
[84] Keynes [1921] 1948: 31, 34.   [85] Keynes 1937: 214.   [86] Kirshner 2009: 532.

worse, entrepreneurial creativity and exuberance or panics showed protean power at work. Uncertainty means that the past is not prologue. Under conditions of uncertainty there is no basis for agents to settle on what the probability distribution looks like. Often experienced as "turning points," new narratives signal the obsolescence of the status quo and undermine the conventional wisdom, with profound consequences for how we think about power.

Despite the widespread acceptance of the behavioral turn in economics that challenges the standard rationalist approach, economists for the most part ignore or dismiss the distinction between risk and uncertainty. The conceptualization of uncertainty and risk that Knight and Keynes advanced in the 1920s has been relegated to the margins of the discipline.[87] Many fields of knowledge developed techniques "to isolate and domesticate" those aspects of the world subject to risk-based analysis, sidelining the rest. Economics, in particular, writes James Scott, has "incorporated calculable risk while exiling those topics where genuine uncertainty prevails."[88] Mainstream economists closed ranks around the assumption that uncertainty was analytically indistinguishable from risk. In an important textbook, Jack Hirshleifer and John Riley, for example, wrote in the early 1990s that Knight's distinction is "sterile."[89] As a result, in the words of George Akerlof and Robert Shiller, "theoretical economists have been struggling . . . to make sense of how people handle such true uncertainty."[90]

Because power is at the center of its concerns, failing to distinguish between risk and uncertainty is a serious problem in the field of international political economy. As in economics and security studies, uncertainty has either been neglected or conflated with risk, thus making protean power dynamics invisible. Not well known in other parts of the world, the paradigmatic American approach to the study of International Political Economy – "Open Economy Politics" (OEP) – moves entirely in the world of risk. In a paper addressing the effects of uncertainty, Lake and Frieden concede that uncertainty increases in crises, and then proceed to argue that risk and uncertainty "are similar enough to be conflated for our purposes."[91] In this way they and many scholars of international political economy follow the long line of economists who treat the difference between risk and uncertainty as semantic rather than substantive.[92]

---

[87] Best 2008.   [88] Scott 1998: 322.   [89] Hirshleifer and Riley 1992: 10.
[90] Akerlof and Shiller 2009: 144.   [91] Lake and Frieden 1989: 6–7.
[92] Ahlquist 2006; Bernhard and Leblang 2006; Bernhard, Broz, and Clark 2002; Koremenos 2005; Koremenos, Lipson, and Snidal 2001; Mosley 2006; Rosendorff and Milner 2001; Sobel 1999. For dissents without repercussions in OPE, see Blyth 2002; Oatley 2011; and Nelson and Katzenstein 2014.

In OEP economic actors have clear preference orderings. Interests are deduced from an actor's position in markets. Policies and outcomes are ranked according to how they affect an actor's expected future income stream. Interests are aggregated by institutions, which in turn structure the bargaining that occurs. The main advantage of OEP is its deductive argument about preferences. OEP scholars start with sets of actors who "can be reasonably assumed to share (nearly) identical interests . . . Deducing interests from economic theory was the essential innovation of OEP."[93] But it stunts political analysis. Capacity, potential and creativity, and the processes by which they circulate are made invisible in a static framework that overlooks protean power dynamics by assuming that the preferences of actors are determined by their structural position.

OEP derives parsimonious theories of politics from sparse economic theory. The flow is from micro to macro in an orderly, linear progression. To simplify analysis, work in the OEP tradition adopts a partial equilibrium analysis by focusing at most on one or two steps in this causal chain and treating the others in reduced form, an analytic simplification that reduces complexity to complication by holding constant many elements that otherwise would make analysis intractable. In principle, however, all partial analyses can be assembled into one integrated whole. Informed by rational expectations theory, OEP thus moves exclusively in the world of risk.[94]

The assumption that interests can be read off the agents' situation in the international division of labor constitutes the "hard core" of the OEP paradigm.[95] In OEP strategic decision-making is modeled as unproblematic because analysts do not know how to model uncertainty. OEP relies on a "reductive translation" of uncertainty into risk, especially when the rules of the game are unclear and their future trajectory is pure guesswork.[96] This is an important reason why the collective performance of the field of political economy in the years before the financial crisis of 2008 was, in the words of one leading scholar, "embarrassing" and "dismal."[97] To be sure, OEP specialists were not alone in missing the signs of the gathering storm. It is nonetheless surprising how little scholars of OEP have had to say about the financial crisis in the post-crisis years. With the exception of one review essay on financial market regulation, the subfield's

---

[93] Lake 2009b: 50; 2009a: 226–27, 230–31. OEP rests on two core assumptions: (1) economic policies produce income effects that are driven by an agent's position in the domestic and international division of labor; and (2) economic agents, once they know what they want, make rational decisions as if they knew the relevant probability distributions.
[94] Kirshner 2015.   [95] Lake 2009a: 231.   [96] Holzer and Millo 2005: 228.
[97] Cohen 2009: 437.

premier journal did not publish a single article on the financial crisis in the five years after the crisis broke out in 2007.[98] This collective silence makes apposite Lawrence Summers' biting criticism of macro-economics: OEP scholars are unlikely to learn much as long as they wear "the armor of a stochastic pseudo-world before doing battle with evidence from the real one."[99] And the real world mixes elements of uncertainty and protean power with risk and control power.

Sympathetic to OEP, yet insisting on the autonomy of politics, Gourevitch and Shinn make an important modification to address the limitations of an exclusively risk-based analysis. In their view, the assumption of OEP about the origins of preferences are too arbitrary in ruling out the importance of political autonomy and its corollaries: creativity and potentiality. Structurally induced economic incentives are not determinative on their own. Often they must yield to the complexities of processes of coalition formations that are driven by an unconstrained politics. "We stress incentives and interests ... the rules of production do influence behavior ... Where we disagree on emphasis is in explaining the origins of those rules (politics for us not ... the 'autonomous' economy pure and simple)."[100] The complex politics that Gourevitch and Shinn evoke center on the dynamics of both control and protean power that escapes the reach of OEP.

Alternatives

Needless to say, the bargaining model of war and open economy politics do not exhaust the field of international relations scholarship.[101] Some empirical studies of world politics have developed arguments that incorporate power dynamics operating under uncertainty. Studies of global value chains, international knowledge creation, and social movements, for example, have pointed to conceptions of power that are not restricted exclusively to the concept of control. In his analysis of global value chains, Mark Dallas, for example, argues that "the strategic-agentic actions of firms can create non-agentic economic structures ... which are both unintended and unpredictable ex ante ... power is simultaneously conceived of as agentic-strategic and non-agentic."[102] In a similar vein, Anna

---

[98] Helleiner and Pagliari 2011. In personal correspondence (February 10, 2016) with the authors, *International Organization*'s then editor, Jon Pevehouse, also expressed his astonishment about the total submission of only nine papers during that period: "it is rather surprising that we received so few in that initial period."
[99] Summers 1991: 146.   [100] Gourevitch and Shinn 2005: 93.
[101] McCourt 2016; Fioretos 2011.   [102] Dallas 2014: 317, 338–39.

Lee Saxenian has observed changes in the creation of international knowledge that have shifted from diffusion or "brain drain" to "brain circulation."[103] Improvisation and creativity in social movements are also highly germane for organizationally or crowd-enabled connective actions that rely on social media to personalize political causes.[104] In today's movement societies, the problem for the organizers of social movements is to create models strong enough to withstand the pressure of their opponents and to create space for spontaneous action by an energized base – control and protean power in action.[105]

Besides empirical studies that resonate with the concept of the circulation of protean power, this book's focus on the relation between uncertainty and power dynamics has an affinity with theoretical and methodological approaches that are open to the improvisational aspects of protean power. Karl Deutsch's cybernetic theory of politics, for example, focuses on steering and control – and their limitations.[106] For Deutsch, control power is about the priority of output over intake, the ability to talk over the ability to listen, to act out rather than modify internalized routines and acquired traits. In short, Deutsch has a dual vision of power. Control power is one side of the coin – the other side is the politics of potentialities, growth through learning.

Such learning can consist of observable, prospective individual or group practices recognized as such at the time. When describing the spread of revolutions, and foreshadowing what Kurt Weyland would subsequently observe in the context of the Arab Spring,[107] Adam Przeworski noted that "the entire event was one single snowball. I mean it in a technical sense: A development took place in one country, people elsewhere were updating their probabilities of success, and as the next country went over the brink, the calculation was becoming increasingly reassuring."[108] Besides Baysian updating, learning can take many other forms. For example, it encompasses also the creation of agency through moral commitment, emotional engagement, and practical improvisation, recognized often only after the fact. In El Salvador's civil war, for example, Elisabeth Wood writes that "pleasure in agency" was grounded in emotional processes, moral perceptions, and values of being an active part in the making of one's own history.[109] Similarly, Silvana Toska's fieldwork during the Arab Spring reports the mobilizational effect of the "euphoria of the moment." James Scott calls these "rare moments of political electricity" that can push millions of people into the streets "in

---

[103] Saxenian 2006.   [104] Bennett 2014; Bennett and Segerberg 2013.
[105] Tarrow 1994: 136.   [106] Deutsch 1966.   [107] Weyland 2012.
[108] Przeworski 1991: 3–4.   [109] Wood 2003: 18, 20.

the teeth of power."[110] Although Wood, Toska, and Scott capture important aspects of power we have called protean, this term does not have only positive connotations. In its many nefarious practices ISIS, too, illustrates protean power dynamics (Chapter 9).

Uncertainty plays a big role in international conflicts. In her book on war, Ann Hironaka writes that "in a startling number of cases, the seemingly more powerful state suffered unexpected catastrophic losses, while the ostensibly weaker state ended up victorious."[111] Erik Gartzke offers an explanation that undercuts a risk-based view of the world. He argues that rationalist models of war must put war in the error term of their equations. "Our ability to predict which crises will become wars will probably prove little better than the naïve predictions of random chance ... Important theoretical and empirical components of war are not knowable."[112] Stacie Goddard develops a theory of legitimation for political conflicts over indivisible territories.[113] It integrates disparate factors such as the material interests and strategies of elites, bargaining, and coalition-building, on the one hand, and cultural resonance, rhetorical action, and legitimation processes, on the other. Not reducible only to calculable probabilities, the interaction between the two sets of factors Goddard identifies leaves space for the play of both control and protean power dynamics. Similarly, on questions of political economy, John Hobson and Leonard Seabrooke have underlined the constitutive effects of everyday political economy practices on states and markets.[114] Elites do not simply provide a script that other economic actors follow. Everyday political economy is also about the protean power dynamics that create unexpected change and novelty. In short, these studies insist that individuals do not constitute the bedrock of social and political life; relationships do. Stored and accessed in a dispersed manner, relationships coalesce to a whole that is not controlled by any one site. As is true of jazz, power dynamics contain elements of creative interaction and improvisation. Jazz bands thus differ from marching bands which are moving to a very different beat and give no space to the circulation of improvisational and innovative practices that protean power thrives on and reinforces.

Conclusion

The theoretical development of our argument in the first two chapters and the empirical case studies that follow alert us to six costly short-cuts and mistakes.

---

[110] Toska 2017: 2–14, fn. 38, 3–23; Scott 1990: xiii.   [111] Hironaka 2017: 34.
[112] Gartzke 1999: 567, 573.   [113] Goddard 2010.   [114] Hobson and Seabrooke 2007.

First, the behavioral short-cut to the analysis of power leads to a tautological dead-end. Observing a set of practices and inferring power effects leads to the trite conclusion that winners have power and losers do not. In our argument, practices are distinct from power. They affect how power reinforces or undermines risk and uncertainty. Second, a truncated view of power focusing only on control power assumes the world to be a closed system amenable to controlled experiments and calculable risk. Yet world politics is not a closed system. Once we recognize it as an open system blending risk and uncertainty, our account of power needs to broaden and take explicit recognition of protean power effects operating in the realm of the unexpected – the central point of this book. Third, it is a mistake to think about power dynamics in terms of binary distinctions – such as top-down/bottom-up or macro/micro. A lot of shifting and changing occurs in the relationship between protean and control power and risk and uncertainty. Fourth, it is a mistake to think that one kind of power is normatively superior to the other; no group of actors inherently occupies the moral high ground. We should be careful not to imbue either type of power with positive or negative connotations. Whether control or protean power produce morally good or nefarious outcomes can be addressed only within the context of specific, empirical investigations. Fifth, we should not think that one kind of power is for the strong, the other for the weak. In fact, such labeling of actors is unhelpful. Which weaknesses or strengths are central? Control power is shaped by various capabilities. Similarly, protean power resides in the agility of actors, the actualization of potentialities, and an openness to accept and promote novel solutions that others might not have thought of or tried out. Discursive frames strategically deployed or spontaneously created can constitute both efficient sources of control and promising actualizations of power potentials. Sixth, and finally, it is a mistake to disregard the potential for processes of power reversals. Control power can be vulnerable even when it appears to be stable. Protean power can be promising even when it seems out-of-reach.

How does our argument connect to two commonly accepted power analyses in international relations? Approaches that seek their inspiration in Hobbes and Foucault focus on power capabilities and the diffusion of mechanisms of control. They offer important and enduring insights. But their different styles of analysis are incomplete as long as they neglect the multidimensionality of power, the heterogeneity of power situations, and the omnipresence of power dynamics. Liberal institutional approaches, focusing on information imperfections, are also partial in their insights. Institutional complexes matter for all the reasons the followers of this approach have explored so energetically. But institutional complexes and meaning indeterminacies also create sites that agile actors can exploit to their eventual advantage. Institutional scholarship falls short when it overlooks how these actors move in and around the nooks and crannies of deliberately designed institutions and take advantage of indeterminate meanings of rules and norms, feeding off and reinforcing uncertainties. In focusing on the relations between control and protean power we hope to add to the insights of two approaches that enjoy broad acceptance among international relations scholars.

Some readers may think that this book is doing both too much and too little. It does too much in stretching the concept of power beyond the notion of control. As we will argue in the concluding chapter, this critique overlooks many compelling arguments for a more capacious concept of power advanced by political and social theorists such as Aristotle, Machiavelli, Hobbes, Arendt, Foucault, and a host of contemporary writers. Furthermore, insisting on the existence of only one kind of control power entails assuming the entire burden of accounting for unexplained, dramatic changes in world politics, a burden that existing scholarship has failed conspicuously to take on board. Keeping such changes exogenous, as is the going practice in the analysis of world politics, is a poor second compared with endogenizing change by recognizing protean power in its own right.

Other readers may find that this book does too little. They may be looking for a full-blown research program that specifies scope conditions, articulates causal mechanisms, and operationalizes variables. This criticism expresses an unrealistic expectation of what one piece of research can reasonably hope to accomplish. Furthermore, this criticism comes with a large amount of unexamined and confining meta-theoretical baggage that, for reasons articulated here and in Chapter 13, we do not wish to take on board in this venture. Our main aim is to shift a way of thinking about power as a core concept in scholarly research and eventually perhaps in public discourse.

More importantly, this criticism betrays a probability-inflected worldview that overlooks the importance of uncertainty and protean power dynamics. Focusing on the dynamics of human interactions, Richard Bookstaber usefully points to four phenomena that underline the limitations of such a view of the world.[115] First, slowdowns on accident-free interstate highways and stampeding crowds point

---

[115] Bookstaber 2017.

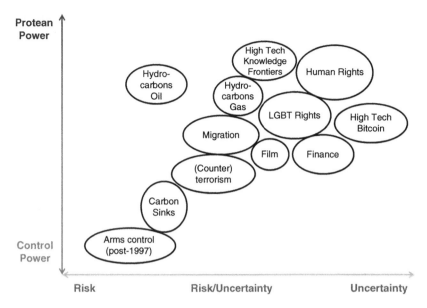

Figure 2.2 Examples of Control and Protean Power in a Risky and Uncertain World

to unexpected results that are not related to human intentions; human interactions can produce "emergent" phenomena. Second, in the social world of constant human interaction probabilities are forever changing; social processes are often not "ergodic." Third, human interactions are so complex that they elude all attempts to anticipate unknown outcomes correctly; the world is filled with "computational irreducibility." Finally, the belief that we live in a world of manageable risk is sheer fantasy; instead, we live in a world often marked by "radical uncertainty" for which the probability of outcomes is simply unknowable. Protean power is rooted in all of these uncertainties as an integral part of political and social life.

We note here that conceptual analysis is the first step in articulating a research program. A second step takes the form of plausibility probes that this book also provides with a dozen case studies presented in ten chapters covering a broad range of security, economic, social, and cultural issues in world politics. Beyond these initial two steps we hope for the intellectual engagement and future work of other scholars who undoubtedly will improve, modify, or reject the line of argument that we have developed here. In an effort to enhance our understanding of the unexpected in world politics, this book offers no less, and no more, than the initial two steps in analyzing the dynamics of control and protean power.

Unfolding under conditions of risk and uncertainty, the empirical case studies in this book cover a broad array of issues: security (terrorism and counterterrorism, arms control); economy (finance, hydrocarbons, environment); society (migration, LGBT and human rights); high-tech (knowledge frontier and bitcoin); and culture (film). Figure 2.2 maps them along two dimensions: risk and uncertainty and control and protean power. Although overly schematic and simplified, this visual presentation conveys variations among the various case studies along both dimensions.

In our study of control and protean power under conditions of risk and uncertainty, this book aims for depth of understanding rather than unobtainable, predictive accuracy. If to the question "how was this possible?" protean power offers plausible, new answers, then this book will have been successful.

Part 2

Protean Power: Embracing Uncertainty

3   Protean Power and Revolutions in Rights

Christian Reus-Smit

Revolutions in rights are always momentous and always surprising. With hindsight, we find ways to explain them: attributing interests, sketching institutional architectures, unearthing material substrata, and artfully tracing key mechanisms and processes. But at the time, on the ground, in the turmoil of real-time politics, revolutions in rights have been either the stuff of dreams – long-term yet evolving objectives, animating activism that is one part strategy, two parts seat-of-the-pants innovation – or barely credible threats, unimaginable transformations of political orders defended by invested elites, backed by material might, and undergirded by old values codified in law. Revolutions in rights are always the product of struggle, generally long and sustained. Yet their triumphs come with a rush. Undercurrents of change break the surface, and suddenly the impossible becomes real: long hostile public opinion swings, new institutional opportunities hand activists unexpected victories, coercion becomes counterproductive, opponents lose the will to fight what was once beyond the pale, and all of a sudden, what constitutes a recognized fundamental right transforms, or the category of humans entitled to such rights expands. The same story has played out time and again: with anti-slavery, workers' rights, women's rights, indigenous rights, and now rights to marriage equality.

The surprising nature of revolutions in rights raises far-reaching questions about the nature of power. Two things stand out. First, how rights are defined and allocated affects the distribution of legitimate power in any social order in which individual rights are the prevailing form of moral and legal entitlement.[1] Rights are legitimate powers. They entitle rightsholders to act in particular ways, and circumscribe legitimate action beyond the domain of rights. They demand the exercise of political authority in some areas, but also circumscribe it. Second, because regimes of rights structure the organization of legitimate power in a social order, struggles for rights are struggles for power, and revolutions in rights

---

[1] All social orders define and distribute entitlements, but these are not always defined in terms of rights and are not always allocated to individuals.

are the product of such struggles. Yet the workings of power within these revolutions is only partially captured by our prevailing conceptions. For Lucia Seybert and Peter Katzenstein (Chapter 1), these conceptions understand power as control, as the ability to exercise control in situations of calculable risk. Evidence of such power can certainly be found in revolutionary struggles for rights: establishment elites have routinely exercised their material and institutional capabilities in calculated attempts to prevent change, often succeeding for long periods of time. The power that ultimately produces change, however, has been far more complex, and cannot be reduced to actors' capabilities exercised under conditions of calculable risk. In all struggles, uncertainty has been the order of the day, and power has come, often unexpectedly, through innovation in an order's cracks and contradictions, not control.

This chapter explores the nature and workings of this "protean" form of power, focusing on a particularly consequential revolution in rights, that associated with the codification of the 1945 human rights regime and the associated reconstitution of the right to self-determination. As I have shown elsewhere, today's global system of sovereign states is the product of successive waves of imperial collapse, the most significant of which were driven by struggles for individual rights.[2] Post-1945 decolonization was the most momentous of these waves: not only did multiple empires collapse, but so too did the institution of empire. Conventional accounts attribute this transformation to a shift in control power: after the Second World War, European powers lost their material capacity to control their empires; the new superpowers, the United States and the Soviet Union, were both anti-imperial; and local anti-colonial struggles raging across multiple empires defeated the European powers on the ground. Common though this view is, it sits uncomfortably with the facts. After the war most imperial powers reasserted their commitment to empire, and their material frailties were evident in some colonies but not in others. Washington's anti-imperialism waned with the onset of the Cold War, and it ended up siding with the imperial powers to oppose any *right* to self-determination. The Soviet Union's rhetorical opposition to empire was contradicted by its own quasi-imperial structure, and its stance in anti-colonial debates was increasingly at odds with that of leading post-colonial states. Local anti-colonial struggles varied greatly in strength, and cannot be credited with the near simultaneous collapse of multiple empires, or the demise of the institution of empire itself. Post-1945 decolonization *was* the product of a struggle for power, but it was protean power, entangled in a complex rights revolution that drove change, not control power.

[2] See Reus-Smit 2011; 2013.

The discussion proceeds in two parts. The first is theoretical. Building on Seybert's and Katzenstein's conception of protean power, I advance three propositions: radical uncertainty is a condition of all systems of rule; some ideas are politically dynamic and defy control; and actors innovate within the cracks and contradictions of institutional complexes, understood as arrays of co-existing, overlapping, but often discordant singular institutions (in this case, the post-1945 complex of persistent empires and the emerging universal institutions of the United Nations [UN], but a phenomenon also highlighted by Phillip Ayoub (Chapter 4) as well as Noelle Brigden and Peter Andreas (Chapter 5). Taken together, these propositions challenge Stephen Krasner's oft-quoted argument about power in a world of normative complexity. States encounter multiple, often contradictory, international norms, he contends, allowing materially powerful actors to select norms that serve their strategic interests. "In an environment characterized by multiple norms, power asymmetries, and the absence of authoritative structures that could resolve conflict, rulers can select among strategies that deploy normative as well as material resources in different and sometimes original ways."[3] Normative complexity thus favors the exercise of control power. Yet in the argument that follows precisely the opposite is true. If the uncertainty inherent to institutional complexes privileges any kind of power, it is protean power not control power. When the meaning of norms is indeterminate, and when multiple norms co-exist in institutional complexes, uncertainty overwhelms the calculable, and innovation in the cracks and contradictions of an institutional complex can challenge the exercise of control. Part 2 illustrates these propositions with reference to the revolution in rights that drove the wholesale decolonization of Europe's empires and the emergence of a universal system of sovereign states.

Radical Uncertainty

Michael Barnett and Raymond Duvall identify four conceptions of power: compulsory, institutional, structural, and productive. Compulsory power "focuses on a range of relations between actors that allow one to shape directly the circumstances and/or actions of another," and institutional power concerns "the formal and informal institutions that mediate between A and B, as A, working through the rules and procedures that define those institutions, guides, steers, and constrains the actions (or non-actions) and conditions of existence of others, sometimes even unknowingly."[4] With structural and productive power, agency is more diffuse and obscure.

---

[3] Krasner 1999: 72.   [4] Barnett and Duvall 2005: 13, 15.

Structural power "produces the very social capacities of structural, or subject, positions in direct relation to one another," while productive power constitutes social subjects "through social systems of knowledge and discursive practices of broad and general scope."[5] While this framework accommodates many of the existing ways that international relations scholars understand power, the "protean" power emphasized in this volume sits uncomfortably within its conceptual distinctions. Control power is easily assimilated within the categories of compulsory or institutional power, but, as we shall see, protean power confounds these categories, particularly institutional power. Furthermore, while protean power can change actor's subjectivities, as well as their structural positions, how this works is not easily accommodated within conventional notions of structural or productive power. Crucially, protean power comes to the fore under conditions of uncertainty, conditions inimical to structural control.

Seybert and Katzenstein distinguish between two kinds of uncertainty. *Operational* uncertainty consists of known unknowns, and can, at least in theory, be transformed by greater knowledge into the world of risk. *Radical* uncertainty is characterized by unknown unknowns, which "are unknowable and cannot be converted to risk" (Katzenstein and Seybert, Chapter 2, p. 41). The closer one moves to the second of these, the more uncertainty appears not simply as a cognitive condition – a lack of knowledge – but an inherent feature of complexity. Some contexts are relatively simple and are amenable to control through the calculation of risk. But increasingly actors must navigate complex, polycentric social, political, and economic contexts in which uncertainty is an existential condition. Furthermore, complex contexts have constitutive effects, creating social subjects. Innovators are not free-wheeling entrepreneurs who step, pre-constituted, into complex environments and work their magic. As Chapter 6 on science and start-ups shows, innovators are products of uncertainty bred of complexity. Innovation is a knowledgeable practice, learnt through engagement with the demands of uncertainty. And "innovator" is a social identity, clearly apparent in Sergey Brin's recent declaration that "Google is not a conventional company. We do not intend to become one."[6]

To understand the workings of protean power in rights revolutions, the concept of radical uncertainty requires further elaboration, as does its distinctive manifestation in struggles for rights. In what follows, I advance three propositions. The first is the general proposition that uncertainty

---

[5] Ibid.: 18, 20.   [6] *The Guardian*, August 11, 2015.

can take radical forms, where unknowable unknowns are hard-wired into complex contexts. The second and third focus on two aspects of radical uncertainty peculiar to revolutions in rights: the open, dynamic nature of rights themselves, and the uncertainty inherent to institutional complexes.

Beyond Cognitive Uncertainty

Some kinds of uncertainty are contextual, others are not. If I sit down to work out a tough problem in mathematics, I am sure to be uncertain about how to proceed: how do I break it down, what techniques do I employ to solve each part, how do I put it all together? My uncertainty is real, but it is not contextual: it derives from the limits of my cognitive capacities, and the puzzling nature of an abstract, deontological equation. This is in contrast to other forms of uncertainty that have less to do with my cognitive limitations than with the social context in which I seek to act. Practice theorists speak of an actor's social competence, defined as socially recognized mastery of a practice or practices.[7] I might be a fully competent actor, a recognized master of relevant practices, but still encounter contexts marked by endemic uncertainty. Diplomats – recognized masters of diplomatic practice – spend most of their time navigating such contexts. No degree of competence renders such contexts controllable arenas of calculable risk: uncertainty is hard-wired into their complex configurations.

As noted above, when Seybert and Katzenstein think about uncertainty and risk, they do so in contextual and experiential terms: from the perspective of the observer, contexts can be uncertain or risky, and actors within such contexts may, or may not, experience them as such (Seybert and Katzenstein, Chapter 1, p. 13, Figure 1.1). This emphasis on experience and context is evident in their desire to accommodate both control and protean power. While they criticize the field's overemphasis on control power, they do not deny its existence or relevance to world politics. Indeed, they insist that some contexts – those that most closely approximate closed laboratory systems – are, from the perspective of the observer, amenable to the exercise of such power, to control through the calculation of risk. Their point, however, is that contexts such as these are far from the norm. World politics is increasingly characterized by complex "open social systems," in which inherent uncertainty defies control and the effective calculation of risk. Uncertainty is thus a feature

---

[7] Adler-Nissen and Pouliot 2014.

of a particular kind of context, and protean power is a product of innovation, a knowledgeable practice impelled by uncertainty.

Uncertainty is not simply an externality generated by particular kinds of context though. Whether or not relevant actors fully experience it, uncertainty can be an intrinsic feature of those contexts. It would be an externality if all that was involved was complexity, where the sheer openness, multidimensional character, and tangled intersections of a context produced a host of known unknowns: what Seybert and Katzenstein term *operational* uncertainty (Chapter 2). Here uncertainty would be a product of unmanageable knowledge demands, impeding reasonable calculations of risk. This kind of uncertainty is common, but it often goes hand in hand with radical uncertainties. An uncertainty is radical if it comprises unknowable unknowns, if it cannot be reduced to attributes of the actors' in the prevailing context, and if it conditions actors' identities, interests, and actions. Quantum theory tells us that such uncertainties are inherent to the physical universe, but they can also be ideational.[8] Indeed, radical uncertainties are endemic to all complex institutional environments, where webs of intersubjective meanings structure social action. This is because such meanings are inherently indeterminate, open to diverse and often contradictory interpretations. Much has been written about the indeterminacy of legal rules, for example. While often touted as the most objective of all meanings, they are rendered indeterminate by both the "semantic openness of legal speech" (words and phrases can be open to diverse interpretation), and by contradictory reasons that generated the speech in the first place.[9]

My claim here is a strong one. Intersubjective meanings, whether embedded in norms, rules, or practices, whether formal or informal, generate radical uncertainties. These uncertainties are more than the known unknowns of operational uncertainty; they involve unknown – and unknowable – unknowns. Even in the realm of common law, where formal processes of judicial interpretation are informed by accumulated precedents, the scope of possible interpretations remains unknowable. This is not only because of the inherent indeterminacy of the law, but because the social domain of interpretation is not confined to formal legal processes. In many areas the meaning of legal rules is the subject of broad political debate, in which the scope and substance of interpretation has a relative autonomy from formal judicial reasoning. This is especially true in the international realm, where authoritative interpretation remains rare. Debate over the legality of the 2003 Iraq War, for example, was not confined to the UN Security Council, and debate within the Council

[8] Wendt 2015.   [9] Koskenniemi 2005: 590–96.

did not determine how the Charter and past Council resolutions were interpreted in the broader political domain.

The radical uncertainty that attends intersubjective meanings is why Stephen Brooks and William Wohlforth are wrong when they claim that the United States, as the unipolar power, can define the terms of its own legitimacy. To be sure, dominant powers – unipoles, hegemons, or the like – have unrivaled capacities to mobilize and codify particular meanings, but this is not the same as controlling meanings. In an artful response to claims about America's declining legitimacy, Brooks and Wohlforth accept the importance of legitimacy, but insist that if transnational advocacy networks can mobilize norms in legitimacy contests, so too can a unipole, with an order of magnitude of greater capacity. "Advantages in power capabilities," they contend, "expand the range and scope of various strategies the United States can use to build legitimacy and mold institutions to its purposes."[10] Put differently, for Brooks and Wohlforth control power determines legitimacy. But even if a unipole enjoys certain advantages in the mobilization of meanings – and Washington's skill in this has been less than striking in recent years – the indeterminacy of relevant norms, and the complex institutional environment in which normative contestation takes place, leaves considerable scope for interpretive innovation and struggle. Indeed, the politics of legitimacy engaged by the United States evinces little evidence of control. To the contrary, American legitimacy has been conditioned by a swirling mix of control and protean power, the latter generated by supposedly weak but innovative actors exploiting the radical uncertainty that attends normative indeterminacy and complexity.[11]

Revolutions in rights have been profoundly affected by the radical uncertainties associated with meaning indeterminacy. To begin with, as we shall see below, the very idea of a general individual right, which has repeatedly animated such revolutions, is inherently dynamic: its constituent ideas provoke ever more expansive interpretation. Again, my claim here is a strong one. It is commonplace to describe some concepts as "essentially contested," in the sense that they can circulate widely, be invoked frequently in public debate, but be understood differently by different actors. Power, culture, democracy, etc. are classic examples. I want to suggest more than this, though: that some ideas, by their very nature, provoke debate, invite ever more expansive interpretation, and defy control. General individual rights are a prime example. Second, actors have mobilized and contested such ideas within multilayered,

[10] Brooks and Wohlforth 2008: 206.
[11] On the challenges a unipole faces defining the terms of its own legitimacy, see Finnemore 2009.

highly variegated institutional contexts: some formal, some informal. These contexts are riddled with cracks and contradictions that enable some forms of mobilization and struggle while foreclosing others.

General Individual Rights   The revolutions in rights that interest me here have all been about general individual rights, of which human rights are a species. Individual rights can take two forms: "special" rights and "general" rights. A special right is one that an individual holds by virtue of a particular transaction or social relationship in which they stand or are engaged. A good example are the rights an individual acquires when contracting to buy or sell a house. The contract of sale grants both the vendor and the purchaser individual rights – rights that would not exist without the contract, and rights only the parties to that contract hold. This type of rights is in contrast to general individual rights. An individual has such rights not because of particular transactions or social relationships, but because they are said to constitute a particular kind of moral being. Human rights are the best examples of such rights. As explained elsewhere, "individuals have such rights because they are human beings: normative agents with the capacity to 'form pictures of what a good life would be' and to 'try and realize these pictures.' Individuals have human rights to protect these capacities, to safeguard their moral 'personhood.'"[12]

Two forms of indeterminacy are built into the idea of general individual rights. The first concerns their scope: what are they rights to? If they are meant to safeguard an individual's moral personhood, what kind of rights are essential to this end? Reaching a definitive answer to this question is probably impossible, as is evident in the persistent debate about what constitute essential human rights: civil and political rights, social and economic rights, or some combination thereof? The second form of indeterminacy concerns the zone of application of individual rights: the group of individuals who, at any given historical moment, are thought to be moral beings worthy of such rights. We now assume that all biological humans are entitled to general individual rights, thus rendering them "human" rights in the full sense. Yet for most of the history of general rights only a portion of the human population has been deemed moral beings with such entitlements. The norm has been for a select group to assert their status as such beings while confidently denying that other human beings qualified. Slaves, followers of other religions, unpropertied men, colonialized peoples, women, indigenous peoples, homosexuals, and transsexuals have all found themselves excluded from the zone of application.

[12] Reus-Smit 2013: 37.

In what follows I am particularly interested in this second kind of indeterminacy. The idea of a general individual right depends on the existence of qualified moral beings. Not only are such beings the bearers of general rights, their perceived needs determine what these rights are. Yet defining what such a moral being is, and who among all biological humans qualify, is an entirely subjective enterprise. All sorts of arguments have been used historically to define the zone of application in one way or another. Religion, race, civilization, property, gender, and sexuality have all been invoked to justify patterns of inclusion and exclusion. None have ever come close to being objective, as what constitutes a worthy moral being can be defined only with reference to other subjective values. Added to this, any non-universal attempt to define such beings, and to draw an exclusionary zone of application, has been politically contentious. As explained above, how rights are allocated in a social order affects the distribution of legitimate power, often in life and death ways. Any non-universal definition of the zone of application simultaneously empowers some while disempowering others, giving the latter powerful incentives to challenge prevailing definitions of the moral subject and expand the zone of application. Herein lies the inherent political dynamism of the idea of general individual rights. Non-universal definitions of the zone of application beg revision, almost always through struggle. And the bounds of such revision, and the potential scope of struggle, is as indeterminate as the concept of a qualified moral being. This is evident in the discussion of decolonization that follows, and in Phillip Ayoub's analysis of LGBT rights (Chapter 4). Even drawing the line around all biological humans has proven to be controversial, as attempts persist to exclude some humans as being morally incompetent or compromised, and calls are made to extend basic rights to non-human species: great apes, for example.

Institutional Complexes If radical uncertainty can be a product of the meaning indeterminacy that attends general individual rights, this is compounded by the institutional environments in which actors have mobilized and contested rights claims. Institutions are commonly defined as "stable sets of norms, rules, and principles that serve two functions in shaping social relations: they constitute actors as knowledgeable social agents, and they regulate behavior."[13] Institutions, so understood, are thought to be embedded in, and reproduced by, actors' routinized social practices: they are the product not only of what actors think and say, but what they do.[14] As the rights case illustrates, actors navigate their way

---

[13] Reus-Smit 1999: 13.   [14] Adler and Pouliot 2011: 42.

through multiple, often contradictory, institutions simultaneously, and since meaning indeterminacy is inherent to all of their constituent rules and norms, radical uncertainty is accentuated, both as an observed reality of institutional environments and the lived experiences of actors themselves (locating the institutional politics of rights in the lower right-hand quadrant of Figure 1.1).

It is common in international relations to theorize institutional behavior as though actors exist within single institutions. Regime theorists studied the regulatory effects of *an* institution – the GATT, the NPT, the EU, etc. – on the actors operating within that institution. Similarly, most constructivist work on the constitutive effects of social norms has focused on single norms: how they emerge, how they socialize actors, and now, how they erode. The idea that actors might operate within multiple institutions features only at the margins. Regime theorists acknowledge that actors forum-shop, jumping from one institutional arena to another in a strategic effort to maximize gains. In the end, though, all this says is that utility-maximizing actors who face a menu of institutional options will gravitate toward the optimal single institution. Constructivists talk about the grafting of norms, how norm entrepreneurs seed new norms by appealing "to values higher than those which they want to justify, by proving that the latter are but an interpretation of the higher values, or that they can be related to these higher values without logical contradiction."[15] These remain stories, however, of the construction of single norms, albeit in association with other extant norms.

In reality, actors exist within, and spend their lives navigating, complexes of multiple institutions. The regulatory effects of any one institution (in the field of climate change, for example) will depend on how it stands in relation to the other institutions actors engage (such as in the area of trade). And how actors are constituted as knowledgeable social agents will be determined by the highly variegated, often contradictory, institutional complexes in which they are socialized, complexes that by definition vary from one individual actor to another. The crucial thing for our purposes is that radical uncertainty in institutional complexes is doubly determined. Not only do the norms, rules, and practices of individual institutions suffer meaning indeterminacy, institutional complexes are riddled with cracks and contradictions, generating yet another layer of uncertainty. This doubly determined uncertainty is evident in current international legal debates, where recognition of the indeterminacy of legal rules is joined by growing consternation about the proliferation of overlapping and contradictory legal instruments and mechanisms that

---

[15] Heller 1987: 239.

threaten to dissolve the international legal order into a fragmented institutional complex.[16]

The Instability of Mixed Worlds

Seybert and Katzenstein (Chapter 1, p. 10, Table 1.1) rightly argue that
pure worlds of calculable risk and control power, on the one hand, and
uncertainty and protean power, on the other, are ideal types. Real worlds
are always mixed. Arenas of calculable risk that permit control always co-
exist with radical and operational uncertainties that demand innovation
and improvisation, producing often transformative circuits of protean
power. To capture this, Seybert and Katzenstein propose an interactive
approach: these "two kinds of power co-exist and co-evolve" (Chapter 1,
p. 5). Nothing in this chapter contests this proposition. I want to suggest,
however, that mixed worlds of risk and uncertainty, and control and
protean power, can be far from stable. Indeed, in crucial cases they are
not only unstable, but pull toward uncertainty, innovation, and protean
power.

   This is especially true in the case of systems of rule. Systems of rule are
the framing arenas for politics, and international systems of rule, whether
we call them systems, societies, or orders, provide the political architecture for international politics. They define the political game – the principal political units, how they stand in relation to one another, and the
bounds of acceptable political action – and their rise and fall alters the
basic parameters of political life. International systems of rule take multiple forms, varying principally according to their organizing principles.
Some are sovereign, some are suzerain, some are heteronomous, and,
importantly for us, some are hybrids. What matters, though, is that stable
systems of rule – whatever their form – cannot rest on control power
alone. The quintessential form of such power is compulsory: the ability of
"one to shape directly the circumstances and/or actions of another,"[17] an
ability derived from the material command of the distribution of risk. But
as Edmund Burke pointed out in a classic statement, "the use of force is
but *temporary*. It may subdue for a moment, but it does not remove the
necessity of subduing again; and a nation is not governed, which is to be
perpetually conquered."[18] Stable systems of rule depend on something
additional, on legitimacy: the "generalized perception or assumption that
the actions of an entity are desirable, proper, appropriate within some
socially constructed system of norms, values, beliefs, and definitions."[19]

[16] Alter and Meunier 2009; United Nations 2006; Young 2012.
[17] Barnett and Duvall 2005: 13.   [18] Burke 1908: 89.   [19] Suchman 1995: 574.

Yet as soon as legitimacy enters the equation, so too does uncertainty. To begin with, legitimacy is in the eye of the beholder. Auto-legitimation is impossible; it always depends on the perceptions of others, and these are difficult to control as millennia of politicians have discovered. At best, perceptions of legitimacy are known unknowns. Second, perceptions of legitimacy, as the Suchman quote indicates, are norm-referential. Actors make legitimacy judgments with reference to interpretations of prevailing intersubjective understandings about rightful agency and action. But this brings us into the realm of meaning indeterminacy, where norms, rules, and practices can be open to diverse, and at times contradictory, interpretations. Struggles over legitimacy sometimes see actors appealing to radically different norms or principles, but often contests are over the meaning of the same norms. Finally, legitimacy is seldom constructed, sustained, or contested in singular institutional contexts. More commonly, the politics of legitimacy plays out within highly variegated institutional complexes. When this is combined with the meaning indeterminacy of legitimating norms, the context of uncertainty moves from operational to radical.

If this is true, surely mixed worlds are likely to be stable? A stable system of rule, for example, might settle on an optimal balance of control and legitimacy, risk and uncertainty. While theoretically possible, two empirical reasons suggest otherwise. Seybert and Katzenstein (Chapter 2) argue that open systems are inherently uncertain and privilege innovation and, in turn, protean power. The openness of a system is generally understood in interactional terms, but systems can be open epistemically as well. New ideas can enter a system through creativity – the artful fashioning of new knowledge out of extant ideational resources – and through cross-fertilization and localization: two forms of innovation. Systems of rule are open systems in both interactional and epistemic terms, and the structures and practices of legitimation that sustain them are always vulnerable to the creation and conscription of new ideas. The second reason has to do with elite incapacity. When the mobilization of new ideas challenges the legitimacy of a system of rule, elites can either recalibrate the system's legitimacy, or they can compensate for a legitimacy deficit by deploying greater control power: most commonly, coercion and bribery. Historically, in the great rights revolutions that have transformed international orders, elites have almost always chosen the second of these paths, ultimately compounding the crisis of legitimacy. For both of these reasons, I suggest, mixed systems, if systems of rule are anything to go by, pull toward uncertainty and protean power, and artful politics is needed to sustain any balance.

Rights and Universal Sovereignty

Today's global system of rule has one feature that distinguishes it from all prior international orders: universal state sovereignty. Systems of sovereign states have been rare in world history, and always regional affairs: Ancient Greece; the warring states period in China; Renaissance Italy; and post-Westphalian Europe. Today's order is unique in being global, and unique in having a single legitimate form of polity: the sovereign state. Furthermore, this novel global order is very young, emerging fully only in the wake of post-1945 decolonization. Prior to this, a hybrid order organized political life across most of the globe, an order in which sovereignty in the European core was institutionally tied to empire in the non-European periphery. The transition from sovereign/imperial order to universal sovereignty was one of the momentous shifts in the global configuration of political authority in world history.

The dismantling of the sovereign/imperial order occurred over several centuries, propelled by a series of great imperial implosions: the eighteenth- and nineteenth-centuries collapse of Europe's empires in the Americas; the early twentieth-century break-up of the Austro-Hungarian, German, and Ottoman empires; and then, most dramatically, the total dissolution of Europe's remaining empires after 1945. Across these waves of imperial fragmentation, the sovereign core of the hybrid order gradually expanded: the number of recognized sovereign states grew, eventually drawing in non-European states, and the institutional norms of the sovereign order clarified and consolidated. It was not until the final act, however – post-1945 decolonization – that empire, as a legitimate form of rule, was discredited. Individual empires might have fallen, each suffering their own distinct crisis of legitimacy, but the institution of empire remained robust well into the second half of the twentieth century. As Edward Keene explains, until post-1945 decolonization, Europeans (and Westerners more generally) were quite comfortable "adopting one kind of relationship, equality and mutual independence, as the norm in their dealings with each other, and another, imperial paramountcy, as normal in their relations with non-Europeans."[20] It was not until the 1960s that these norms were finally undercut, leaving the hybrid order without legitimating foundations.

As noted in the introduction, conventional accounts of post-1945 decolonization emphasize shifts in control power: the waning of metropolitan power; the rise of anti-imperial superpowers; and the diffusion of power to anti-colonial nationalists. According to such accounts, Europe's

---

[20] Keene 2002: 6.

far-flung empires were held together by the imperial powers' material might. After half a century of world war such might no longer existed, and the balance of global power had shifted to the United States and the Soviet Union, both of whom were anti-imperial. Added to this, Europe's grip on empire was undercut by anti-colonial wars in Africa and Asia, wars that the Europeans lacked both the will and capacity to defeat. Common though this view is, it is contradicted by the facts. The Europeans were greatly weakened by a half a century of war, but in most cases weakness encouraged renewed commitments to empire. The United States and the Soviet Union had long touted their anti-imperial credentials, but as the Cold War intensified, Washington fell in behind the imperial powers, and Moscow's brand of anti-imperialism clashed with that emanating from much of the colonial world. Anti-colonial struggles were waged in many colonies, but not all were destined for success, and local struggles cannot explain the wholesale dissolution of Europe's empires.

The greatest failing of these accounts, however, is that shifts in the balance of control power tell us little about arguably the most important feature of post-1945 decolonization: that it involved not only the simultaneous collapse of multiple empires across the globe, but also, and most significantly, the moral disintegration of the institution of empire itself. In the space of two decades, empire went from being the norm, a thoroughly acceptable system of rule, to a moral, if not a legal, crime. The institution of empire suffered a profound crisis of legitimacy from which it never recovered. Scholars debate whether the United States is an imperial power – a move that stretches the concept too far in my view – and some like Niall Ferguson think Washington should come clean and embrace this status.[21] But since the 1960s no state concerned with its moral standing could make such a declaration: "empire" became, and has remained, a term of moral opprobrium.

A focus on control power cannot explain the collapse of the institution of empire, a key factor in the rapid and simultaneous disintegration of multiple particular empires. To understand this collapse, we need to see it for what it was: a collapse in legitimacy. In 1945, the drafters of the UN Charter could still describe Western tutelage of non-Western peoples as a "sacred trust," but by the 1970s, UN General Assembly Resolution 2621 called "the continuation of colonialism in all its forms and manifestations a crime."[22] By 1960, the legitimacy of empire had all but disintegrated, and this in turn undercut the last vestiges of local imperial legitimacy. In the decade following the 1960 UN Declaration on the Granting of

---

[21] Ferguson 2004.   [22] Quoted in Reus-Smit 2013: 156.

Independence to Colonial Countries and Peoples the rate of decolonization tripled, from 1.26 new states per year between 1946 and 1960 to 3.86 per year thereafter.[23]

To understand the crisis that befell the institution of empire, we need to see empires as systemic hierarchies: they rest on an unequal distribution of authority between the core and periphery, and a differential allocation of social and political entitlements between metropolitan citizens and colonial subjects. Elsewhere I call these "regimes of unequal entitlements,"[24] regimes comprising differential special rights (grounded in custom and law, and derived from social position). In empires, a central political challenge sustains the legitimacy of these regimes, both within the metropole and among subject peoples. From the late eighteenth century onward, Europeans justified such regimes with reference to a standard of civilization that in the nineteenth century they codified in international law. This standard, which divided humanity into civilized, barbarian, and savage peoples, placed Europeans at the top of a human pyramid and licensed both their domination/tutelage of the non-European world, as well as the unjust distribution of social and political entitlements within their individual empires.[25]

The dramatic collapse of imperial legitimacy was the product of artful innovation under conditions of radical uncertainty – uncertainty generated by institutional complexity and norm indeterminacy. The struggles over imperial legitimacy that intensified after 1945 took place within a distinctive institutional complex. In the eighteenth and nineteenth centuries, the institutional arena for struggles over imperial legitimacy was predominantly intra-imperial. For example, both the Concert of Europe and the Holy Alliance were concerned with the fate of the Spanish empire in the Americas, but anti-colonial forces had no access to these institutions. It was insurgent Cortes of Cadiz, formed in response to Napoleon's usurpation of the Spanish crown, that provided the principal, intra-imperial institutional setting for debates over the empire's legitimacy. With the Versailles peace negotiations and eventual settlement after the First World War a more complex institutional environment emerged, in which struggles over imperial legitimacy could play out both within individual empires and in the embryonic fora of the League of Nations. After 1945, this multidimensional institutional context received ever greater elaboration, as the UN developed not only an increasingly robust general assembly of states, but also emergent human rights fora charged with negotiating an international bill of rights. Proponents and critics of

---

[23] Quoted in ibid.: 154.   [24] Ibid.: 41–42.
[25] The classic works on this are Gong 1984 and Adas 1989.

empire were thus faced with a highly variegated institutional context, in which local imperial institutions co-existed with new supranational institutional arenas.

This new institutional complex significantly empowered purportedly weak actors, most notably newly independent post-colonial states that joined the UN in its first decade. The emergent institutions of the UN provided unexpected spaces in which to innovate with key norms of international society, particularly those pertaining to membership and legitimate statehood. Crucial here were UN bodies charged with negotiating the two binding international covenants on human rights: the Human Rights Commission and the Third Committee of the General Assembly. As others have shown, the UN's founders were far from anti-imperial, and the early architects of its human rights instruments did not see them as a tool against empire.[26] Yet newly independent post-colonial states found spaces in the UN's emergent human rights bodies in which to redefine and rehabilitate the collective right to self-determination, grafting it onto evolving human rights norms.

After Versailles the right to self-determination was defined as a right of ethnically defined nations, and only those within Europe. This conception emerged from the Second World War as morally and politically denuded. The Nazi Holocaust cast a pall over any claims to ethnic exclusivity, and the idea that only ethnically defined nations could claim self-determination was of little use to colonial peoples in Africa, Asia, and the Pacific, most of whom were ethnically heterogeneous. If such a right was to be of any use after 1945 it had to be reconstituted by placing it on more universalist foundations. Newly independent post-colonial states – such as India, Pakistan, the Philippines, and Lebanon, working closely with key Latin American states – used UN human rights fora to achieve this reconstitution.

There is a long-standing myth, taught to all students of human rights, that the international human rights regime was a Western achievement: a myth that gives pride of place to enlightened liberal powers, especially the United States, and iconic norm entrepreneurs, such as Eleanor Roosevelt. The truth is almost the reverse. The myth holds that African and Asian states favored social and economic rights over civil and political rights. But while this was consistently the Soviet Union's position, key post-colonial states insisted on the primacy of civil and political rights. When debating the Universal Declaration of Human Rights, the Soviet Union tried to subordinate civil and political rights, to which India asserted that it "would never agree to restricting political rights in order

---

[26] Mazower 2009.

to realize social aims."[27] The myth also holds that Western states were strongly committed to the universality of human rights. In reality, Australia, Canada, and the United States joined Europe's imperial powers in seeking to limit the application of human rights norms within colonial territories and federal states. Again, it was newly independent post-colonial states who defeated these moves, thus ensuring a universal zone of application. It was these states who put the "human" in human rights.[28]

What we see here is innovation bred of norm indeterminacy. As noted earlier, human rights, as general individual rights, suffer from two forms of indeterminacy, both stemming from the idea of a worthy moral being. The first concerns the scope of such rights: what rights are essential to protect someone's moral personhood? The debate about the relative priority of civil and political rights over social and economic rights reflects this indeterminacy. The second concerns the zone of application of core human rights; a zone the new UN institutional fora enabled post-colonial states to expand.

Post-colonial states redefined and rehabilitated the right to self-determination by grafting it onto the emergent human rights norms they were fashioning. This enabled them to transform a norm previously restricted to ethnically defined nations within Europe to a norm of universal reach. The connection was first made by Afghanistan and Saudi Arabia in 1950 when they moved a motion in the Third Committee of the General Assembly calling on the Human Rights Commission to study "the right of peoples and nations to self-determination." When the Commission failed to do so, post-colonial states called on the General Assembly to compel the Commission to include an article on self-determination in the draft covenants, arguing that "no basic human rights could be ensured unless this right were ensured."[29] The Commission not only went ahead and included the requested articles in both covenants, but asked the General Assembly to pass a resolution encouraging states to uphold the right. Resolution 637(A), adopted in 1952, states explicitly that "the right of peoples and nations to self-determination is a prerequisite for the enjoyment of all fundamental human rights."[30] In his well-publicized attempt to cast human rights as a post-1970s revolution, and to deny that decolonization had anything to do with human rights, Samuel Moyn misinterprets the meaning of "prerequisite" here. While he assumes that it meant normatively primary, to post-colonial states it meant no such

---

[27] United Nations 1949: 533.   [28] Reus-Smit 2013: 182–87.
[29] United Nations 1951: 485.   [30] United Nations 1952: preamble.

thing. For them, fundamental human rights could not be secured unless people were self-determining, not that self-determination was a higher value than such rights.[31]

In Seybert's and Katzenstein's schema, protean power is an unintended effect of the innovative practices of knowledgeable actors, in which "micro-level" actions produce "macro" outcomes. In revolutions in rights, such as the one discussed above, this played out in complex ways. First, the model suggests that innovative actors can generate transformative protean power unintentionally. Intentionality is complicated in the rights case, though. Actors innovating with rights who intend to produce transformative protean power, or actors innovating with rights with no such intention, do not exhaust the range of possibilities. Rights are not just tools of innovation, they are constitutive values that when actors embrace them transform their understandings of themselves as moral beings. In doing so, rights may generate new circuits of protean power, manifest in new patterns of agency and identification, irrespective of their innovative mobilization. Second, the rights case is a clear example of how innovation under conditions of radical uncertainty produces transformative protean power. But it is also a case of how protean power defies possession. After 1945, newly independent post-colonial states played a central role in constructing today's international human rights regime, but many of these states are now being criticized on the basis of the very norms they helped to define and codify. Put differently, the radical uncertainty that characterized the post-1945 institutional environment encouraged innovation that had transformative effects. Yet, as Figure 1.1 captures (Seybert and Katzenstein, Chapter 1, p. 13, above), this first wave of uncertainty was displaced by a new wave of uncertainty, one that now confronts post-colonial states as they navigate the international human rights norms they helped to institutionalize, but are now mobilized by NGOs, international organizations, and leading Western states.

Conclusion

Those who wield control power are often the most surprised when revolutions in rights transform the social and political orders they have defended with all their might. How are such transformations possible when they, the order's elite, hold all the material cards, and when their lofty status ought to breed its own legitimacy? The answers lie in the diminishing value of control power to arrest crises of legitimacy, especially

[31] Reus-Smit 2013: 165–71.

under conditions of radical uncertainty. A distinct pattern characterizes all the rights revolutions that have driven the expansion of the modern international system: those associated with the Westphalian settlement; the collapse of the Spanish Empire; and post-1945 decolonization. In each case, when the legitimacy of the regimes of unequal entitlements that held imperial hierarchy together was challenged by new rights claims, imperial elites sought control through coercion. In short, while objectively the context was one of radical uncertainty, these elites understood it as one of risk, placing them in the upper right-hand quadrant of Figure 1.1 (Chapter 1, p. 13, above). Not only did this further erode imperial legitimacy, it radicalized anti-imperial groups, pushing them from voice to exit. Furthermore, because these groups were animated by ideas of general individual rights, action took place under conditions of radical uncertainty: the scope and zone of the application of such rights is neither fixed nor amenable to control. Add to this the uncertainty that attends institutional complexity, and one has a realm of political action that privileges innovation. Time and again it has been the protean power generated by the innovations of seemingly weak actors that has driven change in the modern international order.

As Seybert and Katzenstein (Chapter 2) note, control power and protean power relate in complex and often contradictory ways. Brigden and Andreas (Chapter 5) show how in the migration case the two were mutually reinforcing. Just as prevailing systems of border control inspired new modes of transgressive improvisation and innovation, these very same modes also led to heightened transit dangers and ever more coercive means of border control. In yet another example of this complex relationship, Ayoub shows how the institutionalization of LGBT rights in the EU created a new form of control power, which then provoked "affirmation" and "refusal" in several Eastern European states, producing a new regime of control over LGBT communities (Chapter 4). This has, in turn, encouraged innovative new strategies of translation to encourage greater local acceptance of LGBT rights. The revolutions in rights discussed in this chapter suggest a third version of this complex relationship, this time working at the level of systems change from one kind of international order to another. The rights revolution that led to post-1945 decolonization replayed a common pattern: in their attempts to shore up the prevailing hybrid system of rule imperial elites relied ever more heavily on control power. Early withdrawal from some colonies was matched by violent repression in others, and the emerging institutions of the UN were used not to recalibrate the legitimacy of empire, but as sites for rearguard resistance against anti-colonialism. This in turn created new opportunities for early post-colonial states to innovate with emerging human rights norms, enabling them to reconstitute the right to self-determination. Their eventual success, however, replaced one system of rule with another: the hybrid order was replaced by a universal system of states. The architecture of control power thus took a new institutional form and created the structural conditions for the post-1970s politics of human rights; a politics characterized by new manifestations of protean power born of the innovations of transnational advocacy networks.

4 Protean Power in Movement: Navigating Uncertainty in the LGBT Rights Revolution

Phillip M. Ayoub[1]

Few revolutions in rights have emerged as suddenly, and with such intensity, as the sweeping changes we have observed around LGBT[2] rights in the last two decades. In multiple states, these monumental changes have transformed many LGBT people from the proverbial "other" – often perceived as criminal and degenerate – into respected and sometimes even celebrated members of society. Coming out of the depths of the AIDS crisis of the 1980s, few would have predicted the major victories in rights many states afford LGBT people in 2017. From the passage of gender recognition in Colombia and Malta to same-sex marriage in Ireland and South Africa, the diversity of states that address such norms have surprised even the most pessimistic onlooker. As such, LGBT rights constitute an intriguing example of unexpected and transformative social change on a global scale.

What powers, then, have spurred this transformation? Indeed, the theoretical explanations for this striking revolution have often obscured the very real struggle that LGBT people – and the movements that represent them – have experienced on the ground. Too often our theories have focused on concepts closely tied to control power, such as conditionality and the diffusion of formal rules. What is obscured is the resistance that top-down diffusion provokes on the ground and the destabilizing polarization we also see surrounding LGBT rights globally. Undoubtedly, the LGBT rights revolution conforms to the broader characterization of such revolutions painted by Chris Reus-Smit (Chapter 3, p. 59): "Revolutions in rights are always the product of struggle, generally long and sustained. Yet their triumphs come with a rush." A movement's

[1] I thank Peter Katzenstein, Lucia Seybert, Steffano Guzzini, Aida Hozic, Jeffrey Isaac, Stephen Krasner, and Daniel Nexon for their incisive comments on earlier drafts; the remaining shortcomings are my own. The research for this chapter was supported by the Postsecular Conflicts Project, European Research Council Grant STG-2015-676804.
[2] LGBT is an umbrella term referring to lesbian, gay, bisexual, and trans people. I use the umbrella term while acknowledging that the issues of bisexual and trans people have been excluded throughout much of the history of the gay and lesbian rights movement.

struggle consists of the innovative practices and little surprises that come along the way, which taken together explain the big transformations we then remember. By taking protean power seriously, we refocus on the struggle, which has explained more of the path to tangible rights than a singular and homogeneous notion of top-down power. Analyzing a movement's struggle, as it navigates a complex world, aids our understanding, explanation, and interpretation of power.

This chapter thus applies the concepts of protean and control power to understand transnational advocacy surrounding LGBT rights. Using the cases of the European Union (EU) and the Council of Europe (CoE), I rethink the hard mechanisms of conditionality – a type of control power – often associated with the successful transfer and diffusion of rights. Importantly, the control power driving these conceptions of sexuality as human rights can also lead to the inflation of threat in multiple domestic contexts.[3] As such, control power, in the form of hard law diffusion, has had the effects of affirmation and refusal (without internalization), often provoking active resistance and sometimes increased repression. When it does, it changes the experience of actors on the ground, departing from conventional expectations and making their surroundings more uncertain. I argue that these local advocates, embedded in transnational networks, navigate these uncertain and complex terrains with practices of improvisation and innovation that are inherent to the concept of protean power. These actors are attentive to the realities that remain invisible from the top – realities that render control power ineffective on its own – and help to generate transformative change in world politics.

Faced with competing claims about new norms governing sexuality, especially those that problematically conflate sexual rights with the external imposition of "Western" power over "vulnerable" states, local advocates commonly improvise with a practice of translation. They step in where control power falls short to align "external" norms to local contexts. The product is initially movement survival, and sometimes ultimately transformative change, in response to a troubled "one size fits all" approach that can, at times, be counterproductive to the goal of rights recognition. It is the protean power generated by such improvisation that has sustained LGBT movements in times of seemingly insurmountable odds. While improvisation is a common practice in coping with operational uncertainty as activists navigate the unanticipated consequences of control power, its deeper form comes in practices of innovation during radical uncertainty. Radical uncertainty is present when advocates experience a world in which their local surroundings are uncharted *and* the

---

[3] Picq and Thiel 2015.

underlying context of LGBT rights norms is indeterminate. During these times their innovations often feed back up to change the strategies for transnational human rights promotion. Indeed, for LGBT advocates the world in which they operate is constantly changing. Linking back to Seybert's and Katzenstein's Figure 1.1 (Chapter 1, p. 13), their mode of operation in any one cell is rather momentary, shifting between practices of improvisation, innovation, refusal, and affirmation as new obstacles arise and terrains change. In most cases of LGBT activism, however, uncertainty characterizes at least one axis of movement operation (either in context or experience) and control and protean power interact. In sum, protean power and control power complement one another in a relationship that is continuously changing – sometimes alternating and always interacting – under various conditions of uncertainty.

In what follows, I introduce the European LGBT rights regime in the first section; use that empirical case to discuss affirmation, refusal, and improvisation (as effects and causes of power) in the region in the second section; then, I take a step back from the intricacies of the case to reflect on broader processes under conditions of risk, complexity, and uncertainty, and how they relate to LGBT power practices and effects in the third section; before concluding in the last section.

European LGBT Rights Regime

LGBT activism has a long history of generating protean power through niches that innovative actors have created. Centered in Wilhelmine, and subsequently Weimar, Germany, the initial – though small scale and without widespread public recognition – political mobilization around homosexuality dates back to the mid-1800s.[4] During that time, pioneer activists such as Karl Heinrich Ulrichs and Magnus Hirschfeld operated with no compass in a world where homosexuality was invisible in the public sphere. For Ulrichs, responding to the potential proliferation of anti-sodomy legislation that made his sexual orientation illegal, as well as the social sanction that left him without employment prospects, innovation was the only option available.[5] Innovation was central to this process,

---

[4] Beachy 2014.

[5] Anti-sodomy legislation was the early homosexual movement's central battle. Beginning in 1868, leading up to German unification, Ulrichs spoke out against Prussia's anti-sodomy legislation in fear that it would proliferate throughout unified Germany (via Prussia's paragraph 175). Catholic Bavaria, for example, had already decriminalized sodomy following the French Revolution. Despite many near successes (both by Ulrichs and later by Hirschfeld and others), paragraph 175 did become the law of the land in 1871 and was intensified in 1935.

since the desires he understood had no name, prompting his writings – which were published and disseminated using pseudonyms in various pamphlets – on what he would call *urnings* (and later *homosexuals*).[6] His efforts, therefore, offer an example of the *innovation* that produces protean power during *radical uncertainty*, for he was operating in a world where sexual minorities were publicly invisible. Only through interactions with like people did he feel compelled to chart their existence. This ultimately gave his innovation of the *urning* identity the ability to generate movement power – by "offering previously unavailable modes of consciousness" (Emanuel Adler, quoted in Katzenstein and Seybert, Chapter 2, p. 38) and spurring mobilization and research around a new identity – once it was shared and received by others through his writings. In much the same spirit of innovation, Hirschfeld's later research focused on charting the existence of sexual and gender minorities and studying their proclivities. Both Ulrichs and later Hirschfeld had several near successes at repealing the Prussian anti-sodomy legislation (paragraph 175) before it was ultimately enhanced by the young National Socialist regime in 1935.[7] That regime extinguished the movement throughout Europe (except for a small organization in Switzerland) and sent thousands of gay men to concentration camps. The innovative practices of activists like Ulrichs and Hirschfeld has informed many episodes of LGBT movement history, including the more contemporary one – as a case of *improvisation* during *operational uncertainty* – addressed in this chapter. The need for improvisation, in response to severe backlash and resistance is equally apparent in later episodes of the movement.

It was after the Second World War, as part of a post-1945 rights revolution, that sexual minority rights first evolved on the periphery of the broader human rights regime, eventually attaining high political salience across many parts of the world in recent years. Reacting to unresponsive states that had long prohibited access to sexual minorities, LGBT actors in Europe sought out new sources of power outside the state. Because sexual minorities exist in some form across societies, cross-border ties became of paramount importance to political action for post-war *Homophile* and post-Stonewall (1969) *Gay Liberation* activism. Recognizing that several elements of their situations were shared across borders, many activists generated unlikely transformative power by organizing transnationally. In 1978, an enduring transnational constellation emerged as the result of a nationally diverse activist meeting in Coventry, United Kingdom: the International Lesbian, Gay, Bisexual, Trans and Intersex Association (originally IGA, later ILGA).[8] Due to uneven support

[6] From Uranus, Greek god of the heavens. Beachy 2014.   [7] Ibid.   [8] Paternotte 2012.

among their respective states, ILGA activists – and a handful of pioneering states that supported their cause – began targeting European institutions as a venue to challenge the state powers that had previously closed the door to them. These activists were innovative, if not visionary, because they targeted an international organization, the European Community, more than a decade *before* it had the social mandate it would attain after the Maastricht Treaty of 1992.[9] At the time, the odds of finding institutional allies from an economically focused international organization, and on this contentious issue, were low.

Targeting the EU – and other organizations, such as the CoE and the Organization for Security and Cooperation in Europe – did eventually change the underlying international context by creating a place for sexual minority rights at the periphery of the broader human rights regime. Over time, the articulations of a norm that LGBT people are entitled to fundamental human rights, deserving of state recognition and protection, became increasingly clear in both the rhetoric and the legal framework of EU and CoE institutions.[10] Article 13 of the 1997 Amsterdam Treaty introduced the first internationally binding law on the issue: it prohibited employment discrimination on the basis of sexual orientation. The 2000 Employment Anti-Discrimination Directive; the European Charter for Fundamental Rights; the 1993 Copenhagen Criteria; various European Parliament resolutions; European Court of Human Rights (ECtHR) decisions; and European Court of Justice decisions further institutionalized the norm as part of European human rights values.[11] In more recent years, and especially for post-communist states that wish(ed) to join the EU and CoE, the "return to Europe"[12] would mean adopting the universal understandings of the LGBT norm that European institutions now proffered. Having access to new-found institutional control mechanisms of support and sanction, European advocates began operating in a complex world where risk and uncertainty interact: a world of operational uncertainty, where protean and control power meet.

From Effects to Causes of Power

Affirmation and Refusal: Complying with and Resisting the LGBT Rights Norm

While advocates rely on these now dominant systems of knowledge that have legitimated LGBT rights norms in the European polity – especially

---

[9] Ayoub and Paternotte 2014.   [10] Beger 2004.
[11] Swiebel 2009; Wilson 2013; Kollman 2009.   [12] Havel 1990.

in unresponsive states –the "one size fits all" interpretations of such rights have produced varied and unpredictable outcomes across states. On the one hand, the EU has used incentives, such as membership or enhanced political ties, to produce desirable rights outcomes in a calculable fashion. Indeed, such carrot/stick power has produced compliance outcomes: notably the introduction of employment anti-discrimination measures, which now exist across the twenty-eight-state polity. In a different area of civil liberties, the threat of reduced EU regional subsidies may have also compelled the Hungarian government to step back from its calls in 2017 to close the Central European University in Budapest. The CoE, which has also played an activist role in promoting the LGBT norm, has produced major court rulings in defense of LGBT people.

However, affirmation can abruptly shift to refusal, opening small niches for protean power during periods of operational uncertainty. More often than not, such predetermined diffusion models were met with considerable resistance as they were diffused across the CoE, the EU, and their neighborhoods. Importantly, the control power driving these dominant conceptions of sexuality as human rights also resulted in the inflation of threat perception in multiple domestic contexts, making the situational experience of local LGBT advocates increasingly uncertain as new resistances formed. Opposing sectors of societies viewed these models as challenging the fixity of national identity, questioning their national sovereignty, values, and self-understandings – even in a context as open to human rights as Europe, and more so in other regions with less established human rights frameworks. Often portrayed as foreign power over the domestic sphere, emerging counter-movements problematically conflated LGBT rights with "secular" or "Western" imposition.[13]

Reminiscent of the practice of refusal, hard law conditionality around sexual minority rights thus came with sudden shocks that could backslide the early successes of LGBT movements by mobilizing new social actors to challenge them. When such measures were introduced, many new member states responded by simultaneously banning public assembly and even proposing homophobic bills, such as those that proposed removing LGBT people from teaching in schools and constitutional bans on same-sex unions.[14] State authorities did this both because of the recognition of uncertainty in society – and to reap political gains from them – and with the intention of further enhancing it by questioning the validity of the norm. As a direct response to a ECtHR ruling against Russia, for example, Moscow took the opposite position and banned public assembly by LGBT people

[13] See Kymlicka and Opalski 2002 on minority rights in post-communist Europe generally.
[14] Biedroń and Abramowicz 2007.

for 100 years. States have also introduced novel bills intended to protect "religious liberty," sanctify marriage, oppose "gender ideology," and ban the promotion of homosexuality. Refusal by governments creates an indeterminacy surrounding the legitimacy of LGBT norms that also fuels the fomentation of societal backlash domestically. In response, at the societal level, rates of violence against LGBT people in other spheres of life often accelerated, and popular attitudes toward LGBT people often declined. Within the EU, the mean country scores measuring the approval of homosexuality dropped in the Czech Republic, Estonia, Slovakia, and Slovenia in the European Values Survey waves before and after EU accession.[15]

In the EU's neighborhood, Ukraine is the most recent example of this paradox, in which the power of strict conditionality is initially met with a mixed response of affirmation and refusal. In exchange for liberalized travel visas, it was compelled to adopt employment anti-discrimination measures with protections on the basis of sexual orientation. Yet such minimal compliance does not equate with the norm internalization goals set by the LGBT movement. After two failed attempts to pass such a bill in early November 2015, Ukrainian parliamentarians were obliged to make the third time "the charm"; begrudgingly they introduced the bill after immense pressure from state leaders and EU officials. Yet passing the bill came with the simultaneous practice of refusal. Political leadership across parties initially assured their citizens that Ukraine would not introduce any other rights for such minorities, and that tolerance toward LGBT people would not be internalized as part of Ukrainian national values. President Petro Porochenko declared that "family values will remain inviolable," and the "speaker of parliament assured deputies that the law would not threaten 'family values', saying: 'I hear some fake information which says that there may be same-sex marriages in Ukraine. God forbid, this will ever happen. We will never support this.'"[16] In 2016, a march in Lviv was canceled after the state said it could not be protected, prompting activists to flee the city after right-wing groups attended the planned meeting shouting "kill, kill, kill."[17] Societal backlash also ensued, including an arson attack on a cinema during a screening of a gay-themed film in October 2014, as well as targeted attacks on activists.[18] Amid safety concerns spurred by increased repression, Ukrainian LGBT activists opted to protest outside Parliament without the symbolic rainbow flag, a 1970s innovation of the American gay liberation movement that became a global symbol for LGBT people. Indeed, this refusal of typical LGBT symbols – largely because they

---

[15] *European Values Study 1981–2008*, 2011.   [16] BBC News 2015.   [17] Ibid.
[18] Kenarov 2015.

buttressed the Russian Duma's claims that pro-EU Maidan protestors were all "gay" – was so evident that an LGBT organization attributed a flash mob of protestors using the rainbow flag as a provocation organized by pro-Russian groups and the Ukrainian Security Service.[19]

The anti-gay politics of Vladimir Putin's Russia, a member of the CoE, is equally exemplary of refusal, leading to indeterminacy. The state has used the rhetoric of "traditional values" to present Russia as the international protectorate of the new post-secular morality politics, justifying the passage and diffusion of anti-"homopropaganda" laws that center on sexual "decadency" as deviant.[20] This politics of traditional values has been used as a geopolitical tool with which to symbolically distance Russia from Western power. It explains why, as Bateson[21] has described, the Ukrainian "pro-Kremlin media was attempting to portray the pro-EU [Maidan] protests two years ago as a tantrum by LGBT people yearning to join 'Gayropa.'"

Thus, while EU law – and the United Nations' more recent rhetoric and declarations (cf. Hillary Clinton's 2011 speech in Geneva)[22] – might lead us to take for granted that systems of knowledge place LGBT people squarely within universal human rights, this knowledge system does not go uncontested. Contentious debates destabilize new international narratives at local levels, and they can undermine the efficacy of such institutions to engineer change from above. Indeed, there is a multiplicity of centers of control from which such power can be exercised that make norms indeterminate. As the new Russian paradigm of "traditional values" politics exemplifies, refusal as a response to power also leads to what Symons and Altman call "norm polarization."[23] Such polarization refers to a process in which states purposively take contradictory positions on the same norm, leading to norm indeterminacy (see Chapter 3) at the global level. This heightens uncertainty – in this example, beyond operational and toward radical uncertainty – for LGBT advocates in states not firmly embedded in the transatlantic community of states. It is not surprising, thence, that when the American President Barack Obama threatened the material consequences of cutting aid to Uganda for passing an anti-homosexuality bill, Ugandan President Yoweri Museveni replied he would then "want to work with Russia."[24]

Returning to the EU, empirical evidence suggests that hard law mechanisms are only part of the story when relating to the spread of sexual minority rights, and that they are dependent on local translation. If we look at the broader range of the LGBT rights agenda (anti-discrimination,

---

[19] Ibid.   [20] Wilkinson 2014.   [21] Bateson 2016.   [22] Clinton 2011.
[23] Symons and Altman 2015.   [24] Ssebuyira and Kasasira 2014.

decriminalization, partnership, parenting, and hate crime legislation), EU membership conditionality alone did not have a significant effect on advancing the movement's goals.[25] Despite the wide array of formal pressure points associated with EU accession, top-down conditionality was not statistically correlated with transformative legal change. While it does predict changes in anti-discrimination legislation (which states were required to adopt in the three most recent accession waves), it is challenged in predicting wider shifts of incorporating LGBT norms into domestic legal frameworks. By contrast, the presence of activists engaged in the practice of norm translation did aid the adoption of the norm, which I elaborate on below.[26] The powers that have produced tangible and lasting change are not associated only with control power. The work of activists has certainly been facilitated by EU rules and regulations, but processes of change rely on the actors that connect practices of control and protean power. Typically, during operational uncertainty, protean power occupies the spaces created by control power's unanticipated consequences.

It is thus worth emphasizing that responses to the diffusion of LGBT rights norms are rarely calculable, even if LGBT international non-governmental organizations (INGOs) and the institutions that support them hope to perceive them as such. Actors on both the international and domestic levels provide competing views of, and solutions to, the issue of LGBT rights. When LGBT rights first appear in popular discourse, they almost always provoke resistance. Thus, the top-down introduction of LGBT norms – however important that step may be – also produces a set of other unpredictable and undesirable outcomes, ones that control power alone cannot remedy. As the next subsection demonstrates, protean power operates in the periods of operational uncertainty I have outlined above.

Improvisation: Translation during Operational Uncertainty

Experiencing uncertainty with competing claims about new norms, local LGBT activists respond with a process of *translation*, adapting universal norms to distinct local contexts, and *innovation*, when no functioning models exist. This is especially crucial for audiences in which LGBT people have been previously isolated from the public sphere: as an

---

[25] Ayoub 2015: 306. EU conditionality refers to the rules with which prospective member states must comply. A statistical analysis shows how this dynamic plays out. In new EU member states (2004 and 2007 waves), both the application for membership and actual accession to the EU did not have a significant effect on the introduction of higher levels of LGBT rights.

[26] Confer findings for transnationally embedded LGBT organizations in Ayoub 2015: 306.

unknown that, when initially visible, provokes resistance. Two types of uncertainty operate in these common scenarios: *operational* and *radical*. The first (operational) has to do with the uncertainty on the ground for local advocates that emerges from the clash of norms. They face the conundrum of what to do given resistance and backlash, painfully aware both of the expectations of prior legitimate models as well as their unanticipated consequences that they must now confront. The second (radical) is that uncertainty that is built into all levels of the system: both in the underlying context and in actor experience on the ground. It has to do with deep norm indeterminacy surrounding rights at the domestic and international levels: domestic indeterminacy in response to "imposed" and illegitimate norms that clash with local sovereignty, as well as international indeterminacy involving norm polarization. Radical uncertainty questions the very existence of LGBT people and their rights; it typically operates when LGBT individuals first step into the light of local public visibility. Local LGBT actors focus on reducing operational uncertainty, while also addressing the radical indeterminacies surrounding the norm to root the claim's legitimacy.

During these periods of uncertainty, when political opposition intensifies, local LGBT advocates turn to innovation and improvisation to adapt to changing environments. In doing so, they help to interpret norms and create knowledge concerning the societal place of the group they represent. The degree to which this is done can vary from innovation during radical uncertainty (as the Ulrichs example above suggested) to some combination of refusal and improvisation during operational uncertainty. During operational uncertainty, this can mean that actors both dismantle and adapt common attributes of the universal norm, using their local knowledge to *translate* the norm in unique social and cultural terms.[27] Such translation comes into play when universal scripts clash with local ones. It is especially necessary in the case of LGBT rights, since majority populations often turn to traditional social conventions – ones that rarely provide positive etymologies of LGBT people – when "external" LGBT norms are made visible. Translation is the interactive top-down and bottom-up process in which actors package dominant conceptions of sexual rights for distinct audiences.[28] Advocates can balance engaging in translation while maintaining relations with outside actors (including other states and EU institutions)

---

[27] Seckinelgin 2009.
[28] In the diffusion model, commands are obeyed and disseminated because of an impetus from their original source, overlooking the translation work that actors on the ground depend on. Indeed, one problem with the concept of diffusion is the image of particles moving into empty spaces. Conceptualizing the translation process inherent to protean power acknowledges that such empty spaces do not exist in world politics. In the translation model, activists are attuned to the realities that remain invisible to actors wielding control power from the top.

who provide valuable resources and support. Thus, they creatively find spaces to exploit when control power from above produces unwanted outcomes.

An example of this process is the Polish LGBT movement's consistent improvisation as it navigates among various competing groups in periods of intense backlash.[29] Provoked by the perceived imposition of new EU standards, Polish counter-movements framed sexual rights as "external" and incongruent with Polish national identity. This is an aspect of the controlling discourse of universal norms that can perversely limit room for local expression and fan the flames of resistance. During an intense period of politicized homophobia following EU accession, from 2004 to 2007, local LGBT actors worked to reconcile authoritative international demands and create appropriate local meanings for norms. This process is highly improvisational, and it produces protean power to shape new understandings of sexual minorities in the domestic sphere by moving them from the external periphery to connect them to domestic political debates. At the core of this process has been repackaging the norm according to different contexts and forms of emerging opposition.[30] The innovative nature of these movement actors is captured in the practice of translation. It describes how advocates reconcile external and internal understandings of the norm, constantly reshaping the norm's message.

Polish activists have long engaged in a process of translation that connects the universal LGBT norms championed by EU institutions to their local audiences. Leading up to Poland's EU accession, activists framed the issue as one of European values and responsibilities associated with democratization. When public assembly was banned in 2004 and 2005, activists used their transnational networks to mobilize European dignitaries to march in Poland. When these dignitaries were brought to the front of the illegal demonstrations by their respective embassies, the police were compelled to protect them, and thus they indirectly protected the Polish protestors that organized the march.[31] For the strategic local activists, this human-shield technique was imperative at a time when any public assembly was outnumbered by often violent counter-demonstrations. It was a way to generate visibility for local LGBT people who could not safely march otherwise.[32] During periods of Euro-optimism, the LGBT frame was primarily attached to the EU. Protestors donned t-shirts that stated "Europa=Tolerancja" and waved EU flags. Foreign dignitaries were told to refer to themselves as Europeans, which resonated with the wider political discourse of Poland's "return to Europe."

[29] Ayoub and Chetaille 2018.   [30] Ibid.   [31] Ayoub 2015.   [32] Ibid.: 311.

In a later post-accession period, when anti-EU politics intensified, activists shifted gears. By emphasizing that LGBT people were precisely the aspect of "Europe" that was to be rejected, the emerging opposition surprisingly changed the focus of the LGBT movement to the nation. While the Polish cultural counter-movement is a loose conglomeration of religious, political, and nationalist actors, their frames converged around an issue of the nation being "under attack" by external forces – largely in a differentiated response to the international human rights frames touted by the LGBT movement initially.[33] As Agnès Chetaille and I have traced across twenty years of Polish activism, the movement responded to its opposition strategically by emphasizing its Polishness in frames that signal a far more rooted politics of sexuality than before.[34] They used "Catholic" and (increasingly) "national" frames to root LGBT rights as Polish. For example, Poland's largest LGBT organization, the transnationally linked *Campaign Against Homophobia*, changed its logo to mimic the national borders of Poland. In 2016, the organization co-developed a campaign called *Przekażmy Sobie Znak Pokoju* (Let us offer each other a sign of peace).[35] It adapted the locally resonant phrase – used by Polish bishops in a reconciliatory letter to German bishops in 1965, as well as by parishioners as a greeting during mass – placing it over a picture of two hands shaking, one hand adorned with a rosary and the other with a rainbow flag bracket. The campaign, displayed on billboards across the country, generated a firestorm of media attention. Early signs seem to suggest a historic step forward in soothing the oil-and-water relationship between Catholicism and LGBT rights in Poland.

These tactics were contentious within and without the Polish movement, as activists remain hesitant to wash away the decades of harm they have experienced as a result of the Church's vehement opposition. The tactic would also appear ill-conceived to some of the best practice handbooks and directives, emphasizing universality, composed by LGBT lobbyists and policymakers in Brussels (and in Amsterdam, Stockholm, and Berlin). But Polish actors do so in an innovative way that has countered and co-opted the arguments of the resistances that emerged in response to imported and sometimes coercive models of external LGBT activism.[36] At the INGO ILGA-Europe's 2016 summit, the early success

---

[33] Ayoub 2014. While I focus on Poland in this example, scholars have charted similar counter-movement frames of "threat to nation" across new adopter states in Europe. Swimelar 2016; Mole 2016.

[34] Ayoub and Chetaille 2018.   [35] See at: www.znakpokoju.com.

[36] Similarly, local Ugandan and Russian LGBT activists opposed the well-intended external activist calls for boycotts (of Western aid to Uganda, and calls for participation boycotts to Russia's Sochi Olympics) in response to state homophobia.

of the controversial Polish campaign turned heads, with new calls emerging to replicate it in other domestic contexts. It is thus also an example of how protean and control powers are entangled. They both make room for and replace one another, constituting and reconstituting human rights norms.

As Table 4.1 illustrates with the work of Ayoub and Chetaille, activists were consistently improvisational in how they presented LGBT rights according to the changing context in which they functioned.[37] Throughout this process, local actors borrow models that fit (e.g., human rights, democracy, European values) as well as altering and adapting them in an agile process of translation. This is done as they navigate what comes their way in a constantly changing environment of contestation. In the Polish case, frames have become increasingly rooted in response to nationalist local challenges. For the Polish activists, translation becomes an interactive top-down and bottom-up process in which actors present and package dominant ideas and master frames of sexual rights for distinct audiences.

While this example has drawn on Poland, LGBT activists throughout the world respond to ever-changing contexts of uncertainty. Even in the aforementioned Ukrainian case, activists today are debating and adapting the initial strategies they deployed two years earlier.[38] In response to the backlash and a rapidly changing domestic environment, local activists have pursued varied innovative strategies – including invisibility strategies to initially deflect the anti-gay opposition's strategic use of universal LGBT symbols – that have engendered some positive change in recent years.[39] These successes include pride parades in Kiev, an activist conference, enhanced capacity-building for civil society organizations, and some elite political support in the domestic sphere.[40] The same dynamic of translation is true of countries with older LGBT movements. Kelly Kollman has shown, for example, how the LGBT norm, which is often presented in the language of "European values" in the EU, has been reframed according to context. British activists abandoned the frame entirely, framing it in national terms. German activists held on to the resonant frame, shaming Germany for "falling behind" European human rights standards. Dutch activists argued that LGBT rights were a forum for the Netherlands to play a norm pioneer role in European and world politics.[41] In other mainly non-European contexts, activists have rejected the terms "queer," "gay," and "lesbian" entirely for their specific constituency. In the hopes of removing

---

[37] Insights for Table 4.1 are derived from Ayoub and Chetaille's 2018 process-tracing work on the Polish movement's framing strategies.
[38] Bateson 2016.   [39] Shevtsova 2017.   [40] Ibid.   [41] Kollman 2014.

Table 4.1 *Innovative Framing by the Polish movement, 1990–2010*

	1990–2001	2001–4	2004–5	2005–10
I. Changing periods of uncertainty	Democratic transition and the "return to Europe"	Political allies and European accession	New adversaries/ opposition intensifies	Movement– counter-movement interaction
II. Innovative frame attributes	External and universal	External and non-contentious	Contentious and diversified	Diversified, rooted and particular
III. Types of frames used	*Human rights*: universal principles of equality and rights *Democracy*: return to Europe	*Educational*: anti-discrimination, anti-homophobic *Europeanization*: European values and responsibilities	*Defining adversaries*: political parties, nationalist organizations	*Reclaiming localness*: patriots vs. nationalists *National turn*: religion, culture and memory

Source: Adapted from Ayoub and Chetaille 2018.

their "foreignness" or to strengthen their inclusivity, they prefer local language variants or other terms, such as "men who have sex with men" (MSM) or the more inclusive "sexual orientation and gender identity" (SOGI).[42]

In sum, the LGBT rights revolution shows that control power, through the diffusion of formal rules and conditionality, can obscure the experience of local resistance and global polarization around LGBT rights. Uncertainty produced by the clash or misfit between international human rights norms with domestic values has generated protean power impulses for local LGBT activists who translate EU rules and regulations into different national contexts. Faced with emerging counter-movements and competing claims about new norms governing sexuality, local advocates, embedded in transnational networks, developed tools of norm translation to navigate this complex terrain. In recent decades they have engaged supranational institutions when their respective states closed access to them. And later, after successfully securing international support, they translated and localized the norm as it re-entered the domestic sphere. In times of operational uncertainty, they looked for new allies and sought to reframe the norm in a discourse that resonated with local audiences and disempowered the frames used by their opposition. In this interactive process, the practices of LGBT advocates help protean power rise to complement and subsequently reshape top-down control power on their behalf.

Reflections on the Theoretical Framework

Practices of Power under Conditions of Risk, Complexity, and Uncertainty

Stepping back from the intricacies of the cases, this section connects the empirics described above back to the ontological assumptions of Katzenstein's and Seybert's Figure 2.1 (Chapter 2, p. 33, above). In doing so, it navigates the interaction between control and protean powers as a theoretical exercise, while also addressing the counterfactuals of worlds defined purely by risk or radical uncertainty. Empirically, this is a challenging task because there is ample and frequent movement across the length of Figure 2.1's spectrum, with most scenarios operating in between the purest forms of control and protean power practices.[43] Indeed, I occasionally shift into the hypothetical to imagine a world for

---

[42] Seckinelgin 2009.

[43] The same can be said of the constant movement across cells in the related Figure 1.1 in Chapter 1, p. 13, above.

LGBT rights that functions at the extreme ends of the spectrum, when power wielders and the targets of power (roles that are malleable in the real world and often occupied by different actors from one scenario to the next) both operate in settings of calculable risk or radical uncertainty. While I do illustrate scenarios at the extreme ends, the majority of LGBT rights cases fall into the center of the figure, echoing a core argument of this volume: that we live in a world of complexity in which control and protean power are entangled. I should also note that operating in any one space along the spectrum is rather momentary for the LGBT case. For example, and as the Polish case demonstrates, a refusal response is usually met with one of improvisation, and both can continue simultaneously, with creative practices eventually being co-opted by control power actors (though whether a model based on these practices leads to success in a new context is not given). In what follows, I begin at the far left of Katzenstein's and Seybert's Figure 2.1 (*risk*) and move along the spectrum to the right (toward *radical uncertainty*).

Risk   A scenario of pre-accession conditionality comes closest to the example of risk at the far left of the spectrum. In it a state conforms to pressure from the EU, and the INGOs that support it, in adopting some aspect of LGBT rights. The aforementioned case of anti-discrimination based on sexual orientation in the run-up to the 2004, 2007, and 2013 waves of EU accession is a useful example. Here there is a calculation made at both ends, because adopting the norm is tied to a clearly defined set of other material and social benefits that come with EU membership. Thus, both the EU (as a power wielder) and state actors (as a target) can entertain a cost–benefit analysis in a world in which context and experience align. This is an example of the EU's power over the applicant state, and it has led directly to affirmation around some aspects of the LGBT norm. While much literature regarding rights diffusion assumes a power relationship of this nature, most power dynamics surrounding LGBT rights are far more complex. If power operates in moments of a calculable and risk-based world, they are short moments indeed. Affirmation can abruptly shift into backlash locally, which rapidly moves us further right on the spectrum to refusal, opening niches for protean power. It is in the following two scenarios that the interaction between or entanglement of the two kinds of power becomes most apparent.

Complexity: Manifested primarily in Control Power Practices   The more common scenario is one of complexity, in which the underlying context of the world and local actor experience are not in sync – as in the diagonal cells of Figure 1.1 of Chapter 1. With the interaction still slightly favoring control power practices, the more uncertain the underlying context becomes, the more it opens a space for refusal. For example, Russia's new paradigm of moral conservatism has changed the dynamic for power wielders supportive of LGBT rights, amplifying and (re)introducing contestation and indeterminacy around the norm at the international level. As discussed above, instead of an increasingly strengthened international norm, the movement is faced with international norm polarization. While this dynamic is still relatively new, since politics surrounding LGBT movements have been at the grassroots for much of their history, refusals toward LGBT politics are also regularly played out at the international level. This involves one community of states refusing the values of another, making LGBT rights part of a geopolitics in which states co-opt the values that align with "their" side. This can shake the experience of actors at the grassroots level, as their issue is debated, partly unchecked, at a very abstract universal level.

Complexity: Manifested Primarily in Protean Power Practices   Moving further right on the spectrum, we come closer to a type of interaction that is common in the contemporary LGBT case. Here, templates of sympathetic international organizations and human rights INGOs for how to provoke change in multiple domestic realms are contested locally. With uncertainty prevailing on the ground, states and their societies refuse "imposed" norms. This shifts the interaction further away from control power practices. Uncertainty is high in contexts where the LGBT rights norm is still unknown, because LGBT people themselves have been largely invisible on the ground. Such contexts invite a host of societal actors into a debate (e.g., a mix of political elites, religious institutions, nationalist resistance movements) when the norm first diffuses into the domestic space, leading to anti-LGBT resistance and subsequently new uncertainties experienced by local LGBT advocates in the domestic sphere. The approximate sequence is one of diffusion (state affirmation), followed by resistance (societal refusal), followed by translation (movement improvisation). As in the Polish example, here the impetus falls on local advocates, which usually multiply during these times, to translate the norm for a local audience. Innovative power practices involve translation, which can circulate up to sympathizing power wielders, in a world dominated by operational uncertainty.

Yet again, I want to note how *momentary* a world of complexity favoring either control or protean power is. Take, for example, the US criticism of Russia's handling of the Sochi Olympics, an example falling at the left space of complexity. While international condemnation met refusal when challenging Russian domestic policy toward LGBT people, local American actors could shift gears to condemn US policy, which they said sounded hypocritical and hollow in its criticism of Russia, considering the long list of issues facing LGBT Americans.[44] Thus, activists shift us right on the spectrum of Figure 1.1 toward the protean space of complexity. This may have contributed to reshaping the underlying context for advocates on the ground in "the West," where states are now expected to live up to their discourse more than they were before.

Uncertainty   Further right, at the other extreme end, we enter a world of deeply radical uncertainty. Even when there is uncertainty among power wielders, states usually fall into one group or another in a world of regions. A unique example, however, might be a case like Uganda, which has a heated contest domestically around these rights, and power wielders also compete over it at the international level (i.e., the US Obama Administration threatening to cut aid and Russia offering to provide it). At some points in time, the Ukraine case also exemplifies a similar dynamic of being caught between Russia and the EU. Scenarios like these open ample space for innovation by activists, as both the underlying international context and the experience of actors on the ground are deeply uncertain. We could also think back to the late nineteenth and early twentieth centuries when there were no "power wielders" (in the form of *de facto* powerful actors and institutions) to think of that supported the norm. By this I mean no would-be commands exist, let alone provide a model for how to achieve it at any level of analysis. In these cases, LGBT rights advocates have to (re)invent much of the rule book from scratch, innovating new ways of claiming their rights and reconstituting social orders. From this vantage point, the innovation of Ulrichs during radical uncertainty is related – though a much more pronounced version – to the improvisation of Polish activists during complexity. Here protean power practices involve innovation that completely rethinks or recreates models at all levels, in a world that is radically uncertain for movement advocates. Such innovative practices that generate protean power almost always circulate back to change the underlying context of LGBT norm promotion at international and domestic levels.

Conclusion

This chapter has explored the concepts of protean and control power as they relate to the transnational advocacy networks surrounding the issue

---

[44] Ayres and Eskridge 2014.

of LGBT rights. The case of LGBT rights embodies two aspects of unexpected change. The first concerns what the proponents of LGBT rights would consider positive. The sweeping changes surrounding the adoption of norms governing LGBT rights around the globe are truly surprising, and scholarship has grappled with the failure to predict it. At the same time, the second aspect of unexpected change concerns the resistance to these emerging norms. While backlash itself is common, and thus anticipated by movement actors, the various shapes it takes are not. In this sense, it is much like in the case of migration (Chapter 5), where border enforcers react and adapt to the strategies of migrants, or in the case of anti-terrorism (Chapter 9), where states adapt to their failed attempts at control. The constellations of opposition actors and their methods of resistance are unique, unpredictable, and ever-changing across domestic contexts. In many cases of resistance, the opposition is also connected to state actors at an international level, which the example of Russia's normative opposition to LGBT rights makes explicit.

Identifying stagnant, or even central, nodes of power is thus challenging when we consider the diverse realm of contending actors at play in LGBT politics as well as the global polarization of the norm. Just as US state power has been a force for some LGBT people in the Obama years, an array of US non-state actors were responsible for introducing anti-gay bills to various regions in the first place (e.g., anti-gay activist Scott Lively's involvement in early iterations of the notorious Ugandan "kill the gays" bill).[45] Just as activists improvise to defeat domestic opposition, anti-LGBT counter-movements seek out and find new state and non-state allies. And just as states and counter-movements can refuse the promotion of the LGBT norms, so can local LGBT activists refuse and reshape the ways that states and INGOs advocate on their behalf. Thus, the actors exercising and generating power are always interchanging in a complex and uncertain world. Especially for a chapter on a vulnerable population, it is essential to emphasize this important point, that protean power is not only a tool for the "weak" or the "good."[46] As Brigden and Andreas (Chapter 5) demonstrate so well, the protean power practices available to actors via improvisation is likewise available to the various contending actors in this dynamic story.

---

[45] Bob 2012; Weiss and Bosia 2013.

[46] While this chapter focused on the protean power of human rights promoters, it addressed a multitude of different types of actors (for and against LGBT rights) practicing advocacy in different ways depending on their experience of the world as risky or uncertain. In fact, one set of actors that occasionally heightened operational uncertainty for activists on the ground were the well-intended international organizations and INGO allies that tried to advance the norm at the international level.

A core goal of this chapter has been to highlight such contestation in a world of complexity. The institutionalization of LGBT rights has shown recurrent, divergent understandings, even contradictions, of human rights at international and domestic levels. This has created opportunities for innovative political mobilization and the creative grafting of new rights onto local contexts.[47] That is, the control power exercised by the EU and CoE was a necessary (if not sufficient) condition to generate conflict between supranational rights and domestic norms, opening spaces for protean power through the introduction of additional uncertainties. Most episodes of LGBT rights diffusion and circulation are in the spaces where control and protean power interact. While the empirics surrounding LGBT rights advocacy drew heavily from the broader European context in this chapter, we observe a related dynamic of this contestation and indeterminacy in other world regions. As Ashley Currier has demonstrated, the universal underpinnings of LGBT rights norms have also clashed in Namibia and South Africa, where they have been portrayed as colonial and un-African.[48] Palestinian LGBT groups face a similar dilemma under occupation in advocating for gay rights while disassociating themselves from the "pinkwashing" politics of Israel's gay rights promotion.[49]

Navigating such uncertainty generates protean power, embodied in the innovative and improvisational practices that have always been paramount to LGBT advocacy. When international standards of human rights in Europe inadvertently provoked backlash, activists creatively reframed them, often rooting them locally with frames that had previously been seen as antithetical to LGBT rights norm promotion. Depending on the time period and context, different frames helped to facilitate translation to the national level. This was evident in the Polish case, in which activists rooted the universal human rights claims by linking them to the frames used by their opposition.

In doing so, LGBT rights activists resist state repression and thus find the power to, more or less successfully, transform the state's conception of human rights. Often their innovative practices also loop back to amplify uncertainty and influence the strategies of international institutions and INGOs, which may or may not find similar success when they are used again. Thus, the case of LGBT rights in Europe demonstrates how advocates navigate between international and local arenas, translating international norms to local realities. It is under conditions of complexity that most of these interactions between protean and control power occur.

---

[47] Price 1998.
[48] Currier 2012. Paradoxically, colonial Britain introduced anti-sodomy laws to Africa.
[49] Schulman 2012.

In sum, I have emphasized that LGBT rights advocacy predominantly operates in an incalculable and uncertain world that relies on an entanglement between both types of power. As this volume advocates, the case of LGBT rights compels those analyzing power to withstand the temptation to simplify the world to such an extent that it appears to be readily controllable through risk-based strategies. We must acknowledge the existence of uncertainty and the space it gives to the emergence of protean power and highlight the dynamics of power that will always leave room to the disruptions that innovation creates for affirmation.

5   Border Collision: Power Dynamics of Enforcement and Evasion across the US–Mexico Line

Noelle K. Brigden and Peter Andreas

In 2005, Maria,[1] a humble and devout woman from rural El Salvador, embarked on a clandestine journey to the United States. She made a contract with a hometown smuggler, who then subcontracted with a series of guides along the route. While under the care of one of those guides, her travel party took a van across southern Mexico.[2] Confronted with the possibility of being stopped by immigration authorities and questioned, Maria began to pray and sing for their safe passage. She began timidly at first. Upon hearing her shy voice, the guide turned to face her, and demanded urgently and unkindly to know what she was doing. When she explained, his face broke into a broad smile, and he responded, "Yes! Great idea! If they stop us, we will tell them we are a church group." The smuggler, faced with the potential for unpredictable traffic inspections by immigration authorities, seized on the idea. For the rest of the journey in the van, her travel party sang their praises to God loudly alongside their smuggler.

This encounter between Maria and her smuggler unwittingly generated a new survival tactic, one of many novel tactics employed during a clandestine journey to evade capture. Encounters between migrants, smugglers, and the state are often creative moments. New strategies are devised. New trajectories are imagined. New roles are crafted. This creativity emerges from their interaction, as people grapple with uncertainty and danger. Maria's mobility, despite the state's attempt to thwart her passage, is thus an outcome of a power that neither belongs fully to Maria nor to her smuggler, but instead circulates contingent on uncertain social moments.

An analysis of Maria's story, to which we will return later, helps to elucidate why attempts to control the US–Mexico boundary have long

---

[1] All names are pseudonyms. All quotes are reconstructed from shorthand taken during interviews. We return to Maria's story later in the narrative.
[2] Interview, El Salvador, December 22, 2009.

had an ambiguous, and often counterproductive, impact on clandestine flows. An unrelenting unauthorized traffic rolls north across the US–Mexico line. Nevertheless, while a massive allocation of resources to the border has not succeeded in stemming the tide of contraband and migration, it *has* dramatically reshaped these flows.[3] The geographic focal points,[4] modes of transport, protocols, social relationships, and smuggling networks[5] that underpin routes adapt to policing, and policing, in turn, adapts to these adaptations. In the last two decades, border crossings have grown more dangerous for unauthorized migrants, generating a new humanitarian crisis at the doorstep of the United States.[6] Thus, the border remains porous, but policing has altered crossing practices with deleterious consequences for migrants. The exercise of state power has collided with a complex transnational social reality, producing cross-cutting consequences.

Our chapter explores the ambiguous outcome of this collision across the US–Mexico divide. A myopic focus on conventional notions of power, or its failure, contributes to perverse border policies and analytical shortcomings. Public discourse neglects the protean power evident in migrant improvisations, thereby underplaying migrants' agency and vilifying smugglers with deleterious consequences for border policy; the binary of powerless migrants/victims and powerful smugglers/victimizers justifies further escalation of policing to protect both national and human security.[7] Furthermore, this discourse also tends toward historical amnesia about its own origins, highlighting the supposedly unprecedented nature of migration crises and forgetting that the power dynamics evident across the border extend back more than a century. Indeed, the starting point in most analyses is the past few decades.

Finally, scholarship generally highlights the failure of border control, rather than unpacking its complex consequences from different levels of analysis. A broad consensus of scholars focuses on the inevitability that border patrol displaces migration to new terrain and social practice, but we know less about how exactly this displacement takes place, and how it has varied across place and time. While the flow continues, displacement is a disruptive and painful process in the lives of unauthorized migrants. On the one hand, migrants endure tremendous precarity and violence, and they sometimes die. On the other hand, migrants are not passive victims; if they survive the treacherous journey north, their success can often be attributed to a combination of fortuitous circumstance,

---

[3] Andreas 2009.
[4] Eschbach et al. 1999; Cornelius 2001; Madsen 2007; Slack et al. 2016.
[5] Spener 2009.   [6] Brigden 2013; Cornelius 2001; Eschbach et al. 1999; Ogren 2007.
[7] Mainwaring 2016.

intellectual and physical agility, and social flexibility that emerges within encounters with other migrants, smugglers, or state authorities. Scholarship has generally left unexplored how these individual creative moments collectively contribute to displacement.

Moving beyond traditional conceptualizations of power elucidates such moments, and thereby explains the process of displacement over time. The lens of protean power reveals the multifaceted roles played, not only by traditionally powerful actors like the state and organized crime, but also by individual migrants, like Maria, in concert with the social landscape they must cross. Practically, the lens of protean power complicates the binary of victim–villain, and thereby undermines a useful fiction to justify border escalation. Analytically, this lens also provides a window onto the primary mechanism of displacement: improvisation.

Thus, this chapter applies the concepts of protean power and control power in tracing the evolution of the US–Mexico border enforcement and evasion from the nineteenth century to the present. Following the definition in this volume, protean power is the effect of an imaginative agility, which contrasts with traditional notions of power. Protean power navigates a world of uncertainty, where successful responses to danger and/or opportunity must rely, to a much greater degree, on improvisation and a leap of faith. In contrast, control power is rooted in the capacity to manipulate and respond to risk. This capacity presupposes a world of rational calculations and knowable probabilities; under those relatively predictable conditions, control power can be more effectively utilized to incentivize and coerce particular behaviors from other actors.

Combining a historical perspective with more recent ethnographic fieldwork on the experiences of unauthorized Central American migrants, the chapter recasts the escalatory spiral of policing and smuggling at the border as a collision between worldviews of risk and uncertainty, and between protean and control power. The political and bureaucratic theatrics that drive border policing are primarily premised on a world of risk. Policing measures taken at the border are meant to convey an image of control. Smugglers and migrants, however, live in a world of uncertainty, as well as risk.[8] Border policing has increased the probability of dangers befalling migrants on their journey, but it has also intensified the difficulties of judging that probability. Smugglers' and migrants' experiences with and reactions to this hostile and unpredictable environment illustrate the agility and adaptation associated with protean power. Thus, the chapter provides a micro-foundation for understanding the dynamic interaction between the state and unauthorized migration flows.

---

[8] Brigden 2015.

Importantly, we argue that protean power is not an instrument that marginalized people can harness to produce "social justice" in any predictable way. In other words, it is not an effective means to achieve collective political goals or to correct the structural inequities and violence that reproduce the vulnerability of immigrant populations. Migrant and smuggler improvisations generate protean power, but cannot direct or use it to achieve such goals. Despite the fact that they often prove to be capable of resisting and transgressing borders, migrants also experience policing and violence as profoundly disempowering. Therefore, we unpack these consequences for a variety of actors who populate the migration corridor into the United States: migrants, smugglers, crime bosses, and law enforcers. In conclusion, we caution against a celebration of the emancipatory potential of protean power, even as we acknowledge and explore its effect.

The Ambiguities of Power

The level of analysis matters crucially for how we understand this ambiguous outcome of intensified border policing. On the one hand, we can see the resilience of the border crossings when we look at the aggregate. The migration stream continues to flow north, simply changing direction and adapting to the policing with new clandestine practices. Indeed, at the aggregate level, this outcome is easily predictable; the specific form of criminal displacement may be unanticipated, but the general pattern is expected. It is a policy failure foretold. Accepting the inevitability of this general pattern, policymakers have for several decades now pursued border policing that pushes migration routes to less visible terrain and practices.[9] Policymakers traffic in images of control, premised on assumptions of risk management.

On the other hand, migrants may fail to cross the border and, sometimes, they die in the attempt. During their journey from their homeland, migrants sometimes fall victim to treacherous physical terrain or criminal activity, such as kidnappings, extortions, murders, robberies, and rapes.[10] Changes in policing often aggravate migrants' exposure to these dangers.[11] At the level of the individual, the lived experience of the border is very different. The individual experience and personal consequences of the border are not predictable; migrants must function under both conditions of high uncertainty and risk, depending on the situation.[12] Migrants also experience both risk and uncertainty, feeling buffeted both by increased

[9] Andreas 2009.   [10] Brigden 2012; Vogt 2013.
[11] Brigden 2013; Martinez 2011; Ogren 2007.   [12] Brigden 2015.

probabilities of some dangers and the sheer unpredictability of other dangers. From their perspective, policing and subsequent adjustments in smuggling circuits require an improvised response, adapting with agility to changing conditions. Smugglers and migrants traffic in creative subversions of state control, choosing their conduct based on assumptions of uncertainty, as well as risk.

In the risk scenario, the past experiences of friends and family members can offer a reliable guide for future journeys. However, there is little stability in the strategic setting of the clandestine route as experienced by migrants.[13] The diffusion of survival information renders it suspect when criminal predators or state authorities can manipulate it to their advantage. A once-trodden path cannot necessarily be safely traversed a second time. A once-trusted guide cannot necessarily be relied upon a second time. Under these conditions, the trustworthiness of information has an immediate expiration date. In this reality, both migrants and smugglers engage in a reflexive and strategic process throughout the journey. They do not simply rely on information gleaned at the outset of their journey through their existing social networks, but instead improvise new understandings en route. In other words, migrants and smugglers, confronted with a mix of experienced risk and uncertainty, as well as an underlying context that combines risk and uncertainty, exude an extraordinarily malleable protean power.

Indeed, the level of analysis dictates how we see and experience power itself. Control power becomes most apparent when we look from the top down. Control power is the primary instrument of organized collective actors and institutions. However, when we work at the level of individual experience, protean power comes into view, as something that circulates among creative individuals. If we view the state itself through the lens of practice, we can see how protean power constitutes and compliments the exercise of the state's control power, through a myriad of flexible everyday actions conducted by state agents and bureaucrats.[14] Frontline border patrol agents adapt and innovate on the ground, giving rise to protean power that facilitates control. While criminal bosses exercise control power over their territory, their henchmen give rise to protean power as they implement their orders. In other words, depending on whether we look at smuggling gangs and other criminal groups through the lens of an organization or as individuals within that organization, different power dynamics come into view. In contrast, migrants can be understood only as an unchoreographed collection of people engaged in collective practice, not even an approximate of a unified actor. Among the actors caught in

---

[13] Brigden 2015.   [14] Gupta 1995; Migdal 2001; 2004: 20–22.

this border collision, they are uniquely vulnerable and marginalized, depending almost entirely on protean power as a "weapon of the weak."[15] Thus, this chapter pays close attention to how we view the ambiguous consequences of power.

The chapter is organized chronologically. We take the reader through the collision over time, in order to highlight the dynamic between protean and control power. We trace the evolution of border policing policies from the late nineteenth century to the present, showing how such policing has been premised upon assumptions of risk and the projection of an image of control. Against this policy backdrop, we juxtapose the innovations of migrants and smugglers as they adapt to changes in policing over time. Migrants and their smugglers make assumptions of uncertainty and subvert control through improvisation.

However, the alliance between migrants and their smugglers is often an uneasy marriage of convenience and complicated by pressures from other criminal actors and the state. While migrants often improvise together with their smugglers to achieve the shared goal of clandestine passage, migrants also sometimes generate protean power as they resist their smugglers. Indeed, the complexity of these relationships requires us to disentangle the sometimes compatible, sometimes divergent interests of migrants, their smugglers, criminal terrain bosses, and the state. Creative moments emerge from actors' negotiation of these complex relationships and their contradictions. Border control unwittingly spawns new types of criminal characters, who seem to exude both kinds of power to exploit migrants. In Mexico, these struggles have culminated in the arrival of criminal bosses who more effectively control passage across their territory than the state. The existence of multiple actors with cross-cutting interests and capabilities complicates the effects of power.

The Collision in Historical Perspective

The collision between protean and control power across the US–Mexico border is hardly new, though it has certainly intensified over time.[16] Many of the border dynamics of immigration law enforcement and evasion we see today can be viewed as representing the latest chapter in an old story that dates back at least a century – a story that does not simply repeat itself, but nevertheless has a remarkably consistent and recognizable theme: through their interaction, protean and control power have stimulated and reinforced each other. Periods of low control power have typically also been periods of low protean power; likewise, as the exercise

---

[15] Scott 1985.   [16] This section draws on Andreas 2013.

of control power by the state has increased, so too has the presence of protean power. Indeed, protean power is integral to the functioning of control power. Thus, ironically, while seemingly in opposition to each other, these two forms of power have also been symbiotic, creating space for one another.

Given all the attention today over the influx of Mexicans and Central Americans across the border, it is especially striking that the first unauthorized immigrants crossing the border from Mexico viewed by US authorities as a problem were actually Chinese. Efforts to prohibit Chinese immigration in the late nineteenth century mark the beginning of the federal government's long and tumultuous history of trying to keep out "undesirables." The Chinese Exclusion Act of 1882 barred the entry of Chinese laborers, who until then were mostly coming in by steamship to San Francisco. But while this front-door entry was closing, back doors were opening, especially via the US–Canada border and the US–Mexico border. The federal government had no stand-alone immigration control apparatus when the Chinese Exclusion Act was passed, but enforcement of the law would stimulate the creation of entirely new federal administrative capacities.

The US–Mexico border, long a gateway for smuggled goods, was now also becoming a gateway for smuggled people. In 1900, there were just a few thousand Chinese in Mexico, but less than a decade later nearly 60,000 Chinese migrants had departed to Mexico. Some stayed, but the United States was a far more attractive destination.[17] In his investigations, US Immigration Inspector Marcus Braun witnessed Chinese arriving in Mexico and reported that "On their arrival in Mexico, I found them to be provided with United States money, not Mexican coins; they had in their possession Chinese–English dictionaries; I found them in possession of Chinese–American newspapers and of American railroad maps."[18] In 1907, a US government investigator observed that between twenty and fifty Chinese arrived daily in the Mexican border town of Juarez by train, but that the Chinese community in the town never grew. As he put it, "Chinamen coming to Ciudad Juarez either vanish into thin air or cross the border line."[19] Foreshadowing future developments, a January 1904 editorial in the El Paso *Herald-Post* warned that "If this Chinese immigration to Mexico continues it will be necessary to run a barb wire fence along our side of the Rio Grande." The El Paso immigration inspector stated in his 1905 annual report that migrant smuggling is the sole business of "perhaps one-third of the Chinese population of El Paso."[20]

[17] Ettinger 2009: 99.   [18] Quoted in ibid.: 100.   [19] Quoted in Lee 2003: 159.
[20] Quoted in Reynolds 1909: 368.

Some historians note that border smuggling operations involved cross-racial business collaborations, with white male smugglers often working with Chinese organizers and Mexicans serving as local border guides. A 1906 law enforcement report on Chinese smuggling noted, "All through northern Mexico, along the lines of the railroad, are located so-called boarding houses and restaurants, which are the rendezvous of the Chinese and their smugglers, and the small towns and villages throughout this section are filled with Chinese coolies, whose only occupation seems to be lying in wait until arrangements can be perfected for carrying them across the border."[21]

As US authorities tightened enforcement at urban entry points along the California–Mexico border, smugglers shifted to more remote parts of the border further east in Arizona, New Mexico, and Texas. And this provided the rationale to deploy more agents to these border areas (this dynamic would repeat itself again at the end of the century). In addition to hiring more port inspectors, a force of mounted inspectors was set up to patrol the borderline by horseback. As smugglers in later years turned to new technologies such as automobiles, officials also pushed for the use of the same technologies for border control.[22]

Chinese migrants were not the only ones coming through the back door; they were simply at the top of a growing list of "undesirables" that included paupers, criminals, prostitutes, "lunatics," "idiots," polygamists, anarchists, "imbeciles," and contract workers in general. Japanese laborers were banned in 1907. Illiterates were banned from entry in 1917. As seaports became more tightly regulated and policed, immigrants who feared being placed in one of these excludable categories increasingly turned to the back door. Those groups that were disproportionately being turned away at the front-door ports of entry – among them Lebanese, Greeks, Italians, Slavs from the Balkans, and Jews – found Mexico to be a convenient back-door alternative.[23]

The popularity of the Mexican back door received a major boost by new US restrictions on European immigration through the national origins quotas in 1921 and 1924. Passport rules left over from the First World War formalized in the Passport Act of 1918, also now required immigrants to secure visas at US consulates abroad. The Mexico smuggling route offered a way to sidestep these new numerical restrictions and documentation requirements. This sparked alarm in Washington and provided political ammunition for calls for more border enforcement. The commissioner-general of immigration reported in 1923 that each new entry restriction "promoted the alien smuggling industry and

---

[21] Quoted in Ettinger 2009: 60.   [22] Lee 2003: 57–58.   [23] Ettinger 2009: 105.

furnished new and multiplied incentives to illegal entry."[24] The commissioner's report the following year predicted that the Immigration Law of 1924 "Will result in a further influx of undesirable European aliens to Mexico with the sole object in view of affecting illegal entry into the United States over the Rio Grande."[25]

Local media reports reinforced these concerns. A December 22, 1924 article in El Paso's Spanish-language newspaper *La Patria* pointed to the booming cross-border business for "contrabandistas de carne humana" ("smugglers of human meat") in the wake of the new US immigration restrictions.[26] The article (with the headline "Foreigners who want to cross over to the United States have invaded the city of Juarez") described Juarez as a depot for foreigners waiting to enter the United States.[27] The US Congress greatly expanded the immigration bureau's personnel powers to search and arrest along and near the borderline. In a country otherwise wary of increasing the power and reach of government, border control was clearly one realm where there was a push to bolster federal authority.

Political pressure had been building up for a number of years to create a uniformed border patrol force. The US Border Patrol was formed in 1924 with a $1 million budget and a total force of some 450 officers. Its primary mission was to keep out illegal immigrants, especially the smuggling of Europeans. Wesley Stile, one of the first border patrol agents hired in the summer of 1924, later recalled, "the thing that established the Border Patrol was the influx of European aliens." Border patrolmen "didn't pay much attention to the Mexicans" because they were considered merely cheap seasonal farm labor that returned to Mexico when no longer needed.[28] This meant that the growing influx of unauthorized Mexican workers was largely tolerated and overlooked – at least for the time being.

For Mexicans, crossing the border illegally was relatively simple and largely ignored – successful entry did not require much creative agility. Up to half a million Mexicans may have come to the United States in the first decade of the century. The Mexican Revolution, US labor shortages during the First World War, and the continued expansion of agriculture in the southwest fueled a further influx. There was a growing disconnect between the formal entry rules handed down from a distant capital and the realities, needs, and practices along the border. In other words, the "control power" called for in national immigration laws did not translate into its application on the ground.

As a substitute for European and Asian workers, employers considered Mexicans an ideal labor force: flexible, compliant, and temporary – or so

---

[24] Quoted in Siener 2008: 60.   [25] Quoted in McCullough 1992: 51–52.
[26] Quoted in ibid.: 6.   [27] Ibid.: 230–31.   [28] Quoted in Ettinger 2009: 162.

it seemed at the time. Millions of unauthorized Mexican migrants would eventually settle in the United States, becoming a vital source of labor for agriculture and other sectors of the economy but also the main rationale for more intensive border enforcement. It was not until 1929 that US border inspectors even made any real effort to regulate the entry of Mexican nationals; even as late as the 1980s, border controls remained at token levels. US Border Patrol agents could cover only about 10 percent of the nearly 2,000-mile border, and most of those apprehended were simply sent back across the line to try again. Most smugglers caught were simply let go, and those who were not were charged with a misdemeanor.[29]

Anemic enforcement (a bare minimum exercise of control power) meant that illegal entry across the border remained a relatively simple and inexpensive activity: migrants either smuggled themselves across the border or hired a local *coyote*. The use of a professional smuggler remained more of a convenience than a necessity. Hiring the services of a smuggler generally meant a faster and safer trip across the line. Use of a smuggler did involve personal risks (there was the potential for theft and physical abuse), but attempting the border crossing without such help increased the likelihood of assault by border bandits and abuse by authorities.

The long if uneasy border equilibrium between relatively low levels of control power and protean power became unsustainable in the midst of a growing domestic anti-immigrant backlash that culminated in the 1990s, with California (home to an estimated half of the nation's unauthorized migrant population) at the epicenter. Just as the late nineteenth-century backlash against Chinese immigrants began in California, so too did the backlash against Mexican immigrants in the late twentieth century – with the fallout spreading across the entire border.

In the heated early and mid-1990s policy debates about illegal immigration and a seemingly "out of control" border, in which politicians from across the political spectrum were scrambling to outdo each other in proposing tough new immigration-control measures, the federal government launched a high-profile border enforcement crackdown. Long viewed as the neglected stepchild of the Department of Justice, the Immigration and Naturalization Service (INS) suddenly became one of the fastest-growing federal agencies. The INS budget grew from $1.5 billion in fiscal year 1993 to $4 billion in fiscal year 1999, with border enforcement by far the single largest line item. The size of the Border Patrol more than doubled along the border by the end of the decade. The new

---

[29] Andreas 2013: 415.

border enforcement campaign also included an influx of new equipment, ranging from night-vision scopes and low-light TV cameras to ground sensors, helicopters, and all-terrain vehicles. The military also played a supporting role by assisting with the operation of night scopes, motion sensors, and communications equipment, as well as building and maintaining roads and fences.[30]

Congress assured that the border build-up would continue by passing the Illegal Immigration Reform and Immigrant Responsibility Act of 1996. The sweeping law sharply increased the penalties against migrant smugglers, and authorized the hiring of 1,000 Border Patrol agents a year, reaching a total force of more than 10,000 by 2001. Most of these agents would be deployed to the most popular urban entry points for unauthorized migration, such as El Paso and San Diego, with the goal of disrupting and deterring the flow. Left out of this immigration-control offensive was any meaningful focus on workplace controls – in other words, the application of "control power" was highly selective and focused. It was highly visible, but also extremely thin.

Not surprisingly, tighter border controls in El Paso and San Diego pushed migrants to attempt entry elsewhere along the border. These shifts in human traffic, in turn, generated further political pressures and bureaucratic rationale to geographically expand the border-policing campaign. Consequently, a Border Patrol force that had already more than doubled in the 1990s more than doubled again in the first decade of the twenty-first century.

In order to cross a now much more intensively patrolled border successfully, migrants increasingly turned to professional smugglers. As INS commissioner Doris Meisner acknowledged, "as we improve our enforcement, we increase the smuggling of aliens that occurs, because it is harder to cross and so therefore people turn more and more to smugglers."[31] And as the risks and smuggling fees jumped (from hundreds of dollars to thousands of dollars per crossing), smuggling became a much more organized and sophisticated business. Breaking up the traditional routes and methods of clandestine entry turned the once relatively simple illegal act of entry without inspection into a more complex underground web of illegality. Put differently, the greater control power exercised by the state made migrants more dependent on protean power and smugglers.

In turn, US officials went to great lengths to portray migrants as the victims of smugglers, and they used this both to deflect criticism and to provide a further rationale to crack down on smuggling. But this was a much too simple and convenient a characterization of smugglers.

---

[30] Andreas 2013: 301.   [31] Quoted in Andreas 2013: 305.

Migrants generally viewed smugglers as simply a "necessary evil," a clandestine business transaction in which they willingly engaged to evade the expanding border enforcement net. Within Mexico, many considered migrant smuggling a shady business, but one that was providing a high-demand service. Smugglers could be abusive and reckless, and their efforts to bypass law enforcement could place migrants at great risk; hundreds were dying every year in trying to cross the border in the harsh and remote terrain where border enforcement was thinnest. Yet smugglers were hired precisely because they generally provided a safer, faster, and more reliable border-crossing experience.

Smugglers also became more skilled as border enforcement became more intensive. Although some of the local freelance entrepreneurs who once dominated migrant smuggling along the border were being squeezed out by the border-enforcement offensive, they were replaced by better organized and more skilled migrant-smuggling organizations. This, in turn, was used to justify tougher laws and tougher enforcement. The number of smugglers being prosecuted mushroomed, and more punitive sentencing guidelines significantly increased the length of prison terms for smugglers. But this did not translate into a shortage of smugglers. More risks translated into higher smuggling fees. And as the risks for smuggling rose, so too did the incentive for smugglers to use more dangerous methods to avoid law enforcement.

The Lived Experience of Today's Collision

As we have seen, although the collision between protean and control power along the US–Mexico divide is not new, it has intensified. Contemporary relationships between the state, migrants, smugglers, and criminal terrain bosses are themselves an outcome of over a century of these power collisions at the US border. However, the latest chapter of this old story further complicates simple narratives about the interactions of these actors and their relative power. Drawing on ethnographic materials collected in a study of clandestine Central American migration to the United States,[32] we trace the power dynamics within these relationships. This tracing reveals the sometimes contradictory and sometimes symbiotic connections between protean and control power. It also reveals the lived contradictions of protean power, as experienced by migrants themselves.

The on-the-ground *experience* of the US government control agenda is a story of protean power. The everyday practice of policy implementation

---

[32] Brigden 2013.

requires discretion and deft maneuvers on the part of the street-level bureaucrats.[33] Border control is not an exception to this general rule; it too generates protean power. Routines must be adapted to a lived reality, or they are rendered useless; patrols cannot keep a strict schedule and unchanging route without becoming predictable and easy to evade by smugglers. Frontline immigration agents must rely on discretion,[34] their wits, innovations and improvisations on protocols and stereotypes[35] to adapt to unforeseen events at the border.[36] A border official explained the gut feeling that develops with experience, "But people develop a sense. It's like at the border. The agents can see a car coming from half a mile away. Maybe the mannerisms are just not right. It's just that something doesn't feel right. The agents have a difficult time articulating the probable cause. They just know who to stop." After further questioning, the border official explained that, "In law enforcement, we call it profiling."[37] Indeed, the US courts implicitly recognize the necessary role of protean power, by granting border patrol agents greater discretion in their job than any other law enforcement agent.[38] In order to empower them to make judgments and act on their wits at the border, the courts have defined standards for probable cause loosely for US Border Patrol. As the state attempts to increase its control power at the border, this discretion, which creates a space for border agents to exercise their protean power, plays an increasingly vital role in the national security agenda.

In response to the increased control power exercised by the state, smugglers and migrants generate a collective protean power. Indeed, smugglers and migrants sometimes co-improvise migration strategies to achieve their common objectives. The most reputable smugglers behave as service providers, treating migrants as valued customers, protecting them from criminal predators, or settling disputes among travel companions. In turn, migrants generally agree to keep the smuggler's identity secret if they are apprehended by border patrol. For their part, experienced migrants may be called upon to assist smugglers, helping to guide or maintain order in the travel group. Indeed, the boundary between smuggler and migrant may be blurred, when these migrants accept travel discounts, receive upgraded treatment, or other payments for such auxiliary support. Experienced migrants may begin to work as guides. Sometimes migrants co-innovate new migration tactics. As Maria's

[33] Lipsky 2010.   [34] Bouchard and Carroll 2002; Salter 2008: 370.
[35] Gilboy 1991; Heyman 2009.
[36] Interview, El Salvador, September 2, 2010, also quoted in Brigden 2016.
[37] Quoted in Brigden 2016.
[38] On the role of discretion in the performance of Canadian state sovereignty, see Salter 2008: 368–70.

story from the introduction illustrates, collective brainstorming or migrant–smuggler partnerships to devise new ways around unexpected barriers to mobility are not uncommon.

When Maria and her smuggler had devised the plan to sing gospel, she and her companions did not know that far greater dangers awaited them in northern Mexico. At a point just north of Puebla, Maria's guide slipped into the secret compartment alongside the migrants. If stopped, he would pass as one of them, and they had all sworn to protect his identity. His decision to conceal himself among loyal clients proved to be fortuitous. A new guide drove the banana truck in which they were hidden. Squatting in these cramped quarters in the hidden compartment, Maria heard the three gunshots that killed the driver. They had been stopped by a heavily armed group of bandits, dressed in black. Based on their paramilitary appearance and ruthless behavior, Maria presumed these men and women to be the Zetas. Having recently taken control of the territory, this criminal group had not received the appropriate passage fee from the Salvadoran smugglers. Thus, the bandits kidnapped the migrants and held them until family members or friends paid for their delivery. And the bandits began to negotiate with Maria's hometown smuggler for a more regular fee to cross their territory. The kidnappers treated Maria and her travel companions harshly, but Maria was fortunate because this criminal group delivered her to New York in exchange for the smuggling payment. Every year thousands of migrants are not so lucky; kidnappers often release migrants in Mexico, rather than the United States, or turn them over to Mexican migration authorities for deportation after receiving ransoms. Sometimes they keep their victims indefinitely, breaking promises and demanding ever more money from desperate family members. Luckily for Maria, she arrived and lived in New York for several years, before returning home to El Salvador as a local success story. She saved the money to build her dream home and open a restaurant near the center of town, until extortion demands and threats from a Salvadoran street gang forced her to migrate a second time.

When Maria made the return journey to the United States in 2010, she contracted with the same hometown smuggler for the second passage from El Salvador to New York. She did so despite the killing of the guide he had subcontracted and her subsequent kidnapping during the first journey. However, Maria made this choice of smuggling service provider not primarily to avoid US border agents or Mexican migration authorities, but because the hometown smuggler probably knew which criminals to pay to cross Mexico safely. She was primarily frightened of the Zetas drug-trafficking organization operating in Mexico, which had acquired infamy for their kidnapping of migrants for ransom. Ultimately, Maria and her family crossed Mexico, but were captured by the US border patrol.

They immediately filed an asylum claim based on the criminal gang-based persecution they had suffered in El Salvador, and this claim was eventually granted. Indeed, an increasing number of Central Americans turn themselves in to US border agents or allow themselves to be captured in order to file asylum claims. Some smugglers instruct their clients to do so, improvising upon the legal resources made available to migrants by the state. While many of these claims are in fact well-founded asylum cases, smugglers and migrants nevertheless deftly leverage the state's own institutions against its control power. Thus, the "cracks and contradictions" of institutions (Reus-Smit, Chapter 3, pp. 60, 61, 66, 68) provide opportunities for improvisation and innovation; in this case, borders and the refugee protection regime collide, demonstrating how, at the right moment, migrants and smugglers can exploit the nexus of "co-existing, overlapping, but often discordant singular institutions" (Reus-Smit, Chapter 3, p. 61).

In the contemporary context of the escalation of the Mexican drug war (post-2006), Central American migrants like Maria no longer only pay smugglers to resist the control power of the state. Instead, these migrants also pay smugglers to help them negotiate a perilous passage across territory controlled by Mexican criminal terrain bosses. For Central Americans, the danger of Mexican criminal terrain bosses is the primary motivation for contracting a smuggler. Well-informed migrants often pay smugglers not because they know their way around US border patrol efforts, but because their smugglers know which criminal to pay for safe passage.[39] As explained by one migrant, "A good coyote is well connected; he knows who and how to bribe."[40] The control power of Mexican criminal territory bosses, who extort crossing fees from both migrants and smugglers, guarantees that the profession of smuggling will remain profitable. This shift in control to criminal territory bosses illustrates the dynamic between control and protean power over time, and it signals how actors may be impacted by multiple forms of power depending on which relationship they engage.

When the drug war erupted spectacularly in 2006, Mexican territory began to change hands quickly and without warning among competing criminal gangs. The Mexican crime groups splintered with fighting between and within. These gangs began to kidnap northbound migrants for profit. They also kidnapped migrants to renegotiate passage fees with Central American human smugglers. The fees for criminal crossing

[39] Brigden 2015.   [40] Interview, El Salvador, January 24, 2010.

increased in tandem with the intensification of violence, rapid shifts in criminal control, the breaking of old business protocols, and the fragmentation of terrain among competing gangs.

At the same time, beginning in the aftermath of September 11 and continuing into the present, bilateral US–Mexican cooperation for contraband interdiction has intensified.[41] Most recently, in 2014, Mexico launched a reinvigorated "Plan Sur" primarily policing the southern train routes that the poorest and most vulnerable migrants often board like hobos to get to the United States. To give a sense of the magnitude of this policing effort, the number of Central Americans deported from Mexico has exceeded the number deported from the United States.[42] Such immigration enforcement operations have made migrants ever-more reliant on hiring smugglers for successful arrival in the United States.

Despite this massive Mexican enforcement campaign, as well as ongoing fighting within and between gangs, criminals have proven to be more adept at controlling clandestine traffic through their territory than the state. Working through both civilian informants and corrupt state officials, their intelligence networks actively identify smugglers and migrants who have not paid the requisite passage fee. The efficiency of these stealthy networks is legendary among migrants, who sometimes whisper about the spies who travel alongside them to collect information for criminals. Even if US border enforcement were to disappear, human smuggling would now persist as a profession, because migrants – especially non-Mexican migrants – need the smugglers' contacts to negotiate passage across criminal terrain. Ironically, Mexican criminal bosses generate protean power; they deftly manipulate expansive social networks, fluid shifting alliances, the recruitment of former soldiers and police with counterinsurgency skills, violent stagecraft and message murders that project an intimidating reputation, and other flexible tactics. In so doing, the Mexican criminal bosses impose greater control power along smuggling routes than do states.

The ruthlessness of the Mexican criminal bosses is infamous by design, not unlike modern-day terrorist organizations that capitalize on their violent and powerful image with carefully publicized acts (Mendelsohn, Chapter 9). As the drug war has intensified during the past decade, criminal groups have employed increasingly brutal methods to extract money from Central American smugglers and their migrant clients. Capture by border patrol may force migrants to begin the journey again, a terrible prospect after coming so far from home. For migrants with criminal records or multiple crossing attempts, capture by the border

[41] Casillas 2007; Isaacson and Meyer 2014.
[42] Dominguez Villegas and Rietig 2015; Lohmuller 2015.

patrol may even be punished with a lengthy prison sentence. However, these consequences pale in comparison with the torture, trafficking, rape, ransom demands, and, sometimes, murders that occur at the hands of Mexican criminal territory bosses, such as the Zetas or the so-called "Gulf cartel." Ransoms generally cost migrants' families thousands of dollars, often money that had been borrowed to pay smugglers for the delivery of migrants in the United States. Without the migrant to work off the debt in the United States, immigrant families that pay these ransoms may be left financially destitute. To extract sufficient information to make these ransom demands or to intimidate migrants into submission, kidnappers sometimes cut off their victim's fingers or beat them with wooden boards. Female migrants may be trafficked for sex work rather than ransomed. Conditions in the drop houses where migrants are held for ransom can only be described as deplorable. When thinking about making a clandestine journey, US border policing is often the least of Central American migrants' worries.

Criminal territory bosses are not the only non-state actors who attempt to dominate migrants. Despite their shared enemies of the state and dangerous criminal terrain bosses, smugglers have also long been infamous for the exploitation of their clients, imposing control over migrants. This is perhaps even truer today than in the past. Even in early periods of border crossing, smugglers had been known to threaten and intimidate female migrants into having unwanted sexual relations. Smugglers may not keep promises about travel and living conditions en route, subjecting migrants to more suffering than expected. Smugglers sometimes steal from and cheat migrants, abandoning them in dangerous places along the route. They may sell their human cargo to traffickers. Smugglers may collaborate with kidnappers, who demand ransoms from family members in the United States without delivering them there. Finally, smugglers may suddenly attempt to renegotiate their contract with the migrant at a vulnerable moment during the journey, extorting more money than the original agreement had entailed.

At some point during the journey, virtually all Central American migrants experience a deprivation of liberty at the hands of their smuggler, even when the migrant–smuggler contract is consensual, rather than the outcome of a kidnapping.[43] Migrants may be locked inside a hidden compartment of a vehicle, incapable of escaping if conditions turn dangerously hot or oxygen-deprived. They may be locked in an unsanitary drop house with other migrants for days or weeks to wait for an opportune moment to make the

---

[43] For an in-depth discussion of these moments of immobility during mobility during migrant journeys, see Brigden and Mainwaring 2016.

next segment of the journey, or to wait for a payment to the smuggler from US-based relatives.

It should be pointed out that this predatory protean power, benefiting smugglers as well as other criminal organizations, ultimately contributes to the US policy goal of making the border harder for migrants to cross (even as migrants rely on smugglers and the bribing of criminal organizations to make it across the border). In this way, predatory protean power serves as an unintended accomplice in control power objectives. Nevertheless, migrants are not powerless. They resist smugglers and kidnappers. Escape stories abound, as migrants flee buildings that are poorly equipped to hold hundreds of captives or take advantage of drunken debauchery during football matches or holidays to slip past inebriated guards. In interviews, a migrant found a window in a bathroom, another carefully learned the schedule of his captors, and yet another broke through a shoddily constructed wall to find freedom. Acts of collective resistance also erupt in these drop houses, and in one particularly dramatic story, migrants grabbed pitchforks and shards of broken glass to defend themselves against armed assailants.[44] Migrants may submit to their captors outwardly in appearance only, but continue to conspire quietly to regain their freedom.

However, protean power comes at a terrible cost for many migrants. The Honduran man, Maynard, who told the dramatic story of resisting kidnappers with pitchforks and broken glass wept when he remembered how the kidnappers beheaded his co-conspirator; their plan had been discovered prematurely, because a particularly hungry captive had informed on them in exchange for food rations. It had been the second time Maynard had been betrayed by another migrant; a Honduran "friend" had sold him to the kidnappers. Other migrants who survived kidnappings wept, rather than congratulate themselves on their impressive feats of resistance and wit, as they thought of the people left behind or the expense of the ransoms to their families. Migrants often do not experience a sense of empowerment from their capacity to negotiate a humiliating, morally compromising and physically difficult journey.

The physical sacrifices of the journey are common knowledge across the region, leaving lasting scars on the bodies of border crossers. For those that survive the passage, the price of protean power still potentially includes extreme hunger and malnutrition, exposure to the elements or wildlife, illness from contaminated water, suffering assaults, disembodiment from

---

[44] Interview, Mexico, March 12, 2010.

falls from the train, and injuries in the desert. However, these scars often run deeper than the skin and bones of a migrant.

The trauma of the journey can leave lasting social and moral traces in the psyche of border crossers. Even the most successful border crossers must lie or alienate themselves from loved ones to survive. A Salvadoran woman, Ana, traveled with her two small children and a military-age nephew across Mexico in the late 1980s.[45] She tearfully described the ethical dilemmas she faced in transit. Her husband had already fled due to political persecution during the civil war. Her nephew had been a low-ranking infantryman, and he deserted to flee the violence. On the way north, they boarded a bus, pretending to be Mexican. The guide kept them separate, and told them that they must all act like strangers. Her nephew was sitting a few seats from her when police boarded the bus and took him away. At this point in the story, Ana wept remembering how she could only assume that he was being led away to his death, "Imagine pretending you don't know your own nephew ... But that is how it is on the road." To survive, she had to momentarily disavow her kin, silently watching him be led to potential slaughter.[46] She thereby maintained her disguise and continued north, exercising her power to move and protecting her children, but at a terrible emotional and, in Ana's interpretation, moral cost. Her power to migrate was inexorably tied to her acceptance of her powerlessness to help her nephew.

Later in the journey, Ana traveled in a private car with her children and smuggler. Before passing through the highway migration check-point, Ana and her smuggler had to coach her young son. The smuggler instructed the boy to say he was his father if anyone asked. The seven-year-old boy became indignant at the suggestion, "You are not my father! My father is in the US and we are going to him!" The smuggler was patient, but the situation was critical. The boy had to be taught how to lie. While interviewing her, Ana shook her head with sadness at the memory of threatening her son to dissuade him from telling the truth. While she did not say it aloud, perhaps, her thoughts briefly skipped ahead to the rebellious young man he later became, a regret that she had discussed on other occasions. Deception is part of the power that migrants can draw upon, but they do so at a cost. In Ana's estimation, she paid with her son's virtue and her own responsibility as his mother. Teaching her son to lie went against her principles as a mother and a

---

[45] Interviews, El Salvador, November 11, 2009 and January 14, 2010.
[46] The nephew began the journey again as soon as he returned, and he arrived safely in the United States on his second try.

devout Catholic, but morality must be bent (in this case, somewhat gently) in the realm of protean power.

However traumatizing the journey might be for Ana, telling lies to migration police is one of the lesser moral quandaries that migrants face in transit today. In the contemporary context, migrants may be forced to collaborate with criminal terrain bosses and kidnappers. A small minority of migrants become spies infiltrating the migration stream. They lead groups of migrants into ambush or monitor the activities of human rights activists, smugglers, and other migrants for criminal bosses. These co-opted migrants become the eyes and feet of criminal networks along the smuggling route. Migrants' capacity to go undetected among their co-nationals is a form of protean power that comes from the ability to cleverly disguise intentions and improvise upon social expectations and stereotypes to forge new relationships. In turn, this protean power serves as a resource for criminal territory bosses to exert control power over the smuggling route. Such protean power enables the migrant's survival and mobility, but at the expense of others.

This form of collaboration represents neither outright resistance nor acceptance of the control power of the state. Such collaboration on the part of migrants is a survival tactic that mirrors relationships that form across a variety of violent settings, generating what Primo Levi calls a "grey zone," where distinctions between victims and perpetrators become blurry.[47] The fact that this power comes at the price of solidarity among Central Americans and an increase in the suffering of a vulnerable population does not go unnoticed by migrants. As a Honduran woman ruefully lamented, "They are us, same as us: Hondurans, Guatemalans, Salvadorans. My own paisanos are those that rob. That's why you can't trust people in the [Catholic migrant] shelter either." The Honduran woman turned to a Guatemalan girl next to her, "You don't know who they are, your own paisanos."[48] Indeed, a sense of betrayal often accompanies the experience of the journey. A shadowy world of mistrust, chameleon-like characters, and ephemeral alliances is the price of protean power.

Conclusion: Protean Power and Predation

As this chapter has suggested, protean power should not simply be equated with "empowerment." It is worth noting that migrants themselves do not celebrate protean power. They would much rather see a dramatic immigration policy change than be forced to improvise a terrible

---

[47] Levi 1988.   [48] Interview, Mexico, April 11, 2010.

and dangerous clandestine journey. They would rather the state leave them alone than be forced to respond to it with agility and ingenuity. In fact, the practices in which they must engage during the journey are often experienced as profoundly disempowering and dehumanizing. As Maria's and Ana's stories suggest, survival often requires painful compromises of morality or extraordinary physical sacrifices.

Protean power is not a form of solidarity that promises to bring us to a more just or equitable world. It is a fragmented force that enables some individuals to navigate a path to the United States, but does not address the larger socio-economic and political structures that motivate migrant journeys and shape the migration route. Predatory patterns emerge from protean power generated by some migrants as they survive violence at the expense of their compatriots. Such predation may thwart some political projects and undermine a sense of shared identity. Furthermore, protean power seems better fit for creative resistance of control than to capturing and controlling the direction of state policy.

As far as migrants are concerned, "weapons of the weak" are a distant second best to a US immigration policy revolution. For this reason, Reece Jones calls everyday practices that transgress state boundaries, but without an overt political motivation, a form of "refusal" rather than "resistance."[49] Such activities are disruptive and have structural effects, but their participants do not necessarily understand them as resistance or empowerment. Protean power clearly complicates control power. Nevertheless, control power also necessitates and, in an important sense, generates its own antithesis in protean power. Likewise, protean power constitutes control power. When viewed through the lens of experience, even the state requires the protean power of individuals to implement its control. Finally, given the perverse escalation spirals that sometimes emerge from the interaction of the two forms of power, the future structural effects of protean power remain unclear, and may ultimately reinforce control power rather than undermine it. Nevertheless, protean power is creative and, thus, a form of agency that cannot be overlooked if we wish to understand the dynamic process of control and evasion at the border.

Indeed, using different levels of analysis, we have explored the interaction of control power and protean power, showing how their collision has produced a humanitarian catastrophe at the border, not just a failure to curb migration. If we only look from the top down at the border, we see a mirage of control that might be heralded as a victory for policing.

[49] Jones 2012.

Nonetheless, it is a pyrrhic victory of control power, representing a decrease in the visibility of an otherwise continuous flow of unauthorized migrants across the US–Mexico line. Nor, however, can continued border crossings be heralded as a victory of protean power. If we look through an ethnographic lens from the bottom up, where protean power becomes visible for individuals, we have seen the true consequences of the attempt to impose control: dramatically intensified human suffering. The interaction of control with protean power produces this tragic outcome. Shifting the line of sight of our analysis brings the tragedy, as well as the victory, of protean power into focus. Border guards and border crossers both experience profound uncertainty and risk, and ethnographic methods bring this experiential level into view. Thus, for the contemporary period, we augment our historical analysis with ethnographic research on the day-to-day experience of Central American migrants attempting to clandestinely reach and cross the US–Mexico border.

From this analysis, we find that at key moments control power is constituted by protean power. We can see this complementarity when we move up and down the levels of analysis from collective actors to practice. At the level of practice, the state generates the protean power as its individual immigration agents exert control power at the border. These improvised practices constitute the state, and the protean power generated by individuals engaged in such improvisations constitutes the state's control power. Similarly, organized gangs that control territory require the protean power of individual criminals, that is, the smugglers, look-outs, enforcers, and others. Moving up and down the levels of analysis shows us how protean power complements, and in some ways creates spaces for the operation of control power.

In other moments, control power and protean power of various actors interact, leading to a spiral of intensification with yet unpredictable outcomes. As the state exerts control power, it calls protean power into existence. Necessity is the mother of invention, and border control is the mother of improvised smuggling and migration practice. The protean power generated by migrants and smugglers then destabilizes the façade of control, justifying further control effort by the state. We see this interaction by moving across history.

Although beyond the scope of this chapter, this type of analysis could be extended to the recent plight of African and Middle Eastern migrants attempting to enter Europe. Attempts to control illegal traffic across the Mediterranean have had an ambiguous, and often counterproductive, impact on clandestine flows. An unrelenting unauthorized traffic drifts north from the northern African coastline. For the last two decades of policing intensification, the bodies of failed border crossers have washed ashore on European beaches alongside tourists. While a massive allocation of resources to fortify the European continent against these flows has not succeeded in stemming the tide of contraband and migration,[50] it has dramatically restructured the lived experience of migration in ways similar to those survived by Central American migrants seeking to enter the United States.[51] The geographic focal points,[52] social relationships, and smuggling networks[53] that underpin routes adapt to policing.

Since the 1990s, the Mediterranean crossing has grown more dangerous for unauthorized migrants,[54] especially in recent years. In response to the Syrian refugee crisis and a recent series of high-profile calamities suffered by boat migrants during clandestine passages, NATO ships have been deployed to the Aegean Sea to deter human smuggling.[55] Our analysis leads to the expectation that, despite its humanitarian justifications, these militarized deterrence efforts will lead to a formidable increase of suffering, but ultimately prove incapable of halting clandestine flows into Europe. Instead, the complex collision between the control power of the state and the protean power generated by migrants will likely continue to expand and intensify on the periphery of Europe.

Our chapter has shown how a ground-level line of sight helps us to sort out precisely these complex effects of power on diverse actors and their relationships. We find that different forms of power alternate, crosscutting between empowerment and disempowerment at key moments in interactions between state actors, smugglers, migrants, and criminal territory bosses. Furthermore, the ground-level line of sight, at the level of experience, brings surprising instances of protean power into view, sometimes constituting the control power exerted by collective actors like the state. In this way, we complicate the dichotomy between state–non-state actors and their relationship to control–protean power. Recently, much to the chagrin of low-ranking smugglers, more powerful criminal actors have imposed control over clandestine flows through their terrain. The tightened control of terrain by criminal bosses represents a new iteration of, and increasingly complex interplay between, control and protean power. Migrants must sometimes resist the control of their own smugglers, and the very existence of smuggling as a profession is predicated on the imperfect but potent control power of the state and now criminal territory bosses. Power reverberates in often

---

[50] Anderson 2000; Andreas 2009.   [51] Brigden and Mainwaring 2016.   [52] Carr 2015.
[53] Collyer 2010.   [54] Albahari 2015; Carling 2007; IOM 2014.
[55] Schmidt and Chan 2016.

unpredictable ways through these layered and shifting relationships between the state, smugglers, territory bosses, and migrants, as experienced by the individuals implicated within them. Across the US–Mexico border and across the globe, states have tightened enforcement, thereby restructuring these layered and shifting relationships, intensifying the experience of uncertainty along clandestine routes, and often unwittingly complicating (though not undoing) control power by calling protean power into existence.

6   High-Tech: Power and Unpredictability at the Technological Frontier and in Bitcoin

Lucia A. Seybert and Peter J. Katzenstein[1]

In scientific inquiry and technological change the presence of uncertainty, linked to power, is explicitly acknowledged and actively explored. Innovation and improvisation define and constitute manifestations of protean power that are related closely to more familiar control power. The resulting technological and knowledge shifts have important consequences, as actors cope with questions and solutions that arise in the face of risk and uncertainty.

This chapter focuses on these dynamics. They unfold in especially interesting ways when the most relevant actors *agree* that uncertainty is pervasive and unavoidable. Two empirical illustrations, knowledge frontiers and bitcoin technology, explore the different manifestations of protean power in detail. The first example traces improvisation, learning, and advances in science and technology fields, taking us well beyond the narrow bounds of the "controlled" experiments on which they rest. The innovation fueling scientific discovery and start-up industries occurs in contexts so complex that the outcomes and underlying processes remain in the realm of unknown unknowns. The second example explores the bitcoin revolution that combines radical and operational uncertainty, the responses they elicit, and the co-evolution between control and protean power.

Knowledge Frontiers

The drive to improve the human condition unites innovators of all stripes. With each discovery or novel solution, new hurdles arise. Some obstacles can be the direct result, anticipated or not, of changes initially labeled as progress. A common theme across scientific disciplines and fields of innovation is the continuous debate about the adequacy of questions

[1] LS would like to thank David J. Chen, Isaac Kriley, Winnie Lo, and Eric Tran for illuminating conversations about uncertainty in medical science. PK would like to thank Benjamin Cohen, Eric Helleiner, and Jonathan Kirshner for critical comments on the second half of an earlier draft of this chapter.

124

asked and the reliability of answers offered. When a scientist sets out to conduct a series of experiments, she or he cannot know whether she or he will get a publication or the Nobel Prize. When an entrepreneur presents the plans for a new start-up, the viability, profitability, and overall impact of his or her endeavor is unknown. What drives these actors is not a predetermined risk calculation. Instead, curiosity, intuition, understanding of particular conditions, and the ability to spot opportunities as they arise fill the air in science laboratories and start-up incubators. The levels of eventual payoff, if any, are unrelated to actor expectations. The pursuit of solutions and improvements may bring about transformative change that falls well beyond the intended reach. The uncertainty surrounding such projects allows no guarantees; even highly promising projects can disappoint or turn into sources of danger.[2]

This section draws on examples from the outer bounds of science and technology that illustrate the varying degree to which actors seek or relinquish control power. The question is particularly resonant in these areas. Innovators understand better than most that whatever projects they launch, deep-seated uncertainty is their constant companion. They do, however, opt for different approaches in their daily confrontations with unknown or unknowable unknowns. And this produces different types of relations between control and protean power in a context marked by different constellations of risk and uncertainty. The following episodes span the range from attempts at carving out as much control power as possible; to instances where its advantages are exploited with its limits fully recognized, and, finally, to situations where no control is sought in the first place.

DNA Editing

In the form of precision, reproducibility, and efficacy, control goes a long way in scientific experiments. It is therefore not surprising that CRISPR, a gene editing technique that meets all these requirements, swept through the world of molecular biology at unprecedented rates upon its initial publication in 2012. This reaction across many disciplines, led to an innovative and fundamentally agile implementation of the novel method and so endowed its creators with protean power. It altered how scientists handle both operational and radical uncertainty associated with studying living organisms. Without needing years of training or expensive equipment, scientists around the world can now use CRISPR to modify the DNA of any cell in an expedient and deliberate way.[3] Not long ago, such

[2] Baumann 2016.   [3] Ledford 2015b.

technology was a matter of far-flung ambitions or science fiction. Today, the ability to modify genes at will affects virtually all bio-engineering and medical fields, from disease resistance in crops to studying human cancer mutations. Mistakes in editing the genome have been reduced to a minimum. The enthusiasm for CRISPR might suggest full control as all uncertainty has been eliminated.

Yet, despite the impressiveness of this new technique, many scientists have issued stark warning calls to "think carefully about how we are going to use that power."[4] One set of challenges falls into the category of unintended consequences. The "democratization" of gene editing resulting from this new-found accessibility of DNA modification threatens to put the technique into inexperienced hands, with consequences no one can foresee. Similarly, even if proper precautions are taken, there is still the possibility of CRISPR cutting the DNA in places other than those intended by researchers, threatening irreversible changes. Critics of widespread and unregulated CRISPR application refer also to the much discussed issue of matching the break-neck pace of CRISPR applications with ethical and safety standards.[5] Modifying the genetic code of malaria-carrying mosquitos to eliminate their ability to spread the disease or wiping out invasive species in delicate ecosystems has clear advantages.[6] At the same time, the conversation about unanticipated effects relates directly to actor experience of uncertainty, especially in uncertain contexts of inadequate regulation. Altering the germline of an organism is an inherently complex matter, necessitating separate oversight efforts for each species – fruit flies differ considerably from mosquitos. However, the everyday uncertainty of translating scientific insights and expertise is quickly overshadowed by considerations of the uncertainty that disrupted ecosystems would produce.

The desire to control something so fickle and expansive is strong. It is interesting to observe the various attempts at control clashing in the arena newly opened up by CRISPR. At first, scientists wanted better control over their laboratory tasks. Subsequently, the need to regulate both the process and outcomes of such activity brought another element of control to the forefront. And all along, the shocking novelty and broad applicability of CRISPR technology has fueled a fierce battle over patent ownership.[7] This is no minor matter. It affects the particular paths that subsequent developments take, as well as the point of contact at which scientific and regulatory control attempts meet.[8] The result: disregard for key unknowns and

---

[4] Ibid.   [5] Ledford 2015a.   [6] Khatodia et al. 2016.   [7] Ledford 2016.
[8] For a related account about innovation in the context of power over information flows, see Marlin-Bennet 2017.

creation of space for newly creative solutions that may bypass this particular manifestation of protean power and replace it with new ones.

The quest for intellectual property rights is a matter of reaping large financial benefits from commercializing the technology at hand. In the language of power, that means gaining competitiveness in pharmaceutical markets and, importantly, financing additional research and innovation. The self-perpetuating model of research investments seems like it might be capable of bypassing the underlying uncertainty. In practice, however, the picture is not nearly so simple. First, once inventions are streamlined and scaled up to generate profit, the focus shifts away from agile creativity in finding resourceful answers to pressing questions toward generating protean power that is converted into control through the identification of material benefits. Exchange represents one move in the reversible relationship between the two power types. Movement in the opposite direction is fueled by the fact that initial impact of an invention in no way guarantees continued or future success. In the case of CRISPR, the interaction is further marked by regulatory uncertainty stemming from battles over patents and the particular policy stance that governments take on the technology.[9] It introduces pressures from researchers working on still newer methods to match or outperform CRISPR capabilities.

Paradoxically, then, the quest for control has produced additional uncertainty. Fighting for intellectual property rights has underscored the desirability of CRISPR technology and at the same time increased the incentive for others to come up with alternatives. Patent battles will likely result in the development of still newer methods that will bypass this avenue of progress altogether. All obstacles surrounding the adoption of CRISPR gene modification highlight the pervasiveness of uncertainty despite actors' desire to control what limited aspects of it they can, either through patent adjudication or ethics and safety regulations. In this example, control power and protean power are deeply entangled in competitive relations. The shifts from one power type to the other have typically been shaped by actor experiences of their context and fleeting openings for intervention.

Ambitious Journeys

In frontier science, the fundamental interference with probability calculations arises from the very nature of the questions considered.[10] Scientists

---

[9] Falk, Decherney, and Kahn 2016; Jones 2015.

[10] As if the complexity of the questions considered was not enough, researchers face the uncertainty of continued existence of their laboratories. First, there exists a lag between the demonstrability of scientific principle and its commercialization, testing the patience

"control" what they can, but readily admit that an unknown set of unknowns may drive the ultimate success or failure of their work. As a result, many innovators make no pretenses about seeking control beyond a very limited point.[11] In fact, they deliberately open up the playing field for others, realizing that ideas and innovations cannot be forced but, if nudged along a specific path, may follow a semblance of the initial creators' vision. Studies harnessing the immune system to fight cancer at the National Institutes of Health (NIH) are a case in point. Contrary to the common practice of making research information available only following formal publication, Dr. Steven Rosenberg of the National Cancer Institute, himself a pioneer of immunotherapy for more than three decades, has advocated the sharing of unpublished data to expedite progress.[12] Given the complexity and fluidity of both cancer and human immunity, there is too much to be learned from early discoveries. The job is simply too big for any one research team to tackle alone. Aware of the urgency of the endeavor and committed to scientific progress over personal profit, Dr. Rosenberg's leadership acknowledges uncertainty and stops short of seeking to rein it in.[13]

The race to produce human insulin in the late 1970s documents the unanticipated effects that uncertainty can have on the specific pathways scientific discovery takes. The task that would-be innovators faced at the time was to produce human insulin in the laboratory, as opposed to harvesting it from limited livestock pancreases. Several competing companies sought to reap the commercial rewards of reaching the goalpost first, but probabilities of success were incalculable. Scientists had to create a molecule of the insulin protein and find a way to produce it in vast quantities – both extremely high bars to clear. Overwhelming uncertainty and fluidity of actor interrelations shaped the eventual outcome: the race was won neither by major university laboratories nor industrial Goliaths wielding an abundance of conventional resources. Rather, the prize was claimed by Genentech, a start-up David who embraced the unknowns with agility and creative experimentation.[14] The scientists in this small company set up a laboratory in a converted warehouse. They did not work against dominant actors in the industry as they tried to solve a scientific puzzle, and ended up participating in the birth of bioengineering as a field. In what later proved to be a key move, they did not try to clone the insulin molecule from human DNA but instead assembled it

---

of funding sources. Second, as the CRISPR episode illustrated, regulatory obstacles can have an impact on the survival of research programs themselves.

[11] In the context of medical science such an attitude is particularly closely linked to clinical trials of new treatments and techniques. Chadi 2017.

[12] Rosenberg and Barry 1992: 151–52.   [13] Ibid.   [14] Watson 2003.

"from scratch." This decision put them in a position to bypass the exploding regulations requiring high-security laboratories for work combining human DNA with other (bacterial) organisms.[15] As for conventional resources, Genentech had relatively few and ended up generating protean power by not following predictable paths to either scientific or commercial success.

There is one final but important layer in the recombinant insulin story that quite possibly may characterize all potentially transformative scientific discoveries. In the 1970s, the scientific community deemed the uncertainty surrounding the impact of genetic engineering to be extremely high. It convened a conference of experts in 1975 to set out guidelines and limitations based on past laboratory practices and existing risk perceptions. Recombinant DNA work, however, was so fundamentally different that previous knowledge was not particularly useful for setting expectations. The Asilomar conference, along with a panicked public response, ended up temporarily tying the hands of many scientists.[16] Effectively, it choked the usefulness of conventional resources and benefited agile actors who did not have them in the first place. Although the rules were later relaxed, the unique mix of unknowns with which actors had to contend marks the late 1970s in both bioengineering and protean power history.

The products of innovation in early laboratory experiments are not driven by control power. It is only once relatively less complex elements of the initial scientific discovery become recognizable and manageable that they attract resources. Innovations in both science and industry have to be clearly visible if they are to be comprehensible to control power and the financial backing accompanying it. This entangles the relations between protean and control power against a background of deepening uncertainty about future success. Ultimately, this uncertainty is relieved only temporarily by impressions of predictability as solitary breakthroughs make news.[17]

Start-ups

At first glance, there is a clear difference between how scientists and start-up developers approach the uncertain context in which they operate. Unlike the deliberately open, bottom-up, and unstructured attitudes surrounding the birth of new companies, strict methodological approaches like experimental design in natural sciences are meant to reduce most unknowns and offer some semblance of control over the

[15] Ibid.: 115.   [16] Johnson 1983; Watson 2003.   [17] Rosenberg and Barry 1992: 233.

world under study. However, scientists are the first to admit that what is observed in a petri dish does not readily translate into living organisms, and what is true in mice need not be true in humans. Conversely, unconventional office layouts and novel management strategies provide a surprisingly well-grounded approach to stimulating creativity and represent much less of a free-for-all world than we might assume. The key quality that these seemingly distinct fields share is the recognition that scientists and entrepreneurs both operate in a world that combines risk with uncertainty. It therefore pays to cover the bases of what is known to work. Yet by nature of the questions asked and objectives pursued, agility and openness to new discoveries, hunches, and even surprises, are needed to overcome constraints imposed by risk calculations.

In their driving quest, start-ups seek to identify opportunities in the realm of the unknown and unknowable. Their greatest hurdles lie in the incalculability of risk in a wide range of products and services that have great potential in national and global markets. All firms operate within the same environment. Working together in close proximity, as in Silicon Valley, these firms can generate important agglomeration externalities that serve the industry extremely well. Individually, however, start-ups seek to respond to some aspect of the uncertainty that their existing competitors and potential customers also experience. Although these ventures vie for market power, none have the illusion, at the outset, of controlling or dramatically transforming national or global markets, although some, like Google, Facebook, Airbnb, Uber, Tesla, or Chobani, eventually do. Neither the innovators nor their investors know whether any pay-offs will follow. Successful start-ups uncover needs that their prospective clients may not even realize exist. Located at the margins of technological innovation, countries like Peru also develop novel digital practices and global connections. These can yield alternative development trajectories that are truly innovative and do not merely replicate technological futures imagined as universal in Silicon Valley and other global centers of innovation.[18] When tracing the competition of control and protean power among start-ups on a global scale, we do not speak of filling gaps but of creating spaces for riding out the next wave of uncertainty, instead of being swept away by it.

Not attempting even limited control, a number of prominent start-ups deliberately abandon what would otherwise be valued capacities for a partial steering of relevant market segments. When Tesla offered its electric car technology patents for no-fee fair use by those interested in adopting the technology, it did so with the hope (but no guarantee) that

[18] Chan 2013.

everyone would eventually adopt the Tesla platform. The creation of a network of recharging and battery replacement stations is the only viable avenue Tesla has toward reaching big-company status. By giving up control, it effectively expanded the ranks of those working to make gasoline-powered transportation irrelevant. The source of Tesla's power comes from the knowledge that it will continue to evolve together with other innovators who will participate in this spontaneously emerging network. If successful, the process could have a transformative impact on the operation of the car industry as a whole. Similarly, in the late 1980s Intel chose to put its resources behind building a platform for the chip and personal computer industries rather than pursuing a highly promising new product. Promoting a new standard and thus increasing demand provided Intel with a powerful run throughout the 1990s.[19]

Similar tactics have been pursued by other start-ups. Responding to uncertainty by actively encouraging innovation, regardless of who reaps the direct benefits from new ideas, is at odds with traditional approaches to building market power by carefully guarding copyrights and patents. In other examples, "Apple, Google and Amazon are all racing to build computers we can talk to, that'll understand us ... but they face competition from a surprising place – small entrepreneurs using software they're getting for free."[20] Thousands of individual programmers, on nights and weekends, work together on mastering the transfer of human language to computer applications using Wit.Ai software. There is no single actor that possesses control over how the innovative process unfolds. Yet the work being done is something "that could end up ruling the technology universe."[21]

Recognizing the prevalence of everyday and radical uncertainty in global markets, start-ups cannot afford to ignore it, nor can they settle for merely chancing upon solutions that a continually stimulating environment may produce as it challenges established power configurations. Rather, as these examples illustrate, start-ups deliberately give up that control to fully embrace the uncertainty they know they cannot and do not wish to avoid. As Taylor Owen argues, the power that distinguishes high-tech and the digital world is formless, unstable, and collaborative.[22] We call it protean.

Bitcoin: Spinning Gold out of Straw?[23]

Famously, the Grimm Brothers told the story of Rumpelstiltskin, an imp who helped a peasant girl spin straw into gold and could disappear into

---

[19] Yoffie and Cusumano 2015: 90–130.   [20] Henn 2014.   [21] Ibid.
[22] Owen 2015: 37–47.
[23] The distinction between Bitcoin the technology, and bitcoin the currency, is sometimes marked in text by capitalizing the former, not the latter. For reasons of convenience and

thin air. Updating this story for the twenty-first century requires only slight adjustments. Straw then is numbers now, crunched by tens of thousands of computers whirring 24/7 in electricity-rich, Icelandic-cold caves all over the world, but increasingly in China. The imp then disappearing into thin air when the girl guesses his name correctly, now is bitcoin's anonymous Japanese-named creator, Satoshi Nakamoto, who published a paper detailing the bitcoin protocol in November 2008, developed the necessary software in 2009, and took her or his farewell in 2011.[24]

Bitcoin is a cryptocurrency invented to bypass the political and financial centers of power. A prime example of protean power, it came on the scene in 2008–9 at the height of financial uncertainty and with the hope of undermining the state's and financial sector's control over currency. In the words of a former advisor on innovation to Secretary of State Hillary Clinton, Alex Ross, bitcoin illustrates a "wider trend towards networked and globalized power structures that tend to undermine the nation-state-based systems to which we have grown accustomed."[25] Not so. What we have grown accustomed to is overlooking the protean power potentials that are lodged in the controls that the nation-state-based system has always harbored within itself. This case illustrates the close connections between protean and control power that run like a red thread through all the other cases reported in this book.

The resourceful initiatives of a broad assemblage of innovative actors – nerds, libertarians, and cyber-cosmopolitans – seeking to circumvent the control of financial institutions and financial actors undercuts the notion of the unchallenged control by any one sector or group of actors. Admittedly, the new currency may not have lived up fully to some of the more optimistic, initial expectations of revolutionizing the world of finance. Bitcoin's underlying blockchain technology, however, has great potential for the creation of distributed, fully transparent ledgers that could revolutionize many practices of those exercising control in the fields of finance, government, and law. Ironically, banks and financial institutions, the primary targets of bitcoin's mysterious inventor Satoshi Nakamoto and his or her libertarian allies, are beginning to exploit a new technology originally designed to undermine them. The story of bitcoin is one of multi-cornered political struggles, unanticipated effects, and the lack of control.[26]

---

consistency, and because the context makes the difference between the two normally clear, we will refer to bitcoin in lowercase throughout
[24] Nakamoto 2008; Popper 2015b.   [25] Owen 2015: 71.
[26] McKeen-Edwards and Porter 2013: 24–26.

Bitcoin undercuts notions of money as an instrument of control developed, for example, by Talcott Parsons.[27] His consensus theory of power built on an analogy between the circulation of money in the economy and power in the polity. Interested in the nature of power more than its effects, Parsons downplayed conflict and imposed on an inchoate political reality a self-perpetuating practice of affirmation in the political legitimacy of established centers of authority. This perspective catches part of money's power dynamics, but it overlooks both refusal and innovation that mark protean power's disruption of financial and technological routines.

Instead of Parsons, many early users of bitcoin reflect the views of other theorists. Friedrich Hayek, for example, argued that government should not have a monopoly over the issuance of money.[28] Instead, there should be a competitive market in which currencies would be traded at variable exchange rates among both public and private actors. And currencies could be of different kinds: traditional gold- or silver-based, novel commodity-based, foreign, or virtual currencies like bitcoin. Currencies able to guarantee stable purchasing power, Hayek argued, would drive inflation-prone currencies out of business. Anticipating bitcoin by decades, Milton Friedman looked not to markets regulated by the Federal Reserve, but to a computer program as the preferred mechanism for increasing the money supply at a constant and well-publicized rate.[29]

Understood as both currency and technology, bitcoin points to the interaction between protean and control power, as Hayek and Parsons argued. And that interaction is reflected in processes and practices of innovation and refusal as well as affirmation. In a world "where innovation expands and complicates choice ... local forces are in constant motion."[30] The bitcoin world provides a graphic illustration of local forces in motion – with the local here understood to be part of the virtual rather than the geographical world. A twenty-four-year-old bitcoin entrepreneur charged with money laundering and other crimes, Charlie Shrem, has likened Nakamoto to a second Columbus who "gave us the new world."[31] One enthusiastic characterization argues that bitcoin is "about freeing people from the tyranny of centralized

---

[27] Parsons 1963. See also Barnes 1988, 12–20; Giddens 1977: 333–49; Kindleberger 1970: 3–16.

[28] Cohen 2001; Hayek 1976; Rogojanu and Badea 2014: 104–5.

[29] In contrast to Friedman's proposal, bitcoin has a fixed supply of 21 million coins. In an era struggling with deflation rather than inflation, bitcoin's deflationary bias is even more severe than the gold standard and may eventually become an insurmountable problem. Needless to say, bitcoin or other electronic currencies will have to find a way to circumvent this deflationary bias in some form without losing the transparency that the blockchain offers.

[30] Shubik 2014: 11.   [31] Sidel 2014.

trust. It speaks to the tantalizing prospect that we can take power away from the center – away from banks, governments, lawyers . . . and transfer it to the periphery, to We, the People."[32] In the words of a young Argentinian woman trading bitcoins, "It feels good, doing things that you are not supposed to, saying to the structures of power they don't have power over you."[33] In the summer of 2014 there existed reportedly 434 bitcoin meet-up groups with close to 50,000 members in 309 cities and 68 countries.[34]

What is Bitcoin?

In broader historical perspective bitcoin is less radical than it may appear at first glance. Territorial money issued and guaranteed by states has been around for only a couple of centuries. Local and now electronic currencies have been central to financial systems for much longer. "Cross-border circulation of currencies was not only accepted but widespread, monetary policy as such did not exist, and private monies were commonplace."[35] Even today, for monies and near-monies, the state is "primus inter pares and not the supreme ruler."[36]

Bitcoin is the most important of hundreds of electronic currencies.[37] It is an open-source, copyright-free, decentralized, online financial network that is easy to use for sending and receiving payments.[38] Three significant differences set bitcoin apart from more familiar financial networks such as VISA or PayPal that are owned by profit-seeking corporations. First, bitcoin is neither owned nor managed by anybody. It is a peer-to-peer network of computers that processes bitcoin transactions. Second, in contrast to existing financial networks, bitcoin is completely open. If an actor wishes to create new bitcoin-based financial services, no one's permission or assistance is required. Finally, in contrast to existing financial networks that rely on conventional currencies such as dollars, this one comes with its own currency. While the value of bitcoin is uncorrelated with the value of the world's major currencies, thus illustrating the unknowability of outcomes,[39] the denomination of its value in terms of dollars illustrates the close connection between protean and control power.

[32] Vigna and Casey 2015: 8.   [33] Popper 2015d: 53.   [34] Cofnas 2014.
[35] Cohen 2001: 207. See also Helleiner 2003: 42–79; Middlebrook and Hughes 2015.
[36] Shubik 2014: 3.
[37] Deal B%K 2014; Böhme et al. 2015; Castronova 2014; Champagne 2014; Cohen 2001; Dowd 2014; Kelly 2015; Popper 2015a; Tapscott 2016; Turpin 2014; Vigna and Casey 2015.
[38] Lee 2013.   [39] Wu and Pandey 2014: 48.

Bitcoins are electronic tokens created by miners. Collectively, miners keep a decentralized ledger called the blockchain. It is controlled by no one and creates bitcoins. Miners are rewarded for the cost of their computational labor in bitcoins. In the words of Benjamin Cohen "money can be made by making money."[40] What started as individuals operating a few personal computers in their homes has evolved quickly into very large networks of computers, running into the tens of thousands that operate in different locations all over the world. In this manner dispersed, protean power very quickly has mutated into centralized, control power over a vital part of a functioning bitcoin payment system. Expensive chips powering large computer networks are necessary to solve the increasingly difficult mathematical problems that are rewarded by an ever-decreasing number of bitcoins.

Today huge amounts of computing power are needed to mine bitcoins. To receive 25 bitcoins valued at about 6,250 dollars in October 2015, miners must calculate roughly 10 quadrillion (one thousand million million) mathematical equations per second.[41] The computational and energy-intensive underpinnings of the bitcoin currency exist in tens of thousands of computers stretching from environmentally polluting Mongolia to environmentally green Sweden.[42] As early as 2013, the computational power behind bitcoin exceeded by a factor of 100 the combined performance of the world's largest 500 supercomputers.[43] According to one estimate, by mid-century the computer capacities for solving the mathematical problems that would lead to the issuing of additional bitcoins will approach the size of the universe, operating at the speed of light.[44] One of the trickiest challenges in the evolution of bitcoin is to structure the incentives for large-scale miners so that they can make adequate profits and thus continue mining. With the dramatic expansion in the scale of mining operations, the dynamics of protean and control power have shifted. By 2016, four Chinese mining pools accounted for over 70 percent of transactions on the bitcoin network, with the vast proportion controlled by only two companies. China had "effectively assumed majority control of the Bitcoin network."[45] With the price of bitcoin about doubling in 2016 and quadrupling in 2017, topping $4,000 in August 2017, in the second half of

[40] Cohen 2001: 201.
[41] Kelly 2015: 84. Kelly 2015: 16 reports a figure of 50 quadrillion per second.
[42] *The Economist* 2015a.
[43] *The Economist* 2013. In the first five years of its existence, the computing power behind bitcoin reportedly consumed 150,000 megawatt-hours of electricity, enough to keep the Eiffel Tower lit for two and a half centuries (Clenfield and Alpeyev 2014).
[44] Castronova 2014: 162–63.   [45] Popper 2016b.

2016 Renminbi transactions accounted for 98 percent of total global bitcoin trading.[46]

Undergirding bitcoin, the currency, is the bitcoin technology. The bitcoin payment system is a protocol, a series of rules governing the exchange of information among interlinked computers. The protocol is a mathematical construct that cannot be forged. The computer code for the calculations that create bitcoins is open source and gradually evolving. Because any kind of application can be built on top of that protocol, this technology is important, even if bitcoin, the currency, were to fail altogether.[47]

Like alternating currents travelling over the electrical grid, bitcoin's blockchain is a foundational technological infrastructure. Without a roughly simultaneously emerging demand for its use, infrastructure technologies cannot develop. For the bitcoin payment system to evolve, a large and vigorous market for bitcoin currency is a necessity. The light bulb needed to be invented for the electric grid to become a worthwhile investment. Bitcoin currency in the twenty-first century plays the role of Edison's light bulb in the nineteenth century. It makes possible the development of a payment system that bypasses billing processors, credit card associations, banks, and clearing-house networks managed by regional Federal Reserve banks. Thus, it may drastically reduce the need for and power of such intermediaries and the fees they charge, putting at risk billions of dollars of sunk costs and tens of thousands of jobs in existing payment systems.[48]

In contrast to traditional payment systems run by private financial institutions or states, bitcoin technology has evolved with great speed. For one, the advantages of bitcoin are hard to deny. Final financial settlement time approaches near-real-time (an hour or less compared with 2–3 days) and at a fraction of current cost, 1 percent or less compared with 2–4 percent or more; international money transfer costs are even higher, varying between 5 and 11 percent.[49] As an optional form of payment bitcoin is now accepted by firms like IBM, Microsoft, Amazon, Expedia, iTunes, Dell, Bloomberg.com and many start-ups, including Bitpay and Coinbase. The number of American companies accepting bitcoin numbered about 140,000 by the end of 2015.[50] In the United

---

[46] Wildau 2017. Although it is by no means clear that the high correlation between the surge in the value of bitcoin and the weakening of the Chinese currency and capital outflows are causally linked, China's two largest bitcoin exchanges stopped withdrawals of the electronic currency in February 2017, after a warning by the central bank about the necessity of enforcing rules on foreign exchange transactions and money laundering.

[47] Hochstein 2014: 20.   [48] Maney 2014.

[49] Hochstein 2014: 20; Kalmadi and Dang 2015; Shubik 2014: 10.

[50] Kalmadi and Dang 2015; Lee 2013; Maney 2014; Vigna and Casey 2015: 103.

States currently there exist an estimated 500,000–1 million digital currency accounts.[51] In 2014, bitcoins were used in daily transactions worth about $50 million (up from $1 million in June 2011), compared with PayPal's $492 million and VISA's $19 billion.[52] ATM machines offering conversion of bitcoins to dollars have started springing up in several North American cities, including a new bitcoin center near Wall Street.

Bitcoin and the Dynamics of Protean and Control Power

An example of protean power and the most pervasive of a large number of private, electronic forms of currencies, bitcoin was introduced in January 2009, followed by about 700 other cryptocurrencies. As in Wagner's *Rheingold*, below the world of majestic daily global currency flows, measured in the trillions of dollars, many dwarfs were hammering away to create alternative currencies. Bitcoin saw the light of day when confidence in banking systems and central banks hit a nadir in 2008–9.[53] The financial crisis offered Nakamoto a fleeting opportunity for action that did not require having any special foreknowledge or concrete plans. At the height of that crisis, the control power of governments, banks, and large corporations over the economy had evaporated. Bitcoin became "a perfect object for the anxieties and enthusiasms of those frightened by the threats of inflation and currency debasement, concerned about state power and the surveillance state, and fascinated with the possibilities created by distributed, decentralized systems."[54]

Bitcoin was surrounded by plenty of uncertainty itself – about its feasibility, stability, and transparency. Supporters of bitcoin experienced first-hand that "there is no calculus of risk independent of an individual's affective self-reliance to uncertainty."[55] However, bitcoin was attractive apart from the escape it seemed to offer from an all-pervasive disregard of uncertainty. Individuals chose this new technological "infostructure" also because of the hope of reaping the benefits of a relatively egalitarian and open network and of immunity from hierarchical control by state and corporate elites.[56] What bitcoin supporters were seeking was perfect transparency. Thus, they adhered to a contradictory stance: total distrust in political and economic institutions, specifically governments and

---

[51] Cofnas 2014.
[52] Bitcoin can process only seven transactions per second, compared with tens of thousands for VISA. The average bitcoin transaction is about $500 compared with $80 for VISA. See Böhme et al. 2015: 214; Velde 2013.
[53] Weber 2016.   [54] Surowiecki 2011: 106.   [55] Massumi 2015: 4.
[56] Cohen 2001: 205; Hochstein 2014: 21.

banks; total trust in social institutions, specifically networks mediated and facilitated by technology.

Actors such as Goldman Sachs, JP Morgan Chase, and NASDAQ who enjoy enormous control power in the world of finance are less interested in bitcoin the currency than in the blockchain technology on which it rests. UBS, Deutsche Bank, Santander, and BNY Mellon, for example, have teamed up to develop a form of digital cash to clear and settle financial trades.[57] This technology has the potential to replace middlemen and to make redundant all forms of verification in the transfer and recording of financial assets such as stocks, contracts, crowd-funding, property titles, and patents.[58] In addition, computational law may emerge as self-executing computer programs that largely reduce, even eliminate, the need for many ordinary legal services as counterparty risks disappear.[59] A recent report estimates the savings of distributed ledger technology to soon run to between $15 and $20 billion for cross-border payments, securities trading, and regulatory compliance.[60] About 20 percent of the users of a recent start-up, Chain, are developing non-financial blockchain applications, compared with less than 10 percent a year ago. And growing sums of venture capital are flowing into this market. It remains to be seen whether and how blockchain applications will affect or eliminate trusted intermediaries or entire legal, economic, and social structures that currently guarantee property rights. Apple Pay, a digital wallet, signals that bitcoin technology is beginning to reach mainstream consumers.[61] And as it does, the recalibration of protean and control power will proceed apace. Venture capitalists investing in this technology try to convert the uncertainty attending their investment decisions into risk by creating self-fulfilling prophecies. Giving speeches, convening workshops, and stressing emergent network effects are deliberate attempts at shaping beliefs about the blockchain technology that undergirds the bitcoin currency.[62]

Most major banks and some large corporations and central banks, including the Federal Reserve and the Bank of England, have in-house teams that are exploring bitcoin's underlying technology for their operations.[63] An association of big banks called the Clearing House is trying to develop a network among the big banks that would permit instantaneous transfers between all accounts of all network members, thus eliminating the risk and uncertainties of having billions of dollars

---

[57] Arnold 2016.   [58] *The Economist* 2015a.   [59] Hochstein 2014: 23.
[60] Stafford 2015.   [61] Castranova and Fairfield 2014.
[62] With one-third of their investments failing, these rhetorical strategies are only partly successful. Susan Athey interview, April 14, 2015, Ithaca, NY.
[63] Popper 2016c; 2017; Popper and Lohr 2017.

in limbo for days while transactions are settled. In contrast to early bitcoin enthusiasts, these banks are interested in very large payments which account for most of the money moving around the world each day.[64] Harnessing the blockchain for managing transactions in foreign currency markets, for example, with their daily turnover of more than $5 trillion, would increase directly the control power of the financial sector and indirectly that of the state. Innovative applications of the bitcoin protocol to non-financial transactions are potentially far-reaching in fields as different as accounting, music, and law. But for the most part they remain today highly unpredictable.

Bitcoin is thus driven by the interaction of protean and control power as both speculators and investors alike must cope with calculable risk and incalculable uncertainty.[65] Bitcoin supporters thought they had discovered a sweet technological escape from the doomsday scenarios of a world riddled by uncertainties.[66] Yet increasingly bitcoin's underlying technology is driven by the influx of venture capital seeking profitable commercial applications of the blockchain. For now, entrepreneurs can intuit only dimly different applications of the blockchain technology that extend well beyond electronic currencies and payment schemes, such as those for products and services. Despite that unavoidable impediment, in nominal dollars, blockchain technology attracted more than $1 billion in venture capital in 2014 and 2015, dwarfing the funds attracted by the internet at its dawn in 1995, when *Newsweek* ran an article titled "Why the Internet will Fail."[67]

Uncertainty and risk incite some actors to circumvent the reach of the state while at the same time inviting regulatory activities by the state. Bitcoin makes it difficult for governments to "follow the money." It offers avenues for conducting undetectable transfers of funds, possibly for a variety of nefarious purposes.[68] Entrepreneurs like Pascal Reid, Michael Abner, and Charlie Shrem, for example, have been arrested on charges of facilitating money laundering. Bitcoin enthusiast Andreas Antonopoulas has an optimistic take on government efforts to control bitcoin: "first they ignore you, then they laugh at you, then they fight you, and then you win."[69] At the same time, seeking to exercise control, governments are beginning to regulate bitcoin and other electronic currencies in an uncoordinated fashion.[70] For example, the US Internal Revenue Service (IRS) has classified bitcoin as property and thus assumed some regulatory control. The Chair of the Federal Reserve Board, Janet Yellen, in

---

[64] Popper, 2015c; 2015d.   [65] Whitehouse 2014.   [66] Griffin 2014: 33.
[67] Smith 2014; Tapscott 2016: 9.   [68] Chafkin 2014.   [69] Thomas 2014.
[70] Raymaekers 2015: 36.

contrast, has declared that bitcoin is beyond the regulatory reach of the Federal Reserve since it has no ties to any bank. Congressional reactions to bitcoin have been similarly mixed.[71] Foreign governments have also reacted in different fashions. The German Finance Ministry, for example, has recognized bitcoin as a unit of account. In contrast, in 2013 China's Central Bank prohibited the processing of transactions in cryptocurrencies and suspended trading on several bitcoin exchanges, thus causing a collapse in the price of bitcoin and shifting Chinese entrepreneurs, unexpectedly, to become the most important miners of bitcoins worldwide. Hong Kong meanwhile is trying to position itself as Asia's center for bitcoin. Russia has followed the lead of the Chinese government without enjoying a Hong-Kong-style fallback option.[72]

Conclusion

"Money is not some separate force, easily divided from other, more human, concerns. Money is changing now, very fast, but only because we are, too," writes Adam Davidson.[73] Like language, bitcoin is a social technology that is spontaneously and rapidly evolving, and delivers outcomes through competition, imitation, and emulation that no one can anticipate. It undercuts the conventional presumption that only state-issued money is "real." Alternatives to national currencies, typically minuscule, are often local: Ithaca hours and the Berkshare in the United States; Simecs in Italy; Auroracoins in Iceland; QQ in China; M-PESA in Kenya; Tem and Sano in Greece; Peaches, Bees, Wheels, Measures, and Soil in different parts of France; and similar varieties of currencies in Spain are different examples of local currencies that have sprung up, diminished in importance, vanished altogether, or lasted for decades.[74] In many rich countries alternative currencies, such as airline miles, have become durable complements to national currencies. Under-served by banks, poor markets in Africa have seen the emergence of "mobile-minutes" as alternatives to official currencies. In addition, there exist also supranational, regional currencies such as the Euro. Private electronic currencies such as bitcoin offer a global complement to state-issued currencies.

The collapse and utter failure of bitcoin the currency is possible.[75] The fact that its inventor, Nakamoto, remains anonymous should make

---

[71] *The Economist* 2013; Griffin 2014: 33.
[72] The IMF seems ill-equipped to regulate electronic currencies like bitcoin. See Plassaras 2013.
[73] Davidson 2015b: 46.
[74] Cohen 2001: 210; Rogojanu and Badea 2014: 105–7; Shubik 2014: 3–4.
[75] Dowd and Hutchinson 2015; Yermack 2013.

anybody wary of possible insider trading and private information that could mark bitcoin as a gigantic Ponzi scheme that will at some time, somehow, and somewhere explode – unpredictably. Wild gyrations in the dollar value of bitcoin have shown that it is as vulnerable to speculative bubbles, as are other currencies or assets. And these gyrations have been reinforced by serious concerns about repeated incidences of large-scale fraud.[76] Investors on Wall Street and in Silicon Valley are guessing and betting that under risky and uncertain conditions bitcoin will somehow outgrow its current phase as a speculative investment object, while providing enough demand for further development of the underlying infrastructure technology for related and unrelated purposes. Even if bitcoin the currency were to fail altogether, bitcoin the technology, embodied in its central idea, the blockchain, will persist. Hopes for a dawn of democracy brought about by bitcoin the currency after 2008 have been disappointed. And so are the hopes of advocates of blockchain technology as a force for empowerment of the disempowered.[77] The empirical record suggests otherwise. For example, sharp disagreements among influential members of the bitcoin network about the currency's technical protocol, specifically the size of a given block, illustrate the tension between "populists," who are intent on broadening bitcoin's commercial potential, and "elitists," who are committed to posing a radical challenge to existing currencies. And this tension is acquiring an international dimension as it pits American against Chinese firms.[78] Disappointment and disillusionment hang in the air as hacking and even death threats are dividing what a few years earlier had been a tight community.[79] In short, the fight over the future of the blockchain technology illustrates how the co-evolution of currency and technology is shaped by the variable relation between protean and control power.

At the end of the Grimm Brothers' tale, in a fit of total fury, the imp splits himself in half while the peasant-girl-turned-queen and her king live happily ever after. One recent, unconventional application of the blockchain was in fact made in the marriage market. Diamonds, it turns out, are not forever – blockchains are. At least that is what David Mondrus and Joyce Bayo decided when they became the first couple to use a bitcoin automated teller machine to record their written vows in front of fifty guests.[80] In the future, on the way to the altar, taxis may be both self-driving and self-owned – by bitcoin blockchains. Traditional wedding planners, and for that matter, all planners, take note!

---

[76] Kaminska 2016; McLannahan 2015; Soble 2015; Trautman 2014.
[77] Tapscott 2016: 22–25, 86, 227.   [78] Popper 2016b.   [79] Farrell 2016; Popper 2016a.
[80] Ember 2015.

Conclusion

The blending of control and protean power produces interesting outcomes in areas characterized by a consensus about procedures needed to minimize risk, while the majority of actors recognize that uncertainty, and therefore the futility of risk calculations, remains the overwhelming norm. The *Cancer Moonshot* and the efforts to pull off a "Mars-shot" illustrate a different blending of the control power tools that scientists wield and the agility and improvisation that they need. The research teams behind the CRISPR gene-editing technique resorted to extracting what limited control patent ownership might provide. Cancer and space-flight scientists use probability-based calculations sparingly and open their minds to fundamental unknowns. And start-ups do not set out to control the surrounding context at all. The knowledge frontier thus illustrates a range of responses that contradict the notion of effective control power. Seeking to challenge established patterns of (control) power, innovators are agile as they seek to harness potentialities that might help them to take the next step.

Rather than showing that control power has limitations, the bitcoin story is one of fighting fire with fire. The emergence of bitcoin, following the financial crisis of 2007–8, leveraged profound uncertainty about the future of global finance, further complicated by the intricate architecture of interdependent financial systems. Support of the blockchain technology came first from individuals seeking to bypass an irremediably crisis- and inflation-prone financial system and later from corporate actors who instead sought to increase its efficiency. Thus, the creation of an alternative and highly volatile currency was intended to undermine failing financial structures and practices, illustrating the limits to a world of exclusive risk calculations. At the same time, central banks and financial institutions quickly realized the potential of the underlying blockchain technology for future growth and profits.

This study of power in areas that, more than most, hinge on improvisation and innovation reveals that uncertainty affects power dynamics both by the nature of the questions asked and the degree to which actors appear satisfied with the answers they receive. The experience of uncertainty is associated with unexpected threats as much as the promise of novelty and improvement. Both stir human creativity. Accidental discovery, for example, unites the possibilities of a disciplined approach to science while allowing the possibility of interpretation and creative connections that determine its ultimate success. From a different angle, the bitcoin case shows creativity in two important ways. The mathematics undergirding bitcoin the currency was genuinely innovative. It was sprung on the world at a moment of great uncertainty at the height of a global financial crisis. Furthermore, the creativity shown by venture capitalists and bankers seeking to exploit and adapt bitcoin technology was impressively improvisational. It is impossible to know at the outset where such disruptive but generative efforts end up, yet acknowledging uncertainty throughout the process of invention alters the range of the actualization of power potentialities in important ways. We may still be far from finding a cure for cancer, a landing on Mars, or finding a reliable buffer against financial crises, but we can be sure that seeking opportunities in uncertainty mixes elements of protean and control power.

Part 3

Mixed Worlds: Agility Meets Ability

7   Firms in Firmament: Hydrocarbons and the Circulation of Power

Rawi Abdelal[1]

> I can add colours to the chameleon,
>   Change shapes with Proteus for advantages,
>   And set the murderous Machiavel to school.
>   Richard III, William Shakespeare, *Henry VI, Part Three*, III.ii

Power inheres in the markets for hydrocarbons: natural gas and oil. The extraction, transit, sale, and price of hydrocarbons all create geopolitical moments in which agents may exercise control over one another or create new modes of interaction.

Firms extract hydrocarbons from beneath us. Some of these firms are minuscule beasts, privately owned with a handful of technicians and a drilling rig or two. Others are leviathans that employ hundreds of thousands and have varied owners that often include states. The vast majority of these large firms do business across national borders. When they produce outside their home nations, firms rely on institutional environments and often complex contractual arrangements designed to manage their calculable risks of cost and price. Firms that produce at home and sell abroad face symmetrical risks. Governments are ever-present in these markets. Are the firms the masters of the governments, or is it the other way around? Such is a common, but ultimately unanswerable, question.

Governments covet the gas and oil that rest untapped beneath the territories and waters of other nations. That covetousness always results in politicking over the pipelines and shipping lanes through which hydrocarbons are supplied; and sometimes it leads to war. Control over routes can be used to coerce, though it is more often a tool of influence, the subtle reshaping of domestic coalitions and national policy preferences.[2]

[1] For insightful reactions to previous drafts, I thank Jacqueline Best, Noelle Brigden, Christina Davis, Rafael Di Tella, Catherine Duggan, Jessica Green, Aida Hozic, Jeffrey Isaac, Miles Kahler, Peter Katzenstein, Robert Keohane, Stephen Krasner, Daniel Nexon, Leonard Seabrooke, and Lucia Seybert, as well as participants in seminars at Princeton University and the University of Waterloo. I am grateful to Rachel Van Horn and Morena Skalamera for research assistance.
[2] Hirschman [1945] 1980; Abdelal and Kirshner 1999/2000.

Whose power is greater: the government that controls the supply or that which controls the transit? Thus is posed another hopeless question about hydrocarbons and power.

The price of the hydrocarbons affects very nearly everyone. Oil is traded on markets that are essentially global. Already liquid, and thus easy to move from where it is buried to where it is burned, oil is a commodity that comes close to having a single world price. With the notable exceptions of financial market expectations and radical uncertainty about geopolitical supply disruptions, the price of oil results primarily from the intersection of supply and demand. Only a few firms are capable of influencing the price of oil by restricting or expanding supply when they cooperate within the context of the Organization of the Petroleum Exporting Countries (OPEC). One firm, the Saudi Arabian Oil Company, commonly known as Aramco, has sometimes done so on its own.

The price of natural gas is another matter altogether. Naturally occurring in a gaseous state, and expensive to liquefy, natural gas is sold on markets that are local, regional, and global. In the densely pipelined United States, gas is traded on spot prices. So it is in a few gas trading hubs around the world. Liquefied gas can, like oil, travel by ship to the highest bidder. For the most part, however, gas travels from source to consumer through a pipeline that allows for no diversion; the prices for piped gas have generally been determined by complex formulae agreed upon by suppliers and consumers. Until recently those formulae relied extensively on the oil price as the most important reference in an index. Supply shocks – such as the US unconventional oil and gas revolution – and demand shocks – like the pan-European recession and the slowdown of Chinese growth – both influence price. There is, to be sure, power in those prices. Whose is it? Over whom? And to do what? The simpler questions obscure the differences between multiple forms of power that interact.

In this chapter I explore the character of protean and control power in hydrocarbon markets. I first describe the relationships among firms, among states, and between firms and states as constitutive of what we ultimately interpret as markets. In these relationships we find both protean and control power. Then, I narrate briefly four cases that illuminate the effects of protean and control power in hydrocarbon markets: the European–Russian gas relationship over several decades; the geopolitical consequences of the US unconventional revolution; the Sino-Russian energy rapprochement; and the effects on Russia of the sudden, rapid, unintended, largely unanticipated decline in the price of oil amidst the Ukrainian geopolitical crisis. I conclude with some reflections on the paradox that the particularities of natural gas markets render them ostensibly susceptible to control power, whereas in fact protean power is their defining feature.

The Circulation of Power in Hydrocarbon Markets

The participants in hydrocarbon markets experience, promulgate, deploy, and embody power, both dominating and shape-changing. Seybert and Katzenstein (Chapter 1, p. 16) distinguish between two different instantiations of power: between the possibility to "exercise 'power over' (understood here as actual capability) the human or non-human world . . .," and the fact of being "empowered to have 'power to' (understood here as the capacity to actualize potentialities) navigate in that world successfully." Many scholars and practitioners recognize control power in hydrocarbon markets, but the most interesting, consequential outcomes and practices result from the interaction of control and protean power. Power circulates across these ways of being, of seeing, and of doing.

The interplay of these forms of power defines the relationships among states and firms, the transit of hydrocarbon supply to its demand, and the formation of prices. As is true of finance (Chapter 8), hydrocarbon markets comprise moments of probabilistic risk and both radical and operational uncertainty. Firms generally try to write contracts to manage the risks that they estimate. When faced with uncertainty, however, those same firms rely on the depth of their relationships, on trust and habits of thought, and on improvisation to reshape the institutional contexts within which they manage.[3] Technological change in the industry may sometimes seem endogenous, but in fact such change results largely from firms taking seemingly calculated risks that collectively create uncertainty about supply and price. Risk-based behavior leads to systemic uncertainty and unpredictability. Thus, these markets are characterized by elements of both risk and uncertainty. And firms experience both the riskiness and uncertainty as they alternately acquiesce or refuse, improvise or innovate.

Firms and States

The scholarly literature on political economy is composed in part of several enduring debates about the balance between public and private power. In comparative political economy, scholars have interrogated the influence of firms on states. Although political lobbying and regulatory

[3] Herrigel 2010.

capture are phenomena that describe the intentionality of firms, some scholars have identified ways in which the control of firms over political outcomes is pervasive in practice and inherent to the structure of modern capitalist systems. Thus, the structural power of business might rest upon automatic processes in addition to intentionality.[4]

For scholars of international political economy, systemic questions have been preoccupying. Cross-border markets for, say, capital are thought by some to have transcended the authority of nation-states, though others insist that states retain both autonomy from and influence over such markets.[5] Multinational firms might have become more powerful than the governments that created the very possibility of their incorporation, or perhaps instead the states are still masters of the firms.[6]

The implicit and explicit understandings of power that inform these enduring debates have allowed scholars to answer some important questions about the power of one set of agents over another at different moments in varied contexts. The idea of control power is the very basis for the questions that have been asked: power over; higher or lower; and so on. We find those who dominate and others who acquiesce and submit. Control power, in this conception, is an attribute of an agent.

Yet the power that one finds in these relationships is more mutable and multidimensional. It is not merely that the dominant and the submissive switch roles regularly depending on the moment or the issue at hand, though that is true. In fact, power is constantly being renegotiated through acts of creativity and agency. The firms and governments have interests in accomplishing or experiencing outcomes – power to do this or that thing – that often have little to do with insisting or relenting relative to one another. Protean power here is oblique: it is about the effects of unanticipated innovations by agents, innovations that disrupt the practices of control power and unsettle agents' understanding of risk and uncertainty. An understanding of protean power uncovers heretofore obscured elements of the relationships between firms and states in hydrocarbon markets.

Firms also have relationships with one another – relationships of great political consequence and considerable variability.[7] These relationships are, however, almost completely absent from the scholarly literatures on comparative and international political economy. Power circulates among firms as well in a system that is intertwined with the system of states. The managers of energy firms would not recognize the power

---

[4] Lindblom 1977; Culpepper 2011; Culpepper and Reinke 2014.   [5] Abdelal 2007.
[6] This is one of the classic questions of international political economy. See Vernon 1971; Gilpin 1975; Krasner 1978. See also Baldwin 1989.
[7] Abdelal 2015.

dynamics between them as involving or implicating control only. For the firms, power is also protean. Basically, they cannot do without one another, and the formal and informal elements of their relationships are in a state of constant renegotiation. Protean power is the effect of firms' improvisation and innovation as circumstances – and their relationships – evolve in unpredictable, often unknowable, ways.

In these relationships between and among states and firms we find many moments of improvisation. Both the private and public agents – executives and policymakers – tend to believe about the other that there exists a plan with calculable probabilities. But what they believe about themselves is usually the reverse: that they are all at sea, and that their successes are based more on adaptability than foresight. Machiavelli's arguments about *fortuna* and *virtù* reflect these intuitions. If *fortuna* is responsible for half of our actions, then we are left only the other half. And *virtù* defines our ability to improvise and adapt.[8] Machiavelli himself understood power as protean – chameleon-coloring, shape-changing, improvisational – even if Shakespeare's "Machiavel" in *Henry VI* was supposed to be outdone by Richard III. As the political theorist Richard Clegg astutely observes, for Machiavelli any inquiry into power is necessarily ethnographic. Power, in Machiavelli's analysis, is an effect: it is tenuously produced and reproduced as a result of the competencies of agents, rather than merely as a resource that inheres in them. Power is thus to be revealed in the networking of relations among agents.[9]

Whereas risk requires an understanding of probability and decision-making, uncertainty creates, in contrast, a premium on judgment. At the highest levels, executives and policymakers know that technique will bring them only so far. Models and forecasts bring them to the moment when judgment must be exercised, where empathy and intuition must be employed. At that moment, a sense of history, a coherent worldview, and the competence of recognizing patterns are critical. The micro-foundation of this theory of practice is an agency attenuated by an environment of dense, intertwining relationships, as Chris Reus-Smit also shows in the case of human rights (Chapter 3). These agents know that they do not know what they do not know about their environment; they recognize the elements of uncertainty that persist and recur in their market environments. They plan with a language of scenarios of possible futures, rather than of prediction and calculation. Good judgment – coupled with a sense of timing – is not a resource, but a practice.

Thus, the relationships that are the essence of any market are, like all relationships, in a state of constant renegotiation. Nothing ever gets

---

[8] Machiavelli [1513/32] 1998, ch. XXV.   [9] Clegg 1989, chs. 1 and 2.

settled once-and-for all. No one always wins, and no one loses forever. The moments of *Veni, vidi, vici* are passing fantasy. Instead, *Luctor et emergo*: I struggle and emerge. Or, perhaps even more accurately: We struggle and emerge.

A holistic understanding of hydrocarbon markets – and of the circulation of power among firms and states – offers insight into flows of capital. Regardless of the ownership structures of firms in hydrocarbon-exporting nations, their governments rely on receipts in the forms of corporate income, dividends, and tax receipts. The firms and governments of hydrocarbon-importing nations depend on the flows of energy resources to generate the power that underpins output growth. Leaders of exporting nations express concern over the security of demand for their resources, demand that is essential for the fiscal health of the state. In importing nations, however, the security of supply – usually called energy security as shorthand – is the greater risk.

Supply and Transit

Thus is the transit of energy resources the vasculature of hydrocarbon markets. The vast majority of the world's oil is transported by ship. A small, but growing share of the world's natural gas is liquefied and shipped in the same way. Exporters and importers rely therefore on the openness and safety of the world's sea lanes, sometimes called the sea lines of communication. Once under the control of the British, the sea lanes are now maintained largely by the US Navy – a form of control power based on the management of risk. The US government has used its naval predominance to restrict the supply of hydrocarbons to adversaries during war – a practice that reached the height of its effectiveness during the Second World War when Japan was deprived of oil.[10]

The US approach to energy markets and energy security informs the nation's approach to military power. The United States has traditionally not, for example, purchased a significant proportion of its imported oil from the hydrocarbon-rich states of the Persian Gulf. So its military presence in the region, often mistakenly attributed to its direct interest in oil, derives in part from the US interest in the continued flow of oil onto the world's markets.

The United States similarly does not rely on all of these sea lanes for the transit of its own oil imports. So the US blue-water naval presence has not tended to protect directly its own supply. Instead, the United States seeks to maintain sea lanes because of a long-held, poorly defined, but

[10] Barnhart 1987.

preference-revealed approach to energy security. For US practice, energy security is maintained by the liquidity of global markets, on which importers may buy as much as they wish at whatever price happens to prevail.

The Japanese wartime and global postwar lessons are apparent to Chinese policymakers. In the long run, the Chinese government expects its own blue-water navy to challenge US predominance, at least in Asia. For now, however, some 80 percent of Chinese oil imports transit the Straits of Malacca, which are controlled largely by the US Navy and, otherwise, by pirates. Chinese energy firms have, with the strong encouragement of the military establishment, purchased equity stakes in oil fields around the world, including in Africa.[11] This improvisation is to ensure the nation's access to hydrocarbon resources, though whether such a tactic would provide insurance in the case of an all-out naval blockade is doubtful.

The transit of natural gas is far more intimate, for the pipelines cross the territories – and occasionally territorial waters – of sovereign states. The oil politics are largely global; the gas politics are local. Transit states are the middlemen in these producer–consumer relationships: the delivery services essential to the commerce of natural gas. Transit states are always themselves consumers of natural gas, and occasionally they provide their services in exchange for the gas supplies they require. Much more often, however, transit states provide delivery for a fee and pay cash for the gas they consume – the prices for both are subject to negotiation. While in transit, the gas is owned, if not controlled, by the seller. Such an arrangement, as in the varying routes taken by illegal migrants, creates opportunities for fascinating struggles of money, influence, and security (Chapter 5).

Price

Oil has a single price.[12] That price metaphorically pulls the oil from the ground. A high price pulls more; a lower price implies a softer tug. Yes, there are financial market participants who speculate on future prices and thus affect them moment by moment. Overall, though, the oil markets deliver to us a wonderfully simple formula: supply and demand. The demand is not under the control of anyone in particular. The supply, on the other hand, is in the hands of only a few. The challenge of coordinating supply changes, however, has most often proved to be a collective

---

[11] Downs 2000; Taylor 2014; Zhao 2014.
[12] This is basically so. Oil comes onto the market in different grades (heavy or light, sweet or sour) that are not altogether fungible because refineries differ in their capabilities to manage them.

action problem beyond the capabilities of an old, yet still inchoate organization.[13] And supply and demand move in an uneven rhythm of time, since high oil prices invite capital investment that may take several years to come to fruition, by which time the price may have declined just at a moment of burgeoning supply.

Natural gas has, in contrast, a great many prices. One prevails in the liquid, but self-contained, market of North America. Still another, higher price emerges from the fragmented market of Europe. The Asians pay the most. The markets thus are regionalized. Whereas oil is pulled, gas is pushed and relationship-laden.

Consumers of imported gas do not receive the price they deserve; they receive the price they negotiate. Industry practice for fifty or so years was to use the price of oil as the starting point for negotiating the formula for the price of piped gas. In part, this was done to ensure that gas would remain competitive with fuel oil, its closest substitute as gas-powered electricity generation became widespread.

The more important reason for the practice, however, was that gas markets were not very market-like. That is, a natural gas contract commonly involved bringing the molecules from a starting point in an exporting nation through a pipe to an ending point in an importing nation; the pipeline did not serve other nations, and gas could not somehow travel elsewhere. The gas either entered the pipe destined for a single destination, or it did not. So: a market with perhaps only two participants.

And from what might a price emerge in a market with only a monopolist and a monopsonist? Either the monopolist and monopsonist could abuse one another during each passing moment of bargaining position. Or, as it turns out, the two parties could agree to avoid any such thing by settling instead on the price of something else, which itself is formed through the daily interactions of thousands of buyers and dozens of sellers.

So the prices of natural gas would vary with the price of oil, with further influence from the density of pipeline networks and the relationships between the firms that transacted with one another. As more and more pipelines were built, and balancing markets for a few billion cubic meters here or there evolved into more liquid trading hubs, over just the last few years the markets for natural gas have begun to incorporate the spot prices for gas into formulae at the expense of the long-standing practice of the oil index.

The transition from oil to spot-price indexation has introduced some of the simpler dynamics of oil prices, in which exporters may influence price

[13] See, for example, Spar 1994.

through unilateral or coordinated adjustments in supply.[14] And this transition itself introduced an era of intense, complex negotiation over the composition of the formulae for gas price formation. Firms have created new practices and contract structures in ways that affect both their influence over one another and the fortunes and fates of the nations in which they are based.

Stories

Four stories reveal the interplay of control and protean power in the markets for hydrocarbons.

Gas, Red

First is the story of how a handful of European firms went to Moscow at the height of the Cold War to negotiate one of the most historically significant – and fateful – natural gas deals of the last century with the Soviet gas ministry.[15] US policymakers opposed the European–Soviet gas relationship then and in the decades that followed for fear of Soviet manipulation of and coziness with European allies. US control power was employed – unsuccessfully – to undermine or thwart the deal.[16]

Yet the relationship flourished. Soviet and European managers came over time to trust one another. As the Soviet Union collapsed, all of these agents were obliged to recast their relationships with one another. The Soviet gas ministry evolved into the Russian firm Gazprom. The pipeline route that had once spanned a single Soviet state and a handful of Warsaw Pact nations on its way to European markets was transformed into a complex maze of pipelines that crossed multiple sovereign territories.[17] Possibilities for the exercise of control power were ever-present and almost never undertaken.

A newly post-Soviet Ukraine emerged as the most important supplier to Gazprom: of the transit of gas, with some 80–90 percent of Russian gas contracted to European customers traversing its borders. Building on decades worth of trust, European firms continued to do business with Gazprom, which was left with the problem of managing its new relationship with Naftogaz Ukrainy, the firm responsible for the Ukrainian pipeline infrastructure.

Even as gas crises flared in 2006 and 2009, European firms continued to believe that Gazprom was a reliable partner.[18] Operational uncertainty

---

[14] Stern and Rogers 2012; Mitrova, Kulagin, and Galkina 2015.   [15] Högselius 2013.
[16] Jentleson 1986.   [17] Abdelal, Jorov, and Tarontsi 2008a.
[18] Abdelal, Jorov, and Tarontsi 2008b: 2008c.

over the sources of the supply disruptions required firms to interpret and ultimately judge competing narratives. The gas crises resulted from contractual disputes between Gazprom and Naftogaz Ukrainy. The most contentious issues were the fees Naftogaz would charge Gazprom for transit and the price Gazprom would charge Naftogaz for the gas volumes Ukraine consumed. For much of the 1990s, the transit fees and gas prices were contractually linked: each was below the rates that prevailed in western Europe. The value of the transit discount enjoyed by Gazprom was worth much less than the gas discount Naftogaz received.

During spring 2005, some months after the Orange Revolution of late autumn/early winter 2004 brought a pro-Western regime to Kiev, Naftogaz and Gazprom undertook a new round of their yearly negotiations.[19] (Their contracts concluded on 1 January of each new year.) Naftogaz proposed that Gazprom pay for transit at rates comparable to those in the West. Gazprom responded that Naftogaz should also then pay gas prices that prevailed elsewhere, thus bringing to an end the discounts that each had offered the other. Naftogaz refused, for Ukraine could ill afford the higher price for the significant volumes the nation consumed. Having reached a stalemate in the negotiations, 10.00AM on January 1, 2006 found Naftogaz and Gazprom out of contract.

As Gazprom compressed and shipped the amount of gas for which its European customers had paid, it also cut the shipment of gas intended for Ukraine's consumption. Not all of the Europe-bound gas made it through the Ukrainian pipeline. Naftogaz accused Gazprom of exercising crude control power as putative punishment for the nation's Western geopolitical ambitions. Gazprom accused Naftogaz of theft and argued that Ukraine would not be shipped gas until a new contract were signed. Naftogaz, Gazprom suggested, was also exercising control power in the form of extortion, by taking advantage of the nation's near-monopoly of transit.

A similar contractual dispute during spring and autumn 2008 led to an even more dramatic breakdown of the Naftogaz–Gazprom relationship in January 2009. Gazprom's European customers were left with an interpretive puzzle. They could have decided that Ukrainian transit was untrustworthy, that Russian supply was undependable, or that persistent discord between Russia and Ukraine rendered the ascription of guilt moot.

Such was their trust in Russian supply that the solution of the major European energy firms to the problem of Ukrainian transit was to disintermediate Ukraine with new pipelines.[20] The most important of these

---

[19] A fuller recounting of this episode can be found in Abdelal 2013.
[20] Abdelal and Tarontsi 2011a; 2011b.

was the Nord Stream pipeline, a major innovation to the existing system. Long touted by both European and Russian executives as a solution to potential supply disruptions by contentious transit negotiations, the northern pipeline route was pushed along toward completion by the gas crises. Although US policymakers were disappointed, and central European policymakers were downright alarmed, the northern route reshaped the geopolitics of the region.[21] A new proposed route to Ukraine's south, the South Stream pipeline, would, if it had come to fruition, almost fully disintermediated Ukraine. Both Nord Stream and South Stream were joint European–Russian projects. The Nord Stream consortium comprised Gazprom, E.ON, BASF, Gasunie, and, eventually, GDF SUEZ. The South Stream consortium was composed of Gazprom, ENI, and Électricité de France. Ukraine was left in the cold.

In the complex relationship between Gazprom, Naftogaz Ukrainy, and European energy companies, many US policymakers and scholars saw only control power. Either Russia was punishing Ukraine, or Ukraine was extorting Russia, or Russia was threatening Europe. A much more subtle protean power was, however, evident. Rather than a desperate Ukraine and a gas-hungry, dependent Europe, Russian and European energy executives recognized their mutual dependence, the geopolitical and contractual uncertainties of the Ukrainian transit route, and their joint innovative potential to reshape the transit of gas. In the language of this volume, this innovation was a response to a thoroughgoing uncertainty that, so it seemed, demanded more of them than mere improvisation.[22]

The story was thus not primarily one of an agent's exercise of power over another. Instead, multiple agents, which in some ways were constituted by their relationships among one another, creatively found ways to manage their production and consumption dealings – an iterative, protean power that resulted from the underlying uncertainty of the context and the agents' experience of that uncertainty. The result came largely at Ukraine's geopolitical and commercial expense, but even in the Russian–Ukrainian relationship the control power of each over the other failed miserably to deliver any outcome either desired. Russia failed to pull Ukraine decisively toward Eurasia; Ukraine's monopsony gambit failed disastrously. The innovation for which Ukrainian leaders had hoped became merely refusal; Russian leaders' efforts toward Ukrainian acquiescence brought frustration and disappointment. Both sides discovered that when control power failed them, the ground beneath them nevertheless shifted enough to create a landscape that was unfamiliar and undesirable to each.

---

[21] Abdelal 2013.   [22] Abdelal 2015.

Gas, Red, White, and Blue

American exceptionalism is mostly mythological, except for the unconventional hydrocarbon revolution. That revolution has been and will likely remain an exception in its scale and influence. In just the last few years the United States has become one of the largest oil and natural gas producers in the world. The prospect of hydrocarbon self-sufficiency may fundamentally alter patterns of geopolitics, and in a number of ways the unconventional revolution has already done so.

The unconventional revolution was not, however, the result of conscious US policy. The mix of agents, norms, and institutions was exquisitely American. Partly it is a simple story of discontinuous technological change. American firms had known for decades that bountiful natural gas supplies lay within shale rock formations. There was little point in counting up those billions of cubic meters, for no one could really get to them – not until a handful of small firms pioneered the combination of using water to fracture (to frack, that is) the shale and horizontal drilling to extract the gas and, later, oil. The technology was not so fancy. True, the crews with the knowledge and experience to operate the drilling rigs were in desperately short supply. There were not even enough rigs to go around the United States, much less the world. Those remained manageable challenges in the medium run for any nation.

What could not be easily replicated, however, was the peculiar combination of features that defined the US revolution, including the hundreds of small, entrepreneurial energy firms willing to take bet-the-company decisions repeatedly; the vast expanses of sparsely populated territory under which many of the largest shale gas deposits sit; a dense, capacious pipeline network that can bring the gas practically anywhere within the country's borders; and a societal willingness to drill hundreds of thousands of holes (the activity is much more drilling-intensive than conventional oil and gas development) in the earth's crust to get at the resources. Another important institutional arrangement is the subsoil property rights regime, within which, for example, a farmer whose land sits atop shale reserves can sell or lease drilling rights thousands of meters beneath the earth. And, finally, a permissive regulatory environment that has largely required opponents of hydraulic fracturing to prove its dangers, rather than the other way around, as in Europe, where many citizens are mystified that the fracturers did not have first to prove the safety of the practice before regulators allowed it.

The irony is particularly acute for the US government, which tried and failed for forty years to achieve energy independence with a series of ill-fated public policy schemes based on control power. The government sought to exercise control power over its energy market by allowing more drilling for resources, drilling for resources in precarious habitats, subsidizing renewables, and promoting efficiency and conservation. Yet it was innovation in the face of uncertainty, largely uncoordinated, and accomplished by small, under-capitalized firms ignored by the majors that in the end delivered energy self-sufficiency to the United States.

The oil from the unconventional revolution made its way onto global markets and affected their overall supply. Still, US firms are profitable, depending on the basin, only at prices of $45–60 per barrel, and they faced their own uncertain future as oil prices plummeted during 2014 and 2015.

In order to make its way onto world markets, however, US unconventional gas would first need to be liquefied, and then, as with oil, a firm must apply for and receive a license to export. A few licenses have been granted, and some liquefaction facilities are in construction. Thus far, only a few cubic meters of liquefied natural gas have left the shores of the United States, yet the consequences for natural gas markets have already been felt around the world.

Plummeting US natural gas prices and abundant domestic supply led to the diversion of theretofore anticipated liquefied gas deliveries to elsewhere in the world. A collapse in US coal prices led to the export of incredibly inexpensive coal. Combined with a pan-European recession and new liquid gas trading hubs, European energy firms in particular found themselves paying – for the first time – higher prices for piped gas than for spot-market or liquefied gas.[23]

This created a new era of operational uncertainty for both European firms and their suppliers, Gazprom in particular. Would the United States export natural gas in significant quantities? For how long would spot prices stay below oil-indexed prices? Before the recent declines in the price of oil, oil-indexed gas had become relatively expensive.

Europeans proposed two major improvised revisions in their contract structures with major pipeline-gas suppliers. The first was to index the price of piped gas to the spot prices of natural gas, rather than the spot prices of fuel oil. The second was to reduce the role of the so-called take-or-pay clause. With take-or-pay, the customer commits many years in advance to purchase minimum annual quantities of gas: the firm can buy more than that commitment, but not less. This clause provided a kind of security to the customer, since the commitment was bilateral: the producer also was obliged to sell at least that much to its customer at the price delivered by the index, even if, at that moment, there might be a better

[23] Abdelal, Maugeri, and Tarontsi 2014.

price to be found elsewhere. There was also security of demand for the producer, since the exporting firm could count on a predictable stream of revenues.

Exercising their leverage over Gazprom, and out of desperation, European firms managed to undertake several years of renegotiation with suppliers. Another energy crisis thereby revealed the protean nature of power in these hydrocarbon markets. The firms were not engaged in risk-based, arm's-length contract negotiations in which their knowledge and power delivered an outcome. Instead, all the parties were at sea, unsure of how difficult the market environment would become for either of them, yet still embedded in decades-long relationships. Those renegotiations temporarily saved the balance sheets of the European firms at the expense of those of the suppliers. Gazprom, thoroughly dependent on the European market for most of its revenues and essentially all of its profits, suffered most of all from the new contract structures.

One consequence, however, of the arrangement was that the new contract provisions provided little incentive for Gazprom to continue to build pipeline infrastructure to Europe. A contractual arrangement in which European firms offered to purchase whatever amount of gas they needed at whatever price happened to prevail pushed the responsibility for infrastructure development away from Gazprom, which would not be able to rely on a stream of well-understood, if still variable, revenues. Without such a revenue stream, Gazprom and its European partners might not be able even to find financial backing for the project from the banks that usually undertake project finance.

Gazprom's response was, in part, the cancellation of its South Stream pipeline project, which had been a joint Italian–Russian plan to bring gas across the Black Sea. Instead, a joint Turkish–Russian project, Turkish Stream, became Gazprom's preferred route for bringing its gas to a growing Turkish market and near enough to Greece so that the Europeans, at the presumably inevitable end of their macro-economic crisis, might be able to build pipelines to collect it at the Turkish border.[24] Thus, the Turkish–Russian protean reorganization of the eventual supply infrastructure promised to reshape once again the dynamics of the Eurasian gas industry.

The only certainty in the short and medium term was that Europe and Russia would remain bound together by steel pipes and intimate contractual relationships. The contractual arrangements are never definitively settled. As one European energy executive observed: "A long-term

---

[24] Abdelal, Çekin, and Çelik 2015. The downing of a Russian jet by the Turkish military in November 2015 delayed the project, although by 2017 it seemed to be back on track.

contract is a good handshake: we work together for fifty years; we meet from time to time to sort out the price."[25] Each agent is thus creatively, dialogically working through the challenges while embedded in a context of mutual intelligibility but systemic uncertainty. For now, European firms have achieved the contract structures that enhance their viability, while Gazprom began to search for a creative solution to the unpleasant problem of its income statement. Gazprom lamented the demise of its once highly profitable Western market.

A Sino-Russian Rapprochement

At this point Gazprom turned wishfully toward the East. In May 2014, after more than a decade of on-again-off-again negotiations, Gazprom and the Chinese National Petroleum Company (CNPC) finally reached an agreement for gas-rich Russia to supply gas-poor China.[26] The details of the deal are not public, and speculation about the realized price of the gas is rampant. After the uncertainty over the possibility of any deal between the two companies, a wholly surprising chain of events made the improbable finally conceivable. The road to the deal had followed a circuitous path from the supply-and-demand shocks of the 2000s.

The most plausible interpretation of the deal is that Gazprom's desperation in the wake of a European market that had deteriorated for an uncertain, if not indefinite, period of time, pushed the Russians toward accepting a deal. Most likely, the Chinese government had by that point also realized that the prospects of its own unconventional gas revolution were in the short term slim, though uncertainty lingered. Without the pipeline infrastructure to bring the Chinese shale gas to the population centers where it was needed, and without the water that was necessary for the hydraulic fracturing of the shale, Chinese energy firms would have to import gas until enough capital could be spent to create the network of steel or the technology evolved to become less water-intensive.

The Russian government portrayed this deal as part of a broader pivot away from Europe and the West toward Asia. The Russians narrated the adventure as a new era in Russian–Chinese relations and perhaps even a new strategic partnership. This coincided with a variety of Eurasianisms in Russian political thought that lent ideological legitimacy to a Russia that was as much a part of dynamic Asia as it was a part of the lovely

[25] Author's interview with Bruno Lescoeur, CEO, Edison, Paris, June 12, 2013.
[26] Skalamera 2014. Also see Abdelal and Tarontsi 2012; Abdelal, Skalamera, and Tarontsi 2015.

museum of Europe.[27] The Chinese, however, viewed Russia as a junior partner at best.[28]

The post-Ukrainian crisis sanctions regime may not have undermined Russia's commitment to the geopolitical organization of its near abroad, but without infusions of vital technology from the West the ability of Russian firms to honor existing contracts with China remain questionable. Given this uncertainty, Moscow was forced to invent another creative solution to disguise the increasing asymmetry of the Sino-Russian relationship as a form of resistance to an increasingly clear fate.

Thus, Russia's desperation as oil and gas prices plummeted led to an invitation that China take up the slack in investment. Equity was the cost. In exchange for Chinese investment in the fields that would provide gas for the eventual pipeline, CNPC, as one example, was able to acquire a 10 percent stake in Vancorneft, a subsidiary of Rosneft. Chinese firms, as well as the government itself, have committed the financial liquidity that Russian companies need desperately in light of collapsing investment and a severe recession.

The realities of Russia's position vis-à-vis China reveal an unhappily creative reorganization of the relationship. The equity stakes being acquired by Chinese firms will undermine the profitability of the deal for Russian firms. Since China does not depend nearly as much as Europe on Russian gas, price guarantees and upstream equity stakes will likely become essential elements of future gas deals. So, too, will the pipeline routes take the paths preferred by Chinese firms. When, in October 2014, Gazprom announced the likely cancellation of a Vladivostok LNG project, a third gas pipeline to China – in addition to the already agreed Power of Siberia and Altai projects – emerged as its successor. Russian firms had preferred to diversify energy relationships throughout Asia, but instead they are finding themselves bound together more closely with the Chinese market.

The most likely scenario, then, is that Russia will emerge as a resource appendage to China. The partnership, which had once been seen as an alternative to decreasingly profitable Western relationships, is one on which China's seniority in the arrangement requires Russian adaptation to a less attractive, but still indispensable, Asian future. Russia's acquiescence to China's growing leverage has come to resemble resignation.

As the Chinese economic slow-down combines with almost-unbreathable air, natural gas is likely to figure prominently in the leadership's interest in burning less coal without altogether abandoning less expensive, but relatively

---

[27] On the variety of Eurasianisms, see Katzenstein and Weygandt 2017. Also see Laruelle 2008.

[28] Skalamera 2015.

clean fossil fuels. So Russia bet on economic dynamism in China and the Pacific; China bet that its nearby resource-rich, but otherwise rather sad, neighbor will help the nation reproduce a normal, Sino-centric world. They need each other, but the uncertainty about their fates has required extraordinary creativity and improvisation by both about how to proceed.

Eurasian Borderlands

The Ukrainian crisis was a long time in the making.[29] Contemporary Ukraine is composed of territories in the east that had been part of the tsarist empire for several centuries, as well as, at the other extreme, those in the west that had been part of Habsburg Galicia and interwar Poland. Soviet Ukraine's nationalist movement emerged in Ukrainian-speaking Galicia during the 1980s, an agitation that mystified many in the Russian-speaking east. Ukrainians agreed on one basic fact: that they were Ukrainians. But they agreed on little else: not on language, or on history, or on a common geopolitical destiny.

The Putin regime had signaled with emphasis and in vain that the West, broadly conceived, was unlikely to care as much about the geopolitical fate of Ukraine as did Russian leaders. When Vladimir Putin annexed Crimea, thus undoing Nikita Khrushchev's 1954 "gift" to the Ukrainian Soviet Socialist Republic, US and European policymakers were left with a dilemma. Although they could not reasonably hope to dissuade Putin and were unwilling to support credibly western Ukraine's Western dreams, they felt that they must at least signal their displeasure. The United States imposed sanctions on the Russian economy for this purpose, as did, less exuberantly and more expensively, the European Union.[30]

For the Russians, the sanctions were unwelcome and irritating. The sanctions also represented for the Russian leadership the single most vexing aspect of post-Cold War international relations: namely, their sense of American hypocrisy.

At around the same time, the Russian economy experienced a serious crisis, and the ruble declined precipitously – from about 35 to 70 rubles to the dollar. American policymakers were quick to claim credit for Russia's economic troubles, a putative result of the sanctions regime and their employment of control power. And while it is true that the sanctions were consequential, in fact the travails of the Russian economy resulted more from the coincident, precipitous decline in the price of oil. The fall in the

[29] Abdelal 2001; Abdelal, Di Tella, and Tarontsi 2014.
[30] On this logic of economic sanctions, see Baldwin 1985.

price of oil was largely a consequence of oversupply – pulled onto the market by capital investments made when the price of oil was high – and weakening demand, particularly in China and an increasingly self-contained US energy market.[31]

In this episode we find control power in a surface narrative: a Western effort to force Russia to withdraw its territorial claims on the Crimean peninsula and involvement in a bloody armed conflict on Ukraine's eastern border. With Russia's international relations, however, the text is almost always misleading; everything interesting is in the subtext.

Russia's interests in Ukraine have already been largely achieved, and the endgame will likely deliver some sort of federal reorganization of the Ukrainian state. With Crimea as the ninetieth Russian region, there is no longer any risk, however remote it may have been, that the naval base at Sevastopol would be situated in a NATO or NATO-aligned nation. Ukraine's unitary state meant that an eastward-leaning regime could effectively tilt the country toward Eurasia, while a westward-leaning one could turn in the direction of Europe. Given Ukraine's complex institutional and linguistic history, neither definitive resolution of Ukraine's place on the border between Europe and Eurasia would be satisfactory or politically sustainable. A federal Ukraine would be permanently unable to choose, and the non-choice leaves Ukraine not-in-Europe.

Particularly given European reluctance to enforce a comprehensive sanctions regime, the US approach was similarly revealed more by subtext. Few in Washington or Brussels, much less Berlin and Paris, could have realistically believed that sanctions would force Russia to withdraw from Crimea. Yet Western leaders were, despite their vague promises of salvation to Kiev, unwilling to risk a large confrontation with Russia over the geopolitical fate that few consider a strategic priority. Doing nothing would have displayed embarrassing weakness, so sharp words and, for the United States, reasonably costless sanctions represented a language of disapproval and resignation. The coincidence of declining oil prices – a happy one for Washington, alarming for Moscow – provides for a language of serious Western conviction that belied the innovative, subtle conversation that policymakers conducted implicitly.

Conclusions

The world's two most important hydrocarbon markets – oil and gas – are impressively dissimilar. In the first, the molecules naturally occur in a

---

[31] Several analysts anticipated the subsequent decline by evaluating investment patterns in oil fields over the past decade. See Maugeri 2012.

liquid state, so oil can be piped, shipped, even trucked around the world and sold to the highest bidder. In oil markets power is intrinsically entwined with price and, to a lesser extent, the freedom and safety of transit routes used by anyone who has taken temporary or permanent ownership.

The relevant molecules of the second market naturally occur in a gaseous state. Although the gas molecules may be liquefied, shipped in a manner similar to oil, and then re-gasified upon delivery, the relative expense of that process is often prohibitive. So the gas generally remains gaseous. And for gas, it is more accurate to speak of a number of gas markets, rather than a single one. For these markets, producer and consumer are – intimately, literally – bound together, since physical pipelines carry the product of one firm based in one country – and only that country – to another firm and country. In gas markets, the risk to the importing country is not simply that the price will become untenable, but that the gas might stop flowing altogether with no ready alternative suppliers or other ways of generating electricity or heat at hand. Where gas moves in pipelines, it not only crosses borders, but it almost never avoids traversing state territory. It is therefore bound up with government interests, since it is not as regularly subject to the kind of market manipulations that influence the market for oil.

One might, reasoning from first principles, expect that gas markets – in which states and firms are physically bound to one another – control power would be primary, and protean distantly secondary. Yet this intuition is precisely wrong. Rather, in precisely the markets in which one might imagine state interests to dominate and control power to obtain, protean power is far more in evidence. Protean power has organized the response to uncertainty in the form of unforeseeable technological change, unknowable geopolitical transformations, and incalculable price fluctuations.

8   Incomplete Control: The Circulation of Power in Finance

Erin Lockwood and Stephen C. Nelson[1]

Consider two views of the power of finance. From one perspective finance is in the driver's seat. The residue of the sector's control power can easily be glimpsed in the capture of the regulatory and lawmaking processes in the United States by the major players in the financial sector – an achievement made possible by finance's sheer material resources and by the revolving door that brings regulators out of the government and into the sector (and sends former employees of financial firms back into the regulatory organizations).[2] An important byproduct of finance's highly concentrated political power, in this perspective, was the construction of an incomplete and insufficient regulatory system riddled with loopholes even before the crisis of 2008 – and the production of an even more woefully inadequate regulatory system after the collapse that took the world economy into the biggest crisis in seventy years.[3]

Power in finance appears much more fleeting from an alternative vantage point, however. The players in financial markets that look, to many industry outsiders, like all-powerful "masters of the universe" are in fact constantly engaged in struggles to stay afloat in complex environments rife with ambiguities and incalculable uncertainties. For an experienced market player like George Soros, radical uncertainty is an ever-present condition of modern finance and participants can never fully uncover the "hidden generators" that move market sentiments.[4]

The players in sophisticated financial markets face both risk *and* uncertainty. The past distribution of returns in different markets can be relied upon for predictive purposes only insofar as the generating process for those returns will continue to operate into the future. Players in the markets for financial assets, subject as they are to episodic crises and innovative breakthroughs that permanently shift the means of the distributions, impose a (often illusory)

[1] For helpful comments and encouragement we wish to thank Rawi Abdelal, Jacqueline Best, Aida Mozic, Miles Kahler, Kate McNamara, Mark Nance, Dan Nexon, Len Seabrooke, the other contributors to this volume, and – in particular – Lucia Seybert and Peter Katzenstein.
[2] Johnson and Kwak 2010.   [3] Admati and Hellwig 2013.   [4] Soros 2009; Blyth 2006.

sense of stability by relying on market conventions.[5] Financial markets are, in Zuckerman's words, *open* rather than "closed system(s) whereby investors repeatedly encounter the same or highly similar problems of valuation ... Investors must repeatedly manage the uncertainty generated by events that defy categories of existing models."[6]

The pervasiveness of uncertainty and the fleeting nature of the control power possessed by players in finance are leitmotifs in many of the recent ethnographies of financial markets produced by economic anthropologists.[7] The pressure on market players to innovate radically new strategies to beat their competitors is intense. Chong and Tuckett, based on numerous interviews in 2007 and 2011 with professional money managers in the United Kingdom, the United States, France, and Singapore, contend that players in financial markets need to be convinced about the "profitability of the uncertain opportunities for future gain they hypothesize to exist." "Conviction narratives," sharing similar characteristics, become the social conventions upon which managers "depend to feel committed to their beliefs and to manage dependency on the uncertain future. They can then promote themselves as skillful and survive in the industry."[8]

In contrast to conventional views focusing on which actor has more control over the other, we contend that a richer conceptualization of power – one that goes beyond simple dyadic relationships of coercion and control – is indispensable for understanding power dynamics in contemporary globalized financial markets. Like other domains explored in this volume, the financial markets that we discuss are realms of deep, "Knightian" uncertainty. Yet the institutions and conventions that serve to stabilize expectations sometimes lead market players and regulatory authorities to experience their environments as domains of measurable risk. As Lawrence Lindsey, former member of the Federal Reserve's Board of Governors, observed about the run-up to the 2008 crisis: "we had convinced ourselves that we were in a less risky world. And how should any rational investor respond to a less risky world? They should lay on more risk."[9]

Complete control in finance, however, is illusory. Uncertainty cannot be fully eliminated and thus there is space for improvisational and innovative practices by agile actors; these practices, in turn, can generate unpredictable protean power effects.[10] In the next section, drawing on the work of Marglin and Scott, we explore how different systems of knowledge can help us to understand the conditions under which protean power-generating practices can emerge. Financial markets are realms in which there are ongoing struggles to exert control by both private and public actors (each seeking to impose greater stability and predictability on markets), but these attempts to impose

[5] Abdelal and Blyth 2015; Nelson and Katzenstein 2014.   [6] Zuckerman 1999: 1411.
[7] Ho 2009; Riles 2011.   [8] Chong and Tuckett 2015: 310.   [9] FCIC 2011: 61.
[10] Streeck 2016: 25.

control on an open system can generate unanticipated consequences, serving as an endogenous source of uncertainty within financial markets. At the same time, actors who experience markets as more radically open and uncertain than manageably risky devise innovative strategies that confound efforts to "close" systems.

For illustrations of how different configurations of power-generating practices produce unanticipated outcomes and have unpredictable consequences for actors' power potentialities, we look at the markets for over-the-counter (OTC) credit derivatives and sovereign debt contracts. These markets are, in some important ways, a study in contrasts. Credit derivatives markets are massive, largely unregulated, highly innovative, and extraordinarily complex. By comparison the international sovereign debt market – the size of which is still in the multitrillion dollar range – is significantly smaller, less complex, and – given that governments are by definition participants in the market – more politicized. And while the markets for credit derivatives and international bonds issued by sovereigns overlap to a degree (sovereign bondholders can and do offload credit risk by entering into credit default swaps (CDS) with counterparties, paying fees to the CDS dealers who then assume the risk of default on the bonds), the sovereign debt market has been distinguished by its long-standing "reputation as relatively safe, staid, and conservative."[11] Both markets, however, share a key feature: they are realms characterized by quantifiable risks *and* by irreducible uncertainty. Unlike the market for hydrocarbons (Chapter 7),[12] neither sovereign debt nor credit derivatives are material assets, making valuation far less certain and expectations more dependent on stabilizing market conventions. Our analysis of these markets thus helps to illustrate the power-generating effects of practices employed by financial market actors grappling with uncertainty – practices that can often subvert the instruments of control power and that produce surprising outcomes.

Uncertainty, Knowledge, and Incomplete Control in Financial Markets

Viewed through the analytical lens of financialization, the balance of power between the financial sector and the state resembles a seesaw that has, over the past thirty years, tipped away from the "postwar settlement"

---

[11] Dyson 2014: 340.

[12] While the problem of valuation is more acute in financial than in product markets, contracting nonetheless plays an important role in each as a means of stabilizing actors' expectations in an environment of uncertainty. Indeed, this is precisely why commodity derivatives were initially developed in agricultural markets as both farmers and grain buyers sought greater predictability in future grain prices.

arrangement in which finance, "controlled by the state and the rules of the Bretton Woods system," was relatively weak, and toward a new arrangement in which "financial institutions have become increasingly powerful and influential" – a power shift that necessarily involved a significant loss of public control. "The powers and capacities of the financial sector," Morgan observes, "have clearly varied over time according to the degree to which the state has managed to control and regulate its activities and processes."[13]

By focusing exclusively on the struggle for control and domination, the conventional perspective provides only a partial view of power dynamics in financial markets, however. Other scholars of power in finance make similar claims. Nesvetailova, for example, observes that the complexity and uncertainty of globalized financial systems calls for a process-centered understanding of power; as she notes, "it would be mistaken to present the financial industry as some cohesive or unified force that is able to control outcomes ... The industry's power [lies] less in its ability to control the agenda and more in its ability to adapt and innovate in a way that it [is] not harmed by agendas set by others."[14] Likewise, in Woll's comparative study of bank–government relations during the 2008 global financial crisis, thinking about power as a resource that financial actors hold, store, and strategically deploy misses the heart of the story; far more important are the *processes* by which finance enrolled, convinced, and enlisted "people who perform social relations defined in the interests of the financial industry."[15] The protean power framework is better placed to understand innovations that allowed financial players to evade control by outside actors arising from what Johal et al. describe as "a kind of practical bricolage which responds to changing circumstances by mobilizing whatever means are to hand and thereby adds both new capacities and unintended consequences."[16] By bringing the protean power approach to the analysis we can better account for both the specificity and unpredictability of agile actors' navigation of open and uncertain environments *and* the structural consequences that result from the efforts by both private and public authorities to alternately facilitate and crack down on agile players' power-generating practices.

Systems of Knowledge in Financial Practice and Governance

Financial market players' improvisational and innovative practices are purposive responses to environments that are often experienced as highly

[13] Morgan 2016: 211–12.   [14] Nesvetailova 2014: 547.   [15] Woll 2014: 55.
[16] Johal, Moran, and Williams 2014: 400.

uncertain; those practices, however, can change the environment itself in unpredictable ways, triggering responses by other actors that must adapt their own practices to (illusorily) re-establish control in a world they experience primarily as risky – thus contributing to new structures and systems of meaning. To better understand these issues, we turn to the work of Marglin and Scott (writing separately), for whom the existence of distinct systems of knowledge plays a central role in analyzing relations of power and resistance. These forms of knowledge, we contend, underlie the forms of power theorized by Seybert and Katzenstein (Chapters 1, 2, and 13).

Marglin invokes these forms of knowledge to explain "the odd mixture of resistance and accommodation with which workers have received technical changes that have undermined their autonomy."[17] In trying to understand why workers in advanced industrial countries were often complicit in the reorganizations of production that ultimately enhanced managers' control power, Marglin makes the case that dominant "shared cultural assumptions" elevated one form of knowledge (*episteme*) over another, putatively inferior knowledge system (*techne*), allowing management "to restructure production so as to separate conception from execution, the better to bring execution under their control."[18]

Marglin's claim about the socio-cultural underpinnings for the disempowerment of workers is less important for us than the dynamics he associates with each "knowledge system." *Episteme*-type knowledge, in Marglin's ideal-typical conceptualization, is logically deduced from first principles (it is axiomatic); it is decomposable, analytic, impersonal, incremental, and often lays claim to universality. This type of knowledge is geared to external verification, though possession of *episteme*-type knowledge is a key way in which "insiders" are distinguished from outsiders. According to Marglin, "*episteme disenfranchises* those outside. From the universalistic claim of *episteme* it is an easy and direct step to the view that those lacking in *episteme* are lacking in knowledge itself."[19] *Episteme* is suited for (and indeed often presumes) a world of calculable risks.

Techne-type knowledge, by contrast, is practical, personal, and non-decomposable. It is geared much more to unpredictable processes of creation and discovery. "Opposed to the small steps of *episteme*," Marglin argues, "are both received doctrine and the imaginative leaps which all at once enable one to fit the jigsaw puzzle together."[20] The dynamics of *techne*-type knowledge are unpredictable and difficult to control: "the underlying structure of technic innovation, like the *techne*

---

[17] Marglin 1990: 251.   [18] Ibid.: 232.   [19] Ibid.: 234, 236–37.   [20] Ibid.

it modifies, is often hidden from the innovator itself."[21] *Techne* is suited
for (and contributes to) worlds of incalculable uncertainties. Scott terms
this form of practical, adaptive knowledge *mētis*, ascribing to *mētis* the
same phronetic and non-systematic qualities Marglin identifies with
techne. *Mētis* is, in Scott's words, "the mode of reasoning most appropriate to complex material and social tasks where the uncertainties are so
daunting that we must trust our (experienced) intuition and feel our
way."[22]

While Marglin and Scott both identify *techne* with traditional, locally
embedded forms of knowledge, and position it in contrast to (though
simultaneously co-complicit with) modernizing capitalist projects, we
expand this concept to apply to highly technologically sophisticated, de-
localized financial actors. While financial markets certainly depend
on *episteme*-type forms of knowledge for their existence and development
(e.g., through standardized contracts and risk models), the irreducibly
adaptive and innovative aspects of finance strike us as consistent with this
less systematic, more intuitive system of experiential knowledge.

For Marglin, the success of workers' resistance to changes in the organization of production that reduced their autonomy was built on the *techne*-
type knowledge that could not be automated or replicated with "scientific"
management principles. The devaluation of *techne* and the elevation of
episteme in the culture of manufacturing work in the United States was a
key element in workers' greater willingness to accommodate management's promotion of labor-saving (and autonomy-sapping) changes in
production processes. But the two forms of knowledge are ultimately
intertwined; the "*techne* of coping with uncertainty" persisted "as a distinct,
complementary system of knowledge and basis for action ... *episteme*
can never be a self-sufficient system for organizing thought, much less
action."[23] The control power of management was enhanced by the systematic effort to crowd out *techne* in favor of *episteme* – but *techne*'s iner-
adicable nature meant that the protean power-generating effects of
workers' improvisatory and innovative practices were always latent. The
inseparability of the forms of knowledge privileged by wielders of control
power and effective agents of protean power is similarly well captured by
Scott's insight that "formal order, to be more explicit, is always and to some
considerable degree parasitic on informal processes, which the formal
scheme does not recognize, without which it could not exist, and which it
alone cannot create or maintain."[24]

We see evidence of a similar dynamic in the world of finance. From the
late 1970s up to the crisis of 2008 the struggle for control power in the

[21] Ibid.: 236.   [22] Scott 1998: 327.   [23] Marglin 1990: 242, 251.   [24] Scott 1998: 310.

American financial system often, but not always, tipped in favor of the industry's representatives and against the public officials in the bureaucratic regulatory institutions. There is a parallel between the struggle for control over the regulation of finance and Marglin's argument about the elevation of *episteme*-type knowledge over *techne* in industrial production. Self-regulation often meant that market players and regulators alike came to rely on mathematically sophisticated risk models to (illusorily) transform uncertainty into risk.[25] *Episteme*-type systems increasingly provided the instruments of control, as model-based risk estimates supplanted case-by-case judgments. And as in Marglin's domain of production, the effort to squeeze *techne*-type knowledge out of the discussions of finance and its regulation in favor of *episteme* laid the groundwork for greater accommodation of finance's control power by public authorities. Finance's insiders jealously guarded their superior knowledge. "Anyone who questions the mystique (of finance) and the claims that are made," Admati and Hellwig observe, "is at risk of being declared incompetent to participate in the discussion. The specialists' façade of competence and confidence is too intimidating."[26] As one financial specialist told Woll, "the people talking publicly don't know what they're talking about. The people who do know aren't talking."[27]

While the elevation of *episteme*-type knowledge by financial market actors helped to insulate the sector and, by enrolling public authorities in the project to expand finance's reach, increased financial actors' capacity to exert control power, uncertainty in financial markets was not fully transformed to manageable, insurable risks and the agile, improvisatory practices associated with *techne*-type knowledge continued to circulate within financial markets, generating surprising adaptations, innovations, and disruptions.

At the same time as effective control depends on informal processes, financial markets depend on the exercise of control power in order to even function. Processes of commensuration and categorization constitute an essential part of the bedrock upon which *all* markets (not just those for financial assets) rest.[28] But control power in sophisticated financial markets is always incomplete. The instruments of control (such as pricing and risk models) did not actually transform uncertainty into quantifiable risk, though that was the market convention and experience of many actors for some time. Much as Brigden and Andreas observe in the case of migration (Chapter 5), historical data is often an unreliable indicator of future success; like border-crossing strategies, risk management strategies

---

[25] Abdelal and Blyth 2015; Lockwood 2015; Nelson and Katzenstein 2014.
[26] Admati and Hellwig 2013: 2–3.   [27] Woll 2014: 53.   [28] Lamont 2012.

often generate a process analogous to what Donald MacKenzie terms "counterperformativity."[29] That is, a strategy for controlling the future, once used, destabilizes future outcomes. For example, derivatives contracts, once used to hedge investments and reduce risk, in fact, produce systemic risk when they trade at sufficiently high volumes.

Techne-type knowledge could never be fully eliminated from financial markets. Tacit, practical, personal knowledge remained essential in the activities of financial market players, ranging from those involved in arbitrage trading to risk modelers and managers, whose decisions continued to involve a strong subjective component based on experiential knowledge, to the legal technicians responsible for assigning collateral to derivative contracts.[30] The practices of market players grappling with deep uncertainty subverted control efforts better suited to risky environments, producing breakthrough innovations, new sources of profits, and unintended effects that exacerbated markets' fragilities. The interaction of *episteme* and *techne* as distinct systems of knowledge at work in the governance and practice of finance touches off new and unpredictable dynamics and opens up new possibilities for the exercise of power.

Illustrative Evidence from the Market for Over-the-Counter Derivatives

The recent history of OTC credit derivatives illustrates how utterly unpredictable power-generating effects can emerge when the conventional control-oriented practices that enable some actors to experience their environment as more risky than uncertain confront radically disruptive strategies from agile players, under enormous competitive pressure to innovate, who experience their environment as highly uncertain. This section of the chapter traces collateralization practices in OTC markets from the self-regulation of the 1990s and early 2000s, through the 2008 global financial crisis, to the post-crisis regulatory requirement that requires OTC derivative contracts to be cleared through central counterparties (CCPs). Although the mandated shift to central clearing was intended to restore a measure of public oversight and control to a market that was constituted by near-constant innovation, complexity, and opacity, to date the central clearing mandate has been prone to unintended consequences and has itself been a source of uncertainty for market actors.

Derivatives are financial assets, the value of which is derived from an underlying asset or source of risk, such as a bond or interest rate, and

[29] MacKenzie 2008: 19.   [30] Riles 2011.

which effectively allow asset-holders to insure or hedge against the risk of future price changes in the underlying asset. The development of financial derivatives can itself be understood as an illustration of the effects of protean power. Although commodity derivatives have existed in various forms for centuries, the development of financial derivatives can be dated back to the emergence of currency swaps, in which the underlying asset was not a tangible commodity, but rather the risk of future changes in currency values, in the early 1980s. The first of these deals was between the World Bank and IBM, with Salomon Brothers acting as an inter-mediary. This form of financial exchange was an unanticipated innova-tion, and one that disrupted not only foreign exchange markets, but also financial markets more generally as the underlying methodology quickly spread to other forms of financial risk such as interest rates and, even-tually, to credit risk. As Gillian Tett writes, "This new form of trade quickly spread across Wall Street and the City of London, mutating into wildly complex deals that seemed to give bankers godlike powers."[31] The novelty of these products allowed them to elude controls; they did not fit clearly into existing regulatory categories, which allowed banks to persuasively argue that swaps were neither futures nor securities nor loans and could not be regulated under the regulatory regimes for any of those product classes.[32]

The market for OTC derivatives was largely unregulated by public authorities prior to the 2008 crisis. The categorical ambiguity of swaps and derivatives contributed to this self-regulatory outcome, but public regulators, especially in the United States under the leadership of Alan Greenspan, also took an intentionally hands-off approach to regulating the market for these products in the first decades after they were devel-oped and became widespread. Regulatory intervention was thought likely to distort the efficient allocation of risk, and regulators argued that market actors had sufficient incentives to manage counterparty risk on their own. Alan Greenspan's 2003 address at the Conference on Bank Structure and Competition illustrates this regulatory attitude toward derivatives mar-kets: "Market participants usually have strong incentives to monitor and control the risk they assume in choosing to deal with particular counter-parties. In essence, prudential regulation is supplied by the market through counterparty evaluation and monitoring rather than by [public] authorities."[33] Although Greenspan recognized that the limited number of market participants in the OTC derivatives market risked creating concentrations of counterparty risks, "rais[ing] the specter of the failure of one dealer imposing debilitating losses on its counterparties, including

---

[31] Tett 2009: 12.   [32] Funk and Hirschman 2014: 671.   [33] Greenspan 2003: 5.

other deals, yielding a chain of defaults," he asserted that "derivatives market participants seem keenly aware of the counterparty credit risks associated with derivatives and take various measures to mitigate those risks."[34] While perhaps most dominant in the US regulatory culture, the pro-self-regulation view was also shared by the Basel Committee for Banking Supervision, the main international public actor to take up the issue of transnational market regulation. The Basel Committee's recommendations for national regulations included the "[promotion of a] better foundation for self-regulation."[35]

The lack of public regulation of derivatives did not, however, indicate an absence of control power in market governance. Prior to the crisis, the risk of counterparty default was addressed through a series of conventional practices, intended to measure and control risk, and rooted primarily in private authority structures – most notably the International Swaps and Derivatives Association (ISDA), an industry coordinating and lobbying group, as well as the credit rating agencies. ISDA supplied parties to derivatives deals with a standard contract known as the Master Agreement that could be modified to fit the specifics of individual derivative dealings. The ISDA Master Agreement outlined provisions for terminating contracts in the event of counterparty default, most notably permitting parties to "net out" all of their transactions with each other, rather than undertaking a series of payments back and forth that the defaulting party might not be able to complete.[36] Regulators lauded the provision as an example of market-based initiatives to reduce counterparty risk.[37] The Master Agreement also includes an Annex (the Credit Support Annex) that was widely used to govern collateral agreements between counterparties, intended to reduce the risk of large losses in the event of counterparty default.

In addition to the ISDA Master Agreement and its termination and netting provisions, derivatives dealers relied heavily on credit assessments from credit rating agencies to calculate counterparties' creditworthiness. Credit rating played a particularly important role in the market for credit derivatives, which are contracts that protect investors against the risk of default and depend on an estimation of securities' creditworthiness for their value.[38] Finally, derivatives market participants relied on standardized risk and valuation models to accurately price contracts, taking the risk of default into account.

---

[34] Ibid.: 4.   [35] Tsingou 2006: 177.
[36] Zepeda 2014. ISDA netting rules, however, disproportionately benefit derivatives dealer banks over other creditors in situations of insolvency. Carruthers 2015: 390–91.
[37] See, for example, Hendricks 1994.   [38] Partnoy 2006: 73–80.

The inadequacy of these private forms of counterparty risk management through control power was starkly revealed during the 2008 financial crisis, when waves of defaults by insufficiently collateralized counterparties spread through the derivatives market. The system of bilateral private contracts was recognized as overly complex and severely lacking in transparency, as contracts were unwound rapidly and without sufficient liquidity in the system to ensure full repayment. As Andrew Haldane of the Bank of England observed in early 2009, "The financial system is ... a network, with nodes defined by the financial institutions and links defined by the financial interconnections between these institutions ... When assessing nodal risk, it is not enough to know your counterparty; you need to know your counterparty's counterparty too."[39]

In response to this financial contagion and to systemic risk more broadly, the G20 and the Financial Stability Board called for a series of substantial reforms of the OTC derivative market, most notably decreeing that "All standardized OTC derivative contracts should be traded on exchanges or electronic trading platforms, where appropriate, and cleared through central counterparties by end-2012 at the latest."[40] While not all of the G20 proposed reforms have been implemented, public regulators in the United States and the European Union mandated a system of central clearing of most OTC derivatives through central counterparties – private clearing houses that would serve as immediate counterparties to all derivatives transactions. Central clearing was a key component of both the Dodd–Frank Wall Street Reform and Consumer Protection Act (Dodd–Frank) in the United States (section VII) and of the 2012 European Markets Infrastructure Regulation (EMIR) in the EU, which authorized the European Securities and Market Authority to impose clearing obligations on certain classes of OTC derivatives. These reforms were intended to make Haldane's complex networks of counterparties more transparent and to allow for centralized risk management: since each derivatives buyer and seller has the CCP as a counterparty, netting and collateralization are multilateralized and market actors' net exposures are more readily apparent. Although relatively recently implemented, the central clearing requirement has already had a significant effect. By 2016, 62 percent of all OTC contracts were conducted through CCPs, and the Bank for International Settlements estimated that the rate of clearing for interest rate derivatives had more than doubled (and perhaps even tripled) between 2008 and 2016 as a result of the clearing mandate.[41]

[39] Haldane 2009: 5.   [40] G20 2009.
[41] Bank for International Settlements 2016: 22–23.

It is tempting to read this as a straightforward story of weakly regulated markets running amok, followed by the reassertion of control power by authoritative actors. The move to central clearing is undoubtedly rooted in a post-crisis consensus not just among public actors, but also among many private market participants that the OTC market is an appropriate object of public regulation.[42]

But we contend that we can better understand the tremendous power of the financial industry before and after the crisis, as well as the instabilities and uncertainties that continue to characterize financial markets, by looking at interactions between control power and protean power effects. In our narrative of three moments of the recent history of derivatives – pre-crisis, during the crisis, and its aftermath – we observe innovation by agile market players, to which other market players respond, and which triggers responses to uncertainty generated by protean power by actors seeking to re-impose a degree of control. New forms of control, however, breed new forms of adaptation in the market, with unpredictable consequences.

In the pre-2008 period, the market for OTC derivatives was largely unregulated by public authorities, but intentionally so, as the *lack* of public control was essential to the continued profitability of the market and to ensure the efficient distribution of risk. Greenspan's claim ("the benefits of derivatives, in judgment, have far exceeded their costs") is illustrative of this attitude.[43] Derivatives were seen as important tools to enhance economic performance through the global financial system, and this economic performance was directly tied to more traditional forms of state power. It is possible to read public regulators' accommodation of finance's power as a form of financial statecraft, an attempt to, if not harness, at least capture and direct some of the unpredictable but undeniable power of unfettered global capital.

Examining the forms of knowledge operating in the pre-crisis derivatives industry reveals further points of interaction between market practices. Financial markets are often characterized in terms of *techne*, spheres of activity that are systematically structured to reward practices that make use of specific local knowledge deployed in highly uncertain contexts – the kind of knowledge on which arbitrage trading has historically depended. The constant development of bank-specific product classes, portfolio composition techniques, and trading and risk management strategies are sources of profit-making that depend on superior information, gained through experiential knowledge of the market and asset values.

---

[42] Helleiner and Pagliari 2010: 74–90.   [43] Greenspan 2003: 6.

At the same time, however, financial markets should also be understood as structured by standardized, widely diffused forms of knowledge and associated practices that are better geared to risk-based contexts. While *episteme* is often equated with state control, *all* financial markets require some level of standardization to establish the basis for price discovery and adequate liquidity, and private regulation played a key role in the development for the market for OTC credit derivatives. ISDA's Master Agreement (as detailed above) was a key innovation in creating a liquid global market for derivatives. Standardized contracts, basic pricing and risk models, and electronic trading platforms are all innovations that have imposed a measure of standardization and centralization on derivatives markets. Credit rating, which is explicitly intended to render assets and creditors comparable, is a constitutive financial market practice that is clearly in the realm of *episteme*, rather than *techne*, even as it allowed assets to be combined in new and innovative ways. It is precisely these private forms of governance that have served as permissive conditions for the protean power-generating effects of financial market innovation to flourish.

The application of *episteme*-type knowledge to financial markets, shot through with uncertainty and complexity, requires forms of knowledge more akin to *techne*. For instance, while ISDA's Master Agreement structured derivatives deals in a predictable and comparable way, the actual processes through which collateral agreements were reached were in fact sites of considerable uncertainty, stabilized through negotiations by legal technicians and conventional "legal fictions."[44] Although often represented (by market actors) and interpreted (by regulators) as a realm of technical, objective problem-solving, the techniques embodied in the Master Agreement and actually enacted by market participants are a politically consequential mode of private financial market governance.

Examining the pre-crisis market for OTC derivatives through the lens of power reveals a fractal-like pattern, where each interaction of control and protean power-generating practices touches off another dynamic in which seemingly opposing forms of knowledge and power again come together, often in unpredictable ways. Rather than enhancing real economic performance, the assiduous accommodation of the purveyors of control power to the unfettered protean power-creating practices of innovative financial market players was ultimately cited as magnifying the subprime crisis in devastating ways.[45] With this analysis in hand, we are better equipped to make sense of the ambiguous consequences of the move to central clearing.

[44] Riles 2011.   [45] Kirshner 2014.

While ostensibly a move by public regulators to reclaim a measure of control over financial markets, the central clearing requirements in the EU and the United States have struggled to do just that. Rather than centralizing a market formerly seen as overly complex and decentralized, central clearing requirements have produced regulatory fragmentation, as different jurisdictions have imposed different clearing requirements on different timelines, a development that risks a reduction of liquidity in the global market for derivatives. This market fragmentation has been accompanied by significant uncertainty on the part of derivatives end users about what central clearing means for banks' profitability.[46]

Similarly, analysts and market observers have raised questions about the ability of CCPs to effectively mitigate systemic risk. For example, ISDA's then-chair Stephen O'Connor's recent remark that the two major clearinghouses, LCH.Clearnet and CME "probably" have enough capital on hand in case of widespread default of their members.[47] Other commentators have observed that risk is becoming increasingly concentrated in CCPs, raising the possibility that these institutions will become, in effect, too big to fail. Announcements in 2015 by the European Central Bank and the Bank of England that they would backstop CCPs in crises fueled concerns that some of the same problems of moral hazard and excessive risk-taking on the part of investment banks that were cited as conditions of possibility for the financial crisis have merely been transferred to a new set of private financial actors.[48]

Finally, some commentators have observed that large volumes of trading do not even qualify for central clearing. Not all OTC derivatives have large enough trading volumes to ensure the liquidity necessary for centralized clearing and are exempted from the clearing requirements of Dodd–Frank and EMIR. Perhaps more significantly, so-called dark pools of capital continue to be unregulated at the public level.

The shift in regulatory thinking from viewing derivatives as an area in which authorities should not obstruct the protean power-generating innovations pursued by actors on the frontiers of the market to a view shared by influential regulators in the EU and United States that the market for derivatives is an appropriate object for at least some measure of state control is a significant one. Nonetheless, state actors have struggled to assert control over a sphere of social interaction that is constituted by irreducible uncertainty – and thus is a realm of breakthrough innovation by adaptable, agile actors. Having legitimized these forms of privately governed social activity in the 1990s and early 2000s, recent attempts to put the genie back in the bottle have instead touched off new practices

---

[46] ISDA 2015.   [47] Rennison 2014.   [48] See, for example, Jones 2015.

that subvert efforts at bringing the system under control and that have unpredictable effects on actors' power potentialities.

Illustrative Evidence from the Market for International Sovereign Debt

The international market for sovereign debt provides additional illustrations of the dynamics of control and protean power in finance.[49] Control power in the international sovereign debt market manifests in several ways. Certification of the creditworthiness of prospective borrowers is tightly controlled by a small number of key players. As in derivatives markets, three rating agencies (Fitch, Moody's, and S&P) dominate. In addition to the credit-raters who grade sovereign borrowers, an elite group of investment banks serve as the "underwriters" for the issuances. The few "primary dealers" in the market rake in huge fees paid by the issuing governments to arrange the deal with money managers; the market underwriters work with prospective buyers to gauge demand, organize countries' auction schedules, and bring in the lawyers from elite international firms to write the debt prospectuses. Gatekeeping by the elite, market-making primary dealers is intended "to promote liquidity, predictability, and stability in sovereign bond markets."[50] Flandreau et al. identified forty-three different banks that served as underwriters in the sovereign debt market between 1993 and 2007, but the top three primary dealers – JP Morgan, Citi, and Deutsche Bank – handled nearly 40 percent of the deals during the period.[51] Control is highly concentrated in the international sovereign debt market.

Control power is also exercised in the sovereign debt market through the classification schemas employed by market players to differentiate borrowers. The market devices that sort sovereigns into "developing/ frontier," "emerging," and "advanced" categories are powerful instruments of control.[52] The so-called "currency clauses" in sovereign debt contracts, for example, systematically differ depending on whether an issuer is considered an "advanced" country or slotted into a different category of borrower. For the advanced borrowers, the denomination of payment to bondholders is typically the same as the national currency; for issuers in the emerging and developing categories, by contrast, the currency clause in the prospectus requires repayment using one of the

---

[49] This section draws from Nelson 2016.   [50] Dyson 2014: 341.
[51] Flandreau et al. 2010: 60.
[52] A publicly traded corporation, MSCI, generates the annual country classifications that are widely used by international money managers. See at: www.msci.com/market-classification.

handful of "hard" currencies issued by the governments in the global financial centers. Sovereigns in the emerging and developing categories are also obliged to include another clause in their debt contracts: they select a foreign legal jurisdiction (almost always New York or London) under which the transaction will be registered (and which becomes the site for adjudication if the bondholders and issuer get into a dispute).[53] Dominant classification schemas in the market for sovereign debt also govern the term structure of debt issuances: historically, only the countries in the advanced club could float long-dated bonds (exceeding thirty years) on the international market.[54]

The contractual arrangement between the sovereign and private creditor, spelled out in the debt prospectus that accompanies the "coupon" purchased by the bondholder, is clearly a locus for the exercise of control power in the market. But control power, as in other financial realms, is incomplete, and contracts have in recent years become the key instrument for a massive disruption of the market engineered by aggressive, protean power-generating players in the international market for sovereign debt.

The disruptive innovators in the market are newer, more litigious specialized firms ("distressed debt funds," colloquially known as "vulture funds") that set out "to buy defaulted debt at large discounts with the aim of extracting the best possible settlement."[55] Their disruptive capacity springs from three sources: the deepening of the secondary market for sovereign bonds; the erosion of the principle of sovereign immunity; and, most importantly, the contractual terms that we (following Riles) interpret as "legal fictions" that market players employ primarily as a way to deal with Knightian uncertainty endemic in all but the simplest of financial markets.

Riles' work directs our attention to the way in which seemingly arcane, technical, and (ostensibly) apolitical contractual clauses serve as "legal fictions" that enable the transacting parties to act "as if" the ambiguity about what will happen in the (unknowable) future has been mapped out so that the deal can be completed. Legal fictions do not resolve the fundamental uncertainties that parties to a financial market transaction actually face. Rather, the contractual clauses sweep uncertainty – at least for the moment – under the rug.[56] Market participants may not believe in or even fully understand the meaning of a "placeholder" that appears in financial market contracts.[57]

---

[53] Weidemaier and Gulati 2015.   [54] Dyson 2014: 340.
[55] Panizza, Sturzenegger, and Zettelmeyer 2009: 656.   [56] Penet and Mallard 2014.
[57] Riles 2010; 2011.

The *pari passu* clause in sovereign debt contracts is a prototypical legal fiction that, were it not the wellspring for a massively disruptive innovation hatched by a "vulture" fund that many believe is "systematically harmful ... to the market for sovereign bonds," would be of little interest to anyone outside market specialists.[58] In English "*pari passu*" means "in equal step." The clause is typically a single sentence occupying several lines of text, and it appears "in most cross-border credit instruments."[59]

The *pari passu* clause can be interpreted as a means of preventing borrowers from "ranking" debts, such that in a debt rescheduling event one outstanding obligation could not be paid before the others. But the *pari passu* clause certainly has a fictional quality, since "almost no one knows what it [really] means."[60] The fictional element of the *pari passu* is that a bondholder's rights and obligations are clearly defined and enforceable. Rather than resolving uncertainty, the clause introduces other ambiguities: if the sovereign borrower's legislature passes a law preventing the government from paying "holdouts" that do not participate in a debt rescheduling but the debt was issued in a different jurisdiction (in New York, for example), which legal system applies? What happens if the sovereign borrower violates the clause? What constitutes a violation of the covenant?

The clause does not reduce the uncertainty that the bondholder faces; rather, it describes the exchange as a relationship involving rights and obligations of the contracting parties. The *pari passu* clause does nothing to clarify the probability of default or the price of the instrument, nor does it involve making predictions about what will actually happen in the future; rather, it generates the possibility of moving the discussion to the realm of law, and in doing so it empowers some actors and disempowers others. As in Reus-Smit's case of human rights revolutions (Chapter 3), the contractual clause that enabled vulture funds to innovate their disruptive strategy is chiefly characterized by *meaning indeterminacy*. The clause requires interpretation, and since meaning is fundamentally uncertain, space is opened for "contractual arbitrage" in which an

---

[58] Gulati and Scott 2016: 42.
[59] Buchheit and Pam 2004: 871. Gulati and Scott's careful studies of the history of the clause show that there are several different versions that appear in sovereign debt prospectuses over time. The "toughest" version of the clause (in the sense that it is most vulnerable to the legal interpretation that we describe in the next pages) became the most common and now appears in 74 percent of bonds issued by developing and emerging countries (Tomz and Wright 2013: 256). Gulati and Scott's extensive interviews with market players, however, indicate that there was "no bargaining between the issuer and the creditors over the type of *pari passu* (or any other clause that would be used)" (Gulati and Scott 2016: 47). Standardization of the contract is the name of the game in the sovereign debt market.
[60] Gulati and Scott 2013: 3; see also Buchheit and Pam 2004; Varottil 2011.

opportunistic player advances "an interpretation not contemplated by the parties in the *ex ante* drafting process."[61] But activating the clause's latent capacity to function as a politically potent form of private governance requires the willingness and means to pursue a highly improbable legal strategy.

The uncertain gamble that would shock the world of sovereign debt originated with a small fund specializing in distressed debt, Elliott Associates L.P. The fund's now-legendary legal arbitrageur, Jay Newman, was one of the very few in the market who actually read bond contracts.[62] He and the other partners at Elliott identified the obscure *pari passu* clause as the fulcrum in a strategy to extract payment from sovereigns that had fallen into difficulty paying their debts.

In the late 1990s, Elliott Associates sued a Peruvian bank (Banco de la Nación, the issuer) and the government of Peru (the guarantor of the debt) for repayment of bonds the fund had purchased at steep discount just before Peru wrapped up restructuring its external debt under the auspices of the Brady Bond plan spearheaded by the US Treasury. Elliott Associates won its case in a New York court and was awarded a $57 million judgment – but winning a case against a government and collecting on the judgment are two different problems, and the former is easier to solve than the latter.[63] To ensure that it would be paid, Elliott's lawyers constructed a legal argument, built on law professor Andreas Lowenfeld's interpretation of the *pari passu* clause in the Peruvian debt contracts as requiring *ratability* of payments, to prevent any other bondholder (including the vast majority of bondholders that participated in the Brady negotiations) from being paid if Elliott was not also paid in full.[64] Instead of the conventional interpretation of the clause as meaning that a borrower could not accumulate *new* debt that would be paid before the previously issued debts in a restructuring event, Elliott's lawyers argued that "a debtor not yet in bankruptcy that has accepted a *pari passu* covenant must *pay* all its equally-ranking debts equally."[65] In September 2000, a Belgian court ruled in favor of Elliott over Peru, and it ordered the Euroclear system through which the first Brady payments were to flow to European bondholders to freeze Peruvian payments. Caught between two horns – give up its case against the "vulture fund" or miss the Brady bond payment and fall into technical default – the Peruvian government chose to settle with Elliott for over $56 million.[66] Other distressed debt

---

[61] Choi, Gulati, and Scott 2016: 1–2.   [62] Gulati and Scott 2016: 55.

[63] Panizza, Sturzenegger, and Zettelmeyer 2009: 657; Varottil 2011: 227–28.

[64] Buchheit and Pam 2004: 877–78.   [65] Ibid.: 879.

[66] Panizza, Sturzenegger, and Zettelmeyer 2009: 658.

funds noted the extraordinary interpretation of the clause in the Brussels court and a number of similar lawsuits were launched.

Buchheit and Pam lay out a series of criticisms of the Belgian interpretation of the *pari passu* clause.[67] The decision strengthened the position of holdout creditors and worsened coordination problems involved in organizing debt restructuring among far-flung bondholders with different preferences. The decision also conflicted with a long-standing convention in the sovereign debt market: the debt owed to "official" creditors (the IMF, World Bank, and other international financial organizations) is, by custom, senior to privately held debt. The "ratable" interpretation of the clause threw this practice into question. Varottil distills the critical view of the decision: "The overwhelming number of arguments against the judgment in *Elliott* confirms that the court's interpretation cannot stand. The market should therefore be expected to react by clarifying the language in sovereign debt documentation to avoid similar results in the future."[68]

That is not what happened. Instead, the *pari passu* clause was retained in post-September 2000 sovereign debt contracts without any significant alterations.[69] The clause was at the center of the legal case brought by NML Capital (a subsidiary of Elliott Associates) against Argentina. The Argentine government refused to redeem NML Capital's holdings of bonds, purchased on the secondary market at bargain-basement prices, because doing so would contravene the 2005 "padlock" law that prevents the government from paying bondholders that were not party to the country's debt restructurings.[70] In 2011, a judge in New York ruled that the 2005 law was a violation of the *pari passu* clause and moved in 2012 to freeze the country's payments to its creditors, raising the specter, as Peru experienced in September 2000, of another (this time involuntary) default on its international debt. And indeed Argentina did fall into a "technical default" in July 2014 after the US Supreme Court rejected the Argentine government's challenge to the New York court's decision. Argentina was unable to make payments to any of its creditors; as a consequence, the country was locked out of the international debt market, and as the central bank's reserves dwindled the threat of a serious balance of payments crisis loomed.[71]

The major players in the international market for sovereign debt tried to write off the Belgian court's September 2000 interpretation of *pari*

---

[67] Buchheit and Pam 2004: 883–90.   [68] Varottil 2011: 229.
[69] Gulati and Scott 2013.   [70] Gulati and Scott 2013: 170–71.
[71] In March 2016, Argentina's newly elected center-right government paid $2.3 billion to Elliott (on top of the $2.35 billion it paid to other holdout creditors) – a settlement that amounted to a 369 percent return on Elliott's initial investment in Argentine bonds.

passu as an aberration. But the New York court's decision in the *NML* v. *Argentina* case threw the market into a panic. In Gulati and Scott's estimation, "the almost universal assumption of the sovereign debt community of lawyers, academics, and government officials was that the Second Circuit Court of Appeals – traditionally, the pre-eminent court in the country on business law matters – would . . . repudiate the pro rating sharing interpretation of pari passu."[72] When the court affirmed the "aberrant" interpretation of *pari passu* (and the US Supreme Court declined to hear Argentina's appeal) the potentially catastrophic consequences of the fact that Elliott's gamble had paid off began to sink in: given that every issuance in recent decades includes the clause and that a large proportion of emerging market borrowers (and, increasingly, advanced countries) would need at some point to restructure their outstanding debts, the holdout strategy could tie up the market in a welter of lawsuits. The standardized contract in sovereign debt had gone from instrument of market control by a few powerful players to an engine of uncertainty and ambiguity, upon which the newer, smaller players in the market, the distressed debt funds, thrived (while the old guard reeled). As in the case of rights revolutions (Chapter 3), a novel legal interpretation was the source of transformation, illustrating both the incompleteness of the law as a form of control power, as well as the potential for creative interpretation of ostensibly fixed and standardized rules to serve as a generator of protean power effects, with unpredictable consequences for actors' power potentialities. Formerly peripheral players in the sovereign debt market – the vulture funds – have shown that they can use legal arguments about the meaning of boilerplate clauses in debt contracts to hijack debt restructurings and extract large settlements. Sovereign states that cannot fully repay their debts, meanwhile, are likely to have a more difficult time mounting a defense against litigation brought by private creditors – though the Argentine ruling "leaves behind a confused and contested jurisprudence, which will take years to sort out." But one lesson from the episode is clear: "not suing is the one sure path for a creditor to be left out in the cold."[73]

Conclusion

We conclude by reflecting on lessons from the analysis of power in our illustrative cases for two important questions. What drives the high degree of accommodation by political and societal actors to financialization, a

---

[72] Gulati and Scott 2016: 8–9.   [73] Gelpern 2016: 73.

process that has increased the financial sector's material power while simultaneously rendered markets more unpredictable and fragile? And, second, why are financial markets prone to ruptures that surprise insiders and outsiders alike? The empirical sections of our chapter suggest two complementary answers to these questions.

In the OTC derivatives case, we argue that political and societal actors came to regard the innovation and adaptation that fuel the market for derivatives as legitimate, and indeed as socially beneficial, economic activities. The traditional holders of control power have, in effect, carved out a sphere in which *techne*-type knowledge circulates freely – and with unpredictable effects. In one sense, the story of accommodation of finance is the inverse of Marglin's account of accommodation in production: rather than devaluing *techne* in favor of (inevitably incomplete) *episteme*-type knowledge, conventionally powerful actors have recognized and authorized the power of financial actors' creativity – and inevitably, its potential for disruption and crisis. Nonetheless, the imperatives of commensurability and risk management for purposes of price discovery and profitability, even (or perhaps especially) within a highly uncertain market, brought *episteme* back into the picture, wielded first by private regulatory actors such as ISDA and, following the crisis, increasingly by public actors. When confronted with the forms of adaptive and innovative knowledge that partially constitute derivatives markets, however, these attempts at imposing control have not only been incomplete but have, in the case of central clearing, perpetuated uncertainty. The protean power of financial actors represents a likely insurmountable challenge to wielders of control power, even when financial actors' creativity is not directly aimed at subverting control.

The evidence from the sovereign debt market pushes this argument a step further. Disruptive "legal arbitrage" strategies pursued by vultures have not been legitimated or authorized by the traditional wielders of control in the market. The effect of protean power-creating practices in the sovereign debt market has generated responses, in the form of the IMF's recent efforts to get contract writers to use a narrower version of the *pari passu* clause and the UN General Assembly's endorsement of a global set of principles for debt restructurings. But attempts to impose greater control in irreducibly uncertain environments are not only necessarily incomplete, but in fact serve as conditions of possibility for improvisatory and innovative practices that have unpredictable power effects. In sovereign debt, as in OTC derivatives, a market has developed in which risk and uncertainty are central economic objects. The attempt to reckon with the uncertainty of bondholder rights in the future event of debt rescheduling by means of the *pari passu* clause can be read as an effort at asserting control over an uncertain future by means of deploying *episteme*-type knowledge. The clause was intended to move this uncertainty into the standardized, transnationally applicable world of law. However, because the underlying uncertainty linked to the interpretation of the clause was not eliminated, vulture funds were able to leverage this uncertainty to their benefit. And there are other conventional clauses of indeterminate meaning in debt contracts that vultures may use to pursue legal cases against sovereigns.[74] While the particular form of market disruption could not have been anticipated by Seybert and Katzenstein's approach (Chapters 1, 2, and 13), their framework nonetheless attunes us to the possibility that protean power-creating practices, followed by agile, innovative actors operating in contexts marked by incomplete control under uncertainty, can be *endogenous* forces that push financial markets into conditions that are experienced by all – including people with otherwise indirect connections to the markets – as destructive crises.

---

[74] Choi, Gulati, and Scott 2016.

9 Terrorism and Protean Power: How Terrorists Navigate Uncertainty

Barak Mendelsohn[1]

Terrorism is commonly understood as a coercive strategy of armed non-state actors operating under conditions of asymmetry in capabilities.[2] This perspective is grounded in the understanding of power as control; even scholars who advocate complex and more nuanced conceptions of power view terrorists' application of force as a variant of control power.[3] Yet control power tells only a part of the story when considering policy-makers' failure to foresee the emergence of al-Qaeda and the Islamic State (referred to here also as ISIS) as consequential actors on the global scene with tremendous capacities to disrupt the international order. If we only consider one dimension, control power will be a poor explanatory factor.

This chapter argues that in order to understand the interaction between terrorist groups and their state enemies we must view the world as an open system in which actors experience both risk and uncertainty. It demonstrates that protean power – defined by Seybert and Katzenstein (Chapter 1, p. 4) as the effect of improvisational and innovative responses to uncertainty that arise from actors' creativity and agility – does not appear as the result of external shocks only, but also as endogenous and central to state–terrorist dynamics. It shows that protean power could be the effect of actions taken not only by the weak (terrorists), but also by strong actors (states), and that agility and creativity are not the attributes of benign peaceful actors only, but also characterize predatory terrorist entities.

Terrorists try to harness uncertainty to advance their goals. They take advantage of the radical uncertainty of both the international system and its state components to undermine state legitimacy, and of operational

[1] I would like to thank the other participants in this project for their helpful feedback. I am also indebted to Aida Hozic, Jacqueline Best, Stefano Guzzini, Jeffrey Isaac, Miles Kahler, Stephen D. Krasner, Kathleen McNamara, Daniel Nexon, and Leonard Seabrooke for their sharp comments on earlier drafts, and to Peter Katzenstein and Lucia Seybert for their invaluable assistance (sometimes in the form of control power). Ashly Bennett provided much needed editing and Rachel Miller excellent research assistance.
[2] Hofmann 2006: 1–41; Pape 2005.   [3] Barnett and Duvall 2005.

uncertainty to expose the limits of states' control power. And yet, the agility that allows terrorist groups to effectively navigate under conditions of uncertainty does not eliminate the constraints deriving from terrorists' ultimate goal of control. As the experiences of both the Islamic State and al-Qaeda's Yemen branch indicate, the more successful terrorists become, acquiring territorial possessions and the trappings of states, the more vulnerable they become to their enemies' control power. Thus, by moving toward attaining their goals, terrorist groups lose many of the benefits that come from their manipulation of uncertainty: states' resource advantage regains importance, while terrorists' own ability to negotiate protean power weakens.

In contrast, states experience the world as predominantly risky, relying on control power to attain their objectives and fend off threats. When facing agile terrorist actors who improvise and innovate, states are slow to adjust, often failing to understand the threat in terms of uncertainty, to acknowledge the limitations of control power, and to design appropriate responses to power that circulates in unanticipated ways. Yet despite these difficulties, states are not impotent in the face of protean power. Slow as they are, states too can innovate and improvise to amplify their terrorist opponents' uncertainty, thus undercutting the operation and message of terrorist groups.

Interestingly, all actors, even those that are highly adaptable when operating under uncertainty and intentionally seek to magnify the uncertainty of their foes, yearn to reduce their own sense of uncertainty. States often do so by translating uncertainty into risk. Decision-making is complicated and leaders are more comfortable basing their policy choices on probabilities to help simplify it – even if the prevalence of uncertainty means that these probabilities are often a fiction. Terrorists have a similar need to address their own sense of uncertainty. But as disparities in material capabilities turn the odds against them, translating uncertainty into risk is not enough. Instead, terrorists wish to create a sense of certainty and promote the belief that victory is inevitable. Religion can be very effective in producing such certainty and jihadis regularly employ Islam for this purpose, but other ideologies can provide a similar psychological relief in the face of forbidding odds.[4] The need of both states and terrorist groups to reduce their own sense of uncertainty comes with a price. It can easily lead them to misinterpret the underlying context, adopt failed policies, and then to misidentify the causes behind their failures.

Even as my analysis below emphasizes states and terrorist groups, it is important to note that they are not the only relevant actors: terrorist

---

[4] Kennan 1947.

groups articulate a narrative of inevitable positive outcomes – victory or martyrdom – to assuage the fear of supporters and operatives. At times, their plans require inspiring unknown and uncontrollable individuals to take uncoordinated action that would increase states' uncertainty. Yet reliance on such lone wolves also enhances terrorist groups' own uncertainty because they do not know if and to what extent their calls will be answered, and whether such attacks will promote the groups' objectives or backfire. Similarly, states are not the only actors to engage in counter-terrorism. A vast infrastructure to combat terrorism depends on the functioning and knowledge of street-level bureaucrats in airports, local FBI offices, street corners, and elsewhere. Moreover, to confront amorphous threats, states empower a long list of societal actors – including civilians, high-tech companies, and banks – turning them into counter-terrorists. Yet when protean power resulting from societal responses manifests in deepening social cleavages, Islamophobia, and hatred of refugees, it could undercut governments' efforts.

The remainder of the chapter is organized around the two facets of uncertainty that Seybert and Katzenstein present in Chapters 1 and 2. I first discuss how terrorist groups, particularly those that seek to overthrow the Westphalian state system, respond to its radical uncertainty by innovating within cracks and contradictions of institutional complexes. The following section examines the role of religion in mitigating the psychological effects of uncertainty. Although Jihadis find religion a useful tool for replacing uncertainty with certainty, such efforts come with a price. At the same time, states' attempts to respond to the religious messages are complicated by their amorphous audience and the decentralized nature of authority in Islam. The final section analyzes the links between lone wolves, suicide bombing, social media, and operational uncertainty, emphasizing not only terrorists' efforts to increase operational uncertainty, but also the way states' responses to terrorism mirror these efforts.

Terrorism and Radical Uncertainty

Radical uncertainty concerns those unknown unknowns that inherently defy calculation. As both the state and international society – the main targets of terrorism – depend on legitimacy, the resulting meaning indeterminacy creates a space for agile terrorist groups to leverage this uncertainty: they identify cracks and contradictions within these institutions and seek to amplify them. Terrorists chip away at states' control power, challenging their legitimacy, and forcing them to search for effective responses to protean power.

In their quest for security, states are accustomed to looking at rival states – traditionally, the only threat to state survival. They build militaries to address threats emanating from other states, and design rules to manage interstate conflict. But measures designed to enhance predictability and stability in interstate relations present terrorist groups with opportunities to challenge states and erode their legitimacy. They take advantage of the tension between the anchoring of states' legitimacy in the goods it provides – primarily security – and states' inability to deploy the full extent of their control power when facing actors who seek to influence state calculations *indirectly*. They seek to force states to choose between unappealing options: appearing incompetent or controverting their own rules. From the terrorists' perspective, either choice weakens the state's legitimacy.

By using violence against innocent civilians, terrorists seek to shock their enemies, persuade them that the conventional dynamics of control power no longer apply, and intimidate them into submission. Turning all locations into a potential arena for violence, terrorists force states into a struggle in which the traditional deployment of forces to the front does not provide a viable solution: when every crowded street and shopping mall is a potential front, traditional defense becomes obsolete.

Twisting convention to their own ends, terrorists harness ideational developments such as the spread of the norm against the killing of civilians (primarily among democracies) to advance their cause. This norm, perceived as advancing human security by limiting the scope of legitimate violence, led to an unanticipated increase in the shock value of targeting innocents, inadvertently giving terrorists an effective tool to shape public opinion and pressure states into submission. Terrorist actors can engage in ever more gruesome violence, capture it on camera, and distribute it widely, multiplying the impact. Citizens' fear of terrorism and states' emphasis on this threat leads to disproportionate responses, such as the lockdown on Boston after the 2013 marathon bombing. Indeed, one of the most astonishing aspects of protean power is how the actions of terrorists, states, and ordinary people are mutually reinforcing, creating disconnects between the experience and actual threat of terrorism.[5] That states and individuals emphasize terrorism while accepting much more lethal threats – such as mass shootings, car accidents, and even accidental gun deaths at the hands of toddlers[6] – as unfortunate yet inevitable facts of life stands as a testament to terrorists' ability to stoke fear.

Since states are constrained by norms regarding the application of force, responding to terrorism in kind, by violating rules of appropriate

[5] Mueller and Stewart 2016.   [6] Ingraham 2016.

behavior, is likely to come at a stiff price. The flexing of a state's control power only weakens its impact, as observers respond to the state's over-reaction by reconsidering both the competence and legitimacy of the state. Indeed, in fighting terrorism, the state can easily lose the moral high ground. The reliance on drone strikes to target terrorists has undermined users' claims of moral superiority, because of the collateral damage and portrayals of it as extrajudicial killing that weakens the rule of law. The legitimacy of the state's fight against jihadi terrorism has been further challenged by the very limited legal protections for detainees in US-run black sites and Guantanamo Bay, the torture of suspects, and the abuse of detainees in the Abu Ghraib prison.

The limitations on a state's coercive power are particularly pronounced in Western countries that came to redefine their security obligations as encompassing the personal security of their inhabitants.[7] A state expected to protect the safety of its citizens and their property, not just of the state itself, is highly vulnerable to terrorist acts. Rising expectations regarding states' responsibilities coincide with their declining ability to protect individuals. Thus, terrorists demonstrate agility by leveraging these normative changes. Protean power exposes the state's inadequacy in providing an expansive security blanket and results in the erosion of people's trust in their government. Terrorists expect states to ultimately understand the futility of their counterterrorism efforts and comply with terrorists' demands.[8]

The impact of states' control power is further weakened when terrorist groups manage to shift the public discourse from the illegitimacy of their actions to a comparison between states' morality and terrorist practices. Such efforts are aided – unintentionally rather than by terrorist groups' design – by self-interested state leaders who exploit the illegitimacy associated with the term *terrorists* to label their opponents (including human-rights activists) as such. When accusations of terrorism are bandied about freely, they become less credible and may even normalize terrorism.

States are trying to readjust domestic and international law to revitalize their control power and open a new space for anti-terrorist action. This process is slow and difficult. In many countries, especially in the West, it involves contesting established norms regarding the relations between states and their citizenry, as well as the balance between security and personal freedoms. States' responses to terrorism raise serious questions about the nature of the social contract that delineates what states owe their

---

[7] Fingar 2011: 29.
[8] On the futility of state control efforts to stem unauthorized migration, see Brigden and Andreas (Chapter 5).

people, and the limits of legitimate state rights to reduce personal freedoms. Terrorists exploit the ambiguity and uncertainty that characterize states' scramble to find an answer to terrorism, as well as the time it takes for new norms to take hold. American overreach following 9/11 proved to be particularly useful for recruiting individuals to join the jihadi cause.[9] Although the United States and the international community have been trying to recalibrate their response to jihadi terrorism and make more measured adjustments of international law to allow for fighting terrorism while preserving personal freedoms, the damage done by the initial over-reaction – in particular, the launching of expansive, costly, and unwinnable wars based on shaky legal foundations – has not been easily undone.

And yet terrorists are hardly the masterminds that the media portrays. They tend to exaggerate both states' weakness and their own prowess (or the appeal of their cause). While demonstrating agility in turning rules of international society against its members, terrorists are confronted with the uncomfortable reality that the working of protean power is unpredictable and often results in changes that could undermine their own objectives. Indeed, rather than the high level of interstate tensions al-Qaeda expected, post-9/11 counterterrorism featured greater cooperation and even a revolutionary attempt to revamp the state-based order, including the start or acceleration of regulating spheres of activity that they had largely avoided.[10]

Despite the task's broad scope, in the financial sphere, for example, cooperation among states managed to cut down terrorist funds. Agile groups, however, still find ways to subvert the rules. Kidnapping for ransom is a particularly effective terrorist response, with Western states facing a difficult dilemma: when they pay millions of dollars for the release of their citizens, they finance the same groups they fight and subvert their own rules. But when states refuse and the terrorists gruesomely execute the hostages, often in front of cameras, these states face accusations that they have abandoned their people. Moreover, as states pursue different policies – the United States, Canada, and the United Kingdom refuse to pay ransoms, whereas most European countries pay them – terrorists increase friction between allies.

The structural advantage of states is perhaps the greatest detriment with which terrorist groups must contend. States' control power does not stem merely from their superior capabilities, but also from their primacy among the various political entities populating the international system. By defining international order as state-based and assuming the role of international society's gatekeepers, states assume exclusive rights that

[9] ODNI 2006.   [10] Mendelsohn 2009.

non-state actors lack, thus weakening the ability of the latter to attain authority on their own terms.

States' ideational hegemony extends to the question of legitimate use of force. Through law and discourse, states reserve the right to use coercive means while denying it to non-state actors, consequently crippling non-state actors' ability to confront states on an equal footing. International law narrows legitimate non-state violence to resistance against occupation. Meanwhile, states delegitimize non-state violence by largely exempting themselves from the term *terrorism* and by labeling armed non-state actors as terrorists even though many – including Jabhat Fath al-Sham (previously known as Jabhat al-Nusra) in Syria and al-Qaeda's branches in Yemen and Somalia – are primarily insurgent groups, a term with more positive connotations. Even when armed non-state actors manage to gain control over a territory and govern it (e.g., the Taliban in Afghanistan 1996–2001 and Islamic State since 2014), their viability often depends on international acceptance, which in turn requires these actors to submit to the norms guiding the Westphalian order.

The combined effect of states' material advantage and ideational hegemony over non-state violence is that even when non-state actors decide to challenge states, they usually accept the dominance of the state-based order and ultimately seek to become states and join the international society. A byproduct of these limited aspirations is self-imposed limitations on terrorist groups' violence as they balance conflicting needs: unauthorized violence advances coercion, but respect for norms – such as the prohibition on using WMDs – is necessary to gain international legitimacy.[11]

Thus, although terrorist groups aptly expose the tensions inherent to the operation of states when facing terrorists, utilizing radical uncertainty to undermine states' legitimacy, they often succumb to the structural strengths of international society and its state components; as they get closer to attaining their most common objectives – independence or capturing state power – they become increasingly vulnerable to the socializing power of international society and pressured to accommodate states' demands. Indeed, protean power has its limits; legitimate and viable membership of international society means a greater need to experience the world as one of risk, and greater susceptibility to the coercive power of other states.

Religion and the Production of Certainty

Uncertainty also has an emotive element. Actors design plans to advance their interests in a highly complex social environment, but they also look

---

[11] Mendelsohn 2005.

to satisfy psychological needs for some control over their environment. To overcome "fundamental uncertainty," and a threat to one's ontological security, actors might respond with exaggerated certainty.[12] Terrorist groups try to mitigate uncertainty's negative psychological effects. The coping mechanisms they develop to allow them to operate despite forbidding odds simultaneously amplify the anxiety of their enemies' populations. The language of religion is particularly effective for such a dual use, boosting members' and potential recruits' confidence while reinforcing an image of uncompromising zeal that terrifies their foes. Religious discourse uniquely challenges states: limited in their ability to control the message or identify those likely to succumb to it, states utilize multiple channels without ever knowing to what extent their efforts were successful. The decentralized nature of religious authority in Islam further weakens states' control efforts.

Terrorists, Religion, and Certainty

Terrorists seek to magnify their foes' radical and operational uncertainty, but the effectiveness of their actions depends on the ways in which states and individuals experience uncertainty psychologically. The same is true for the terrorists themselves; already disadvantaged in a world of risk, they experience the adverse effects of uncertainty as well. To facilitate their continued operation – attract and retain members – they must resolve the challenge. Given that the odds are against them, fictitious translation of uncertainty to risk is insufficient. Instead, they aspire to a sense of certainty. Ideological beliefs are a common means for reducing uncertainty, but religion, with its appeal to a higher all-knowing authority, is uniquely suited to overcoming the psychological effects of uncertainty[13] by replacing it with certainty.[14]

Religious beliefs address psychological needs by mitigating the fear of death.[15] They also reassure terrorists – the group and its members – that their cause is just and that eventual success is guaranteed. In this way, religion strengthens terrorists' resilience: they can accept distant time horizons and escape the demoralizing effects of defeats. Meanwhile,

[12] Mitzen and Schweller 2011.
[13] For how religion helps to reduce uncertainty for migrants, see the contribution of Brigden and Andreas (Chapter 5).
[14] Contrast the way in which actors attempt to transform inherent uncertainty to a calculable risk through legal fictions in finance, and mutual understanding by negotiating sides in energy deals that the terms of their agreements will have to be renegotiated in the future. See the contributions of Abdelal (Chapter 7) and Lockwood and Nelson (Chapter 8).
[15] Vail III et al. 2010.

they send enemies the message that because jihadis love death more than their rivals love life, resistance is futile, as the dead are quickly replaced by others who long for the afterlife. Religion is particularly important for those jihadi groups seeking to re-make the world order, by casting the division of the world into states as illegitimate in the eyes of God and, perhaps more importantly, by providing ways to reconcile the ambitious agendas of these groups with their meager capabilities.

The role of religion encapsulates the complex interaction between the worlds of risk and uncertainty. Terrorist leaders can use religion strategically to enhance their control power. They rely on religion to mobilize followers and to create a focal point guiding and controlling members' actions. Because protean power can take one only so far, both al-Qaeda and ISIS believed that they need the masses to realize their plans to fully restore the caliphate – an objective associated with control power.

Jihadi groups turn to the Quran and oral traditions to persuade their constituency that they are fulfilling a religious duty, countering the risk of one's life and the unattractiveness of joining a group weaker than its foe. Muslims are not called to fight for mundane purposes such as material gains, rather, their fight is jihad and as such a form of great worship. Because jihad is not recognized among the five pillars of Islam (Shahada, prayer, charity, fasting, and Hajj), jihadis have long sought to elevate its status to attract more volunteers.[16] Some have even portrayed jihad as a sixth pillar,[17] and ISIS has taken the additional step of claiming that there is no act of worship equal to jihad.[18]

Yet religion serves as more than a cause for mobilization. It enables jihadi terrorist groups to shape followers' experience as one of certainty, promising inevitable personal gains. The fighter is assured that there is no risk in jihad, only positive outcomes: victory or martyrdom. Jihadis try to persuade potential volunteers that fighting is desirable even if they will lose their lives. Death is presented not as a price one pays but, rather, as an event that comes with great rewards.[19] Jihad death is not the prosaic act of passing from this world but the heroic act of expressing one's devotion to God. Biological death is thus transfigured into divine martyrdom; it erases past sins and guarantees a place in paradise and the ability to intercede before God on behalf of family members. Jihadis also repeatedly remind Muslims that the afterlife is eternal, whereas life on earth is only momentary.[20]

The conviction that they are fulfilling God's wishes also helps all ranks of religious terrorist groups to confront the demoralizing condition of

---

[16] Al-Sahab 2007a.   [17] Jansen 1986.   [18] Al-Adnani 2015.   [19] Al-Sahab 2007a.
[20] Al-Sahab 2007b.

isolation. Operatives are assured that they should not worry about popular negative responses. Following divine orders is important; pleasing people who fail to follow God's way is not.[21] Members of jihadi groups who see how even fellow Muslims strongly oppose them are told that popular opinion should not bother them. Because Islamic traditions claim that one small sect from God's believers will remain loyal when all others turn from his commands, the small number of jihadis transforms from a sign of weakness to confirmation that they are the righteous ones who will emerge victorious.[22]

However, attempts to produce certainty also have downsides. As they praise the virtues of martyrdom, leaders may witness members exercising individual (and at times flawed) judgment that undermine a group's political objectives. Reflecting on the war against the Soviets in Afghanistan, Mustafa Hamid, a prominent jihadi veteran, has argued that the quest to become a *Shahid* (martyr) can come at the expense of strategic planning to achieve victory on the battlefield. In an example of how micro-level action can have macro-level consequences, he criticized the inclination of many volunteers to simply seek death rather than use their death to promote battle objectives.[23] At other times, lone wolves, self-starting cells, or simply undisciplined operatives might focus on martyrdom instead of its desired political effects. Acts of martyrdom could even harm the terrorists' cause; instances of killing innocent Muslims, such as the Amman bombing (2005), led to reduced support in the Arab world for al-Qaeda's cause and the tactic of suicide bombing.[24]

Sometimes terrorist leaders' own beliefs about the inevitability of victory cripple terrorist efforts. Because religious terrorist groups attribute the outcome of the fight to the will of God, leaders can easily explain away failure in battle. Such an attitude could boost actors' resilience by assisting them in coping with defeats. As ISIS spokesman Abu Muhammad al-Adnani clarifies, God did not promise those fighting in his name victory on all occasions. In fact, God ordained that days of victory and defeat alternate. Defeats are tests for those loyal to God. Although setbacks are inevitable, the victory of Allah's servants is predetermined.[25] However, the belief in ultimate victory is counterproductive when it leads jihadis to move ahead with their plans without presenting a fully developed causal theory of war outcomes or seriously considering the implications of material power imbalances. Additionally, a sense of certainty is likely to undermine actors' interest in learning from mistakes. Thus, jihadi

---

[21] Al-Adnani 2015.   [22] For example, see Islamic State 2015b: 52–54.
[23] For example, see Brown 2007: 57.   [24] Gerges 2005; Wike 2015.
[25] Al-Adnani 2015.

terrorists are particularly prone to enter confrontations without a solid strategic foundation. In such cases, states are likely to be surprised by the initiation of terror campaigns but also able to successfully thwart the terrorists' goals.

Responding to Religious Certainty

Religion is not a given, it is interpreted, and as such open to discursive contestation, the realm of radical uncertainty, and protean power. Terrorists seek to legitimize their religious interpretation while confronting other claimants for religious authority, some of which hold considerable material, institutional, and ideational resources in another meeting of control and protean power.

Confronting terrorist actors holding strong religious convictions is challenging and often requires confronting their religious message head-on. Such efforts are particularly difficult because states appeals are directed at a faceless audience rather than specifically targeted individuals; Muslim states may dissuade most people from joining jihadi groups, but even a small minority could have a tremendous impact, and states are usually unable to identify those pockets of resistance early enough. Additionally, the decentralized nature of Islamic authority empowers radicals and defies states' control efforts.

Secular countries are unlikely to persuade religious terrorists that their group misrepresents their religion. However, countries in which religion plays a central role, while more vulnerable to the allure of religious terrorism, are also better positioned to confront it because their delegitimation of terrorists' religious narrative is perceived as more authentic. Importantly, these states can use religious institutions under their control to condemn the terrorists and declare that they have the "correct" understanding, whereas the terrorists distort the religion. For example, to reduce the danger of recruitment by firebrand preachers, Muslim states have tightened their supervision of mosque imams, requiring preachers to undergo special training focused on moderate versions of Islam, dictating sermon content, and spying on preachers to assure their compliance.[26]

But these attempts at control have their limits, sometimes simply pushing jihadis' recruitment underground. Ultimately, states' measures involve a high level of uncertainty as they compete with the jihadis over a largely faceless audience sitting in front of their computer screens. The jihadis seek to mobilize this audience to action, whereas states wish to keep them loyal to state authorities and the official versions of Islam they

[26] *The Economist* 2014: 52.

promote. States have no way to truly assess the effectiveness of their efforts; after all, success is manifested in keeping people away from radical groups – that is, in a non-event.

De-radicalization programs to change the position of jihadi terrorists are somewhat easier to evaluate. In these programs – established in Saudi Arabia, Malaysia, Yemen, and elsewhere – jailed terrorists deemed to be reformable engage in direct dialogue with Islamic scholars who "correct" the prisoners' understandings of Islam. The state also presents important inducements to reformed radicals, including early release (often under the supervision of the terrorist's family, in an attempt to increase his commitment to the deal with the state), financial support, vocational training, and even assistance in finding wives.[27] In such programs, states rely on risk assessment before they graduate participants and release them, but even low rates of recidivism could result in devastating terrorist attacks that, in turn, undermine public support and, as in the Yemeni case, cripple the whole program.

Recantations by former jihadis are another tool to undercut jihadism's appeal. Over the past two decades, imprisoned jihadi leaders from the Egyptian Gama'a Islamiya, the Libyan Islamic Fighting Group, and the Southeast Asian Jema'a Islamiya have published numerous books articulating their revised position regarding the Islamic legality of their past terrorist activities. In addition to explaining why it is wrong to assassinate Muslim rulers, target foreign tourists, and kill ordinary people, they criticized al-Qaeda and other groups.[28] Al-Qaeda tried to dismiss these works as coerced and part of deals to mitigate prisoners' suffering, rather than as sincere reflections. Nevertheless, at times it was so troubled by these works that its leaders intensely sought to refute them.[29]

States' efforts to contest the extremist messages of groups such as ISIS were often ineffective. A video titled "Welcome to ISIS Land," produced by the US State Department's Center for Strategic Counterterrorism Communications, sought to counter the caliphate's self-portrayal as a haven for devout Muslims by showing its brutality and challenging the worthiness of its cause. Although it had close to a million views on YouTube, scholars and practitioners doubted its usefulness and even warned that it could actually appeal to ISIS supporters.[30]

The lack of clear religious hierarchy in Islam (in contrast to, for instance, Catholicism) further complicates countering the jihadi message.

---

[27] On the Saudi program, see Rabasa et al. 2010: 56–77.
[28] For an example of criticism of al-Qaeda, see Al-Gama'a al-Islamiya 2004.
[29] Al-Zawahiri 2008.   [30] Miller and Higham 2015.

States experience heightened uncertainty, struggling to identify both a persuasive anti-jihadi message, and Islamic scholars who would be viewed as its legitimate and reliable conveyers. Islamic universities such as Egypt's al-Azhar and positions such as the Saudi Grand Mufti accrued considerable influence over the years, but they do not have ultimate authority and their ability to reach young Muslims is limited. Jihadis enhance this uncertainty with concerted efforts to challenge the authority of the state-sponsored *ulama'* (Islamic scholars), and labeling them as collaborators of un-Islamic apostate rulers.

The accelerated erosion and fragmentation of Islamic authority following the revolution in communications technology and the rise of social media is adding further complexity. No one actor could control information and completely suppress undesirable views. Moreover, new claimants of religious authority utilize widely available platforms and reach vast audiences far beyond the areas where they live. The result has been a remarkable opening of the market for interpreting Islam. The new platforms seem to particularly favor virulent and extreme voices that can offer their followers easy-to-understand messages (preferably in 140 characters). A new class of jihadi scholars, many with little religious training but with charisma and great oratory skills, is overshadowing not only mainstream scholars but also jihadi old-guard scholars. Agile actors such as the Islamic State exploit the new landscape, while old-school scholars struggle to capture the imagination of a young, frustrated generation of Muslims. In this context even prominent jihadi scholars such as the Jordanian Abu Muhammad al-Maqdisi and Abu Qatada al-Filistini, who try to dissuade young Muslims from adopting the ultra-radical ISIS version of Islam, struggle to assert their authority.[31]

Improvisation, Agility, and Operational Uncertainty

Whereas terrorists' strategic logic involves the exploitation of radical uncertainty, in their tactics they harness operational uncertainty – the de facto unknown unknowns. Agile terrorist groups improvise, developing tactics such as suicide bombing and lone-wolf attacks that rely on the inevitable limitations of states' control. They also subvert and repurpose originally benign tools such as Facebook and Twitter for predatory purposes, recruiting members, promoting violence, and spreading fear.

[31] Al-Maqdisi 2014; Abu Qatada al-Filistini 2013.

Terrorism, Tactical Improvisation, and Social Media

Suicide bombing and lone-wolf attacks are two principal examples of how terrorists respond to and publicly expose the futility of states' control efforts. Both tactics are extremely hard to defend against due to inherent operational uncertainty: states may be on high alert for terrorist threats, but they are unable to disarm bombers wearing suicide vests or to identify individuals without direct organizational links before they go on a killing spree. Furthermore, by directing operatives to attack "soft targets," terrorists force states to defend an incalculable number of targets. When states inevitably fail – no matter how successful they were previously – terrorists reveal their inability to provide citizens absolute security.

Suicide bombing turns perpetrators into "smart bombs" able to insert themselves in the middle of civilians and produce a high number of fatalities. Because almost any individual can become a suicide bomber with little training, and because suicide bombers view their actions as altruistic self-sacrifice and are knowingly and happily going to their deaths, identifying bombers in time and thwarting such attacks is extremely difficult. Indeed, suicide bombing has proven to be an effective fighting tool, causing more deaths than unmanned bombs[32] and terrorizing foreign occupiers into compliance.[33] The use of suicide bombers strengthens terrorists' claims that their foes are fighting an unwinnable war; bombers' quest for martyrdom prevents states from maintaining security.

Lone-wolf attacks are another manifestation of protean power, based on the belief that the aggregation of uncoordinated autonomous acts can produce strategic effects. Such attacks are a form of swarming: the group does not need to plan all terrorist attacks or even know the perpetrators. Instead, it encourages individuals to attack on their own.

Al-Qaeda has long called for lone-wolf operations but has been largely unsuccessful. Its interest in "leaderless jihad" stemmed from post-9/11 operational constraints, drawing on the ubiquity of the Internet and the innovative thinking of Abu Musab al-Suri and his book *The Call for a Global Islamic Resistance.*[34] Military action and crackdowns led al-Qaeda to envision completely disconnected, invisible, infinite task forces, each responsible for the part of the mission for which it is best equipped. The realization of this vision required training, but since bombing drove al-Qaeda from its Afghanistan safe haven and training camps, the organization sought to reconstitute them in cyberspace. Using the Internet, it disseminates training manuals and instructs followers on how to carry

[32] For example, see Institute for Economics and Peace 2015: 32–35.   [33] Pape 2005.
[34] Lia 2007.

out attacks. The Saudi branch of al-Qaeda even designated a journal, *Mu'askar al-Battar*, as a virtual training camp. In another example, its Yemeni branch's *Inspire* magazine included instructional articles such as "How to make a bomb in the kitchen of your mom."[35]

Nevertheless, centralized dissemination of information is susceptible to disruption. The next logical step, therefore, was to decentralize knowledge-sharing. Al-Qaeda calls on individuals to use the vast information available online to identify material and instructions that will facilitate assembling explosives, producing toxins, forging documents, building jamming devices, and other activities that utilize rudimentary dual-use, widely available material (such as car parts, gardening equipment, plumbing tools, building material and other hardware). Once information and material are gathered, volunteers are asked to record an instructional video, presentation, or document and upload it online to provide others throughout the world (particularly non-specialists) with access to basic how-to knowledge, and, through comparison, to "best practices." Sympathizers are also urged to share information about enemy weaknesses and how to exploit them. Indeed, participants on jihadi forums often raise ideas for attacks based on perceived Western weak spots.[36]

Despite its calls for lone-wolf attacks, al-Qaeda appears more comfortable encouraging its supporters to assist in propagating the jihadi message. It empowers sympathizers by assuring them that with even limited technological knowledge they can "change history right there from your home town, under the cool air of your air-conditioner, safe and sound away from any danger or fear."[37] The media warriors would collect statistics about "America's filth" to remind Americans "how evil and disgusting they are and why the mujahideen will do anything to kick them out from the Muslim lands." They would also prepare statistics on the "crimes" the United States had committed throughout its history, and American servitude to the banks and the lobbyists (particularly the Israeli lobby). Muslims too should be targets for independent propaganda efforts, encouraged through simple messages to help their brethren and join jihad. These media efforts should be customized to the language and norms in each target country and spread through all media platforms available, including Facebook, Twitter, and blogs.[38]

Al-Qaeda's ambivalence regarding lone wolves might be the result of its bitter experience with rogue agents. The indiscriminate violence of Abu Musab al-Zarqawi, the leader of al-Qaeda's Iraqi branch until his death in 2006 and the forefather of ISIS, harmed al-Qaeda's brand and taught the

---

[35] Al-Qaeda in the Arabian Peninsula 2010: 33–40.   [36] Al-Somali n.d.   [37] Ibid.: 3.
[38] Ibid.: 14–15.

group's central leadership a valuable lesson about the hazards of uncontrollable agents: an effective decentralized campaign of terrorism requires its leaders to first articulate clear guidelines to insure that its followers' attacks are in line with the group's strategic plan, and that their actions will not end up backfiring. Indeed, in 2013, Ayman al-Zawahiri introduced a document titled "General guidelines for jihad," although these guidelines hardly guarantee that agents will acknowledge the boundaries of "useful" violence.[39]

In comparison, ISIS is less apprehensive of agents' overreach, because it has few qualms about the use of indiscriminate violence. Moreover, whereas al-Qaeda promotes selective targeting, the Islamic State embraces and encourages extreme and indiscriminate brutality against the West, Shia, and even other Sunni jihadi groups. If inflicting pain is the only thing that matters, control is unnecessary as any lone-wolf attack could be a valuable contribution. The group does not worry about the psychological reasons that drove some of those who answered its call, or how well they fit its ideal model of Islamic behavior. The only thing ISIS asks from lone wolves is that they leave behind a message (such as a Facebook status update or YouTube video) paying homage to the group and its self-styled caliph Abu Bakr al-Baghdadi.

The Islamic State seeks to produce a self-sustaining dynamic in which one lone-wolf attack inspires other individuals to carry out their own operations, thus making the fight less dependent on the activities of ISIS itself. Although it has inspired such attacks throughout the globe (including the United States, Germany, France, Australia, and Canada) they are still relatively uncommon and have failed to generate the momentum that would turn them from isolated events into a strategic threat. ISIS has been more successful in using lone-wolf attacks to amplify societal cleavages. ISIS wants to erase the "gray zone" and create a clear division between friends (Muslims) and enemies (non-Muslims).[40] By persuading Muslims to abandon their national identity for its version of Islamic identity and to attack the society in which they live, ISIS is feeding doubts regarding the loyalty of Muslims to their states of residence and respective societies. And yet growing suspicion and even outright hostility toward Muslims, over which states have only limited influence, has yet to produce clear radicalization among Muslims, which would then lead to further terrorist attacks.

Terrorists' agility is also apparent in their use of social media. They embrace platforms such as YouTube, Facebook, and Twitter while repurposing them for malignant use. Such platforms enable the bypassing

[39] Al-Zawahiri 2013.   [40] Islamic State 2015a.

of traditional media channels with their restrictions on the presentation of graphic violence, limits on time allocated to each news item, and other editorial considerations. They can disseminate information and propaganda independently. Al-Shabab's attack on the Kenyan Westgate shopping mall was even live-tweeted by the perpetrators, adding to the drama and terror.[41]

ISIS is particularly adept at utilizing social media. It produces numerous videos and magazines in several languages, and distributes them independently online, sometimes reaching an audience far greater than it would have had it relied on TV stations. The organization also uses manipulation to increase the visibility of its message. For example, it uses twitter bots to amplify the effectiveness of tweets, so that a tweet is retweeted automatically and at specifically tailored intervals in order to make it trend. The message then reaches a broader audience and strengthens the sense of ISIS's omnipresence.[42] Co-opting hashtags (e.g., the hashtags for the World Cup games #Brazil2014 and #WC2014) extends ISIS's reach.[43] ISIS also uses social media in a more targeted way, trying to reach out to individuals and, through online interaction, recruit them to come to its "caliphate" or to carry out terrorist attacks in their country of residence.[44]

Agility and Improvisation in Counterterrorism

States have invested vast resources in counterterrorism in recent years, with technological developments boosting their control power. Drones, for example, have become a prominent counterterrorism tool for both surveillance and targeted killing. Technological innovations also enhance states' ability to guard their borders.[45] Radical content online is closely monitored, and, notwithstanding legal limitations, electronic surveillance is rampant. The United States compelled (or went around) tech companies to make their data available for government investigations, seeking "back doors" into their programs and forcefully discouraging them from offering the public encryption programs that protect from state surveillance.[46] It was only after the Snowden leak revealed the extent of American online spying that the government began facing pressure to constrain its online surveillance.

States are gleaning information about radicalized youth who are looking to join terrorist groups by combing through Facebook statuses. They

---

[41] Higham and Nakashima 2015.   [42] Stern and Berger 2015.   [43] Ibid.: 147.
[44] For example, see Callimachi 2015.   [45] Mendelsohn 2009: 161–84.
[46] Barrett et al. 2014; Nakashima and Gellman 2015.

also collect intelligence about individuals who have reached jihad arenas and the arenas themselves by examining Facebook pages, Instagram pictures, and YouTube videos. Technological advancements allow the bringing together of huge amounts of information, while computing helps to make sense of the collected intelligence. Network analysis, for example, enables states to identify clusters of terrorist supporters and routes to join jihadis in conflict zones.

States also embrace protean power. Creatively, they improvise and innovate in an attempt to generate favorable effects. However, hierarchical structures and bureaucratic rigidness sometimes undermine their ability to steal from the playbook of their agile non-state enemies. Countering terrorists' narratives, for example, is an objective that practitioners endorse yet struggle to implement for many reasons, including the danger that engaging terrorist claims would lend legitimacy to terrorist groups, and the need to quickly cut through bureaucratic hurdles to provide immediate responses to jihadis' messages.[47]

States achieve greater success in their attempts to magnify and exploit the uncertainty that terrorists face. Intelligence agencies have become adept at turning Internet forums into a source of information about the identities of jihadis, their ideology, and even internal debates. In lightly moderated forums, intelligence agents, using assumed identities, were able to confront radical messages. In more restricted password-protected forums, states utilized their superior technological capabilities to become privy to members' discussions, expose their locations and identities, and even attempt to sow discord among forum participants. Because such engagements happen in cyberspace, penetrating jihadi circles has become both easier and safer for state agents. States also tried to erode users' confidence and inflame relations between participants of different forums by temporarily shutting down some forums and not others and by spreading rumors of penetration.[48] These successes reached their limit as terrorist groups largely abandoned the forums and shifted to social media and to direct communication through encrypted messaging platforms (primarily, Telegram).

However, the expansion of the Islamic State's manpower presented states with the opportunity to plant spies in its ranks. The fear of spies, magnified as the group started suffering defeats, is fomenting internal divisions and even leading to purges. As a result, foreign fighters that are loyal to ISIS nevertheless end up defecting to save themselves from their suspicious and ruthless fellow ISIS members.[49]

How protean power circulates across different levels of analysis can be seen in the creation of new private actors dedicated to combatting

---

[47] Miller and Higham 2015.   [48] *The Economist* 2007.   [49] Sengupta 2016.

terrorism. Many such actors operate out in the open and in the bounds of the law. Others, however, work in the shadows and their actions sometimes violate state laws. Although such empowered actors could undermine some states' counterterrorism efforts, they can take actions that states avoid due to political and legal considerations. Shortly after 9/11, an operator of gambling and sex websites took advantage of al-Qaeda's failure to re-register the domain name of its website al-nida.com to snatch it and replace its content with a picture of an American flag. This move was consequential: al-Qaeda responded by piggybacking unsuspicious websites and putting its content in their back pages, before later moving on to relying on chat rooms as the next generation of online jihad.

The London-based International Centre for the Study of Radicalisation and Political Violence has been at the forefront of private efforts to identify European foreign fighters. In another case, the hacktivist group Anonymous declared war on ISIS and launched a campaign to identify and report (to intelligence agencies' chagrin) ISIS-linked Twitter accounts.[50] Hacktivists also take a more direct approach, identifying websites, blogs, videos, and social media accounts and disrupting them through denial-of-service attacks.[51] Naturally, the most important private actors to impact counterterrorism online are the social media companies, primarily Twitter, Facebook, and Google (which owns YouTube). Driven primarily by financial considerations, they interact with governments and provide information to intelligence agencies. Moreover, they design policies regarding prohibited content and take down the accounts of suspected terrorists and terrorist groups, as well as their material.

A comprehensive and persistent campaign by Twitter to take down radical accounts has significantly limited the reach of ISIS propaganda.[52] In response, many ISIS sympathizers transitioned to Telegram, which has weaker terms of use and stronger encryption. Although Telegram provides jihadis a safe haven in cyberspace, ISIS leaders are calling on followers to return to Twitter.[53] The suspension of accounts makes retaining followers an onerous task, but giving up on that platform means abandoning the efforts to mobilize new crowds. As long as most of the individuals whom ISIS wishes to mobilize stick to Facebook and Twitter – a trend over which jihadis have very little control – the group must stay there.

The recent wave of Palestinian terror attacks and Israeli reactions to it exemplifies the unpredictable and often negative effects of this new class of counterterrorist actors. In response to knife attacks by young lone-wolf Palestinian terrorists, most acting on their own initiative, Israeli leaders called on their people to assist in neutralizing attackers. Civilians'

---

[50] Griffin 2015.   [51] Cottee 2015.   [52] Berger and Morgan 2015.   [53] Bunzel 2016.

responsiveness created an awkward situation in which the state is outsourcing the provision of security to individuals it does not know before they take action. Moreover, empowered and often undertrained Israelis, fearful of any Palestinian-looking individual, ended up killing instead of subduing attackers and, consequently, further inflaming the atmosphere. Discrimination and sometimes outright violence directed at Israeli-Arabs amplified tensions within Israeli society. Additionally, cases of mis-identification led to the lynching and shooting of innocent Israeli residents. It is a cautionary tale for the way enhancing state capabilities through broad mobilization of the public could backfire; terrorists can be stopped faster, but the strengthening of a state's capabilities could enhance uncertainty and produce unanticipated dynamics that might result in increased motivation to commit terrorism as well as the amplification of societal and racial cleavages.

Conclusion

Terrorism could be understood as a creative resistance to the control power of the state. On the face of it, terrorists are better equipped to exploit uncertainty than their state opponents. State legitimacy strongly depends on its ability to demonstrate control, predictability, and accountability. No wonder it prefers to view the world through the lens of risk. But such inclination is a source of weakness given the prevalence of uncertainty. States might try to address this uncertainty by planning for the worst-case scenario and throwing resources at the problem, implicitly translating uncertainty into risk. As it is impossible to show that a particular means used was successful or not, such a damaging dynamic could continue for a long time, costing the state considerable resources without necessarily making it safer. Ultimately, states repeatedly fall into the trap of terrorists who expose control power's limitations.

Notwithstanding the greater agility of terrorist groups, they are confronted with the fact that protean power is very hard to control. As a result, protean power can become a double-edged sword, manifesting in unanticipated and undesirable effects (in the eyes of those harnessing uncertainty). Furthermore, terrorists' agility does not guarantee success. Terrorist groups can survive online by jumping between different social media platforms, thus defying control attempts. But Telegram allows them to only communicate with each other or post their propaganda; it does not offer channels to the much broader Muslim audience whom ISIS must mobilize if it is to attain its objectives. As long as most young Muslims stick to platforms that do not tolerate ISIS, it must fight to stay on Facebook and Twitter.

Even more problematic from the terrorists' perspective is the fact that most of them seek control power and thus must still grapple with their weaker material capabilities. It appears that protean power is more meaningful as an effect of subversion, designed to undermine local and international order. But when terrorist groups seek to establish their preferred order, it is the logic of control power that dominates. In fact, the greater the trappings of a state that terrorist groups attain, the less relevant their ability to negotiate protean power and the more vulnerable they become to their enemies' control power. This could explain how terrorists can wreak havoc yet still often fail to achieve their political objectives.

The turmoil in the Middle East is a testament to states' struggles to handle flaws and internal contradictions at the heart of the international system. The Arab revolutions involved great uncertainty from the start as individuals took to the streets long before they could enjoy the safety of numbers. But this was only the beginning of the story as the toppling of regimes further enhanced an already pervasive uncertainty. The regional system is in flux as control power diminishes and greater space for protean power opens. Regimes throughout the region have been unable to re-establish control power, but are also ill-equipped to harness uncertainty. Whether due to the sovereignty norms, fears of entanglement, or the complexity of recreating functioning states that could provide their people security and other services, members of international society appear unable to find a solution to the chaotic aftermath of the revolutions. In contrast, jihadi groups, who thrive in this chaos and benefit from exacerbating it, have been quick to capitalize on the uncertainty and fill political and security vacuums. But the loss of territories that ISIS and al-Qaeda had controlled in Iraq, Syria, Yemen, and Libya show that as long as terrorist groups keep looking to achieve control at the expense of others, they will find that, like their state enemies, they also are vulnerable to both control and protean power.

10 Slumdog versus Superman: Uncertainty, Innovation, and the Circulation of Power in the Global Film Industry

Lucia A. Seybert, Stephen C. Nelson, and Peter J. Katzenstein[1]

You know Hollywood, you are likely familiar with India's Bollywood, and you may have heard of Nigeria's Nollywood. There is also Chollywood in China, Wellywood in New Zealand, Lollywood in both Pakistan and Liberia, and several more in Africa. Such labeling of regional film industries reveals more than an attempt at a catchy gimmick. The reference to Hollywood in all these cases is clear, but so is the alternative desire to produce films that the Los Angeles-based studios are unable or unlikely to offer. Similar reinvention efforts have rebalancing consequences for the film industry, often beyond what their initiators intended. Each of the many "woods" caters to diverse tastes, some more and some less specific than those of Hollywood's traditional target viewers. Most importantly, non-Hollywood film production undermines the pretense of control over cultural templates and meanings that move global audiences and even pushes traditionally powerful actors to abandon the assumptions of calculability. The underdogs of the movie world introduce a decisive degree of fluidity to cultural, economic, and political competition. They thrive on the uncertainty that incumbent Hollywood seeks to reign in, although they are not themselves immune to unexpected challenges at the next creative turn.

The quintessential underdog story that both emerged from and symbolized such ongoing power shifts was the Oscar triumph of *Slumdog Millionaire* (2008). Audiences around the world found themselves cheering

[1] We are indebted greatly to Aida Hozic and Stefano Guzzini who over several years helped us enormously in clarifying our thinking about movies and power. Without their help this chapter would not have seen the light of day. For their engaged readings and critical comments on successive drafts we also thank Michael Barnett, Susan Christopherson, Matthew Evangelista, Harvey Feigenbaum, Peter Gourevitch, Jeffrey Isaac, Jonathan Kirshner, Daniel Nexon, Nissim Otmazgin, Toby Miller, Galia Press-Barnathan, John Sayles, Len Seabrooke, Etel Solingen, David Spiro, and all of our fellow authors in this project. Kirat Singh was an outstanding research assistant for Peter Katzenstein. Lucia Seybert relied on excellent research assistance from Robert Vainshtein.

for protagonists in the Mumbai story of unlikely success. *Slumdog Millionaire*, directed by a British director, based on a book by an Indian author, tapping international production talent, and featuring local actors also reveals boundary-blurring trends in moviemaking that provide opportunities for capitalizing on high levels of uncertainty. Power need not come from a single center and flow in one direction only. In fact, we should differentiate between an order that is made and one which forms itself as a result of apparent regularities and their reconfiguration.[2] *Slumdog Millionaire* illustrates the role of geographically and culturally dispersed activity in enhancing innovation, adaptation, networking of international talent and, ultimately, power.[3]

What our account employing the concept of protean power captures is that seemingly stable systems can be reconfigured quickly through decentralized innovative moves.[4] Such changes turn the tables and send challenged leaders scrambling to restore their primacy. Their search for full control, however, may be illusory. Outcomes in such struggles are unpredictable. Analytical quandaries of how to explain and interpret shifting constellations of international power emerge with great regularity. The theoretical framing of this book calls for an additional vantage point for examining power dynamics. Other contributions to this volume aptly illustrate that all too often power does not inhere in the measurable attributes of the actors wielding it. Rather, it rests in the dynamic interactions between the controlling and the controlled.

Without wishing to diminish in any way the importance of control power, we highlight the explanatory significance of protean power. It is diffuse in its effects and lacks an identifiable core as it operates from multiple, often uncoordinated sites. Ultimately, this power can enhance political conformity and social stability while also engendering political innovation and social change. Protean power links actors and networks with distinctive discursive structures. It comes into effect through creative individual or collective actions that tap into the distinctive capacities of and relationships among dispersed actors that do not necessarily mirror the apparent distribution of control power or the propensity to use it.

We explore the dynamics of protean power in a heuristic case study, the American[5] film industry. At the nexus of commerce and culture,[6] its

[2] Hayek 1973: 27.   [3] Gerybadze and Reger 1999; Hayek 1945; Ostrom 2010a.
[4] Ostrom 2010b: 552; Ostrom 1961.
[5] Our discussion necessitates one note on conceptual clarity. In this chapter's terminology the "United States" references the state and often stresses the central role of the executive branch of government. "America" refers to social actors and their variegated practices. Located in the "United States" and bearing unmistakable traits of "America," Hollywood is not an actor but a site that permits us to observe power processes.
[6] Kindem 2000b: 1; Nowell-Smith 1998: 1–2.

political and cultural significance make it an important subject for social science analysis.[7] Are a small number of capitalist and cultural entrepreneurs located at the center of the American movie and media industry controlling the world with films infused by American ideas, norms, and values? Or are foreign governments, producers, directors, and audiences developing effective strategies to circumvent, adapt to, and innovate around American control? The first question is indebted to theories of cultural imperialism with a long pedigree in Marxist theory; the second to contemporary discussions of cultural and economic power. Yet, rather than operating like ships passing at night, control and protean power typically are interacting and co-evolve. Control power of American producers and directors aims at foreseeable consequences that is often undermined by creativity and innovation, characteristic hallmarks of protean power coursing through global viewing publics and non-American film producers.

Although the American film industry enjoys a position of unrivalled primacy in global markets, this does not diminish the radical uncertainty it faces when releasing its movies. This uncertainty stems from unattainable knowledge about the changing circumstances that encompass much more than just audience tastes. In a global marketplace the need for rapid adaptation to such change is greatly facilitated by decentralization.[8] Innovation and improvisation are bypassing rather than controlling uncertainty. At the same time, the fluidity of relations between actor experiences and the context in which they operate alters the nature of the underlying uncertainty further, making it important to examine the link between culture, markets and power.

Deploying Control Power By and Against Hollywood

To talk about power and culture is a subject fraught with difficulties. Josef Goebbels reportedly reached for his gun when he heard the word culture. The philosopher Slavoj Žižek reaches instead for culture when he hears the word gun.[9] Political philosopher Kwame Anthony Appiah uses less martial imagery but also conveys the challenge of working with the

[7] Chase 2008; Christopherson 2011; Christopherson and Storper 1989; Flibbert 2007; Hozic 2001; Kirshner 2012; Leaver 2010; Scott 2005; Wasko 2003.
[8] Hayek 1945: 524.
[9] Žižek 1999: 4. Popular culture and the arts more generally have elicited an aesthetic turn in international relations theory that is indebted to post-modernism and that differs from the argument developed in this chapter. The aesthetic turn focuses on cinema, literature, visual art, music, and other forms that encompass high art and extend into popular culture. Sensibility, imagination, and emotion are all part of aesthetic approaches, complementing cognition, knowledge, and reason. The aesthetic turn insists on the unavoidable necessity of interpretation that links the values of the perceiver to the phenomena she

concept: "It's reached the point," he writes, "that when you hear the word 'culture,' you reach for your dictionary."[10]

Compulsion, institutions, and structures are three different faces of control power. Compulsion occurs in relations of direct interaction of control by one actor over another. Institutional power is found in the control that actors exercise indirectly over others, including through controlling the process of agenda-setting in various institutions.[11] Structural power affects directly both the context and the conduct of actors.[12] It often entails its opposite, structural uncertainty, which frequently makes it difficult to translate successfully policy intentions into action with predictable consequences. Structural power in no way guarantees success. Hollywood's all-too-many failed or middling movies show this clearly.[13] This section focuses on historical episodes of control power deployment by the American film industry, with particular attention to why such strategies would have seemed viable and the reasons why they ultimately proved to be inadequate.

In the 1920s and 1930s, Hollywood gained the upper hand over its competitors by standardizing film production through the adoption of more capital-intensive technologies aiming at greater economies of scale. Brand loyalties flourished together with the star system and the ever-widening appeal of the nascent Hollywood studio complex's products.[14] Regional concentration and later subcontracting in and around Los Angeles were efficient "for an industry where standardization is important to keep costs down, but innovation remains critical as a hook for audiences."[15] The production complex that had emerged in California during the 1920s and 1930s was thus well positioned for extending its reach nationally and internationally.[16] The high cost of producing movies generated an advantage for established players in both production and promotion.[17] This advantage was reinforced further by American dominance over channels of distribution.[18] Taken together these added up to a powerful structural advantage of American moviemakers.[19]

In the annals of the history of movies, compulsion plays a role in times of war and postwar reconstruction. Before the Second World War the

---

or he seeks to illuminate. Aesthetic approaches focus on the gap between the object of representation and the form of representation not as a problem to be overcome, but as the location of a profoundly important politics. And that politics should be made accessible to all human faculties and not just human reason. Since representation is always also an act of power, as Foucault has reminded us, scientific realism should be subjected to questioning and the aesthetic turn in cultural studies provides us with one such opportunity. Bleiker 2009: 18–47; Steele 2010.

[10] Appiah 2005: 114.   [11] Barnett and Duvall 2005.   [12] Hay 2002: 185–86.
[13] Leaver 2010; Litman 1998.   [14] de Grazia 1989: 61.   [15] Moran 1996: 77.
[16] Waterman 2005: 272.   [17] Berra 2008: 17; Cowen 2002: 7.   [18] Flibbert 2007: 52.
[19] Christopherson 2012.

German movie industry dominated European markets and Josef Goebbels built on that strength to construct an imposing propaganda machinery. In the midst of the Second World War American movie moguls planned, with the active support of different branches of the US government, to establish European markets freed from German, though not American, influence. According to Geoffrey Nowell-Smith this was little more than "a cover for obstructing the revival of any [European] film industry."[20] Since film was an essential tool of the government's de-Nazification campaign, government and industry were engaged in a relationship of competitive cooperation.

"Studio bosses like Darryl L. Zanuck demanded the total destruction and unlimited prohibition and elimination of their strongest pre-war rival, the German film industry."[21] Somewhat reluctantly, the Information Services Division (ISD) of the American occupation authorities obliged and insisted on a total dismantling of the Ufa conglomerate, the center of German movies in the Weimar Republic and a docile instrument in the hands of Josef Goebbels after 1933. After 1945, West Germany was soon fully permeated by American culture, including movies.[22] But only after the US Army gave in to Hollywood's most far-reaching demands in 1949, did the studios release Hollywood movies in the German market in large numbers.[23] The result, in T. P. Elsaesser's words, was that after 1945 "Hollywood stands at the very heart of the New German Cinema becoming a national cinema."[24]

Some German filmmakers resented the decartelization of the German movie industry, modeled after the change in America's domestic film industry in 1948; others welcomed it as offering an escape from the meddling of local conservative state and religious leaders.[25] By being free to join Germany's central film industry trade organization during the military occupation, American distributors enjoyed a unique advantage which gave Hollywood an effective veto over German film policy. It is therefore hardly surprising that American film companies had a profound influence over West Germany's cultural policy.[26] This manifest success of control power in Hollywood's penetration in postwar Germany justified its continued prioritization and expectation of efficacy.

There were parallel attempts to adopt the strategy of structural positioning, institutional backing, and economic muscle to protect the rising dominance of Hollywood studios in America and abroad. This power has been widely recognized. Aspiring presidential candidates, especially of

[20] Nowell-Smith 1998: 6.   [21] Wagnleitner 1994: 202.
[22] Cooke 2007b: 26–27; Fay 2008; Fehrenbach 1995.   [23] Wagnleitner 1994.
[24] Elsaesser 1994: 284.   [25] Fehrenbach 1995: 52–53.   [26] Segrave 1997: 209–10.

the Democratic Party, make Hollywood a regular stop on their fund-raising trips. With ready access to the halls of power, the lobbying of the Motion Picture Association of America (MPAA) has been very successful.[27] By trying to have movies covered under the catch-all rubric of intellectual property rights, the US government, for example, has backed the industry's demand at the international level. Such interventions were often without great success;[28] however, that is not a reflection of the limits of control power wielded by Hollywood but rather that of the US government.

The recognition of Hollywood's control power resulted in valiant efforts to resist it. Both comparatively strong European producer countries (such as Britain, France, and Germany) and weak ones (in Latin America, Africa, and the Middle East) have relied on a panoply of direct and indirect protectionist and promotive measures.[29] What Anne Jäckel describes for Europe holds also for other parts of the world. Most countries "continue to implement some form of protection for their national film industry . . . films are considered far too socially important to be left to market forces."[30] Yet, because non-American audiences have come to share American tastes for films and genres that translate well across national borders and different subcultures, political resistance against the import of American movies often has been half-hearted and short-lived.[31] Informed or instructed by the preferences of viewing publics, American and foreign producers and governments are thus enmeshed in an unending game of probing and adaptation.[32]

Hollywood studios have also used their dominance to shape markets.[33] For example, exclusive distribution of "one-size-fits-all" movies, selected by a few leading distributors, spurs markets that favor "a homogenized film product that can be profitable everywhere" and generates pressures that leave only limited market segments available for international competitors of American movies.[34] These developments set the stage for a profound transformation of global cinema in the 1980s and 1990s. Film production, financing, and distribution have each become increasingly global, and are dominated by America's major studios. This has created a system in which the national production of movies abroad, through different commercial linkages, became an integral part of the American industry.[35] Film production in the United States has long been seen as a

---

[27] Wasko 2005: 14.
[28] Flibbert 2007: 159; Miller, Kurunmäki, and O'Leary 2008; Miller et al. 2001: 38–39.
[29] de Grazia, 1989: 54, 86; Flibbert 2007: 8, 19.   [30] Jäckel 2003: 1.
[31] Flibbert 2007; Puttnam and Watson 1998.
[32] Cooke 2007a; Kindem 2000a; Moran 1996.   [33] Cowen 2002: 75–77.
[34] Flibbert 2007: 138; Iordanova, Martin-Jones, and Vidal 2010.   [35] Moran 1996: 6–7.

template for corporate and industrial change.[36] The advent of the era of conglomerates allowed for the development of digital technology,[37] which further boosted Hollywood's distribution system.[38] More recently, the combined effect of big-budget moviemaking and expanded marketing opportunities that include the full range of media and sales outlets[39] has extended the reach of Hollywood to secondary markets in soundtracks and other paraphernalia, creating additional advantages for the American movie industry.[40] The movie industry is part of a thriving American popular culture complex that includes television programs, rock, rap and pop, theme parks, sports, clothes, fast food, advertising, the internet, and social media that easily reach customers across national borders.[41] Across a broad front, Hollywood has frequently succeeded in muting refusal to submit to its control by cajoling actors abroad.

The fact that Hollywood has benefitted greatly from the different kinds of control power does not mean that key representatives of the industry followed a strategic plan. As Michael Storper writes, "outcomes need not be intended or planned by large firms; if new production techniques are superior, at a given moment, to what they replace, the path taken can be the outcome of short-term strategies or even accidents."[42] This describes accurately the workings of protean power as partially intended and at the same time unanticipated in a situation shot through with fundamental uncertainty. As we argue here, while the effects of control power are real, fundamental uncertainty is not eliminated by measures focusing on market share and risk calculations.

In attempts to retain control by preserving and expanding its primacy, it is easy for Hollywood executives to overreach in their international ambition. Structural power can have unexpected consequences. Outside the United States there exists, for example, considerable resistance to treating movies as normal economic commodities that should be traded freely.[43] In the words of one French movie director "the majors have been laying the foundation for future domination by infiltrating countries with cartel power. As a result, audiences get accustomed to US production values and *voila*, the Yanks control the world."[44] That sentiment is likely to be even more pronounced in culturally different and institutionally distant international markets, China and India most prominently, possibly limiting the industry's widely touted growth opportunities abroad.[45]

---

[36] Hozic 2001: xvi.   [37] Allen 2003: 36, 220.   [38] Hozic 2001: 22–27.
[39] Wasko 1994: 242.   [40] Aksoy and Robins 1992; Kunz 2007; Litman 1998.
[41] Press-Barnathan 2013.   [42] Storper 1993: 291.   [43] Flibbert 2007; Scott 2005.
[44] Wasko 1994: 226.   [45] Leaver 2010: 474.

Whatever the dominance over global markets by Hollywood creators and the blockbusters they produce, it does not make the American film industry immune against unknowable fluctuations. On the contrary, a lack of knowledge about the preferences of global audiences makes the industry often operate under conditions of radical uncertainty.[46] Hollywood has set key standards for the global film industry, gaining considerable market control, only to find that the markets for which the strategy was devised may follow an entirely different course. "Much of what Hollywood does," Prindle writes, "can be interpreted as a series of strategies to replicate the unpredictable ... People in Hollywood ... face the incalculable every day." As in the crisis-prone markets for sophisticated financial products with highly uncertain future values, in which agents' expectations are often (contingently) stabilized by market conventions (see Chapter 8), Hollywood producers thus have developed strategies to cope with the fact that few movies actually make a return on the invested capital. "Brand loyalty" and "star power,"[47] specific genres, sequels, and series to tap into stable audiences,[48] cutting production costs, expanding markets, control over distribution channels and finance,[49] high production and advertising budgets and moderately priced stars[50] – all make the list of practices and strategies employed by predictability-seeking Hollywood producers.[51] Yet De Vany's statistical analysis of the covariates of Hollywood films' box office performances rejects as useless nearly all of these strategies, without weakening the tenacity with which they are pursued.[52] More recent (and ever-more sophisticated) attempts at forecasting the performance of films have proved to be similarly unsuccessful.[53] The bi-modal (and unusually long-tailed) shape of the distribution of box office returns is captured in Figure 10.1. The figure plots the box office performances for 8,401 films

---

[46] Cassidy 1997.

[47] Statistical script testing is the latest illustration of these beliefs. "It takes a lot of the risk out of what I do," says producer Scott Seindorff (quoted in Barnes 2013).

[48] Prindle 1993: 18–29.   [49] Aksoy and Robins 1992: 13.   [50] *The Economist* 2016a.

[51] Uncertainty is reduced also by vertical integration of production, distribution, and exhibition; careful audience research – test screenings and focus groups on rough cuts of films; completion guarantors – companies that, for a fee, guarantee money necessary to finish production; negative pickup – major studios agree to pay part of the costs of the movie's production upon the delivery of the negative; creative accounting techniques to mask the true net loss and profit of a film; developing ancillary markets like video and DVD; and increasing access to foreign markets. See Acheson and Maule 1994.

[52] Cassidy 1997; De Vany 2004.

[53] For example, two physicists developed a machine learning algorithm to pre-assign films (based on publicly available information) to different categories (ranging from "flop" to "blockbuster"); when they compared the actual performance to the prediction, they found that the routine correctly classified only about one-third of the films in their dataset of over 5,000 films. Pan and Sinha 2010.

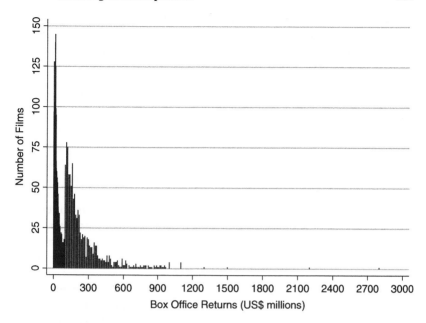

Figure 10.1 The Distribution of Box Office Returns, 1950–2010

released between 1950 and 2010.[54] The data confirm that many films earn little, a few do well, and a very, very small number become global blockbusters – and no one can predict in advance of the release into which category a film will fit.[55] Screenwriter William Goldman encapsulated the radical uncertainty that defines the modern movie business in his best-known *bon mot*: "nobody knows anything."[56]

Despite Hollywood's dominance in select areas, like box office revenues, which enhance control in domestic and international markets, the battles for survival are hardly won. Returns on investments are low, and the ability to reach global audiences and retain their loyalty has been a

[54] Bamman, O'Connor, and Smith 2013. The film data used to construct the figure can be accessed at: www.ark.cs.cmu.edu/personas.

[55] And what is true for Hollywood is true for Bollywood as well: "fewer than 8 out of the 800 films made each year [in Bollywood] will make serious money." Torgovnik 2003: 6.

[56] Asked seventeen years later whether the *bon mot* still held true, Goldman replied "now more than ever." Quoted in Lavin 2000. The micro-level evidence on the total unpredictability of audience tastes is strong. Experimental evidence shows that slight shifts in social cues can move audience valuations of cultural objects in wildly divergent directions. These micro-level studies shed additional light on the "pervasive 'nobody knows' problem, whereby even sophisticated cultural industry insiders have difficulty predicting which cultural products will become highly popular and which will fail." Zuckerman 2012: 226.

source of permanent anxiety among Los Angeles film producers. Analyses of the movie industry stress its history of instability.[57] Although fewer films are made today than two decades ago, competition within the industry remains fierce, and is aggravated by competition with television, Blu-ray, online streaming services, other entertainment industries, and with piracy. The unpredictability of consumer preferences in Hollywood's domestic and foreign markets is also well known.[58] In a complex market place, the frequency distribution of profits and losses in the film industry is non-Gaussian and has very long tails.[59] Hollywood's film producers may try to exert control power, and they have been assisted in this endeavor by the establishment of a template for global blockbuster movies that has helped to create key markets in its viewing public, as well as aspiring moviemakers wanting to create global hit movies. But they are often frustrated when their competitors have a better view of the (moving) target, or once creative entrepreneurs in other sites of protean power master, perfect, and substitute the tools devised by Hollywood to reach the widest audiences.

Put differently, Hollywood's control over global markets and audiences is not limited only by the counter-power of state and corporate actors seeking to evade its control and to impose their own instead. It is also limited by a protean power that circulates among producers, directors, and viewing publics and that can, at times, also course through Hollywood, although not as a result of deliberate strategies. That protean power operates in a decentralized manner and indirectly, appearing to lack identifiable agents, and often results in novel practices.

Both control and protean power are, therefore, deeply intertwined. To focus only on one or the other type of power impairs our understanding. It is the dynamic relation between the two kinds of power that best elucidates developments in the movie industry. "Movies are both art and commerce."[60] Existing studies typically provide either an economic analysis of the system of production and distribution[61] or focus on the movies themselves, the culture of consumption and the ultimate arbiter, the moviegoer.[62] The analysis of the movie industry should, however, capture both economic relationships and cultural exchanges.[63] Economic and cultural crosscurrents reveal clearly power's two different and complementary facets and practices that enhance the circulation of power.

---

[57] Allen 2003: 37.   [58] Swann 1994: 181.   [59] De Vany 2004: 2–3, 6.
[60] Kindem 2000b: 1.
[61] Chase 2008; Christopherson 2011; Christopherson and Storper 1989; Flibbert 2007; Leaver 2010; Scott 2005.
[62] Hozic 2001; Kirshner 2012; Wasko 2005.   [63] Nowell-Smith 1998: 1–2.

Protean Power

The uncertainty that Hollywood faces comes in forms that are not fully captured by market competition. Cultural producers tackling the problem of competitiveness head on and relying on risk-driven shortcuts are often frustrated. Those strategies fit the template for exercising control power, which is not ineffective but limited both as a practical guide, evidenced by Hollywood's struggle for dominance, and as a conceptual framework, since it neglects the dynamic complexity characterizing the world of global film. Control power would suffice if specific market moves met with predictable responses that could be thwarted and neutralized by still more calculated action. No global actors, and certainly not Hollywood, operate in such a laboratory-like environment where controlled experiments produce transparent results. Rules of the game and of "competitiveness," if they are set at all, remain temporary and the creative content of films offered to diverse audiences is only the most visible manifestation of the impossibility of anticipating success. Behind this fluidity, we find control-eluding improvisation-turned-innovation, which both sustains and unravels the relations of power between actors.

Film producers operating in other national and international markets do not necessarily compete with Hollywood's domination head on. Films produced for specific audiences, like those of Bollywood, "have carved out an autonomous history alongside American popular films on an international and now an increasingly global scale."[64] For example, in serving their respective diaspora communities, the Chinese and Indian film industries harnessed Hollywood's content-standardizing strategies that generate product according to the "most-exportable" formula.[65] Cairo, Mumbai, and Hong Kong have significant cultural divides that differ from Hollywood's, which helps to explain "why producers in these cities have been able to sustain distinctive product lines and survive the onslaught of a much more powerful competitor."[66] In striving to become their own force, prospective competitors to Hollywood in India, China, and Korea adapt the organizational content of Hollywood films, sometimes unwittingly. Their power lies in their less-than-fully-deliberate revision of audience tastes and their tapping of local talent, both moves that unintentionally end up transforming practices in major Hollywood studios as well.

---

[64] Baumik 2007: 202. In fact, Bollywood is an inaccurate label. India actually produces films in thirty languages and multiple genres. Hindi movies have a supportive audience even in Pakistan, despite India's troubled relationship with that country.

[65] Curtin and Shah 2010.

[66] Curtin 2007: 19. Powerful, we would add, only if measured as control-power linked to financing capacity and advertising clout, not audience impact.

For example, the rise of the Nigerian film industry since 1992 has been a totally unexpected development in the global film industry. The emergence of "Nollywood," decidedly low-budget and rooted in Nigeria's informal economy,[67] is popular throughout Africa and even generates worries about the continent's "Nigerization."[68] Within two decades the film industry has displaced Hollywood films not only in Nigeria but throughout Africa. It has become the second largest sector of Nigeria's oil-dependent economy and employs about 200,000 people directly and 1 million indirectly. In 2013, it generated $800 million.[69] Between 1992 and 2009 it released about 11,000 full-length features, which made Nollywood the world's leading producer of digital video films. Production costs typically are well below $50,000 and the average production time is seven days. Low-quality is a hallmark of Nigerian movies. In the words of veteran Nigerian director Eddie Ugbomah, "you don't produce 20 films a week. You must be producing rubbish."[70] Movies are produced in English and in one of Nigeria's 521 native dialects. Customized to existing markets, they sell about 50,000 copies, successful ones ten times more. Without a strong property rights regime creativity has flourished. And competition is weak in Africa's most populous country. The entire country has less than fifty movie theaters. Programming on state-run TV is unappealing. Internet connections are slow and unreliable. And about two-thirds of households have either VHS or VCD players. Piracy is widespread and discs now sell for about a dollar. Distribution networks are highly decentralized and have regional and even global reach.[71] Typically, within two weeks of their release date new films are distributed across the continent.[72]

Actors from other African countries, mostly living in Lagos, are hired to enhance the appeal of Nigerian movies in markets throughout Africa.[73] Still, times are changing and competition is bound to emerge from other African countries. Filmmakers in South Africa, Tanzania, and Cameroon are producing hundreds of movies a year. And in an exercise of creative self-branding, South Africa, Ghana, and Kenya are describing their own nascent film industries as "Sollywood," "Ghallywood," and "Riverwood." Uganda's "Wakaliwood" is taking this development to its extremes;

---

[67] Lobato 2010; McCall 2004.   [68] Onishi 2016.   [69] Rutschman 2015: 693.
[70] Ang 2016: 225.
[71] Arewa 2012: 3–4, 7, 9, 12, 15–16, 22–23, 25–26; Olopade 2014: 23–26.
[72] *The Economist* 2010.
[73] The success of the Nigerian movie industry is in contrast to the experience of other African countries where resources are too limited to support state-of-the-art filmmaking equipment; poorly organized distribution and exhibition sectors have forced the government to assume most or all of the production costs; and direct governmental control over the content and style of filmmaking have stifled creativity. See Diawara 1992.

emblematic of the growing industry is Isaac Nabwana's dusty backyard in Kampala's Wakaliga neighborhood, where he has written, directed, shot, and edited forty-seven movies since 2008, the last one at a cost of less than $200 (selling 20,000 copies in the first week after release before wide-scale piracy took its toll on sales of the film).[74] Film has become Africa's dominant popular cultural medium, ahead of music and dance.

In short, in Africa Nollywood rather than Hollywood came out on top. Though we usually fail to notice until it has already happened, when the shift occurs, the innovative sway of protean power can be so forceful that it may transform even what newly empowered actors do, perpetuating the uncertainty of the environment surrounding all film producers. The direct connection to audiences, the low-cost operation, and the ambition to penetrate markets beyond Nigeria has also exposed Nollywood to the vulnerabilities stemming from uncertainties only seemingly separate from film production.[75] The emergent threat of Boko Haram, for instance, necessitated agile responses that Nigerian military leaders hoped to borrow from Nollywood.[76] In an attempt to tap access to viewing households and gain valuable legitimation, the army has sought cooperation in portraying the fight against Boko Haram in Nollywood films.[77] Interestingly, a parallel strategy is being pursued by Pakistan's army, whose soldiers work as extras in otherwise low-cost productions and participate in spreading a deliberately positive picture of anti-insurgent operations.[78] Although it is only a matter of time until audiences see through such efforts, this additional layer of resourcefulness and innovation in addressing terrorist threats reinforces the argument made by Barak Mendelsohn (Chapter 9). The profound uncertainty that gave rise to Nollywood is exacerbated by growing security challenges, opening new territory not only for market–political relations but also redefining threat, with an impact on the future uncertainty within the sector.[79]

Protean power does not denote direct or actor-specific effects. It speaks to the degree to which the attempted transfer of values sets free creative processes that generate new capacities as the values in question are examined, breached, negotiated, affirmed, and undermined. The flow of ideas and information as well as fashions and fads on a global basis, with American society as an important node, thus reflects protean power's face. It is partly shaped by the spontaneous preferences and practices of ordinary people.[80] Just like imported movies, the international success of the TV-series *Dallas*, for example, illustrates the ability of

[74] *The Economist* 2016b.   [75] Tsika 2015.   [76] Klein and Palmer 2016.
[77] Abulude 2016.   [78] *The Economist* 2016c.   [79] Klein Murillo 2016.
[80] Wagnleitner and May 2000.

non-American viewers to interpret, select, resist, and adapt to the themes of a quintessentially American television show to suit their own distinctive institutions, values, and practices.[81]

The lack of an overarching strategy that marks protean power, given the right circumstances, is readily discernible in the case of American cinema and supports our core point about the co-evolution of and interaction between control and protean power. In the words of film historian Vanessa Schwartz, the globalization of culture produced a "'cosmopolitan' cinema ... this term denotes multinational production teams making films that represented subjects, themes, and plots that underscored a transnational cultural experience and perspective rather than a discrete national experience of culture that contributed to separate national identities and rivalries."[82] While this cosmopolitan cinema is neither anti- nor un-American, it retains unmistakable American traits. David Puttnam, a producer, puts it this way: "The norms and values embodied in Hollywood films have come to be absorbed as universal ... American films have always been consciously tailored to a multicultural audience; in the early days they had to be simply because of the high proportion and diverse mix of immigrants in America. In defining itself in acceptable national terms, the US domestic industry quite naturally tended to be international."[83]

It would be unfair and inaccurate to argue that Hollywood has misguidedly used control power only and has been immune to the opportunities resting with protean power. In fact, what may seem as a structural advantage is an element that has been exploited by both Hollywood and its competitors. They all watched the dynamic unfold with some intention, but without any ability to anticipate the full extent and depth of the resulting impact. Exemplifying this dynamic in the case of Hollywood, the polyglot character of American culture may well have greater access to and be more readily accessible by members of other communities. Looking well past structural power, Janet Wasko singles out not only the effects of Hollywood's diverse cultural milieu, but also the role of English as a *lingua franca* that enhances the narrative transparency of American movies.[84] As film director Sidney Pollack observed while reflecting on the American obsession with remaking foreign films: "You can't understand a lot of Japanese movies unless you understand Japanese culture. You don't have to understand American culture to understand our movies."[85] The narrative transparency of many American movies is a great asset in global markets. "Transparency is defined as any textual

---

[81] Liebes and Katz 1990.   [82] Schwartz 2007: 5.   [83] Puttnam and Watson 1998: 277.
[84] Wasko 2003: 175–81; de Grazia 1989: 59–61.   [85] Quoted in Allen 2003: 85.

apparatus that allows audiences to project indigenous values, beliefs, rites, and rituals into imported media or the use of those devices. This transparency means that American cultural exports ... manifest narrative structures that easily blend into other cultures."[86] Protean power thus reflects the very construction of American fantasies and the illusions of control and pleasure that cannot be actualized anywhere.[87]

Returning to the de-Nazification example, elements of protean power underpinned much of that success as well. Even under the extreme circumstances of US occupation German audiences did not passively accept or imitate Hollywood norms. "Hollywood was a cultural palimpsest upon which local audiences construed their own readings."[88] Jennifer Fay writes in a similar vein that "German spectators and filmmakers did not merely imitate Hollywood examples; they reinterpreted, adapted, and domesticated these fictions. German directors even managed to subtly mock, boldly contest, and at times empty these constructs of American citizenship by inverting the conventions of Hollywood genres."[89] This has also happened under more normal circumstances in recent decades.

Protean power helps us to understand why Hollywood's control over domestic and international markets remains limited. Protean power sets unavoidable limits to the notion of control that focuses on the mechanisms of compulsion, institutions, and structures. It has decentralized and indirect effects. These effects create the innovations and unpredictabilities in a world marked not only by calculable risk but also unavoidable uncertainty.

Conclusion

The American film industry illustrates a puzzle. Hollywood controls the global industry by many conventional measures such as screen time, artistic and technological inventiveness, prestige, and access to capital. Yet the confidence that control should instill is not what Hollywood experiences. The American film industry operates in an uncertain environment marked by the intersection of control and protean power. In entertainment, Nate Silver states, "statistics do not provide all the answers; you have to measure the uncertainty in a problem."[90] Overstating a good point, Taleb emphasizes uncertainty even more when he writes that "what we call talent generally comes from success, rather than its opposite ... a large dose of nonlinear luck makes the movie."[91] Control power, therefore, is an incomplete guide for fathoming the direction of the next big wave of hot cultural

---

[86] Olson 1999: 5.   [87] Hozic 2001: 28.   [88] Swann 1994: 184.   [89] Fay 2008: xvii.
[90] Caro 2013.   [91] Taleb 2010: 30–31.

products that will capture the imagination of consumers, directors, producers, and investors. The statistical effect of the wisdom of the crowds on the
revenues a film generates is ten times stronger than the reviews of film
critics.[92] Crowds thus have agency in shaping Hollywood, but in an attenuated sense of that term.

As this chapter has sought to demonstrate, the world of movies is
marked by the intersection between control and protean power. Despite
its formidable compulsory, institutional, and structural resources, protean power stands in the way of the American movie industry's secure
control of markets and recurrent attempts to transform radical uncertainty into manageable risk. Thinking of power in differentiated terms
highlights dynamic relationships between power types that can be
mutually reinforcing, undermining, or indifferent. As a practical matter,
in the film industry, America's institutional and structural power is more
important than its compulsory power. Still, the former two operate in
direct interaction with protean power – the greater the push to streamline
production processes and bet on previously proven horses, the greater the
inclination to assume away important changes in market context, thus
opening up room for innovative interventions. As such institutional and
structural power are both enhanced and set back by the dispersed and
indirect effects of protean power.

The American and global movie industry is an institutional complex
full of conflicts and contradictions revealed in both the refusal of national
governments to submit to US pressure for unfettered access to protected
national markets and the improvisations and innovations by foreign producers and moviemakers, setting free protean power dynamics. The
historical trajectories of the movie industries in different parts of the
world diverge widely in both the scope they reached and the means they
use, while subject to the scrutiny of choice-wielding audiences. The
American and European film-production complexes date back to the
beginning of the twentieth century; Nigeria's cottage industry saw
the light of day as late as 1992. The difference in timing, scale, and
audience responses has a lot to do with the balance between centralizing
and decentralizing movements in each industry and in its links to global
networks, from finance to diasporas. Uncertainty has typically defeated
efforts at forecasting audience preference with the help of risk-based
models. Yet it is that same uncertainty that provides a fertile ground for
the exercise of creative, innovative, and improvisational protean power.

The existence of and configuration between different types of power is
helpful for rethinking what we mean by the term Americanization and

---

[92] *The Economist* 2016a.

how processes that this concept describes link to the broader world. Rather than arguing that America made the world[93] or extolling that world's flatness[94] in imposing one best standard, the analysis of different types of power points to two perspectives. First, the transnational movement of American film elucidates how and why American culture is an important part of global culture. The broad context of world politics connects local and global domains of social and political life. Local practices remake global culture just as global culture remakes local practices. It is unhelpful to think of national cultures as stable and global culture as intrusive. Contested local and global cultures change as they travel. Second, the protean power of American society interacts with the control powers of the United States. Circulation is not a one-way process. Just as American society affects others, so do others affect American society and the United States. Protean power can be genuinely creative, innovative, and original in developing new social practices, knowledge regimes, and policies.

Like the American imperium of which it is a part, Hollywood is remarkable for the open access it grants to outsiders.[95] Distinctive of the contemporary American movie industry is the fact that most of its studios are foreign-owned; many of its most distinguished directors are non-American; and many foreign producers can come to make "Hollywood" movies for non-American audiences. The intimate relation between the American movie industry, foreign producers and directors, and global audiences expresses widely shared commonalities and differences across boundaries that make global viewing publics both receptive and resistant to the industry's products.[96] Located in America and belonging to the world, Hollywood thus embodies very different and complementary faces of power in contemporary world politics.

---

[93] Kagan 2012.   [94] Friedman 2005.   [95] Katzenstein 2005: 149–78.
[96] Acland 2003: 11.

Part 4

Protean Power between Risk
and Uncertainty

11 Changing History?: Innovation and Continuity in Contemporary Arms Control

Jennifer L. Erickson[1]

In 1997, a coalition of state and non-state actors concluded the Ottawa Treaty, a comprehensive ban on anti-personnel landmines (APL). Considered impossible less than a decade before, it passed with surprising speed and popularity. In doing so, lead campaigner Jody Williams argued in her Nobel Peace Prize Lecture that the landmine coalition had "changed history."[2] It brought new actors into the center of arms control negotiations, established innovative diplomatic strategies, and produced a new standard of "good" arms control policy, all of which have since facilitated treaties on cluster munitions (CM) and conventional weapons transfers. These treaties mark a distinct break with the Cold War. Although some acknowledged the human costs of landmines, cluster munitions, and the arms trade in the 1970s, humanitarian arms control failed to overcome opposition both within and between states. Since the end of the Cold War, however, the primary focus of multilateral arms control agreements has been to ameliorate the adverse humanitarian effects of conventional weapons and protect human security.

Why were advocates successful in pushing humanitarian arms control only after the Cold War? Explanations that rely simply on the end of bipolarity miss out on the power interactions that have shaped post-Cold War security governance. I argue that the initial, radical uncertainty of the post-Cold War security environment provided the political space for smaller states and non-state actors to use diplomatic innovation to bypass institutional constraints, frame problems, and mobilize support to make new agreements possible. Advocates were intentional and strategic in seeking new treaties, but their success, speed, and widespread support in negotiating them was unexpected. The Ottawa Treaty created the model, strategies, and momentum to pursue humanitarian controls on other weapons. Nevertheless, advocates have had to adapt the landmine

[1] The author would like to thank Peter Katzenstein, Lucia Seybert, Jacquie Best, Noelle Brigden, Aida Hozic, Miles Kahler, and Len Seabrooke for their helpful comments.
[2] Williams 1997.

campaign's strategies to respond to larger skeptical states' efforts to tamp down – with some success – on the scope of subsequent agreements.

More than a decade after the APL ban, the CM Convention and Arms Trade Treaty (ATT) demonstrate both the lasting influence of the Ottawa Treaty and the limits of protean power as it interacts with control power in the complex post-September 11 security environment. Skeptical states with significant military capabilities have used their institutional, political, and economic resources to weaken post-APL agreements. In some cases, their technological resources have allowed them to work around (and therefore make acceptable) new regulations and prohibitions. In the absence of viable work-arounds, however, they have exerted their control power to weaken agreements. In turn, pro-control coalitions have adapted their strategies to the realities of control power, just as NGOs have had to do in the climate negotiations described by Jessica Green in Chapter 12. As a whole, these negotiations thus reflect a push and pull between control and protean power in global security governance, with important consequences for the design and effects of contemporary arms control agreements.

Risk, Uncertainty, and Complexity in International Security and Arms Control

Conventional weapons restrictions tap directly into the heart of control power, limiting a key source of states' coercive capabilities. Humanitarian arms control agreements can therefore be a difficult sell to security-conscious states. Moreover, the states with greater military capabilities also tend to be the states with greater formal agenda-setting and voting privileges in international institutions. Thus, they possess a wide range of control power resources, which can allow them to block agreements they dislike from being adopted or even discussed. Not surprisingly, these states have typically been the most hesitant to negotiate conventional weapons restrictions. Instead, smaller states and NGOs have been the primary source of arms control initiatives seeking to promote humanitarian values and protect human security. Yet although big states' control power has largely persisted, the effects of protean power have altered its utility and strength in shaping post-Cold War arms control.

It is therefore not enough to argue that the end of bipolarity caused the shift in the focus of international arms control. Rather, Cold War bipolarity and its end are linked to changing experiences of risk and uncertainty in international security, which in turn provide changing opportunities and constraints for the interaction of power. In the radical uncertainty of early post-Cold War international politics, political space

opened for innovative state and non-state actors to pursue new strategies and policies. Of course, small states have often had to be more agile
and creative in order to manage their vulnerability to changes in their
external environments.[3] Yet the post-Cold War security environment
enabled their partnerships with NGOs and other diplomatic innovations
to create arms control agreements once thought impossible. At the same
time, bigger states' control power has remained a force of resistance and
placed limits on the extent to which other actors can push new agreements, especially in recent years as radical uncertainty has subsided in
favor of operational uncertainty (see Chapters 1 and 2).

Cold War Security Environment

The Cold War international security system was marked by clear leadership, an absence of major power war, and broad consensus over the
nuclear threat as the predominant international security concern.
Whether due to the bipolar distribution of material capabilities[4] or
nuclear weapons,[5] the international security environment at this macro-
level was seen as stable. To be sure, superpower war had the potential to
end in mutually assured destruction. As a result, however, attacks "out of
the blue" were seen as "so improbable for a nuclear age as to approach
virtual certainty that it will not happen."[6] As Schelling and Halperin
famously argued, war was seen as the result of decisions mitigated by
the logic of deterrence theory.[7] This "risk-based understanding of
chance," Katzenstein and Seybert note, has in turn "had a pervasive
influence on the theory and practice of nuclear deterrence for the last
half century" (Chapter 2, p. 42). Arms control thus served to "slow the
tempo of decisions," improve communications, and provide assurances
between adversaries to better assess risk and reaction.[8] Certainly, the
Cold War was not without a keen sense of threat and insecurity, but it
was generally viewed as a "known" threat in which risk could be calculated, managed, and even manipulated.

By the 1970s, this security environment had fostered an arms control
culture led by the superpowers and focused on managing the risk of
nuclear war. The superpowers (and sometimes the international community more broadly) reached agreements to limit nuclear arsenals, testing,
and proliferation. By maintaining strong weapons programs and negotiating strong arms control agreements, argue McNamara and Bethe,

---

[3] Cooper and Shaw 2009; Ingebritsen 2006; Katzenstein 1985. [4] Waltz 1964.
[5] Gaddis 1986. [6] Brodie 1978: 69. [7] Schelling and Halperin 1961: 15–16.
[8] Schelling and Halperin 1961: 16.

"the risk of nuclear war will constantly recede and confidence that we are masters of our fate will be rebuilt."[9] In the meantime, crisis scenarios could be laid out and responses planned (at least in theory). Thus, the superpowers used arms control as a tool to impose greater control over state security in a high-risk world.

In this control-power dominated world, the arms control agenda was set principally by the superpowers. Other states could choose between security relationships with one of two centers of power or independence through armed neutrality,[10] but they largely accepted the nuclear-focused agenda. For Soviet client states in Eastern Europe, threat of military intervention formed a clear-cut social system based on control power and policy acquiescence. United States' domination of its clients' security affairs was more varied in form but generally founded on promises of material assistance. Moreover, some former colonies were simply too new and ill equipped to exercise political leverage.[11] To the extent that non-superpowers attempted to deploy diplomatic innovation, resources focused on "[dissipating] conflict between the two blocks."[12] As the case studies show, in this security environment, humanitarian weapons restrictions failed to gain broad political traction against superpower preferences.

Post-Cold War Security Environment

The sudden collapse of the Soviet Union upended the established bipolar system and introduced radical uncertainty into the global security environment: what world order would replace the old order; who would take a leadership role; and what would be the primary threat to systemic stability? Scholars debated whether the system would be unipolar or multipolar; if multipolar, which state (or states) would lead; the prospects for international stability; and the security consequences for individual states and regions.[13] Threats became diffuse and connected to weak actors in regions previously seen as the periphery. Societal instability and internal conflict challenged traditional understandings of interstate security, the relevant actors in world politics, and the relevant policy tools to manage conflict. Scholars wrote about "the coming anarchy," "the clash of civilizations," the anti-democratic but conflicting trends of "Jihad vs McWorld," "organized chaos," "new wars," and "the contest between forces of integration and fragmentation."[14]

[9] McNamara and Bethe 1985: 44.   [10] Rickli 2008.   [11] Fox 1969.
[12] Ingebritsen 2006: 10.
[13] For example, Buzan 1991; Friedberg 1993–94; Hyde-Price 1991; Krauthammer 1990–91; Kupchan 1998; Layne 1993; Mearsheimer 1990; Waltz 1993.
[14] Kaplan 1994; Huntington 1993; Barber 1992; Keen 1996; Kaldor 1999; Gaddis 1991: 103, respectively.

Suddenly, the system was in flux and more open to small states and NGOs taking a prominent role, diplomatic innovation, and the generation of protean power.

With the post-9/11 focus on global terrorism, states' security environment has become more complex (Chapter 1, pp. 16–25), oriented toward operational uncertainty and the interaction of control and protean power. Threat is both known and unknown, connected to geographically diffused and often-fluid violent non-state groups with agile networks operating outside established diplomatic rules and norms (Chapter 9). Militarily strong states have confronted that growing complexity with a reassertion of control power and attempts to exert military means of domination. Militarily weaker states and NGOs, in turn, have had to respond to its control-power endowed opposition and improvise on their strategies of the 1990s.

As post-Cold War international security has undergone this evolution from uncertainty to complexity, protean and control power have increasingly interacted. Certainly, the scope of potential policy outcomes remains noticeably broader than in the 1970s. Yet the space for new actors to implement new strategies and comprehensive arms control policies against big-state wishes is somewhat more constricted relative to the 1990s. Bigger states continue to rely on control power resources as a means by which to grapple with complexity, advancing new defense technologies while downsizing military forces. They are therefore reluctant to limit their access to and development of new weapons. Smaller states continue to rely on cooperative military relationships to respond to their changing security needs and secure their own access to arms.[15] In doing so, however, they have been less beholden to superpower alliances in defining their foreign policy preferences than in the past.

As a result, small states and NGOs have been more willing and able to engage in creative policymaking[16] to achieve cooperative responses to security challenges relevant to their own interests and values. Reshaping arms control to focus on humanitarian goals has been one key way in which coalitions of "like-minded" small states and NGOs have innovated in response to the causes and consequences of local instability and international uncertainty. In addition, the radical uncertainty of the 1990s enabled these actors to apply information, resources, and mobilization strategies to pursue their arms control agendas. Bigger states have had to adapt to these policy initiatives and, in more recent years, have employed control power to limit them. In the process, their varying degrees of resistance also demonstrate the limits of protean power. Where possible,

---

[15] Rickli 2008: 308.   [16] Buchanan 2010: 256; Cooper and Shaw 2009: 5.

they have harnessed technology to make new weapons restrictions either acceptable or inapplicable. Absent technological work-arounds, they have more directly sought to block or weaken humanitarian restraints to protect their own interests.

Case Studies

Three key humanitarian arms control agreements demonstrate the evolving relationship between control and protean power in the post-Cold War international security environment: the 1997 Ottawa Landmine Treaty, the 2008 Cluster Munition Convention (CMC), and the 2013 ATT.[17] The first two agreements outlaw anti-personnel landmines and cluster munitions, respectively. The third, the ATT, outlines humanitarian criteria to guide states' transfers of small and major conventional arms.

Attempts to address all three during the Cold War failed as nuclear risk dominated the international security agenda. However, varying interactions of control power and protean power effects after the Cold War have shaped the campaigns, negotiations, and outcomes of each of these agreements. The experience of radical uncertainty enabled coalitions of smaller states and NGOs to develop innovative diplomatic strategies to win support for the historic Ottawa Treaty. Later, as radical uncertainty subsided, these coalitions improvised on their landmine strategies to pass the CMC and ATT. Although skeptical big states are no longer able to use their control power to keep humanitarian arms control initiatives off the table, they have used it to weaken negotiation results. Their success in doing so thus demonstrates the limited effects of protean power as it interacts with control power in a complex international security environment.

Anti-Personnel Landmines: Diplomatic Innovation

The 1997 ban on the production, use, stockpiling, and trade in APLs broke all past expectations of arms control rooted in Cold War nuclear risk management and came about with surprising rapidity after the International Campaign to Ban Landmines (ICBL) was formed in 1992. APLs are mines designed to kill or maim foot soldiers, and, until 1997, were commonly employed by military forces around the world as a low-cost means to protect territory from invasion. Landmine use dates back to the

---

[17] Carpenter (2011) attributes the selection of these issues to transnational advocacy networks' internal issue-vetting processes.

US Civil War, but concern over their effects on non-combatants first surfaced in the 1970s – but with little effect. It was the radical uncertainty experienced in the initial post-Cold War years, I argue, that opened up the political space to make the Ottawa Treaty possible and that allowed advocates to establish new diplomatic strategies that – in modified forms – would later facilitate the CMC and ATT negotiations.

Attention to landmines during the Cold War resulted from the efforts of a few state and non-state actors. From 1974 to 1977, the Swiss government convened a series of meetings to increase protections for non-combatants during armed conflict. In preparation, nineteen governments requested the International Committee of the Red Cross (ICRC) to "consult with specialists on the problem of conventional weapons which may cause suffering or have indiscriminate effects," including APLs.[18] The ICRC's 1973 meeting (which did not include a US representative) concluded that "certain uses of antipersonnel mines ... can lead to indiscriminate effects and injuries far in excess of what is required to put combatants out of action," and called for "intergovernmental discussions ... with a view to possible restrictions upon their operational use or even prohibition."[19] However, at meetings in 1974 and 1976, states disagreed about whether APLs should be banned as inherently indiscriminate, or whether built-in self-destruct mechanisms could resolve the problem. If there could be a technological fix, the logic went, the weapon need not be banned.

The political opportunities and interests for smaller powers to assert initiatives that contradicted superpower preferences were absent in Cold War multilateral institutions and alliances. In the end, the 1977 Additional Protocols to the Geneva Conventions did not include any weapons restrictions. The major powers argued that the APL problem was confined to the irresponsible practices of less-developed militaries and guerilla groups.[20] Evidence demonstrating the extent of the problem came only in the 1980s, after the Soviet invasion of Afghanistan and as Western aid organizations gained access to areas affected by the US war in Vietnam.[21] Although small states like Sweden had wanted prohibitions, they failed to attract broader support against superpower opposition. NGOs were also limited in number, and the primary organization, the ICRC, "[seemed] to have decided not to touch the law relating to different types of weapons."[22] Even so, the 1977 meeting led to the 1980 UN Convention on Certain Conventional Weapons (CCW), prohibiting indiscriminate APL use and restricting mine placement to outside

[18] Maresca and Maslen 2000: 19, 20.   [19] ICRC 1973: paras. 247, 248.
[20] McGrath 2000: 15–16.   [21] Ibid.: 14.   [22] Draper 1977: 10.

populated areas. However, the CCW has been considered ineffective, filled with loopholes, and too limited in its membership.[23]

Thus, the APL problem predates the end of the Cold War, but it did take the end of the Cold War to produce an international security environment conducive to concluding an APL ban against great power preferences. This time, the political space was more open to small states and NGOs reorienting discussions about international security and arms control to include human security, mobilizing public opinion, and leading diplomatic initiatives. The rapid success of the ICBL[24] in coalition with like-minded states in pushing through the Ottawa Treaty in 1997 is well known.[25] Advocates made up for their lack of traditional control power sources in international institutions by coordinating innovative diplomatic strategies. For example, the ICBL relied on victims' personal stories and celebrity advocacy to mobilize public opinion, and used information and expert testimony to counter skeptical governments' arguments against a new treaty. In doing so, these actors took advantage of the radical uncertainty surrounding threat and leadership in post-Cold War security politics, in which other threats and superpower interests did not overshadow attention to or discourage interest in the humanitarian side of arms control.

Importantly, unlike the 1970s, advocates were able to support arguments with extensive evidence that APLs were inherently indiscriminate and caused harm to civilians long after conflicts ended. They also strategically connected – or "grafted"[26] – that information to arguments that an APL ban would fall within states' existing obligations under international law. Finally, they brought in retired military leaders to argue that APLs were unreliable weapons of little strategic value. APLs did not need a technological work-around; they simply were not needed.

These arguments, however, only partially overcame big-state opposition. The United States in particular saw continued strategic value for APLs and refused to support a treaty without exceptions for its specific security interests. This time, however, advocates proceeded without bending to US demands. When the 1996 CCW review conference failed to achieve consensus on a total APL ban, Canada proposed a meeting of pro-ban states outside the UN framework, excluding opposing states and

---

[23] Mekata 2000: 144; Rutherford 2011: 19.
[24] None of the six ICBL-founding organizations came from the traditional disarmament community; they were humanitarian organizations working in mine-affected countries. Mekata 2000: 146.
[25] For example, Bower 2012; Bryden 2013; Maresca and Maslen 2000; McGrath 2000; Mekata 2000; Price 1998; Rutherford 2000, 2011; Tepe 2011.
[26] Price 1998.

shedding consensus requirements in order to create the strongest possible treaty. Canada also coordinated a group of eight small core states with the ICBL and ICRC.[27] In contrast, the United States failed to keep negotiations in its preferred venue, the UN Conference on Disarmament, where it could better control meeting outcomes. Russia and the United States attended the extra-UN meetings as observers only, and China stayed away from the process. Organizers refused to grant the United States any concessions, not wanting to water down the final treaty text. Nevertheless, given the initiative's popularity and the low overall strategic value of APLs, big opposing states seemed disinclined to actively block it. The final product – a full, legally-binding APL ban – quickly gained widespread support, with 122 states signing on in December 1997. As of 2017, it has 162 members. And although states with the most control power continue to refuse to join, many have generally complied with its provisions.[28]

Cluster Munitions: Definitional Improvisation

The Ottawa Treaty initially appeared to have changed the course of arms control history, introducing new actors and diplomatic strategies to achieve humanitarian arms control in the face of big-state opposition. In doing so, advocates believed that the landmine campaign had opened up a more certain way forward on small arms and cluster munition controls. However, the 2008 Cluster Munition Convention was negotiated in the more complex post-September 11 security environment. Advocates faced a need to compromise and alter their strategies in order to deal with opposing states' reassertion of their control power. A cluster munition is a conventional munition "designed to disperse or release explosive submunitions."[29] They have been in use since the Second World War and briefly came to international attention during the US war in Vietnam, once again with no policy response. While the success of the 1997 landmine ban did galvanize and shape the CM campaign, advocates had to contend with the more direct mobilization of control power in opposition to a comprehensive treaty. As a result, the CMC is a less far-reaching treaty in terms of scope and membership than the APL ban.

Cluster munitions were first discussed along with APLs in the 1970s. At this time, CM technology was limited to the United States, Britain, France, and Germany.[30] Experts at the 1973 ICRC meeting noted CM's

[27] Tepe 2011: 90.   [28] See Bower 2012; Morley 2014.
[29] Full text of CMC available at: www.clusterconvention.org/files/2011/01/Convention-E NG.pdf.
[30] Herthel 2001: 238.

"obvious and uncontrollable tendency toward indiscriminateness."[31] At the 1974 meeting, seven states proposed a ban. The initiative was led by Sweden, which had convened its own domestic group of experts in the early 1970s, prompted by public concerns about the conduct of the Vietnam War.[32] Yet although fewer states were using CMs and there was more awareness of the CM problem, cluster munitions were not included in the CCW. The proposal managed to gain support from only thirteen states by the 1976 meeting, where it lacked the consensus to move forward.[33] By dropping it, Borrie argues, "pragmatism appears to have prevailed": proponents decided to back other less ambitious CCW proposals seen as more likely to succeed.[34] The United States and the United Kingdom especially sought to downplay and deflect questions about CM use and effects.[35] Thus, more information about their effects did not save CM controls from failure in this period; like landmines, superpower interests got in the way.

After the Cold War, CMs eventually made their way back onto the international agenda, despite their more widespread possession and use. At least thirty-four countries produced cluster munitions, and at least seventy-seven stockpiled them.[36] But although Human Rights Watch began following CMs during the 1991 Gulf War, the ICBL feared that including them in the landmine campaign might prompt some states to withdraw.[37] It was not until 1999–2000 that NGOs began to organize more widely around CMs,[38] propelled both by landmine treaty success and by their widespread and sharply criticized use in Kosovo and Chechnya. Efforts gained further momentum in 2006 after Israel's use of cluster munitions in its war with Lebanon,[39] again showcasing CM use as a persistent landmine-like problem. Importantly, the success of the landmine treaty now made additional humanitarian arms control initiatives appear politically possible, set a new reputational standard by which to pressure states to commit, and supplied proponents with proven strategies to generate public attention and governmental support.

Thus, the CM campaign was neither a case of innovation born of the effects of protean power nor of "habit" created by APLs, but rather one of deliberate decision-making built on learning from an important success. The campaign did not invent new strategies, using instead what had worked for landmines and improvising on those strategies when met

---

[31] ICRC 1973, para. 150.   [32] Borrie 2009: 12–13.
[33] Hulme 2009: 220; Docherty 2009: 938; Borrie 2009: 14.   [34] Borrie 2009: 15.
[35] Borrie 2009: 11; Breitegger 2012: 21.   [36] Docherty 2009: 938.   [37] Borrie 2009: 40.
[38] The formal "Cluster Munition Coalition" did not form until 2003.
[39] For example, Barry et al. 1999; ICRC 2000. US cluster munition use also drew criticism in the 2003 Iraq War.

with control-power opposition. Like landmines, advocates framed CMs as problematic under existing international law, due to imprecise and therefore potentially indiscriminate targeting and to unreliable detonation, which might allow explosives to remain dormant but hazardous for long periods of time. Some small states adopted domestic bans as an example for others,[40] and together with NGOs framed the problem in ways similar to APLs (including as "de facto landmines"). Also like landmines, small states and NGOs led the creation of the Oslo Process outside the UN in 2007 after attempts to create a comprehensive ban within the CCW stagnated due to opposition from bigger states.[41]

Skeptical states used control power to reassert their opposition in the CM case, however. The United States, Russia, and others actively used CMs in conflict, saw them as useful weapons (a narrative advocates found more difficult to change in this case), and were even more resistant to restrictions on their military capabilities in the post-September 11 world. Rather than a total ban, the United States and other skeptical states advocated for CCW regulations, pointing to possible "technological fixes" for the indiscriminacy problem.[42] Once again, the CCW presented institutional advantages for these states. First, its decision-making rules allowed them better control over negotiation outcomes. Second, the institution had a much more lenient approach to weapons regulations in general, "wherein even the hypothetical possibility that a certain weapon might be used in a manner appropriate under [international humanitarian law] had been enough to argue against attempts to establish prohibitions."[43]

Although skeptical states' control power was again insufficient to keep negotiations in the CCW, it was sufficient to convince negotiators that they needed to temper opposition (or even win support) through compromise with some influential states. Advocates made creative use of definitions in the treaty text to allow for the comprehensive ban they sought with a scope restricted enough to appease some of its opponents. The CMC thus lays out a comprehensive ban for weapons falling within a carefully specified definition of CMs, thereby excluding all other munitions from the ban. This concession left open the possibility of legally developing "smarter" CMs with electronic self-destruct mechanisms and more accurate targeting,[44] without sacrificing the underlying legal and normative foundations of the ban.

Control power thus played a more prominent role, interacting with the effects of protean power, in the CMs case. Compared with the landmine

---

[40] Petrova 2007.   [41] Bolton and Nash 2010: 178.   [42] Mull 2008.
[43] Rappert and Moyes 2009: 246.   [44] Hulme 2009: 223.

treaty, support was not as widespread for the 2008 CMC, with its 107 original signatories and 100 state parties as of 2017. On the one hand, control power enabled skeptical states to push advocates to improvise on the Ottawa template and accept a less comprehensive agreement. On the other hand, control power made it possible for skeptical states to accept a compromise solution at all.[45] By providing the means to develop and integrate technological advances into their military arsenals, skeptical states could accept (and in some cases even sign) the CMC. Similar to APLs, the CMC has also further stigmatized CM-use, including by non-signatories, even as CMs have been recorded most recently in conflicts in Yemen, Syria, and elsewhere.[46] Yet, as the ATT case will show, without such technological alternatives, agreements may be even more restricted in scope.

The Conventional Arms Trade: Accommodating Control Power

The process of creating the 2013 Arms Trade Treaty gained momentum in 2006, overlapping with CMC negotiations. Yet from the start, advocates had to do even more to accommodate the preferences of states seeking to protect their control power resources. Small and major conventional weapons are a broad category of weapon, including guns, tanks, ships, military aircraft, and many more. States have never entertained a blanket ban on the trade or use of *all* conventional weapons, and, unlike APLs and CMs, NGOs have largely accepted regulations rather than prohibitions as their policy goal in order to make some kind of agreement possible. The rare multilateral initiatives to regulate the arms trade before the late 1990s came from major powers seeking to control access to clients and strategic regions, but failed to take hold as their political interests clashed.[47] Like the CMC, "responsible" arms trade initiatives have built on the success of the Ottawa Treaty and the changed expectations for "good" policy it created.[48] Yet the general public has been less engaged in the ATT process, and major powers have been much more integrated and accommodated. As a result, treaty scope and strength have been more restricted, pointing once again to limits on the effects of protean power in the complex post-9/11 security environment.

During the Cold War, conventional arms transfers were seen as a tool of superpower foreign policy and an economic necessity for European

---

[45] It is also worth noting that the global unpopularity of the United States in the late 2000s perhaps made its opposition less of an obstacle than it might have been, a dynamic that also unfolded with the ATT. Instead of seeing the United States as an example to follow, it was seen as an example to avoid.

[46] For example, HRW 2015.   [47] For an overview, see Erickson 2015.   [48] Ibid.

producers. Most states were therefore reluctant to place limits on their arms transfers, a policy tool associated directly with control power. The only activity came under US leadership during the Carter Administration, in response to the 1976 US presidential election in which the American public voiced unusual opposition to what it saw as "out of control" US arms exports to unstable regions.[49] The Carter Administration established unilateral criteria, including human rights, to restrict US arms export decision-making. It also proposed multilateral Conventional Arms Transfer (CAT) talks with the aim of restricting the volume of arms transfers to specific world regions.

Yet while control power might have enabled the United States to bring conventional arms to the table during the Cold War, it was insufficient to overcome significant internal and external opposition – also backed by considerable control power – to grapple with the issue. European arms producers declined to participate, wanting the superpowers to accept restrictions first. US–Soviet talks were stymied by clashing strategic interests between the two countries, who still wanted to use arms transfers to manage their alliance and client relationships, and by bureaucratic opposition in the United States over policy disagreements. The CAT talks finally fell apart as the Soviet Union invaded Afghanistan. Carter's unilateral attempt to link human rights performance to US arms transfers was also widely considered a failure, constantly sacrificed in order to use arms transfers to meet US security interests abroad.

Arms export controls returned to the international agenda after the end of the Cold War in two phases. First, the 1991 Gulf War shone an unexpected spotlight on "irresponsible" arms transfers to Iraq during the 1980s, which generated early – if less well-coordinated – momentum to identify and limit destabilizing arms transfers. The absence of the strategies and coalitions that would grow with the ICBL, however, meant that the first policy phase remained limited. In response to calls for arms trade transparency, the UN adopted a Register of Conventional Weapons in 1991, sponsored by Japan and the European Community. On the one hand, this was a path-breaking response to post-Gulf War public pressure: states had long considered confidentiality to be necessary for a smooth-functioning arms trade and their reputations as reliable arms suppliers. On the other hand, in order to encourage broad participation, transparency measures were voluntary, did not ask for information on price or type of weapon, and were not accompanied by any export control criteria. At first, they did not "even provide a precise definition of what constitutes an arms transfer or when a transfer takes place."[50] Broader,

---

[49] Pierre 1982: 46.   [50] Pierre 1997: 384.

more innovative initiatives were stopped in their infancy. Canada suggested involving more exporting states and more importing world regions, but the United States quickly limited the idea to the P5 exports to the Middle East only. Even then, the P5 talks failed to overcome politics and competition between the major powers, leaving arms export regulations seeming as elusive as ever.[51]

The second post-Cold War phase began with the success of the Ottawa Treaty, which generated momentum for dealing with humanitarian arms export controls directly. NGOs highlighted the control of small arms and light weapons (SALW) as the next arms control target after landmines.[52] They also took advantage of growing arms trade transparency, which yielded more information about states' export practices. The issue proved much more difficult than landmines, however. Unlike APLs, SALW are a broad category of conventional weapons, a cornerstone of states' military and police forces, a more profitable market, and impossible to categorically characterize as inherently indiscriminate.[53] In addition, NGOs were more divided on message and strategy, and public attention was more difficult to attract on the bureaucratic nuances of regulations rather than a clear-cut absolute ban. States were therefore the primary advocates in this case – still in partnership with Control Arms campaign-affiliated NGOs – but less willing to push initiatives as far as pro-control NGOs might have been on their own. Lead states, like the United Kingdom, did unexpectedly expand the initiative from SALWs to include both small and major conventional arms in 2005. But – with the exception of bringing relevant non-state actors (NGOs and occasionally defense industry representatives) into their negotiating delegations, in a sense co-opting them for both political insight and political cover – they also tended to stand by more conventional diplomatic strategies and avoided breaking away from UN negotiation frameworks.

In this case, bigger states most overtly invoked control power to resist policy initiatives and protect their ability to transfer arms in support of their domestic and foreign policy goals. Their less accommodating stance stemmed from two interrelated causes: the complex post-2001 security environment, which exacerbated their perceived need to preserve their arms export flexibility; and the lack of technological alternatives to work around broad export restrictions. The United States was the primary opponent of a legally binding treaty until late 2009. It used its institutional control power and dominant arms market position to squash multilateral controls on licit SALW transfers in 2001 and 2006, hold up formal ATT

---

[51] On the 1991–92 talks among the P5, see Pierre 1997.
[52] Lumpe 1999; McRae 2001; Renner 1997.   [53] Garcia 2006.

negotiations until late 2009, and delay finalizing the treaty in 2012. Yet proponents were reluctant to pursue a treaty without support from at least one of the world's top exporters (the United States or Russia), which they believed would have limited the ATT's support base, legitimacy, and potential effectiveness. ATT leaders therefore adapted their strategies in response to US opposition, delaying negotiations until US support could be acquired in late 2009. Later, to keep the United States on board, they modified treaty language in response to US preferences for flexibility, excluded provisions on non-state actors (a "red line" issue for the United States), and kept negotiations within UN consensus rules at US insistence.

Thus, ATT negotiations appear much more "traditional" and dominated by control power than its predecessors. Although the ATT owes its existence to changing policy expectations established by the landmine treaty, the process was more state-based and less NGO-driven. Leaders also deliberately held negotiations within the UN framework and left out provisions that might strengthen treaty content at the expense of its membership base and US support especially. As a result, the ATT excludes provisions on transfers to non-state actors, provides significant flexibility for national interpretation of its export criteria, and lacks enforcement mechanisms. Perhaps its most protean power moment was leaders' decision to move the final treaty vote from the consensus-based negotiation forum into the majoritarian UN General Assembly. Although the United States supported the ATT at the end of negotiations in March 2013, Iran, North Korea, and Syria blocked the consensus needed to open the treaty for signature. Institutional rules favored these weaker states in the context of consensus but were easily overridden in the April 2013 General Assembly vote, 154 to 3 (with 23 abstentions). The ATT came into effect in December 2014 and, in 2017, had 130 signatories (including the United States), with ninety ratifications/accessions.

Conclusions

Post-Cold War arms control has reflected an evolving interaction of control power and the effects of protean power, as state and non-state actors have responded to changing experiences of uncertainty in the international security environment. In the 1990s, small states and NGOs unexpectedly captured and redefined the international arms control agenda to reflect their values and interests, which they had been unable to do in the risk-dominant, control power environment of the Cold War. NGOs initiated the Ottawa Treaty and used innovative diplomatic strategies to generate public and governmental support. The outcome was both intentional in advocates' careful strategizing to make it possible and surprising in its rapid success. This success, in turn, has shaped subsequent arms control discussions, provided diplomatic strategies, and changed the standards by which "good" arms control policy is judged.

Yet the application of APL advocates' strategic innovation to later humanitarian arms control initiatives has been met, to varying degrees, by control power resistance. Advocates have had to adjust their strategies and compromise treaty contents in order to reach agreements. As a result, the competitive push and pull between control and protean power has had important consequences for the design and effects of humanitarian arms control agreements. When militarily strong states were able to rely on technological resources to work around CMC restrictions, those restrictions were less of an obstacle for negotiations, and the agreement was substantively stronger. When these states were unable to adapt to proposed ATT restrictions, however, they sought to weaken the agreement with more accommodating language and a further reduced scope. In this regard, the ATT case especially illustrates limits on the effects of protean power as it interacts with control power in complex security environments. Actors without control power may only be able to push so far against those that have it.

Moreover, while states and NGOs have been the primary players in the humanitarian arms control story, it is important to point out that defense companies have also played a significant, if quieter, part. Support from APL producers, for whom the expenses of landmine removal promised more profit than the sales of cheap landmines, helped to remove roadblocks to the Ottawa Treaty. In the ATT case, the defense industry worried first and foremost about its sales. Defense industry representatives therefore sought to have a say in treaty design and were more directly integrated into negotiations. Representatives from some lead states – who already faced national or regional "humanitarian" export criteria – also joined diplomatic delegations to promote similar criteria with defense industries in skeptical states and "level the playing field" for their own exports. While their support did not cause governments to commit to humanitarian arms control, the absence of their opposition made it politically and economically easier for many governments to do so.

What are the implications for pending arms control issues? In 2017, a group of non-nuclear weapons states and NGOs negotiated for a humanitarian ban on nuclear weapons, a popular proposal modeled on the APL and CM agreements. Nuclear weapons states and their allies opposed the treaty, however, and it seems unlikely that past strategies will produce similar effects on an issue they see as core to their national defense, especially absent an obvious technological work-around. In addition, some non-state advocates have begun to campaign to ban lethal autonomous weapons systems, or "killer robots." A ban would certainly tread new ground: it would be imposed on a weapon not yet in use, based on the presumed problem of assigning legal liability and responsibility for harmful effects they might cause,[54] rather than on established humanitarian consequences. This analysis suggests that NGO campaigning alone may be insufficient to move a ban forward without also acquiring substantial state support. Discussions have been introduced in the CCW, but states have been unwilling to do more than support a Group of Governmental Experts to study the issue. Many oppose outright a ban. Drones and cyber weapons also raise ethical and legal questions – but are weapons already in use. Norms may emerge in both cases.[55] Yet again, however, state support for formal prohibitions or regulations has so far appeared minimal. Indeed, the development of these weapons may partly be a response to pressures to regulate warfare more generally, reduce fatalities, and (in theory) improve targeting precision. In all cases, pro-control advocates will have to contend with opposition from big states and negotiate the interaction between control and protean power.

New and old weapons will continue to pose such problems, challenging the boundaries and agility of existing arms control laws and norms, and pitting the desires of some states to maximize their control power against the innovative tactics of those who seek to curb the destructive potential of violence. The outcomes will likely depend on the prevalence of risk and uncertainty in the international security environment and developments in defense technology. In this sense, history has changed more gradually than 1997 might have suggested at the time, as both sides continue to draw on and contribute to the circulation of power in world politics to resist, cope with, and promote change in international arms control policy.

---

[54] HRW and International Human Rights Clinic 2015.
[55] On cyber norm emergence, see Maurer 2011; on the need for drone norms, see Abizaid and Brooks 2014.

12 From Green to REDD: Protean Power and the Politics of Carbon Sinks

Jessica F. Green

Forests cover approximately 30 percent of the globe. Estimates suggest that deforestation and unsustainable use of forests are responsible for between 15 percent and 20 percent of annual greenhouse gas emissions.[1] And yet, until recently, deforestation has played a relatively small role in the international rules to govern climate change. From the negotiations on the Framework Convention on Climate Change in the late 1980s and early 1990s, through the development of the carbon markets of Kyoto, only a tiny fraction of intergovernmental efforts has focused on maintaining or enhancing the world's forests. Addressing deforestation seriously entered the climate agenda about eight years ago – despite the fact that carbon "sinks" are a critical component in managing climate change.

Why did this happen? How was the issue of carbon sinks transformed from a footnote in the climate regime to the lead story? This transformation was, in part, the result of the emergence of protean power stemming from the actions of environmental NGOs. Using past experience in forestry and their political acuity, NGOs responded to political defeat in their advocacy efforts with improvisation. In so doing, they helped to bring the issue of sinks to the fore. The end result was the eventual incorporation of protean power within a more traditional frame of control power. This "nested" relationship between the two forms of power shows that this is a limited case of protean power, where complex layers are only evident through an historical analysis.

This chapter demonstrates that NGOs' role in sinks policy is a limited case of protean power, which arose because their material endowments – a virtual monopoly on expertise about the measurement of carbon sinks early in the policy process – eventually coincided with a political window of opportunity, which they recognized and acted upon.

NGOs were the first to develop methods to measure carbon sequestered in carbon sinks, such as forests and grasslands. Since measurement

[1] Intergovernmental Panel on Climate Change (IPCC) 2007.

is a prerequisite for market transactions, these NGOs possessed a body of knowledge that intergovernmental bodies did not. When carbon sinks were virtually eliminated from the global carbon market created by the Kyoto Protocol, NGOs became regulators in their own right, creating a separate "voluntary" market for carbon offsets, which included carbon sinks. (Since NGOs are serving as private regulators, I use the two terms interchangeably throughout the chapter.)

The surprise in the carbon sinks story is that the voluntary market did not exist only in parallel to the Kyoto markets. The twists and turns in the intergovernmental climate negotiations, coupled with NGO improvisation resulted in protean power: ultimately, environmental NGOs moved beyond the realm of partnering with corporations to shaping interstate bargaining as it evolved. Here, protean power emerged as an effect of NGOs' response to a fluid political situation.

Moreover, and consistent with protean power, these outcomes could not have been anticipated at the outset. NGOs were engaged in a constant process of evolution and adaptation, as a way of maintaining their strategic relevance through the ebbs and flows of the intergovernmental process. Yet, in the end, the practice of protean power was firmly nested within control power. A hierarchy was established, in which practices developed by NGOs were translated and then appropriated into the intergovernmental process. In this sense, the sinks case is an outlier among other cases in the volume as an example of relatively limited protean power.

The role of uncertainty in this case is also somewhat of an outlier. Climate change is perhaps the *most* uncertain of all issues discussed in this volume. The radical uncertainty surrounding increased concentrations of greenhouse gases in the atmosphere is profound, including the threat of abrupt changes in the climate and accelerating positive feedbacks. *Even if* scientists could predict temperature changes accurately, there would still be uncertainty about the consequences of these changes. Wagner and Weitzmann illustrate this contrast quite clearly, noting that "as recently as 2007, consensus science predicted an Arctic free of summer sea ice by the latter half of the century. Today, we are on track to have this occur in closer to ten than fifty years, even though our temperature estimates have not changed."[2]

Yet the policy responses to climate change do not reflect the reality of this radical uncertainty. Indeed, the intergovernmental process appears to be almost willfully blind to it. In general, traditional approaches to policymaking (i.e., control power) do not mix well with radical

[2] Wagner and Zeckhauser 2016.

uncertainty. As Sabel and Victor note, deep uncertainty about the "feasibility of achieving policy outcomes, such as lower emissions, at acceptable costs" makes policymaking under conditions of radical uncertainty very challenging.[3] A common response, then, is to focus on what is knowable, assuming a world of risk, rather than one of unknown unknowns. In "risk-based models of power-as-control [actors] assume that they are playing the odds" (Chapter 1, p. 12). Such assumptions, though perhaps inapt, make decision-making easier.

Ironically, this is precisely what happened in the case of climate policy – where radical uncertainty is profound and pervasive, though conspicuously absent from the policymaking process. Most discussions surrounding carbon sinks were limited to operational uncertainty, over which actors can attempt to assert control. Though this is not the usual condition that facilitates protean power; in the instance of carbon sinks, private regulators were able to leverage this operational uncertainty by developing policy tools to create and successfully commodify carbon sinks. This initial operational uncertainty about how to *do* carbon sink projects enabled the emergence of protean power. This is distinct, however, from power that might emerge from the radical uncertainty surrounding the broader effects of climate change. Unable to access the underlying context of radical uncertainty, protean power did not generate more uncertainty, as is described by Bridgen and Andreas in the migration case (Chapter 5). Innovation quickly abated, and was circumscribed – and ultimately nested within the larger ambit of control power.

The relatively restricted role of protean power is both a story of the success of control power as well as one of limiting uncertainty to a less radical form, though in practice it is difficult to disentangle the two. Either way, the effects of protean power are fairly circumscribed. The incorporation of private rules on carbon sinks into public regulations is small. Thus, it fails to catalyze the generative effects that Seybert and Katzenstein describe (Chapter 1, pp. 10–11). Only a small number of public policies on carbon offsets draw on private rules, and, even then, they do so largely for voluntary, rather than compliance-based programs.[4] In this case, protean power results from improvisation, but is then promptly subsumed into traditional hierarchical models of authority. Thus, in the end, *protean power as an effect of private actors' efforts is indistinguishable from the status quo of control power*. Without looking at the provenance of individual rules, it is impossible to detect the fingerprints of improvisation and early innovation.

[3] Sabel and Victor 2015: 4.   [4] Green 2017.

Carbon Sinks: An Early History

Carbon sinks sequester carbon dioxide in living matter, such as forests, grasslands, and other terrestrial ecosystems. Given that land-use conversion and deforestation comprise such a large fraction of global emissions, slowing this process through the preservation of carbon sinks is a potentially powerful tool for combatting climate change.

Using carbon sinks as a policy tool is not a new idea. As early as the 1980s, a number of international environmental NGOs created "debt-for-nature swaps." The precursor to the commodification of carbon was conservation projects, which paid developing country governments to keep trees in the ground. NGOs raised money to purchase the debt of a developing country. In exchange for the cancellation of debt, the developing country agreed to enact conservation measures, usually in the form of protecting large swathes of forests.

The first debt-for-nature swap agreement was concluded in 1987 between Conservation International (CI) and the government of Bolivia. CI purchased US$650,000 of Bolivian debt (for US$100,000) and in exchange, Bolivia enhanced legal protections of the Beni Biosphere Reserve, and created surrounding protected areas. It also provided local funds to finance the activities therein.[5] By the early 1990s, these types of transactions had become a significant phenomenon; twenty-three debt-for-nature swaps were active in 1992 in fourteen countries, ranging from South America to Africa.[6] All were initiated by environmental NGOs. These efforts were focused more on the preservation of biological diversity than on the climate benefits of sequestering carbon; indeed, climate change had barely appeared on the international agenda at that time.

In addition to debt-for-nature swaps with governments, a number of international NGOs cooperated with large corporations to help them offset their carbon emissions. Applied Energy Services worked with the World Resources Institute, CARE, the Nature Conservancy, and Oxfam to plant trees, fund conservation zones, and promote proper land titling to indigenous peoples to preserve tropical rainforests.[7] The Nature Conservancy also created one of the longest-running carbon offset projects in concert with a Bolivian NGO and three energy corporations, the Noel Kempff project.[8] The project has been operating continuously since 1997, and is expected to avoid emissions of 7–10 million metric tons of carbon over thirty years.[9] It has since been

---

[5] Resor 1997.   [6] Deacon and Murphy 1997.   [7] Moura Costa and Stewart 1998.
[8] See at: www.forestcarbonportal.com/project/noel-kempff-mercado-climate-action-project.
[9] The Nature Conservancy 2009.

re-born as a pilot project under the UN REDD program. REDD is shorthand for "reducing emissions from deforestation and forest degradation, and is a fancy way of saying "keeping trees, grasslands, and other carbon dioxide-absorbing plants in the ground." UN REDD is one of the many REDD-related programs, and serves as an umbrella organization for the large swathe of international organizations working on REDD.

These activities were the beginnings of protean power that would unexpectedly emerge in later phases of the climate regime. Through the creation of debt-for-nature swaps and other offset projects, environmental NGOs developed both expertise and know-how not present among other actors; this laid the foundation for their future role as private regulators.

As we will see, in later phases of the climate regime, states became interested in reviving carbon sinks as a policy, but lacked the key knowledge to implement it. The first phase of carbon sinks history demonstrates one key characteristic of protean power of this case: actors' knowledge is not homogeneous. Information available to NGOs was not available to others; their early experience in establishing tools for measurement and creating and commodifying carbon sinks provided them with key knowledge that would be the source of protean power to them in future phases of the climate regime.

Negotiating the Kyoto Protocol: Leveraging Expertise

Environmental NGOs' early experiences with carbon sinks quickly began to pay dividends. In the negotiations on the Kyoto Protocol in the late 1990s and early 2000s, they were able to parlay the expertise they had cultivated into a decisive force in the intergovernmental negotiations. This force was not so much protean power – since radical uncertainty about the effects of climate change was far removed from the policy debates – but at the nexus between protean and control power. The fluidity of the negotiations allowed NGOs to exercise considerable influence over the discussions around sinks, and, eventually, to ensure that sinks were effectively *excluded* from the market mechanisms of the Kyoto Protocol.

In the intergovernmental arena, the issue of carbon sinks first surfaced in the drafting of the Framework Convention on Climate Change in 1992, but at that point they were discussed only in the most cursory fashion. The real debate about sinks did not begin until the negotiations on the Kyoto Protocol, and, specifically, in the design of the Clean Development Mechanism (CDM). The CDM is one of three market mechanisms created by the Protocol.[10] It allows developed countries to meet their reduction targets by paying for emissions reductions in the developing world. However, when it was agreed to in 1997, the CDM was little more than an idea. The so-called "Kyoto surprise" was agreed to at the last minute, without any details about how it would actually function.[11] As a result, the role of sinks in the CDM was not discussed until after Kyoto was signed, with the bulk of the debate occurring between 1997 and 2001.[12]

The last minute insertion of the CDM was critical in many respects. First, it made the whole agreement possible; it provided a much needed "escape hatch" in the event that countries were unable to meet their reduction commitments domestically. Second, it created a great deal of policy uncertainty. Though states agreed to the basic principles of the CDM, major decisions about how it would actually function were postponed until later. Third, despite postponing key design issues, states did agree to incentivize an early start to the CDM. Article 12, paragraph 10 of the Kyoto Protocol states, "Certified emission reductions obtained during the period from the year 2000 up to the beginning of the first commitment period can be used to assist in achieving compliance in the first commitment period." This language indicates that early actions could be counted under the CDM, even before the Kyoto Protocol entered into force, and even before states figured out what "counting" really meant.

Thus, even before entry into force, the creation of the CDM set new processes in motion. Those who sought recognition for early action would need ways to demonstrate that action. Thus, shortly after the signature of the Kyoto Protocol in 1997, the process to draft rules began.

The rule-making period was extremely contentious, largely because of an acrimonious debate about the appropriate role of sinks in the CDM. States quickly divided on the issue. The negotiating bloc representing the largest group of developed country emitters strongly supported the use of sinks as a way for developed countries to meet their reduction targets.[13] The G77 and China, the largest negotiating bloc of developing countries, objected to their use on the grounds that the Protocol should not include any joint measures, but rather should focus solely on developed country

---

[10] It should be noted that the Kyoto Protocol created two other market mechanisms: joint implementation and international emissions trading. However, the CDM was by far the largest and most complex of the three; as such, I limit my inquiry to the CDM.

[11] Werksman 1998.

[12] For a technical account of the issues from an insider perspective, see Fry 2002; 2007.

[13] This was the so-called JUSCANNZ bloc – Japan, the United States, Canada, Australia, Norway, and New Zealand.

action.[14] Indeed, in its proposed negotiating text, it removed all references to sinks.[15]

In addition, most civil society groups participating in the negotiations were also opposed to the inclusion of sinks in the CDM on scientific, moral, and efficacy grounds. Under the auspices of the transnational advocacy network, the Climate Action Network (CAN), they initially pushed for safeguards and other policies that would ensure that sinks projects would not threaten biodiversity or indigenous peoples, and that projects actually produced emissions reductions. Once it became clear that such rules would not be included, they lobbied against the inclusion of sinks as an allowable type of offset project in the CDM. CAN argued that sinks would be hard to measure, would absolve developed countries of obligations to reduce emissions domestically, and, in the end, might not actually reduce overall emissions.[16]

From a moral perspective, they argued that sinks would effectively serve as a loophole, allowing developed countries to avoid strong emissions reductions policies at home. (Since technically, there is no limit to the supply of offsets, prices would not necessarily rise in response to increasing demand.) Indeed, domestic inaction was a distinct possibility, depending on the amount of reductions allowed via sinks and other types of offset. The efficacy arguments suggested that the challenges of calculating the level of emissions reductions against a hypothetical baseline (how much carbon would be emitted in the *absence* of the project?) would mean little in the way of actual reductions.[17] One prominent member of CAN, speaking on behalf of his organization, argued that the inclusion of sinks combined might even permit an *increase* in emissions.[18]

These different views were further exacerbated by a relative lack of scientific consensus on the matter. In 1998, as states began to consider the design of the Kyoto Protocol, and its market mechanisms, the Subsidiary Body on Scientific and Technical Advice (SBSTA) asked the Intergovernmental Panel on Climate Change (IPCC) to prepare a special report on land-use change and forestry (i.e., sinks) to help inform the

---

[14] The exception was a small group of Latin American countries that supported the inclusion of sinks. For further details on various nations' positions, see Boyd, Corbera, and Estrada 2008.

[15] UNFCCC 2000. It is worth noting that there were some notable dissenters within the bloc, including the heavily forested nation of Brazil.

[16] These arguments are made repeatedly in the newsletter published by CAN, which was, at the time, the main transnational advocacy network active in the climate negotiations. Some members of CAN, notably those in the United States, did not support the proposed exclusion of sinks, and lobbied for other outcomes. However, the majority of CAN members were in fact opposed. See Duwe 2001; Pulver 2002.

[17] Lecocq and Ambrosi 2007.   [18] Earth Negotiations Bulletin 2000.

negotiations. Many hoped that clear definitions of basic concepts such as forests, afforestation, reforestation, and deforestation would help states to build political consensus.

However, when the report was released in 2000, it did little to advance the collective discussion on sinks. One scholar notes that the IPCC special report "had not brought an end to the epistemic chaos generated by the sink concept."[19] The lack of scientific consensus contributed to an unanticipated chain of events, and, as we will see below, this provided the opportunity for protean power to emerge. In the absence of epistemic consensus, states staked out different approaches to the measurement of sinks, using approaches consistent with their political preferences.[20] This hodge-podge approach continued, and provided the space for the increasingly vociferous objections of environmental NGOs. Their objections almost derailed the negotiations.[21]

The result of this controversy is that sinks play a very limited role in the Kyoto Protocol. Although they are permitted in the CDM, sinks are limited to afforestation and reforestation activities – or more simply, "the establishment of trees on non-treed land."[22] This meant that "avoided deforestation" – that is, keeping trees in the ground – was not permissible under the rules. Sinks projects were also limited temporally to the first commitment period of Kyoto, and quantitatively to 1 percent of 1990 emissions levels times five.[23] These restrictions are evident in the data on the CDM: less than 1 percent of registered CDM projects fall under the category of afforestation and reforestation.[24]

A conventional reading of this debate is one of failed (or only semi-successful) advocacy by NGOs – a classic case of control power. But a more accurate interpretation, seen through the longer timeline, is as an incomplete case of protean power. Environmental NGOs had worked on sinks initiatives long before the arcane debates surrounding the CDM arose. As a result, they had both knowledge and expertise that others involved in the rule-making process did not. Even the IPCC – ostensibly the designated expert – did not make authoritative claims to knowledge that were expected of it. Thus, the common knowledge assumption operating in conceptualizations of control power did not hold. In one view, environmental NGOs had a relative monopoly on expertise around sinks: they were among the few who had actually *done* the work on these types of offset projects.

Yet, as Seybert and Katzenstein note, protean power generally operates under conditions of radical uncertainty; this scope condition is more

---

[19] Lovbrand 2009.   [20] Fry 2002.   [21] Boyd, Corbera, and Estrada 2008.
[22] Watson et al. 2000, ch. 2.   [23] UNFCCC 2002, Decision 17/CP.7.
[24] See at: https://cdm.unfccc.int/Statistics/Public/files/201605/proj_reg_byScope.pdf.

complex in the sinks case. Though clearly, there is radical uncertainty surrounding the effects of climate change, the intergovernmental negotiations took place within a simpler context of calculable political risk. Thus, there is room for protean power, even in cases of operational uncertainty. As they note, protean power is generated in specific moments (Chapter 1, p. 10). The pitched political battle over sinks in the CDM created one of those moments.

The epistemic advantages enjoyed by environmental NGOs can therefore be seen as conferring capabilities in probabilistic situations (intergovernmental negotiations) nested within a more uncertain context (the tangible effects of climate change on the planet). Risks nested within a larger context of radical uncertainty did not enable protean power: private regulators did not use agility to improvise or adapt to uncertainty until *after* their efforts at sinks advocacy had failed (see next section below). However, they were able to refuse the complete exercise of control power (Chapter 2, Figure 2.1). The result was the near-exclusion of sinks from the rules governing the CDM.

Parallel Relations: The Rise of the Voluntary Market

The bulk of the debate about sinks was concluded in 2000 in Marrakesh, Morocco.[25] In addition to settling on the rules for the CDM, states also decided that the new market could become operational, even though the Kyoto Protocol had yet to enter into force. The logic to the early start was not only to get the CDM market off the ground, but also to incentivize early reductions, which could eventually be counted toward compliance requirements once Kyoto was legally binding.

The effective exclusion of sinks projects from the CDM, coupled with its early operation, spurred a new phase in the development of sinks in policy and practice. As the Kyoto markets got underway, NGOs involved in early sinks projects and in the debates over CDM design turned to a new strategy: creating their own rules to govern and sell forest carbon.

This "voluntary" market existed alongside the compliance market of the Kyoto Protocol, and grew quickly in the early 2000s. The voluntary market targeted actors – mostly firms – that *chose* to offset their emissions, even though they were not (or not yet) legally bound to do so. Most participants were (and remain) corporate actors gesturing toward their

---

[25] UNFCCC 2002. There were still outstanding technical decisions to be taken about the definitions of afforestation and reforestation, which would affect the CDM; however, the major components of the institution had been agreed upon.

"greenness" through the purchase of offsets in the voluntary market. Some are NGOs, and a small number are individuals.[26]

The voluntary market grew quickly. Between 2000 and 2014, almost forty private offset standards were created, many focused on sinks.[27] The value of the voluntary market, though much smaller than the CDM market, also exploded in the early 2000s, in the limbo years before Kyoto took effect. By 2008, the voluntary market had transacted more than fifteen times more carbon credits than the CDM.[28] Many of the private standards that govern offsets in the voluntary market aim to achieve goals beyond the reduction of greenhouse gas emissions. For example, some promote sustainable livelihoods, while others seek to preserve biodiversity. In short, many of these private regulators have chosen a "niche" not covered by the CDM.[29]

Moreover, despite a very limited role in the CDM, sinks comprise a major part of the voluntary market for carbon offsets. In 2013, the voluntary market transacted US$140 million in forest carbon credits (i.e., sinks). By contrast, the equivalent figure for the CDM market was just US$0.2 million.[30]

Not only does the voluntary market deploy sinks projects widely, they are considered part of best practice. The International Carbon Reduction and Offset Alliance was created in 2008 "to promote best practices in the [voluntary carbon] market."[31] Since then, it has created a code of good practice for carbon management, which includes standards on carbon offsets. The code endorses five private offset standards, all of which include sinks. In other words, as private regulators seek to ensure quality and bring uniformity to their rules and standards, they have chosen to include sinks as part of this definition.

Early experiences with debt-for-nature swaps and corporate conservation efforts generated expertise among these NGOs, which they then parlayed into private authority – where non-state actors make rules and set standards that other actors in world politics adopt.[32] Their monopoly on expertise provided claims to legitimate authority, and hands-on experience when others had none. These demonstrable successes were critical in the rise of protean power: they were able to overcome the operational uncertainty surrounding sinks – which, as we will see, was important in future phases of policymaking.

Consistent with protean power, improvisation is evident in the rise of the voluntary market. The political losses in the CDM negotiations prompted a new tack by environmental NGOs. Affirmation bred

---

[26] Hamrick and Goldstein 2015.   [27] Green 2017.   [28] Hamilton et al. 2010.
[29] Abbott, Green, and Keohane 2016.   [30] Goldstein and Gonzalez 2014.
[31] See at: www.icroa.org/About-ICROA.   [32] Green 2014.

improvisation. Previous failures at control demonstrated that a new tack was needed, one in which the probability or type of success could not necessarily be calculated *ex ante*. NGOs transformed themselves from advocates to regulators.

From Green to REDD: Translating Private Practice to Public Rules

As the voluntary market gathered steam, carbon sinks re-entered the intergovernmental climate negotiations – this time in the form of "REDD": reducing emissions from deforestation and forest degradation. This third phase of sinks policy, marked by the rise of REDD, demonstrates yet another shift in the relationship between protean and control power.

In the third phase, protean and control power interact in two ways: through translation and appropriation. As Seybert and Katzenstein note, translation occurs when power is exercised across heterogeneous groups, often through non-central actors. Rather than delegating power from one group to another (an example of control power), translation occurs when "agents observe would-be commands, following their own specific reasons as they translate, or are enrolled into, the projects of those who wield control power" (Chapter 2, p. 32). Private actors in the voluntary market used REDD as a mechanism to translate their preferences and experience into the evolving practice of sinks policy, as elaborated by states. Conversely, states appropriated the work done in the voluntary market as part of the broader REDD initiative. In this way, protean power was circumscribed within a broader structure, dominated by control power.

Translation

As the third phase of sinks policy demonstrates, private actors' limited protean power took yet another new form when the political context around sinks changed. States' renewed interest in sinks created a window of opportunity for private actors, who were now serving as regulators of the voluntary carbon offset market. They were able to leverage their long-standing experience and know-how; as such, translation gave rise to protean power.

In 2005, Costa Rica and Papua New Guinea (PNG) – two heavily forested countries – proposed that states consider additional ways to reduce emissions by addressing one of its largest sources: deforestation.[33] They founded and were soon backed by a larger "Coalition for Rainforest Nations," which advocated for new policies to address avoided deforestation and forest

---

[33] UNFCCC 2005.

degradation – the very activities that were excluded from the CDM.[34] These categories of activities were excluded at the outset for fear that they would create perverse incentives for developing countries to threaten to cut down forests in order to receive funding for their "protection."

In the proposal, Costa Rica and PNG insisted that "their emphasis is on carbon emissions, not 'sinks.'"[35] Yet REDD is clearly a sink by another name: what was once avoided deforestation was reborn with a new name and lots of political support.[36]

REDD was a clear call for experimentation – a way to reduce states' uncertainty about how to "do" sinks policy. Local uncertainty was a factor in REDD's creation: states had only limited knowledge about sinks; this would have to be corrected if REDD were to be adopted as climate policy. The Costa Rica and PNG proposal was an incremental and non-binding way to correct this "operational" uncertainty.

Thus, in 2007, following the lead of Costa Rica and PNG, states endorsed a multifaceted approach, encouraging parties "to explore a range of actions ... including demonstration activities" to preserve carbon sinks.[37] The decision also provides guidelines on the methods and approaches to use. However, the breadth and flexibility of the guidelines indicate that they are essentially a carte blanche to all those interested to go forth and experiment.

A number of international organizations have organized REDD programs – viewing this as a way to participate in climate policy, and potentially garner more resources.[38] The most prominent is UN REDD, which was launched in 2008 to run demonstration projects to ascertain how REDD could be carried out in practice. It is a collaboration of the Food and Agriculture Organization, the UN Development Programme, and the UN Environment Programme. There are now national programs in sixteen countries, funded by approximately $US120 million in contributions by Denmark, Japan, Norway, and Spain.[39] There are a variety of other efforts by international organizations, including the Forest Carbon Partnership Facility (run by the World Bank); the Forest Investment

---

[34] The Coalition for Rainforest Nations began as Bolivia, Central African Republic, Chile, Congo, Costa Rica, Democratic Republic of the Congo, Dominican Republic, and Nicaragua, and has since expanded considerably into an intergovernmental organization comprising both developed and developing nations.

[35] UNFCCC 2005.

[36] There has been an evolution from RED to REDD to REDD+, where each successive version includes more activities. RED included only avoiding deforestation and was the acronym describing the original Costa Rican and PNG proposal. REDD adds the additional category of forest degradation. REDD+ includes other measures to sustainably manage forests.

[37] UNFCCC 2007.   [38] Jinnah 2011.   [39] See at: www.un-redd.org.

Program (run jointly by multilateral development banks); and the International Climate and Forest Initiative (funded by Norway). The Global Environment Facility also funds projects on sustainable forest management and REDD. The Coalition for Rainforest Nations, the original proponents of REDD, also have a host of activities to promote its implementation at the national level.

The intergovernmental call and international organizations' response can be viewed as a classic example of control power. States took a decision, setting an agenda for action, and empowering agents with the appropriate capabilities and resources to respond. The flexibility in agents' choice of response should not be conflated with protean power, since the structures clearly indicate and circumscribe the desired outcomes. Direct action leads to a set of anticipated, though not previously specified outcomes: control power in practice.

By contrast, the involvement of environmental NGOs and other private actors in REDD can be viewed as an act of translation and an effect of protean power. The voluntary market, somewhat unexpectedly, became an important site for implementing REDD. Private actors were able to use their existing knowledge and activities through unanticipated channels – yet these were in the service of the exercise of control power.

Following the Costa Rica/PNG call for experimentation, there was a precipitous increase in the amount of forest carbon traded on the voluntary market. In 2009, the think-tank EcoSystem Marketplace noted that despite measuring transactions since before 2002, two-thirds of all market value for forestry credits occurred between 2007 and mid-2009.[40] This significant uptick clearly coincides with the emergence of REDD on the intergovernmental agenda. Moreover, their research shows that in 2009, 96 percent of all carbon sink projects came from the voluntary market.[41] What was once a separate market, created largely in response to the discontent with control power, now became the primary locus for sinks activities. By contrast, and as noted earlier, sinks projects were nearly non-existent in the CDM: fewer than 1 percent of all CDM projects were sinks projects.

Indeed, a more careful look at the voluntary market demonstrates how private regulators were able to translate their existing activities into REDD activities. For instance, despite the fact that REDD was initially a state proposal, to be incorporated into the intergovernmental climate regime, a private regulator, the Verified Carbon Standard, was the first entity to transact REDD credits.[42] In addition, some of the earliest conservation projects have been converted by private actors into REDD projects under the intergovernmental regime. For example, the previously

[40] Hamilton et al. 2009: xii.   [41] Hamilton et al. 2010.   [42] Reuters 2011.

mentioned Noel Kempff conservation project was initiated by environmental NGOs in 1997; it has since been transformed into a REDD project under the auspices of the intergovernmental regime.

In addition, two privately created carbon standards, the Verified Carbon Standard and the Climate, Community and Biodiversity Alliance[43] (CCBA) created rules governing REDD, specifically for the purpose of being integrated into domestic regulatory regimes. The CCBA standard, called REDD+SES, is specifically designed to be used by governments at multiple scales: "to support the development and implementation of effective social and environmental safeguards for government-led strategies and action plans for REDD+."[44] Five nations – Ecuador, Nepal, Tanzania, Brazil, and Indonesia – are currently implementing the standard. All but Indonesia have government representatives participating in the standards committee, which oversees standards development and implementation.

The Verified Carbon Standard is also targeting governments as end users of its standards. It has created what is referred to as a "nested REDD" standard, which allows bottom-up REDD projects to nest within existing regulatory frameworks. This name is appropriate, given that it can also be construed as a manifestation of the nesting of protean power within the broader ambit of control power. According to the program's website, it "establishes a clear pathway for existing and new subnational jurisdictional activities and projects to be integrated (or 'nested') within broader (higher-level) jurisdictional REDD+ programs."[45] Like the REDD+SES standard, it is being piloted in multiple nations. Its advisory council includes representatives from states as well as NGOs.

In sum, the renewed interest in sinks, now dubbed REDD, allowed for a happy coalescence between control and protean power. The voluntary market became a legitimate place where a once-ostracized policy could be successfully implemented. This allowed private actors to engage in translation – bringing their "outsider" efforts within the ambit of control power.

Appropriation

From the perspective of states, now demanding the incorporation of sinks into intergovernmental policy, the intersection of control and protean power can be viewed as an act of appropriation. By the time the REDD proposal emerged, carbon sinks projects were now a long-standing policy,

---

[43] Technically, CCBA is a "tag," not a carbon standard. It enumerates criteria for carbon reduction projects to ensure their sustainability, but does not contain rules for measuring emissions reductions.

[44] See at: www.redd-standards.org/redd-ses.   [45] See at: www.v-c-s.org/JNR.

vetted by many, and increasingly bought and sold on the voluntary market. With less operational uncertainty surrounding them, they could be safely brought into the ambit of control power.

The reversal is striking. The Costa Rica/PNG proposal did not spark the same acrimonious objections that surrounded the CDM negotiations. In fact, the opposite was true: previously opposed actors embraced REDD. The EU had opposed all manner of flexibility mechanisms, including sinks in the CDM. By contrast, in July 2008, the EU tabled a proposal to promote REDD activities, which emphatically endorsed the potential of sinks to combat climate change: "We shall not, in the EU's view, succeed in limiting global warming to 2 degrees Celsius without efforts in all sectors. This includes action to reduce emissions from deforestation and forest degradation."[46]

China also did an about-face. As part of the G77, it had earlier tabled a proposal that systematically deleted all references to sinks. Now, China called for "innovative incentives . . . for emission reductions from avoided deforestation, conservation, sustainable management of forests and enhancement of forest carbon stocks in developing countries."[47]

Finally, the CAN followed states' lead. It had lobbied extensively to exclude sinks, and particularly avoided deforestation from the CDM, but it also changed its views. In 2006, it tabled a position paper in which it "strongly welcomes the initiative to discuss reducing emissions from deforestation as proposed by PNG and Costa Rica and discussed at COP-11 in Montreal."[48] Shortly thereafter a representative of Greenpeace addressed the plenary on behalf of CAN, noting that a discussion about deforestation was "long overdue."[49]

Conclusion: The Productive Intersection of Protean and Control Power

By 2006, the acrimony and contention surrounding sinks had all but disappeared. While a full explanation of this shift is beyond the scope of this chapter, the improvisation of private actors, in their creation of the voluntary market was at the very least a contribution to this renewed enthusiasm for sinks in a number of different ways. The early entry of private actors in the world of carbon sinks led to several unanticipated, and arguably unintentional, outcomes.

First, their expertise led to strong views about what was and was not desirable in the realm of forest carbon. In turn, this led to the mobilization

---

[46] UNFCCC 2008a. See FCCC/SBSTA/2008/MISC.4.   [47] UNFCCC 2008b.
[48] CAN 2006.   [49] CAN 2007.

of advocacy efforts, and successful refusal: in part due to their advocacy efforts, private actors were able to keep most sinks projects *out* of the CDM. As Seybert and Katzenstein point out (Chapter 1, Figure 1.1), their successful refusal was a preliminary step – and likely a necessary condition – for the innovation that later produced protean power.

Second, with the knowledge developed through early "green" conservation projects, private actors seized upon the exclusion of sinks in the CDM as an opportunity. They reoriented their efforts, transforming themselves from advocates to regulators. This shift cemented their protean power, albeit in a limited fashion. The voluntary market became *the* locus for sinks projects, rendering the intergovernmental markets (i.e., control power), all but irrelevant. Instead of further fights over what the regulatory framework for sinks would look like, would-be consumers simply took their preferences to the voluntary market. Since the emissions reductions required by Kyoto were relatively modest, sinks did not *have* to be part of the bargain. An easier solution, recognized by environmental NGOs, was to create a market for willing participants where they would not be bogged down by political constraints.

In the first two phases of sinks policy, the effects of NGO improvisation were certainly limited. The voluntary market was (and remains) a fraction of the size of carbon markets created to comply with domestic and international climate regulations. The voluntary market, while an important realm for policy experimentation, was politically at the margins of the climate debate. Until it wasn't.

The gridlock in the negotiations led states to look for new policy areas upon which they could begin to build consensus and action. Sinks, previously abandoned as too politically contentious and too difficult to measure, were resurrected. The new emphasis on finding common ground, coupled with an understanding of the limits that uncertainty imposed, created yet another shift in sinks policy – and an opportunity for a largely compatible confluence of protean and control power.

This confluence is consistent with experimentalist accounts of governance, which identify uncertainty as an important driver of successful cooperation. Sabel and Victor describe an "experimentalist governance" approach to climate policy: "Experimentalist governance emphasizes that regulator and regulated, alike, rarely know what is feasible when they begin to tackle a problem under uncertainty; it prizes a diversity of efforts rather than monopoly. It identifies and continuously improves upon solutions that work."[50]

---

[50] Sabel and Victor 2015: 4.

This relatively easy arrangement can be attributed to the fact that protean power was translated and nested within the overarching framework of control power. Environmental NGOs and others in the voluntary market translated their goals into those that were compatible with the larger objectives of REDD. Ayoub (Chapter 4) makes a similar point about translation in the context of LGBT rights in Europe. Despite the universality of human rights, advocates had to engage in the translation of universal norms to "local" practice. This local tailoring of rights-based claims allowed LGBT advocates in Poland to overcome homophobic claims that sexual rights were incongruent with national identity.

The nesting of protean power within control power met the political aspirations of all the actors involved, without any serious challenges to the status quo. As a result, there was minimal pushback. Nesting resulted in the appropriation of private rules by states. In a way, appropriation can be viewed as the desired pinnacle of protean power in the case of sinks: private rules are legitimated through their incorporation into public rules. Protean power becomes invisible, taking on the mantle of traditional hierarchical structures.

By contrast, Erickson's (Chapter 11) case on arms control shows how protean power directly challenged states' freedom to defend themselves in the manner of their choosing. As a result, powerful states developed technological work-arounds to arms restrictions wherever possible, and, absent the ability to dodge new rules, they challenged them directly. In the sinks case, such challenges were rendered moot through processes of appropriation.

In cases of limited uncertainty, such as this one, nesting is perhaps the most desirable outcome for private regulators. Radical uncertainty is a scope condition for protean power, but it was simply too far removed from the political discussion to have any generative effects. The radical uncertainty surrounding the effects of climate change is a separate consideration from the nuts and bolts of carbon markets. Thus, private regulators – those exercising some degree of protean power – did the best they could, given the constraints they faced.

This is not to say that protean power is absent from the story of sinks. Two decades of experience with carbon sinks produced a surprising, and initially unknowable, outcome – the nesting of protean power within a larger framework of control power. The de facto uncertainty of previous phases of sinks policy helped environmental NGOs to develop the expertise, and eventually the power, to create and implement rules governing carbon sinks. As Seybert and Katzenstein note, the unforeseen outcomes of previous activities are emblematic of protean power: "Under conditions of uncertainty it is not necessarily strategic actions but their emerging byproducts that create the most consequential effects" (Chapter 1, p. 16). *Ex post*, as observers we can see that NGOs' loss on their campaign against sinks was a decisive moment in the production of protean power. It precipitated their shift from advocates to regulators and further embedded their operational expertise.

Moreover, there were some unanticipated outcomes along the way. Despite the expansive set of rules created by the Kyoto Protocol – easily conceptualized as control power – sinks policy never operated within that domain. Indeed, the voluntary market continues to be an important player for sinks projects. And some of the private actors involved in it have become increasingly involved in rule-making at the national and subnational levels. The interrelationships established between public and private, protean and control power will not be easily undone.

This limited case of protean power can be read as a revised recipe for successful advocacy in a world of control power. Though protean power is by definition unpredictable, important patterns emerge. First, advocates often seek to shift the framing of issues so that they are more amenable to their goals. In this case, reframing worked in the other way. States set the frame (choosing to revive sinks policy through REDD), and private regulators sought to populate that frame with a specific meaning (or in this case, set of practices) – their existing forestry projects.[51] Second, as is often highlighted in the social movements literature, environmental NGOs moved between "inside" and "outside" the halls of policymaking. This movement (and, perhaps, the blurring of who was where and when) allowed protean power to emerge even within established channels of control power.

[51] Tarrow 1994.

Part 5

Conclusion

13   Power Complexities and Political Theory

Peter J. Katzenstein and Lucia A. Seybert

This book opened with an invitation to think afresh about power and uncertainty in world politics. This concluding chapter summarizes in its first section the findings of the twelve empirical case studies (in ten chapters). Since actors regularly have to tackle *both* risk and uncertainty, control and protean power are closely related. The efficacy of control power is not in question; the persistent neglect of protean power's agility and potentiality is.

In its second section, this chapter probes the writings of ancient, modern, and contemporary political theorists on the issue of control and protean power. During the last half century, conceptual and explanatory inquiries into power have failed to plumb the insights of political theorists. International relation scholars are a partial exception to this generalization, but even their interest has been limited to a handful of theorists, such as Hobbes or Kant. Focusing largely on arguments about the possibilities for war or peace, they have typically bypassed the broad contributions that political theory has made to the analysis of power. Our brief discussion bolsters this book's central point. Ever since Aristotle, the distinction between the actualities and potentialities of control and protean power has been a subject of theoretical inquiry.

The chapter ends with a brief interpretation of the United States and America as exemplars of control and protean power. Since 1945 the challenges to US control have waxed and waned. Many disruptions of US primacy are linked to developments in American society, its transnational engagement as well as its nationalist confrontations. American society is protean in its multiple traditions and coalitions and has surprised the world again and again, as in the elections of Barak Obama and Donald Trump in 2008 and 2016. The dynamics of control and protean power are thus exemplified by the dynamics of the relations between the US state and American society.

Control and Protean Power: Evidence from the Cases

The case studies in this book do not clinch an argument. They illustrate and help us to recognize patterns, an important avenue for an understanding of power dynamics in world politics.[1] Spanning security, economic, social, and cultural issues in diverse arenas of world politics, the case studies highlight relations between control and protean power that are too often overlooked. They are summarized here under the headings of congruence or incongruence of experience and context, different relationships between control and protean power, operational and radical uncertainty, power dynamics in different social settings, and the reversibility between protean and control power. Moved by different intellectual and political commitments and interests, scholars can make world politics look like a well-trimmed garden or an overgrown park. However, when we impose only one of these two logics, sensibilities and sets of practices on all the flora and fauna of world politics we will fail to understand important parts of its ecology. It is the complexity of that ecology that produces effects that are often unanticipated.[2] Control power often fails to recognize the next big wave. The surfer's solution is to temper the urge to look for the perfect ride, to be attentive and stay attuned, and to ride cascades building from all directions.

Why is this book using the empirical findings of the case studies both in the development of the theoretical framework in Chapters 1 and 2 as well as in this summary section of this concluding chapter? Guided by the case studies, we developed in the first two chapters a substantive theoretical, empirically grounded framework for the analysis of power. But we did not fully mine the evidence. The review of the case studies in this section thus records patterns that may prompt other scholars preferring an empirical, hypothesis-testing approach committed to the identification and reduction of observed variance, to also use the ideas and findings of this book. This dual approach reflects the book's eclectic and pragmatic stance on questions of ontology (open rather than closed systems) and epistemology (broader notions of explication rather than narrower ones of explanation). This approach, furthermore, is also reflected in the book's case studies. While all the authors worked creatively with the core ideas advanced in this book, some of the case studies have enriched the book's theoretical framework by making distinctive contributions of their own. Meaning indeterminacy (Chapter 3), power reversibility (Chapter 5), judgments versus decisions (Chapter 7) and *techne* versus *episteme* (Chapter 8) are obvious examples. Furthermore, the case studies

---

[1] Cartwright 2007: 24–42.   [2] Jervis 1997: 91.

of hydrocarbons (Chapter 7), film (Chapter 10), and carbon sinks (Chapter 12), are presented in a narrative style particularly apposite for capturing the fluidity of the power dynamics they analyze.

Experience and Context

What do the twelve case studies tell us about the relations between control and protean power under conditions of risk and uncertainty? Our answer to this question should avoid the common mistake of inferring power outcomes from observed political practices. To insist that the party that prevailed in a political contest is the party that had more power collapses the distinction between practice and power and encourages the spinning of tautologies. Political practices are generating power dynamics, not manifesting them. The case studies track political practice to the risk- and uncertainty-inflected experience and context of actors and from there to variable configurations of control and protean power.

In a few cases, the power story is relatively clear-cut. The history of human rights (Chapter 3), for example, is understood best in terms of the protean power potentials that inhere in innovative practices shaped by institutional and meaning indeterminacies. The situation is somewhat complex because imperial actors experienced the context as risk, sub- altern actors as uncertainty. It is this divergence of departure points that accounts for attempted (and failed) control on the part of the colonizers and system-transforming, protean power-generating innovations by actors encountering the inadequacies of existing governance structures. In other words, by not relying exclusively on control power Chapter 3 helps to explain the observed outcomes: the rapid collapse of the institu- tion of empire after 1945 and the stunning victory of anti-imperialist insurgents. Still, meaning indeterminacy as the primary source of uncer- tainty in the context of the rights revolution does not necessarily surround the formulation and promotion of other international norms. As described in Chapter 11, the framing of the landmine ban as a human rights issue did not launch a cycle of repeated norm revisions that would open up room for further improvisation. On the contrary, state actors continued to experience and describe arms control as falling into the realm of risk. As a result, their corresponding practices of (in)action at the international level reinforced the context attributes upon which such reasoning was based and made the deployment of control power not only a reasonable but also an effective response. In light of these two norm evolution accounts, the conditions under which meaning indeterminacy swings the balance toward protean or control power remains unanswered. The utility of both perspectives on power, however, is clear.

In the case of over-the-counter derivatives and sovereign debt (Chapter 8), the story is a bit more complex. In derivative markets some actors develop conventions, such as risk models and ratings, that make it possible for them to experience an uncertain context as risk. At the same time other actors experience the same context as profoundly uncertain and respond with innovative products and strategies with unpredictable and power-generating effects. In moments of financial crisis or panic, all actors experience totally unpredictable markets for what they are. But soon after, post-crisis arrangements restabilize experiences and generate a sense of control over governable risks. Thus, they set the stage for a new cycle of financial instability, where control is an incomplete and elusive goal. In sovereign debt, comparable power dynamics are at play. States and large corporations experience markets for the most part as manageable risks, bordering only occasionally on uncertainty. This leads to a mixture of affirmation of established strategies and a dose of improvisation when needed. In contrast, so-called smaller distress debt funds, peripheral players compared to primary dealers and sovereigns, experience profound market uncertainties. Refusing to be sidelined, one of them introduced innovative legal arbitrage strategies that, unpredictably, set free protean power dynamics and changed the game for everybody.

An experience of crisis, however, does not inevitably lead to a deepening of the surrounding uncertainty, nor is it always met by further improvisational practices by agile actors. The politics of carbon sinks (Chapter 12) shows that even in the context of climate change mitigation, the effects of context attributes and actor experiences on one another remain fluid. This occurs in a nested policy domain in which governments reformulate issues marked by radical, epistemic uncertainty in risk terms. Experiences thus affect the corresponding power outcomes differently at each stage and do not necessarily generate protean power. In the intergovernmental negotiations leading up to the Kyoto Protocol, control power prevailed in a context of risk. NGOs experienced it as such and failed in having governments adopt new rules. In the post-Kyoto period of parallel relations of government- and NGO-initiated rules, the rise of a voluntary market for carbon sinks was the result of improvisation as NGOs remained uncertain what would follow from their adoption of practices that were no longer constrained by the politics of intergovernmental negotiations. In the final phase, the context became more uncertain for governments that were now committed to taking some action on forests but had no clue how their actions would play out in the end. Experiencing the new situation as risk, NGOs seized on this opening – in a circumscribed way they capitalized on their prior improvisation and translated their efforts into an evolving intergovernmental regime that, itself control-driven, still provided some room for protean power.

In other cases, evolving practices reveal different power dynamics over time, as the history of LGBT rights (Chapter 4) illustrates. Poland's LGBT activists and their opponents relied on improvisations and refusals that played out in risky and uncertain contexts and experiences, generating different power dynamics. Most notably, the story of LGBT rights promotion in the context of EU enlargement illustrates the limits of control power. There was a short-lived period of EU and INGO policies in the run-up to and in the wake of EU accession that we can characterize as affirmation of existing expectations. As the inadequacy and one-sidedness of membership conditionality became apparent, local activists found themselves readjusting to the unpredictable blending of external pressures with local sentiments. In contrast, unable to tap any external discourse, however controversial, for support, the original German LGBT movement in the 1860s was marked by more easily detectable innovation from the outset. The long-term evolution of LGBT rights is a story of the actualization of various power potentialities, deriving from actor experiences of risk and uncertainty. Crucially, it shows that the interaction between actors and context generates practices that result in adjustments in power outcomes that either reconfirm existing constraints or challenge them through protean power and repeated shifts in the unknown unknowns.

Terrorism and counterterrorism (Chapter 9) show a complex picture marked by overlays rather than a temporal sequence of different power constellations. Reinforced by political expedience and bureaucratic inertia, states encounter and describe uncertain security contexts as risky. Their default response of enforcement can evolve in principle, but such change requires the confluence of otherwise unyielding factors. As a result, governments remain tethered to the domain of imagined risk management and control power, even though leaders may recognize in private the futility of their public promises to eradicate all terrorist threats. Terrorists, by contrast, experience and operate in a context of uncertainty requiring innovation and generating protean power. When they succeed, however, terrorists are pulled back into the experience of a risky world while the context remains, for the most part, unavoidably uncertain. The politics of terrorism and counterterrorism thus set in motion complex mixtures of protean and control power dynamics.

What distinguishes the counterterrorism account of protean power are distinctive patterns of agency that impact on the interactive fluidity of the context in which actors operate. In a similar way, the story of Hollywood's fluctuating prominence in the world of film (Chapter 10) also displays opposing sets of actors, variously endowed with control power resources, yet interacting and transforming the very landscape in which their competition unfolds. The co-dependence between producers of cultural content and its consumers creates patterns seemingly amenable to profit-making. Yet, as the limited reach of Hollywood's strengths illustrates, the resulting control is short-lived at best and illusory at worst. Global audiences, as a whole, and also in their cultural or regional subcontexts, play a key role in shaping patterns of innovation countering affirmation, even complacency, at the other extreme. Sometimes filmmakers adopt established means of reaching their audiences and so reproduce risk-based assumptions about how the industry operates. Despite such measures, however, the fickleness and short half-life of best practices is apparent, and without seeking to dominate, actors carving out new paths prevail in the constantly changing world of film. Their success, unexpected and often fleeting, can be labeled as protean power in retrospect. It arises from responses to local challenges, niche markets, and unique audience tastes with the impact of their creative contributions magnified by their previous neglect.

Actor awareness of "knowing how little we know" is explored in Chapter 6 on the technological frontiers conquered in science, start-ups, and bitcoin. There are several layers to this uncertainty. First, it stems from the very questions asked and challenges tackled. Second, the recognition of the profound gaps in our knowledge creates ambiguity about the appropriateness of regulation, further altering the course of invention. Does it make sense to consider the relative risks and costs of pursuing individual innovations? How much of the resulting change is based on deliberate moves and how much of it is the outcome of creative improvisation and intuition? Are there ways in which inefficient regulations can be bypassed altogether? The chapter offers a continuum of responses to such questions, mapping the degree to which actors allow their experience of uncertainty to guide their actions. Battles over intellectual property rights seek to fence in precious discoveries but at the same time increase incentives for the emergence of still newer alternatives. In a different approach, scientists who make their findings readily available do so because they are reluctant to hold further advances hostage to narrow interests that would favor confined lines of inquiry. Start-ups take the innovation game still further. They not only seek to meet existing technological or other needs but create entirely new ones. Finally, in explicit recognition of the failure of the formal banking system, especially at times of crisis, bitcoin offers an alternative currency, a fundamentally novel technology, and a transformed environment of unpredictability in which, to date, it has thrived. Construing these high-tech vignettes as attempts to stay ahead in the uncertainty game, we must not forget that those who succeed and briefly hold protean power do not anticipate this at the outset. A scientist may dream of getting the Nobel Prize but she or he can hardly plan on doing so. The decision to adopt bitcoin is deliberately disruptive and introduces new power potentialities. Depending on their position, actors exploit or bypass ever-changing unknowns. No "win" is a guarantee of future success.

Hydrocarbons (Chapter 7) show sequenced and layered power complexities that conventional analyses of the control powers of large corporations and states largely miss. In the 1950s and 1960s innovations by European governments and the Soviet gas ministry created a new infrastructure of pipelines, practices, and market relations. Subsequently, refusal and improvisation created control and protean power dynamics that acted back on the experience of actors and the context they faced. The break-up of the Soviet Union and a number of Ukrainian gas crises made Russian and European executives acutely aware of their mutual dependence, the geopolitical and contractual uncertainties of Ukrainian transit routes, and the advantage of developing joint innovative practices to reorganize gas transits from Russia to Western Europe. In sharp contrast, in the United States a number of small gas producers experienced only uncertainties as, for more than two decades, they were searching for a commercially viable way of extracting gas from shale. Paradoxically, then, a relatively inflexible gas market invited radical innovation to bypass long-standing technological and market constraints. Improvisation in the face of a slowly-unfolding crisis generated protean power dynamics and produced new uncertainties for all actors operating in global hydrocarbon markets. In reaction, European and Russian firms made still more changes to long-standing contractual practices that led to further unanticipated consequences. Finally, Western sanctions imposed on Russia after the annexation of Crimea and a very large Sino-Russian gas deal were, for the most part, improvising protean power-producing moves adopted in the face of profound uncertainty about future price movements in hydrocarbon markets rather than the exercise of effective control power.

The case of migration (Chapter 5), finally, reflects all power complexities in great clarity, implicating all practices in contexts and experiences of risk and uncertainty. The analysis of illegal migration sits at the intersections of improvisation, innovation, refusal and affirmation, and of risk and uncertainty, generating continuous protean and control power blending. In resonance with the counterterrorism case (Chapter 9), the account of migrants making their way through fluid landscapes erases any suspicion of specific normative assumptions of protean power dynamics.

Although protean power rests in the ability to find channels of possibility where established means of control fail, it is not somehow designed to topple structures of domination by default. Protean power may be more visible if generated by actors who otherwise lack the attributes of control power. Yet *any* agents, not just weak ones, can find themselves responding to uncertainty in a shape-shifting way. In the setting of migration through Mexico, uncertainty mixes with risk and actors are faced with responding to both simultaneously. They convert innovations and improvised solutions into established and reproducible responses, only so these can be overturned again with the arrival of the next train, bus, or truck. Chapter 5 also allows us to observe the internal heterogeneity among actors, suggesting that any specification of their experiences of the surrounding context might need to be fine-tuned even further. For example, state agents operating in different contexts can encounter entirely different conditions that influence their interactions with migrants, smugglers, and crime cartels. The journeys described in this chapter represent always changing sequences of sometimes fatal decisions, illustrating that neither protean nor control power will ever prevail and that they often operate concurrently.

Relations between Control and Protean Power

The case studies of migration, bitcoin, hydrocarbons, finance, terrorism, film, arms control, and carbon sinks (Chapters 5–12) show the relevant actors to be interacting. In the human rights and LGBT cases (Chapters 3 and 4), the identities of actors wielding control power and actors demanding new rights or exploring new practices are entangled. The recognition of uncertainty in science along with a desire to advance knowledge and bypass narrow uses of technology also bring entanglement to the forefront (Chapter 6). And in the case of carbon sinks, NGOs shifted from advocates to regulators, adopting a new identity in the policy process (Chapter 12).[3]

Relations between control and protean power can be both competitive, as in all cases but migration, oil, and carbon sinks (Chapters 3, 4, 6–11), or complementary, as in all cases but human and LGBT rights, finance, and arms control (Chapters 5–7, 9, 10, and 12). In some instances, such as high-tech, gas, terrorism, and film (Chapters 6, 7, 9, and 10), both relationships unfold at the same time. In the case of terrorism (Chapter 9), for example, states and terrorist groups are in highly competitive relations,

---

[3] For reasons of length not reported in Chapter 5, the migration case also shows evidence of entanglement as migrants adopt new ways of thinking of themselves and their goals in life after confronting the violence they encounter on the route. See also Brigden 2013.

Table 13.1 *Relations between Control and Protean Power*

		Types of relations				
		Interactive	Entangled	Competitive	Comple-mentary	Parallel	Nested
Ch. 3	Human rights		x	x			
Ch. 4	LGBT rights		x	x			
Ch. 5	Migration	x			x		
Ch. 6	High-tech/ knowledge frontiers		x	x	x		
Ch. 6	High-tech/bitcoin	x	x	x	x	x	
Ch. 7	Hydrocarbons/gas	x		x	x	x	
Ch. 7	Hydrocarbons/oil	x			x	x	
Ch. 8	Finance	x		x			
Ch. 9	(Counter-) Terrorism	x		x	x		
Ch. 10	Film	x		x	x	x	
Ch. 11	Arms control (post-1997)	x		x		x	
Ch. 12	Carbon sinks	x	x		x		x

even though complementary power dynamics are also in play. States develop counterterrorism tactics that cultivate unexpected practices, for example, in the use of social media. And ISIS has tried to organize a caliphate state in parts of Iraq and Syria. Similarly, in the gas industry (Chapter 7) states and corporations are typically linked in various competitive economic and political relationships spawning protean power dynamics. But the innovative fracking technology developed by small American producers has also had very positive effects on the control power of the United States in energy markets. We observe a similar pattern in the case of both bitcoin and scientific discoveries (Chapter 6). And while studios and film producers compete intensely in national, regional, and global markets, Hollywood also provides film templates that foreign producers can and do exploit profitably (Chapter 10).

Rounding out the possibilities, a few cases show that the relationship between control and protean power can evolve in parallel as in bitcoin, hydrocarbons, film, and the 1997 landmine treaty as one important episode in arms control (Chapters 6, 7, 10, and 11) or be nested as in carbon sinks (Chapter 12). Conceived initially as a fundamental challenge to financial institutions and states, major corporate actors and governments adapted quickly to explore the blockchain technology underlying bitcoin's electronic currency (Chapter 6). Serving the energy needs of large parts of the world, oil and gas markets operate in parallel and with different political logics (Chapter 7). In the 1997 landmine treaty (Chapter 11) control was temporarily slipping out of the hands of major states as other actors established a forum that bypassed the traditional UN venue for negotiations. Finally, in carbon sinks (Chapter 12) the markets for carbon trading were developed and operated by NGOs at first without and, later, with state support.

The empirical case studies reported in this book resonate with the findings of other scholars working in variegated empirical domains. In different cases of transnational advocacy networks, banking, and consumer politics scholars have pointed to "unexpected power,"[4] "the power of inaction,"[5] and "the political power of weak interests,"[6] that could all be interpreted as different manifestations of diverse relationships between control and protean power in empirical settings as different as insurance, climate change, science and technology policy, environmental law, and genetically modified food.[7] Together with the plausibility probes offered in this book, these studies provide suggestive evidence for the importance of protean power dynamics under conditions of uncertainty.

Operational and Radical Uncertainty

Political actors encounter two kinds of uncertainties. Operational uncertainty speaks to the complexity of the world. Political choices and practices often evolve in situations in which the secondary and tertiary consequences of particular actions are mind-boggling and next to impossible to calculate. Experienced intuition and feelings prevail. "Bounded rationality" and "satisficing" are social science concepts that acknowledge the prevalence of educated guesswork in much of world politics.[8] Although in principle such known or knowable unknowns lend themselves to probability calculations, for many practical purposes they often do not. Radical uncertainty is of a different kind. Unknown unknowns are by their very nature not susceptible to any form of calculation.[9] For example, in arms control the end of the Cold War provided a radically new context that informed differently the experience of various state and non-state actors (Chapter 11). In contrast, operational uncertainty in the run-up to the financial crisis of 2008 was not deemed to be salient. Actors and analysts overlooked important elements of

---

[4] Hertel 2006.   [5] Woll 2014.   [6] Trumbull 2012.
[7] Everson and Vos 2009; Heal and Milner 2013.   [8] Scott 1998: 327–28.
[9] For a typology of forms of not knowing, see Beck 2007: 126–27.

uncertainty in a context they had come to experience only in terms of risk (Chapter 8). More generally, actors have different theoretical or practical knowledge about the settings in which they operate. What is visible to some actors remains invisible to others as in migration (Chapter 5), LGBT rights (Chapter 4), and carbon sinks (Chapter 12). Unsurprisingly, therefore, actors adopt different instruments to cope with uncertainty through sophisticated model-based risk estimates in credit derivatives markets (Chapter 8); treaties and contracts in individual rights (Chapter 3), hydrocarbons (Chapter 7), and sovereign debt markets (Chapter 8); and rights in LGBT movement politics (Chapter 4).

Most of the case studies in this book offer evidence of political actors coping with both operational and radical uncertainty. In a few cases, however, one or the other kind of uncertainty holds center stage, shifting the center of gravity closer to risk or uncertainty. To the extent that empirical enquiry has to focus on snapshots in the fluid continuity between uncertainty and risk, this is not surprising. Complex arms control negotiations over cluster munitions and conventional arms sales posed for governments and NGOs plenty of risks and operational uncertainties but no radical uncertainties (Chapter 11). The same is true for oil producers (Chapter 7). Future oil prices were highly unpredictable and affected by myriads of factors, but they were in principle knowable. Trust-inflected, long-term relations imbue actors with intuition and empathy, counterweights to the knowledge that they do not know.

By contrast, the politics of human rights are marked by a radical uncertainty that is grounded in the meaning indeterminacy of all discourses and texts (Chapter 3). During the last century successive redefinitions of what it means to be human have been at the center of evolving human rights declarations and treaties. And that evolution was shaped profoundly by protean power. In the case of LGBT rights that indeterminacy can have domestic roots when contested international norms are experienced as imposed, and international ones when norms are polarizing (Chapter 4). Hydrocarbon markets show how firms, taking what appear to be calculated risks, collectively create systemic uncertainty and unpredictability of demand and supply (Chapter 7). Similarly, indeterminacy inheres in the legal fiction of the *pari passu* clause in sovereign debt contracts (Chapter 8). Once its implausibly innovative legal interpretation was backed by court rulings both in Europe and the United States, a "vulture" fund playing arsonist in the house of sovereign debt destabilized fundamentally global markets for sovereign bonds. Sharing a deep affinity with the profound (Knightian) uncertainty pervading the finance industry, film producers and directors also operate under conditions of radical uncertainty as they have no way of knowing which of their films will be a hit (Chapter 10). As is true of other complex systems, the distribution of returns in the global film industry is highly non-normal and "fat-tailed." "Nobody knows anything" quipped screenwriter William Goldman many years ago; asked years later he doubled down and said "now more than ever."[10]

Finally, carbon sinks illustrate how operational uncertainty about climate change mitigation efforts is embedded in the radical uncertainty that defines the issue of global warming (Chapter 12). This means that political actors can choose to frame uncertainty one way or the other. And that frame can be consequential for political mobilization and demobilization strategies. Radical uncertainty about the future of planet Earth may have the effect of demobilizing government action while operational uncertainty may not. Or the logic may work in reverse, as Krugman argues. "When it comes to climate change uncertainty strengthens, not weakens, the case for action now."[11] Conversely, migrants experience the many choices they face – where to travel, how to travel, with whom to travel – as operationally uncertain (Chapter 5). Yet along their routes they experience many instances of radical uncertainty that are embedded within the larger operational uncertainty frame. Table 13.2 summarizes the distinction between two kinds of uncertainty across the different cases.

Institutional and Social Settings

Under conditions of risk and uncertainty actors devise creative practices that help them to navigate social settings marked by both control and protean power. In his analysis of the institutions organizing US nuclear deterrence, Scott Sagan, for example, has shown that highly interactive and tightly coupled complexity makes us "expect that the unexpected will occur, that unimaginable interactions will develop, that accidents will happen."[12] Although high reliability organization theory operating on the assumption of risk makes us believe otherwise, Sagan's empirical studies found its optimism wanting. His findings support instead normal accidents theory. Institutions are often inhabited by individuals operating in fluid systems of participation with often inconsistent preferences. Complexity makes the unknown – accidents – unavoidable. In Charles Perrow's words "complex social systems are greatly influenced by sheer chance, accident and luck ... and most attempts at social control are clumsy and unpredictable."[13] Barry Posen's analysis of uncertainty

---

[10] Chapter 10, fn. 56.   [11] Krugman 2013.   [12] Sagan 1993: 3.
[13] Quoted in ibid.: 31.

Table 13.2 *Operational and Radical Uncertainty*

	Operational uncertainty	Radical uncertainty
Human rights (Chapter 3)		x
LGBT rights (Chapter 4)	x	x
Migration (Chapter 5)	x	
High-tech/knowledge frontiers (Chapter 6)	x	x
High-tech/bitcoin (Chapter 6)	x	x
Hydrocarbons/gas (Chapter 7)	x	x
Hydrocarbons/oil (Chapter 7)	x	
Finance (Chapter 8)		x
(Counter-)Terrorism (Chapter 9)	x	x
Film (Chapter 10)		x
Arms control (post-1997) (Chapter 11)	x	
Carbon sinks (Chapter 12)	x	

management in military organizations preparing for conventional war is in broad agreement with Sagan's. Organizations seek to address the problems posed by uncertainty through a variety of mechanisms of control and coordination. But the struggle to manage uncertainty is undercut by the fact that "those with formal authority over the organization are a cause of uncertainty" because of their pursuit of independence from and power over those on whom they depend.[14] Protean power dynamics thus can thrive in institutional settings.

Students of international political economy have downplayed the fact that economic institutional complexes exhibit similar power dynamics. One of the proponents of a rational design approach to the study of institutions conceptualizes uncertainty in the following way: "parties always know the distribution of gains in the current period, but know only the probability distribution for the distributions of gains in future periods."[15] This approach assumes, implausibly, either that complexity is low because of the simplifying assumption that uncertainty is the same as risk, or that uncertainty is reflected only in poor information.[16] As long as analysis views economic organizations and institutions apart from the political processes in which they are embedded, it tends to over-emphasize

---

[14] Posen 1984: 45.   [15] Koremenos 2005: 550.

[16] In his trenchant critique of Koremenos et al. Alexander Wendt points out that "the Rational Design framework seems to treat the nature of uncertainty as unproblematic and ends up with a conceptualization that effectively reduces it to risk." Wendt 2001: 1029. See also Seabrooke 2007: 373.

the importance of constraints and stability at the expense of creative choice and recompositional change. In their analysis of the emergence of genuine novelty, John Padgett and Walter Powell, for example, argue that "logical cognition, no matter how useful for refinement and improvement, is unlikely to be a fundamental process for generating novelty, because logic can only use axioms that are already there."[17] Since outcomes such as the information revolution are simply unthinkable before they occur, "institutions," Yuen Yuen Ang writes, "are designed not merely to cope with cognitive limitations but rather to harness and activate the creative potential of the unknowns."[18] In short, institutional models of coherence overlook the power dynamics that inhere in uncertainty and do not fit the logic of institutional complementarity.[19]

Depending on the pervasiveness of the cracks that institutional settings provide, the case studies of human and LGBT rights, migration, terrorism, arms control, and carbon sinks all point to protean power dynamics (Chapters 3–5, 9, 11, and 12). Notably, the rise of protean power is detectable in actors' agility to explore institutional openings that exacerbate underlying uncertainties. The two rights cases (Chapters 3 and 4) document in considerable detail power dynamics linked to institutions and issues of legitimacy. The migration case shows how migrants and smugglers can exploit some of the inherent contradictions between border and refugee protection regimes, thus leveraging the state's own institutions against its control power (Chapter 5). The international state system offers numerous normative, discursive, and geographical sites for terrorists to implant themselves (Chapter 9). In the run-up to the signing of the 1997 Ottawa Landmine Treaty, advocates compensated for their lack of control power by coordinating on innovative strategies of persuasion that took advantage of the uncertainty around issues of threat and leadership after the end of the Cold War (Chapter 11). Specifically, small states and NGOs marshalled extensive evidence showing that landmines caused indiscriminate harm to civilians long after the cessation of hostilities. The end result was a treaty that overcame the opposition of the major states and, in particular, of the United States as the remaining superpower.[20] Finally, although in carbon sinks NGOs played a lesser role, they did exploit uncertainty to their own power advantage, extracting what probability estimates they could out of their unique position and expertise (Chapter 12).

The case studies of film and hydrocarbons, by way of contrast, analyze power dynamics that are operating on open social terrains marked by an

---

[17] Padgett and Powell 2012: 1.   [18] Ang 2016: 275, fn. 15.   [19] Herrigel 2005.
[20] Subsequent efforts on cluster munitions and conventional arms trade were less successful.

absence of institutions. Nigerian film producers, for example, have competed with Hollywood, unencumbered by institutional contexts such as theater chains controlling the screening of movies (Chapter 10). And in hydrocarbon markets firms tend to rely on the depth of their relationships, improvisation, and innovation to mitigate the operational and radical uncertainties they encounter, thus reshaping the broader context in which they operate (Chapter 7). Intense and complex renegotiations of contracts among firms with long-term relationships and considerable amounts of trust are an integral part of coping in settings that indelibly link risk with uncertainty.

Reversibility

Finally, the case studies point to the importance of power reversibility. They illustrate that actors qualifying as powerful in control terms, such as the resources they possess, can nevertheless show sufficient agility to generate protean power effects. Conceivably, control and protean power can even reinforce one another in the case of such well-endowed actors. Similarly, while control may be limited in the case of traditionally peripheral actors, one consequence of their ability to improvise could be the uncovering or creation of new control power resources. In hydrocarbons (Chapter 7), innovative natural gas producers in Texas had to cope with gut-wrenching uncertainties and protean power dynamics. And so did credit rating agencies in finance (Chapter 8). Conversely, terrorist groups like ISIS have exercised control over a caliphate state spanning Syria and Iraq (Chapter 9). Skeptical major states in the negotiations over a Cluster Munition Convention proved to be agile. They pushed for limiting the treaty's scope and exploited various technological fixes (Chapter 11). Surprisingly, matters did not turn out as skeptical states had expected. Signed by 107 states in 2008, the use of cluster munitions has become stigmatized since then even by non-signatories, as many signatories have completed the destruction of their stockpiles before treaty-mandated deadlines.

Going beyond simple reversibility, some cases also show how control and protean power are mutually constitutive. In migration, viewed through the lens of practice, the protean power of migrants creates the state's control by making possible innumerable, flexible, everyday actions of state agents and bureaucrats (Chapter 5). The same holds for hydrocarbons. Abstract logics of control are worked out on the ground, through everyday fluid relationships between firms, governments, and consumers (Chapter 7). This agrees also with the basic facts in the world of finance (Chapter 8). Uncertainty is a pervasive feature of financial markets that are open rather than closed. Control power simplifies and stabilizes complex uncertainties in various ways, including the invention of stabilizing categories (rating) and practices (reliance on risk models). Protean power dynamics can undercut their effectiveness quickly, however, especially in volatile moments of crisis.

The relations between control and protean power are reversible. In shifting fields of power possibilities, some actors who are taking advantage of protean power dynamics are intent on exercising control. Others exercising control improvise and innovate, taking advantage of protean power dynamics. Activists pressing for human rights during the decolonization movement of the 1940s and 1950s, for example, succeeded in seizing political control, thus preparing the ground for heart-breaking human rights violations of their own. Focusing on actor attributes – strong or secure and weak or precarious – tends to conceal reversibilities in positions that changing relations and practices in fields of multiple power configurations and power potentialities can make visible.

Control and Protean Power in Political Theory[21]

Why another neologism describing power? Is power not about different kinds of control as the different faces of power discussion, briefly reviewed in Chapter 1, illustrates? The conceptualization of power dynamics offered in this book suggests otherwise. The faces of power debate was really about control in two different forms: as action in power's first face (most clearly expressed in the behavioral approach of Dahl) and as social order as power's second, third, and fourth face (articulated in different ways by Bachrach and Baratz, Lukes and Hayward); as action and order control power directs and diffuses. Protean power is about the passing from potentiality to actuality of an actor and about the effects of actuality on the future potentialities of the same actor or others; as the actualization of potentialities, protean power creates and circulates. Neglecting for a moment the world of pure risk and pure uncertainty, worlds where actor experience and context attributes match up, both power types operate in a world of risk and uncertainty. At the point where control and protean power meet risk and uncertainty, power becomes the source of the unexpected in world politics.

---

[21] Most of what we write here derives from readings and discussions in a seminar that Professor Jill Frank taught together with Peter Katzenstein in the fall of 2016; PK's extensive and deeply clarifying conversations with Anna Wojciuk; and a set of profoundly penetrating and immensely helpful comments by Stefano Guzzini.

We build on Stewart Clegg's argument that focuses on the difference between Hobbes and Machiavelli as epitomizing two strands of thinking about power in political theory. Control power is central to Hobbes and his mechanical, scientific approach aiming at universal laws. Protean power is the focus of Machiavelli and his insistence on the exercise of power and historical contingency. Hobbes is interested in what power is, Machiavelli in what power does.[22] We develop this insight further by including a number of other theorists who have focused on the relationship between what we call control and protean power.

Although they differ greatly in their arguments, Hobbes and Foucault are the inspiration for realist and critical security scholars who focus largely on capabilities and order as two forms of control power. Speaking in different registers and voices Clausewitz and Machiavelli point to the limits that chance and imagination impose on control power. Arendt, Deleuze, Deleuze and Guatarrie, Aristotle, and Agamben push further and draw our attention to potential capacities and protean power. Our brief discussion of such a diverse group of thinkers is selective and designed solely to highlight our central point. Rather than offering substantive, extended engagement, it serves as a reminder of the existence of a variegated and distinguished lineage of political thought that is rarely read, let alone discussed, by scholars of international relations. In contrast to those wedded in their view of control power exclusively to Hobbes and Foucault, we hold that political theorists of very different persuasions have theorized extensively protean power, in different ways and with different terminologies. Thinking of control power only in terms of capability and order overlooks the importance of protean power as the capacity to actualize potentialities. In fact, it is the issue of potentiality that has interested political theorists throughout the ages. The concept of protean power is therefore not a faddish neologism, but a useful reminder of an important topic in the debates among political theorists and in the world we seek here to illuminate.

Control Power and Chance

Power in international relations is often thought of in Hobbesian terms, as an actor capability. In this view actors deploy control power by drawing on capabilities to produce desired outcomes susceptible to probabilistic calculation. For Hobbes, for example, power is unitary, homogeneous, unidirectional, and asymmetric. It is checked only by the power of other sovereigns. Unlike Hobbes, who sees power as a purely external

---

[22] Clegg 1989: 5–7, 21–38, 202–7. See also Hindess 1996.

constraint on a subject's will as her ultimate passion, for Foucault power is formative of a subject's will; he analyzes the internal processes by which subjects are created. Hobbes focuses on the sovereign's hierarchical control of subjects; Foucault on the creation of self-controlling subjects through the diffusion of control mechanisms that render sovereign policing of subjects superfluous. Hobbes focuses on the individual and "power over;" Foucault on the system and "power through."

Hobbes' anarchic state of nature is marked by radical uncertainty ruled by passion.[23] Among all of man's passions fear is the most important. Unbridled quests for control power make life unbearably hard. Individuals are thus ready to transfer all of their rights to all things to one sovereign with unlimited power of control.[24] In speaking God's word, interpreting the laws of nature, and fixing the meaning of human speech the sovereign's power is total and expresses the unity of a people. In one magical moment subjects are thus transported from a condition of unpredictability and diffuse fear of everyone in the state of nature to a condition of predictability and concentrated fear of the sovereign in the commonwealth. Not so the sovereign who remains in the state of nature, but is now endowed with an unlimited control over her or his subjects who remain prone to indulge their many other passions. The sovereign thus must always guard against the possibility that things can fall apart.[25]

We can find passages in the writings of other theorists that resonate with Hobbes' line of argument. Aristotle, for example, includes might (*kratos*) in his extensive and nuanced treatment of different kinds of power.[26] So does Thucydides in a famous passage in the Melian Dialogue, which realists like to quote in support of their claim that international relations is determined only by material capabilities and power politics: "the strong do what they can and the weak suffer what they must."[27] Machiavelli, too, is often claimed as an advocate of an amoral power politics. He insists that all states rest on "good laws and good arms." War is the main business of rulers.[28] In *The Prince* Machiavelli uses the concept of *potestà* – admittedly only once in the entire text – to describe the authority to exercise unrestricted physical

---

[23] Hobbes 1996: 3–11, 24–46, 62, 86–129, 145–54, 183–94, 214–16, 483–91.

[24] The solution is paradoxical since a contractarian, bottom-up derivation of the Leviathan cannot happen in a true state of nature; its occurrence only shows that there exists no true state of nature. However, Leviathan can also be justified *ex post* and top-down, and is then designed to avoid the state of nature. The solution of anarchy at home only intensifies its problem in international relations. We thank Stefano Guzzini for this point.

[25] Hobbes 1996: 221–30.   [26] Aristotle 2000: 1324b, 25–29.

[27] Strauss 2008: 5.89, 352.   [28] Machiavelli 1998: 48, 124–25.

domination that Cesare Borgia grants to Messer Remirro de Orco "a cruel and ready man, to whom he gave the fullest power."[29]

With his reconceptualization of sovereign as disciplinary power, Foucault focuses on systems of repressive governance that produce political order, although one shorn of the notion of political action.[30] In the middle and late years of his writings there occurs a notable shift from power as outright repression to power as productive practices of individual self-cultivation.[31] The Panopticon is a place for the exercise of total control and an ideal setting for scientific experiments uncontaminated by uncertainty.[32] For Foucault, as for Hobbes, predictability rests in knowledge and scientific expertise, which buttress control power as the characteristic mode of contemporary governance.[33] Knowledge and expertise operate top-down through the invention and acceptance of categories, such as social deviance. However, in contrast to Hobbes, in much of Foucault's subsequent writings disciplinary power is no longer conceived of in centralized, unitary, homogeneous, and unidirectional terms.[34] Power is not actor-centric, direct, and specific; it is impersonal, indirect, and diffuse.[35] It works through a variety of social complexes such as the family, medicine, psychiatry, education, and business, locations of epistemic regimes that shape political life recursively through what Ian Hacking has called "looping effects."[36]

Disciplinary rather than sovereign power thus becomes the center of Foucault's analysis.[37] It is constituted by surveillance and social classification, as foundations of social order rather than coercion and territorial exclusion.[38] Unlike Hobbes, Foucault downplays the importance of direct, coercive action. He stresses instead the systemic aspects of government (or governmentality) to determine the subject's conduct indirectly, through the cultivation of specific dispositions and the instilling of specific norms.[39] Its Christian, pastoral legacy prompts the European welfare state to "constantly ensure, sustain, and improve the lives of each and every one."[40] Depending on the "micro-relations of power,"[41] disciplinary power is a diffuse and impersonal force. Operating through systems of

---

[29] Ibid.: 28. According to Harvey Mansfield, personal correspondence October 13, 2016, the same concept appears twenty-nine times in the *Discourses*.
[30] Guzzini and Neumann 2012.
[31] The first and the last two volumes of Foucault's *History of Sexuality* illustrate this shift.
[32] Foucault 1977: 202–5.   [33] Foucault 1982: 78–84.   [34] Foucault 1977.
[35] Guzzini 2012: 21.
[36] Foucault 1982: 78–84; Guzzini 2010: 8–10; Hacking 2004: 279.
[37] Foucault 1977; 1980: 89–108.
[38] Best 2008: 358–60; Digeser 1992; Larner and Walters 2004: 496.
[39] Rose 1999: 3; Foucault 1982: 789.   [40] Foucault 1981: 235–36; Walters 2012: 21–29.
[41] Foucault 1980: 199; Walters 2012: 21–29.

expert knowledge, it is both pervasive and productive.[42] Disciplinary power is pervasive because it relies on systems of self-governance and self-policing of the citizens themselves. It is productive because the individuals through which it passes are normalized by its effects.

Far from making power disappear as in current writings on international relations that focus on diffusion, for Foucault diffusion magnifies power by enhancing its productivity in the reconfiguration of decentralized practices. A widened and deepened system of rule applies to and works through actors whom it both governs and empowers.[43] The ubiquity of disciplinary power meeting acceptance and resistance leads to iterative adjustments of an impersonal system of all-encompassing governance. The recalcitrance of the political will of elites and the intransigence of individual assertions of freedom yield unending adjustments in the mechanisms of control.[44] Innovations in disciplinary mechanisms lead to an ever more far-reaching form of internalization of the knowledge by which subjects govern themselves and each other.

The logic of power entails both discipline through rule by abstract categories and refusal of abstraction.[45] Individuals are both objects and subjects, experiencing and exercising power. Contextually, specific and focused on power practices, Foucault's analysis prefers granular treatments of singular moments to grand theoretical narratives. His analysis does not start from the assumption that some actors have power and others do not. Instead, it focuses on sites and relationships that reveal power plays, struggles, reversals, evasions, and innovations. Techniques of exercising power and tactics of subverting power co-evolve.[46] For Foucault, we are all the products of power that moves through the capillaries of society.[47] Power "is never localized here or there ... Power passes through individuals. It is not applied to them."[48] In his analysis of disciplinary power Foucault thus focuses on how it constitutes or creates subjects not under the watchful eyes of a Leviathan, but through largely uncontrolled mechanisms and techniques.

Especially in the last years of his life, Foucault at times seemed to point to the limits of control power and the possibility of the actualization of power potentialities spurring subversive creativity and innovative resistance that could move around or outwit control.[49] Since the power to control is all-pervasive and operates even within subjects, Foucault argues that the state was never "sufficiently in one place to be seized, that the

[42] Foucault 1977: 194.   [43] Guzzini 2012: 2, 8–9, 16.   [44] Gordon 1991: 5.
[45] Foucault 1982: 781, 785.   [46] Walters 2012: 14.
[47] Foucault 1980: 109–33; Lipschutz 2007: 230.
[48] Foucault 2003: 29; Debrix and Barder 2009: 404.
[49] Digeser 1992: 984–85, 991, 1003.

state was everywhere and that therefore the 'revolution' had to be every-where, ubiquitous as well as permanent."[50] At another point he writes that zones of incorporated resistance show governmental power to be somewhat elastic, though not infinitely so, as contestation creates "an incitement to political creativity."[51] In revealing protean power potential, enterprising subjects can cope with the "immediate enemy" without having far-reaching plans.[52] Relying on a constitutive analysis of the formation of actor identities and the drawing of boundaries of what is possible, Foucault's analysis encompasses processes of empowerment not expressly granted by a sovereign but through self-activated practices. Individuals have the choice to diminish or enhance unavoidable friction.[53] Empowerment through improvisation and innovation occur in a system of control and self-monitoring that is stretching its octopus arms, like Hobbes' Leviathan, through all of the nooks and crannies of a self-governing society, made orderly by all-pervasive processes of disciplining.

As Clausewitz writes, in contact with chance, friction is a formidable opponent of those seeking unhindered control, both in war and politics.[54] "Chaos and control featured centrally in his writing," and he was con-flicted by their opposing realities.[55] Uncertainty, the singularity of con-text, emotions, and cognitive limitations made a mockery of all systematic attempts to calculate and predict behavior. Agility in developing the original idea informing a military campaign under constantly changing circumstances was the most promising avenue to success. Yet, in Clausewitz's thinking, power also had to navigate around contingency by relying on probabilities. Planning was the attempt to adhere to strate-gic aims by comprehending particular situations, a positive exploitation of fortune. Routine and imagination were both necessary to cultivate, in Michael Howard's words, "the capacity to adapt oneself to the utterly unpredictable, the entirely unknown."[56] Besides emotion and rationality, for Clausewitz war is defined by "the play of chance and probability within which the creative spirit is free to roam."[57] Clausewitz thus points to a power that operates in the domain of the unexpected.

Many political theorists of power have probed that type of power. Since control power is often upended or evaded, they expand the analysis beyond actual capabilities to include also actors' potential capacities, understood both as creativity in the actualization of potentiality in the present and enhanced potentialities for future action. Machiavelli, for

---

[50] Foucault 1981: 253; O'Malley 2000: 261; Sheridan 1980: 111.   [51] Walters 2012: 43.
[52] Foucault 1982: 780.   [53] Digeser 1992: 995.   [54] Clausewitz 1984: 120.
[55] Porter 2016: 252.   [56] Quoted in ibid.: 255.
[57] Clausewitz 1984. Evidently, for Clausewitz as for Weber (see Chapter 1, pp. 11–12, fn. 42), "chance" is not coterminous with "probability."

example, shares an affinity with Clausewitz in his analysis of power. Rather than focusing on the common good, as does Hobbes, Machiavelli is interested in the art of the possible. Besides referring to *potestà*, though only once, throughout *The Prince* he invokes numerous times a ruler's *potentia* – his capacity, ability, or strength exercised in many different contexts.[58] In contrast to Hobbes, for Machiavelli "might does not make right." *Potentia* is a dispositional capacity to do or not to do. It is activated by a prince's acquired, calculating, discretionary *virtu*, his political ability, and physical strength. This is power-in-action rather than power-as-order.

Power derives from the opportunity that chance (*fortuna*) provides and is actualized by the prince's ability, or *virtù*, to seize the moment. This is an excellent characterization of protean power. Since the concept of risk had not yet been invented, Machiavelli is not interested in assessing the epistemic aspect of fortune as risk or uncertainty.[59] This does not stop him, however, from theorizing about it. Fortune is like a destructive river. To protect against it requires strong dikes.[60] Precaution serves the ruler well in the domain of known unknowns; there will always be floods or foreign invasions. Prudent action guided by both resilience and partial control provides the best antidote for a world full of contingency. Not so in the domain of unknown unknowns; there caution or impetuousness are the proper response. And since there are no universal principles that govern a world of indeterminacy, Machiavelli leaves it at that.[61] Man does not have to accept chance with passive resignation. He is an agile dancer with an unpredictable partner. And thus he exercises power (*potentia*) in the face of uncertainty. "Fortune is arbiter of half of our actions ... she leaves the other half, or close to it, for us to govern."[62]

Protean Power and Actualized Potentiality

Power talks and speech has power. For Hannah Arendt the power of speech is the starting point for an individual who has the courage to reveal her or himself in the public realm.[63] Power cannot be stored. Power emerges as the actualization of a potentiality when people act in concert. It actualizes in common projects through speech and action. Arendt

---

[58] Machiavelli 1998: 12, 15, 16, 29, 138. In a few places Machiavelli refers also to two other kinds of power: *potentato* applied to a self-directed and self-enclosed agent or power-holder, as in potentate, normally a government (pp. 45 and 72); and *potente* (p. 43), meaning one who is strong or powerful, not necessarily a prince or ruler. On this point and many others we are indebted to Jill Frank's astute reading of the text.
[59] Bernstein 1996.   [60] Machiavelli 1998: 98.   [61] Lockwood 2013: 16.
[62] Machiavelli 1998: 98.
[63] Arendt 1998: 175, 178–79, 186, 189–90, 194, 199, 200, 205–6, 220.

agrees with Machiavelli, Foucault, and Deleuze: in the dynamics of the creation and evolution of power, it is not only outcomes that matter but processes of power actualization. It takes individual speech to start a work of politics; it takes a joining together to end it. Along the way, and to great frustration, the unexpected is bound to happen. Power is not static. It requires actualization of potentialities. Power is revealed and exhausted in the performance of bringing people together. In politics, as in Christianity, against all odds the new and unexpected is a potentiality that is always on the cusp of being born.[64]

Gilles Deleuze is also interested in speech and the chance events it can create.[65] In developing the concept of power, he updates and dissents from Foucault. Deleuze argues that control over communication is even more individualizing and repressive than disciplinary power. Yet even though speech and social communications are thoroughly dominated by corporate actors, they still offer the prospect for authenticity and independence through acts of "fabulation" and imagination that can add up to refusal.[66] "Rebellious spontaneity" can upend control. Deleuze thus argues that "we've got to hijack speech ... The key thing may be to create vacuoles of noncommunication, circuit breakers, so we can elude control."[67] Echoing Machiavelli, Deleuze envisages new kinds of events "that can't be explained by the situations that give rise to them, or into which they lead. They appear for a moment, and it's that moment that matters, it's the chance we must seize."[68]

But speech is inherently indeterminate and easily stunted. Students of international law have debated at great length the degree of indeterminacy that inheres in norms and laws.[69] Treaty negotiations, for example, often yield international agreements that are unclear, incoherent, or ambiguous. Some scholars hold that the process of international negotiation eventually forces an unambiguous interpretation or enunciation of an agreed-upon norm to specific situations.[70] Others demur and argue that on politically contentious issues no such force exists in an anarchic international system or a weak international order; relevant norms will remain

---

[64] In criticizing Arendt, Judith Butler has suggested that we must avoid identity essentialism by acknowledging the plurality of the self and include in political analysis things Arendt's emphasis on action and speech in the public realm slights: performative aspects of bodily speech, the precarious, the private, and economic and social rights. Butler 2015: 66–98.
[65] Deleuze 1995.   [66] Ibid.: 174.   [67] Ibid.: 175.   [68] Ibid.: 176.
[69] Kardon 2017: 64–66. In behavioral arguments of international relations and politics more generally, this is known as the problem of multiple equilibria. Game theorists try to solve the problem by deriving focal points for coordination that are rooted in common knowledge. To the extent that common knowledge is collective and requires meaning determinacy, the solution, though widely accepted, lacks full persuasive force as Chris Reus-Smit argues in Chapter 3.
[70] Koh 1997: 2646.

indeterminate as does the entire edifice of international law. The forces that bring about unambiguous interpretation of legal outcomes are thus profoundly political.[71] Between these two positions weaker versions of indeterminacy arguments hold sway.[72]

Because speech can be stunted, Deleuze and Guattari's diagnosis of power develops an entirely new and idiosyncratic conceptual vocabulary.[73] It aims at side-stepping and undermining all hierarchies of established thought. For Deleuze and Guattari the centralization of modern society "overcodes" the segmentation of traditional society. Politics thus penetrates all segments and all individuals. Stable and predictable "molar" macro-structures of the state are deeply interrelated with unstable and unpredictable "molecular" processes or "flow quanta" and "line segments." The molar structures of the capitalist welfare state do not "control" flows of capital and information, but render them legible and manageable by "coding" or "overcoding" them. Molar state structures thus are creatively adapting to changes and transformations in the molecular flows and their micro-politics. At times, however, molecular processes escape adaptable molar structures by taking a "line of flight." For Deleuze and Guattari small is not beautiful. Instead, the molecular is often proto-fascist. Deleuze and Guattari play up the importance of potentiality and the unexpected. Although they develop an esoteric terminology to escape from the shackles of conventional speech and thought, their insistence on the intersection of molar and molecular worlds and lines of flight resonates deeply with this book's insistence on the intersection of control and protean power and the importance of the unexpected in world politics.

Shifting our perspective, Aristotle and Agamben find power not only in the relations between but also within subjects as well as between subjects and objects.[74] Far from disavowing the importance of the public realm, they place it in the encompassing political significance of human potentialities and impotentialities in the many sites where power dynamics create and intersect with the unexpected.

---

[71] Koskenniemi 1989: 35–40, 59, 590–91, 597.   [72] Solum 1987.

[73] Deleuze and Guattari 1987: 224–27. We are deeply indebted to Anna Wojciuk for making us understand better this difficult text. Like Guattari and Deleuze, Martin Heidegger calls for a new language that does not suffer from the tyranny of the public, thus setting free the dormant power of the potential. Heidegger 1977: 193–99.

[74] The distinction between and within subjects and objects does not map cleanly onto the difference between inter-subjective and intra-subjective. Unlike Aristotle, contemporary theorists deal with the intra-subjective only in the sense of there being no subject that describes an empty signifier (Lacan), pure contingency (Agamben), or an assemblage (Deleuze and Guattari). We thank Anna Wojciuk for helping us appreciate this point.

For Aristotle the self is not a unified agent ready for action.[75] The self is instead plural, subject and object, doer and being done to.[76] Whether and how power remains a potential capacity waiting to be actualized (*energeia*) depends on the context. It is through actualization or "being-at-work" that the self creates potentiality. There exists then a dynamic and reciprocal relationship within each person between his or her actuality and potentiality. For Aristotle the final end and cause (*telos*) that humans aim at as they find themselves in unending chains of inter- and intra-subjective relationships is "happiness" or well-being (*eudaimon*). And agents have at their disposal cornucopia of power potentialities to achieve well-being. Aristotle's soul exists and reveals itself only in the specificity of each individual's practices grounded in dynamically evolving actualities and potentialities. For Aristotle there is no universal plan or playbook for attaining happiness. It needs to be struggled for and chosen with every step we take along life's path. His thinking is relational and relativist with respect to the world of inter-subjectivity. It is relational and non-relativist with respect to a person's desire (*orexis*) or conscious choice (*prohairesis*).[77]

Drawing on and interrogating Aristotle, Giorgio Agamben theorizes individual choice even further by developing the concepts of impotentiality and destituent power.[78] Impotentiality is the power of not doing, of deciding not to run before the race begins or not to end with the finish line in sight. Agamben draws on Aristotle who writes that "every potentiality is at the same time a potentiality for the opposite ... Everything which is capable may fail to be actualized. Therefore that which is capable of being may both be and not be. Therefore the same thing is capable of being and not being."[79] For Agamben destituent power, or not doing, is an activity rather than its negation; the two concepts are linked. Inoperativity exists in a zone of indeterminacy best described in the Greek middle voice, lacking in English, which is neither active nor passive. This is a space for useless use that relates to both the active self and the self of potentiality. A modest act of distancing by not doing is not a liberation of the individual. It points instead to a dialectics without movement as a condition of change. Although it may seem small, for Agamben this act has great political significance. It demarcates a sphere of "destituent" power that de-activates the machinery of the state. If constituent power is describing the politics of revolution and insurrection, a violence that creates a new order on the terrain of the old, destituent power has the task of imagining

---

[75] Frank 2005.   [76] Ibid.   [77] Aristotle 1933: 1048a11.
[78] Agamben 2014; 1999, 177–84.
[79] Aristotle 1933: 1050b9–11. See also 1019b17–21 and 1046a30–35. We thank Professor Frank for finding textual support for our intuition.

an entirely different still-to-become politics.[80] It is a radical form of an-archaic power. Drained of nature, essence, and a stable identity, the subject of control power thus becomes both the center and the agent of a process that "accomplishes something which is being accomplished in him."[81] For Agamben agrees with Aristotle that what is true of agents is true of the world they inhabit. Both are actual and filled with enormous potentialities and impotentialities. "This is the origin (and the abyss) of human power."[82] Individual choice thus activates the unpredictable in time, space, and politics.

The purpose of power analysis for a political theorist is to think about the nature of the polity, including questions about organized violence and the common good, freedom, and responsibility.[83] The purpose of expla-natory theory is to think about micro-theories of action and macro-theories of domination with a specific focus on the behavior and outcome of social action. The first engages in constitutive, the second in causal analysis. This section has fallen squarely in the domain of political theory; the discussion of the different faces of power in Chapter 1 in that of explanatory theory. The distinction is not ironclad. Lukes' third face of power, for example, spans both types of theory as does Hobbes' theory of sovereign power. And so does the pragmatic and eclectic stance we have articulated in the opening of this book. Re-specifying the concept of power, as in this book, is not the same as developing a theory of power. It is folly to chase the chimera of a general theory of power. The best we can do is be aware of how a specific concept of power fits into different theoretical traditions or orientations, and how those traditions or orienta-tions are then remade by that concept.

Power and Imagination

Fictional expectations are an important mechanism that activate the unpredictable. Economic sociologist Jens Beckert probes the "how-possibles" in Aristotle's and Agamben's world of potentialities. *Imagined Futures* emerge from collective economic practices rather than individual stories. They are make-belief imaginaries with which actors stabilize an unknown future.[84] Risk-taking and capitalist growth depend on the inter-pretive frames that help actors to cope with contingency and uncertainty through imagining a future that is familiar. Actors pretend a future present that instills confidence to act under conditions of uncertainty. As in literary fiction, a present future is a world all of its own. The radical contingency of

---

[80] Agamben 2014: 70.   [81] Ibid.: 68.   [82] Agamben 1999: 182.   [83] Guzzini 2016b: 27.
[84] Beckert 2016: 8–12, 61–67.

that world is stabilized by a variety of everyday mechanisms and practices, which in moments of crisis can collapse overnight, as was true at the height of the financial crisis in 2008. Fictional expectations thus help actors to coordinate their behavior. They affect the future directly in performance – through enactment in practices and by existing institutions. This challenges how we normally think about the seeming efficacy of control. It is protean rather than control power that captures the volatility inherent in uncertain environments and that taps the agile responses of actors with their often fictional expectations.

Similarly, Annelise Riles has documented how uncertainty has shaped legal fictions surrounding the posting of collateral that is central to the functioning of global derivative markets.[85] The problem of temporality in financial contracts is solved pragmatically by quotidian legal practices that create a legal fiction of calculability that delimits the uncertainties and indeterminacies in financial markets. As a matter of practice, collateral is a chain of legal fictions about the rights of parties that appear well understood when, in fact, they are not. Such fictions are placeholders communicating a collective commitment among market participants to an arrangement that is useful though false. Although they are problematically related to markets, legal fictions are readily accepted and thus become reliable predictors and indeed creators of market realities.

More than in the social sciences, the concept of imagination is central in the arts. To be sure, economic and literary fiction are not the same. "Design fiction" implemented by collective actors focuses on their practical credibility; "mere fiction" told by an individual storyteller intent on creating an inherently persuasive story is not.[86] Both, however, point to a world richly filled with potentialities. In his play *Constellations*, for example, writer Nick Payne creates a multitude of possible worlds all hanging on different turns of phrases spoken at different times by the play's two protagonists, a bee-keeper and a quantum physicist. Specifically, Payne plays with the notion of time reversibility. The basic laws of quantum physics do not know past or present. "Time is irrelevant at the level of a-atoms and molecules. It's symmetrical."[87] The possibility exists "that we are part of a multiverse . . . at any given moment, several outcomes can co-exist simultaneously."[88] In that multiverse every choice made or not made exists in an ensemble of parallel universes too large to imagine. And yet, in that vastness honeybees live their intensely short lives with "an unfailing clarity of purpose."[89] That raises the bar enormously for a

---

[85] Riles 2011. Lockwood and Nelson (Chapter 8) discuss the importance of "legal fiction" and the world of make-believe in the world of finance.
[86] Beckert 2016: 71.　[87] Payne 2012: 74.　[88] Ibid.: 22–23.　[89] Ibid.: 47.

predictive science of politics. Tom Stoppard's play *Arcadia* also engages issues of potentialities. For Valentine, the play's mathematical biologist, "the unpredictable and the predetermined unfold together to make everything the way it is."[90] In the arts, the creation of a pretend reality is shared by author and audience. In politics the pretend reality of Donald Trump's "alternate facts" and Adolf Hitler's "Big Lie" is the product of deliberate political manipulation. The relation between fiction and reality is complementary. In inventing their own reality, fiction and politics enhance the possibilities that inhere in uncertainty. Far from negating it, fiction and politics enlarge the heretofore unimagined. The potential and the actual, power capacity and power capability are deeply intertwined.

The study of power, in the words of Robert Dahl, is grounded in observations that "don't defy the laws of nature as we understand them."[91] That view of the laws of nature continues to be shaped profoundly by a mechanical understanding of the political and natural universe, equilibrium models, and classical probability theory dating back to the seventeenth century. Conventions of scholarship have congealed into a worldview, with more (reliable and valid indicators and innovative measurement and modeling techniques permitting replication) and less (applying significance tests to populations rather than samples and reporting only positive findings because negative ones are next-to-impossible to publish) admirable traits.

But as Immanuel Wallerstein and his colleagues argued in *Open the Social Sciences*, what is truly remarkable is how old-fashioned and out-of-step with current scientific beliefs and practices this view of natural science is.[92] Many natural scientists actually believe in non-linearity rather than linearity, complexity rather than simplification, the impossibility of distancing measurer from measurement, and, occasionally, the superiority of qualitative, interpretive capaciousness over quantitative, rigorous precision. This shift in the perspective of nature as active and creative rather than passive and repetitive makes the mechanical, "scientific" construction of the social world in international relations appear like a superstitious oddity handed down from ancient times. The resolute belief that the micro-world aggregates up to explain the macro-world looks incongruous when complexity and massive perturbation mark that macro-world.[93] The natural and the social world is a complex rather than a complicated system. It is creative and active in its self-organization. It is not resting inertly at or near a fictitious point of equilibrium. Novelty and the unexpected play a large part in the contemporary scientific

---

[90] Stoppard 1993: 47.   [91] Dahl 1957: 214.   [92] Gulbenkian Commission 1996: 60–63.
[93] *International Organization* 2017.

understanding of "the laws of nature as we understand them" that Robert Dahl invoked half a century ago. The actualization of protean power potentialities in a world of the unexpected fits right into this contemporary scientific conception of nature.

This is Alexander Wendt's fundamental point in his book *Quantum Mind and Social Science*. Wendt makes a bold argument establishing the possibility of a unified ontology for the natural and social world that links the one real world we inhabit inextricably to an infinity of possible worlds from which the real world emerges once we measure it.[94] Human beings and their experiences are for Wendt not given but potential realities deserving close study. Experience is not grounded in a world of separable, constitutionally pre-social individuals struggling to achieve sociability in a context of competition, atomism, and efficient causation. Rather, experience is grounded in a world that is relational, social, and political through and through. In this account of human experience, Wendt agrees with "pre-classical mechanics classicists" like Aristotle who rely on a logic of "both/and" rather than "either/or." He similarly avoids post-Enlightenment dichotomies such as subject–object, mind–body, part–whole, desire–reason.[95] One central aspect of the reality Wendt and Aristotle study are ongoing potentialities or powers (*dunameis*). In this book we have identified protean power as one such ongoing potentiality that is always ready for actualization in the in-between spaces of an always shared world.

Wendt attacks the unchallenged, reigning assumption that social life is governed by the laws of classical physics. A century after the quantum revolution this is not a far-fetched argument. For example, Kenneth Boulding's orderly "loss of strength gradient" stipulates that power diffuses as an actor's strength diminishes the further he or she moves away from home base.[96] Experimental advances in quantum physics, however, have confirmed quantum entanglement, the notion of "spooky action at a distance," strange and unpredictable effects that show separate particles to be completely entangled at very long distances.[97] Expressed by wave functions, quantum probabilities are entirely different from classical probabilities into which they collapse only at the limit. Quantum probabilities offer complete descriptions of all potential realities. Classical probabilities are incomplete descriptions of one, existing reality. To be sure, wave functions exist only at the level of subatomic particles. But the experimental evidence in physics has firmly established quantum theory as the reigning view of how nature works. The implications of that view,

---

[94] Wendt 2015.
[95] Ibid.: 4, 31, 34, 35, 37. Professor Frank, personal communication, March 5, 2017.
[96] Boulding 1962: 262.   [97] Markoff 2015; Wendt 2015: 53–54.

however, remain a subject of intense debate. Experimental evidence in a variety of social science fields such as quantum decision theory and quantum consciousness theory are beginning to accumulate. It is much too early to assess whether various branches of quantum theory will withstand sustained scientific testing in the social sciences. But as Wendt points out, in their early stages some of the results look intriguing, even promising, in accounting for otherwise jarring incongruities.

As radical and unfamiliar as this view may appear to international relations scholars today, it would not have surprised Aristotle. Going beyond Hobbes' sparse and unidimensional view of power as control, he probed in different ways the relation between actual power capabilities and the actualization of potential capacities. Important thinkers of contemporary society and politics have similarly sought to go beyond a one-sided conceptualization of power as capability or hierarchical order. John Dewey, for example, writes about power as "the sum of conditions available for bringing the desirable end into existence."[98] Judith Butler invokes a power that circulates "without voice or signature."[99] Zygmunt Bauman writes that "liquid life is a precarious life, lived under conditions of constant uncertainty;"[100] in modernity "the prime technique of power is now escape, slippage, elision and avoidance."[101] And William Connolly explores the fragility of things revealed by self-organizing processes that foster unpredictable, adaptive creativity.[102]

A generation ago, politics typically occurred in macro-institutions, be they liberal, statist, or corporatist. In today's volatile world power is shifting from the macro- to the micro-level. Institutions are evaluated for their effectiveness in shaping the incentives of individual action rather than their collective purposes. Resilience has become the central concept in addressing the radical unknowns and unpredictabilities in ecology, finance, and security.[103] Under conditions of inescapable uncertainty states must "insure against the fallibility of their assumptions, marshal their power more conservatively, and prepare for the likelihood of predictive failure by developing the intellectual capability to react to the unknown."[104] Differing on any number of important issues, the late Foucault and Hayek agreed on this one: individuals and their immediate communities are becoming ever more important to the problem of

---

[98] Dewey 1980: 246. We thank Alex Livingston for sharing with us his unpublished paper and pointing out the similarity between Dewey and the concept of protean power. Livingston (2017: 12) writes that "energy is not a unified substance. It is a placeholder for the plurality of material, social and emotional interactions that define the contours of particular practical situations."

[99] Butler 1997: 6.   [100] Bauman 2000: 1–2, 11.   [101] Bauman 2005: 11.

[102] Connolly 2005; 2013; Dewey 1980; Livingston 2017.

[103] Walker and Cooper 2011; Chandler 2014.   [104] Porter 2016: 239.

governance under conditions of man-made risk and uncertainties.[105] The resilience of society and the adaptability of individuals are ever more important, and with it – for better and for worse – protean power potentialities awaiting their actualization. Today's behavioral economics, big data and nudges prepare the ground for the future of brain research and neuro-technologies applied to human happiness. These developments, our analysis implies, may shift the sites of protean power, but they will not reduce the unpredictabilities brought about by the dynamics of protean and control power.

Across the ages political theorists have acknowledged power and uncertainty, rooted in the infinitely variegated relations between actual and potential power. This book's argument about power and uncertainty resonates with that rich tradition. Little is gained by insisting on the primacy of one or the other kind of power or to view one kind of power as a parasite of the other.[106] What matters is the intermingling of their risk- and uncertainty-enhancing effects. Protean power intersects with control power in the overlapping domains of uncertainty and risk, thus both enhancing and illuminating the unexpected in world politics.

The United States and America

The last half century has seen a prolonged, inconclusive debate about the unavoidable decline or continued primacy of the United States and American society. With particular focus on its military, economic, and diplomatic dimensions, the rise of the Soviet Union in the 1950s, Japan in the 1980s, and China in the first decade of the twenty-first century have fed into US anxieties and self-doubts reflected in animated and anguished debates. In the late 1980s, for example, public debate was captivated by the cyclical theory of the rise and the fall of great powers. China's recent and India's anticipated rise have raised new questions about the nature of their power. China has been called a "partial," India a "modest" power.[107] Furthermore, the unexpected calamity of the financial crisis of 2008 and a slow recovery in its aftermath as well as the spread of ISIS have spurred new disagreements about the role of the United States and America in the evolving international order. Like rafts that ride the rip currents of world politics these debates persist without any prospect of ever being resolved.

---

[105] Chandler 2013.
[106] Isaac 1987: 6; Morriss 2002: xiii; Pansardi 2011; Dahl 1957: 206; Ringmar 2007: 195–96.
[107] Shambaugh 2013.

Whatever the state of this conversation may be, the American president continues to wield enormous powers. He exerts control over others by commanding the US military, tapping enormous economic resources, negotiating at the highest levels of diplomacy, getting broad media coverage, and presiding over one of the largest, wealthiest, and most dynamic societies in the world. Admittedly, presidential power is not unlimited. The assessment of how far that power reaches and what it controls varies, depending on when and where one looks or whom one asks. International relations scholars explain, and sometimes predict, such limitations by pointing to inadequate resources and strategies. Yet it is often the case that actors armed with ample resources and carefully crafted strategies fail.

Despite its position of primacy, the United States is unable to avoid the effects of protean power. In former President Obama's words "America, as the most powerful country on earth, still does not control everything around the world."[108] His approach to American foreign policy accepted ambivalence and ambiguity as unavoidable byproducts of a complex international system. He was a realist when necessary in the military defense of US vital security interests. He was a liberal in his efforts to strengthen multilateral approaches and international norms. Weary of American self-righteousness and mindful of the need for US leadership, Obama tailored US policies to specific situations. He preferred tactics to strategy. To put it in terms of this book's argument: Obama did not think that the United States could control world politics, but had to adapt flexibly to unpredictable protean power dynamics.

President Trump speaks of Obama as a spineless pragmatist and feckless opportunist whose lack of a sense of national greatness made him accept or create power vacuums, violence, and volatility throughout the world. Trump's approach to politics is to produce such volatility deliberately and exploit the uncertainties it creates. He channels information almost randomly to create uncertainties and thus unbalance and defeat his opponents. Trump has little knowledge of or interest in directional policies. Instead, he aims at maximizing volatility so that he can make "great deals." His approach to politics merges a ruthless pursuit to control others with the tactic of unpredictability.[109] He is wagering that a transactional approach to international relations and unwavering commitment to American greatness will be effective. It is a bet placed on the success of unrestricted, unilateral control power and of protean power dynamics creating heightened volatility and unpredictability.

Explicit acknowledgment of protean power processes is an important step in developing an approach that does not aim only for unachievable

[108] Baker 2014, A1.   [109] Lee 2016.

levels of political control, but allows also for practical guides to political creativity. Neither kind of power is inherently morally desirable or undesirable. But in their interaction both create unpredictable change and "forms of everyday political engagement and mobilization" that are crucial for a comprehensive analysis of world politics.[110] Prudence requires getting ready for the unexpected by investing in the resilience of both state and society. In the face of the unpredictable, Obama placed his confidence in America's resilience and capacities.[111] Trump aims instead to rebuild US capabilities and restore US greatness, whatever that may mean. The moral purposes that imbue both Obama's localized cosmopolitanism and Trump's assertive nationalism are indispensable for the articulation of normative political orders that will unavoidably remain exposed to the dynamics of control and protean power processes.

One important example of protean power in world politics is the unmatched dynamism and transnational spread of American practices. Virtually unknown today, during the First World War Randolph Bourne was an early observer of this aspect of American power when he published an essay under the title "Trans-national America."[112] America was the first "cosmopolitan federation of national colonies," combining American patriotism with internationalism. A century later, the ideas and practices of the American trans-nation are affecting and being affected by processes that spread around the world with greater ease than ever before. Economic globalization and popular culture in its many manifestations have created what Aida Hozic has dubbed "Hollyworld" and made America an irresistible empire of mass consumption – persistent savings and current account deficits included.[113] The distinguishing characteristic of America's trans-nation lies in its active engagement of the world.

But that is only one of America's several faces. Another is America's fierce nationalism, steeped in the Jacksonianism of right-wing populism. Like liberal transnationalism it, too, is an enduring part of America's multiple traditions. Today, American politics is going through one of its periodic realignments. The cycle of presidential power shifts from Clinton to Bush, Bush to Obama, and Obama to Trump has occurred with increasing intensity and without producing large majorities. Out of the fractious politics within and between the different parts of America will eventually emerge, currently still unfathomable, something new. Protean power processes are churning in American society, upending all predictions and conventions. Walt Whitman captured this internal

---

[110] Howard and Walters 2014: 400.   [111] Goldberg 2016.
[112] Bourne 1977: 248–64. See also Keck 2016.   [113] Hozic 2001; de Grazia 2005.

division of America in the *Song of Myself:* "Do I contradict myself? Very well then I contradict myself; (I am large, I contain multitudes)."[114]

This is not to argue that either US or American ideas and practices are imprinting the world. Rather, their transfer sets free processes that generate new capacities as those ideas and practices are being examined, breached, negotiated, affirmed, and undermined. For better and for worse, American society is a vital node in the global circulation of protean power that illustrates the creative and destructive capacities of Americans and others to affirm, refuse, improvise, and innovate. What is true of cultural projects and practices holds more generally. "Although American popular culture necessarily carries the imprint of the society which produced it," writes C. W. E. Bigsby, "its movement beyond the confines of America changes both meaning and structure. It becomes plastic, a superculture, detached from its roots, and widely available for adaptation, absorption and mediation."[115]

The secret of the products and practices of America's ever changing technology complexes, knowledge industries, popular culture sites, and politics, among others, does not rest only in America as it exists but also in America as it is imagined. Narratives about American exceptionalism and the American dream are forever changing. For both US primacy in military, political, and economic affairs and America's hegemony in technology, knowledge, and entertainment are weakening not compared with any other state or society, but compared with the dynamism of a global system increasingly shaped by the influences of many other actors and processes. Yet America remains the only New World, spelled with capital letters. It is not merely a white brand – as is Shanghai with its 5,000 skyscrapers. The New World is an act of imagination and psychological rebellion against local living conditions and political arrangements throughout the world. Statues of Liberty, real and imagined, symbolize the enduring appeal of the New World and remind us of the often glaring distance that separates the imaginary from the real America.

How do we align these contrasting, even contradictory, observations about US and American power and the attempted homogenization and continuing pluralization of global politics through control and protean power? Modern technology is not only a superficial equalizer, but a wedge that opens up new spaces for the articulation of new commonalities and differences in and through political power. This creates a politics of hybridity rather than purity.[116] The tensions between and overlays of control and protean power illustrate that hybridization is neither spontaneous nor apolitical. It entails different forms of political struggle

---

[114] Blodgett 1953: 97.   [115] Bigsby 1975: xii–xiii.   [116] Pieterse 2004: 74–77.

reflected in practices of affirmation, refusal, improvisation, and innovation that are often heterogeneous and unpredictable.

International relations scholarship often focuses on US control over resources measured by territory, populations, GDP, the defense budget, market size, and other such indicators. This neglects protean power dynamics that America has enabled and that circulate widely in world politics. The dynamics of power in world politics are shaped by this US–American complex. The control exercised by power wielders is often upended by the spontaneous practices of their targets.[117] Since both aspects of power are deeply intertwined, to focus on one or the other impairs our understanding of the significance of and tensions between US and American power in world politics.

The coincidence of processes of Americanization and anti-Americanism shows that the United States and America are jointly creating a world that is simultaneously emerging into greater similarity *and* persistent diversity. In these processes the United States and America both win and lose. They are unable to bet confidently on the control and protean power dynamics marking world politics. And, deeply enmeshed with them, they are also unable to leave the tables at which the poker and roulette games of world politics are played.

---

[117] Aalberts 2012: 240.

References

Aalberts, Tanja E. 2012. Revisiting Sovereignty and the Diffusion of Power as Patterns of Global Governmentality, in Stefano Guzzini and Iver Neumann (eds.), *Diffusion of Power*. Basingstoke: Palgrave, 229–55.

Abbott, Andrew. 1988. Transcending General Linear Reality. *Sociological Theory* 6 (Fall): 169–86.

Abbott, Kenneth W., Jessica F. Green, and Robert O. Keohane. 2016. Organizational Ecology and Institutional Change in Global Governance. *International Organization* 70(2): 1–31.

Abdelal, Rawi. 2001. *National Purpose in the World Economy: Post-Soviet States in Comparative Perspective*. Ithaca, NY: Cornell University Press.

2007. *Capital Rules: The Construction of Global Finance*. Cambridge, MA: Harvard University Press.

2013. The Profits of Power: Commerce and Realpolitik in Eurasia. *Review of International Political Economy* 20(3): 421–56.

2015. The Multinational Firm and Geopolitics: Europe, Russian Energy, and Power. *Business and Politics* 17(3): 553–76.

Abdelal, Rawi and Mark Blyth. 2015. Just Who Put You in Charge? We Did: CRAs and the Politics of Ratings, in Alexander Cooley and Jack Snyder (eds.), *Ranking the World: Grading States as a Tool of Global Governance*. Cambridge University Press, 39–59.

Abdelal, Rawi, Esel Çekin, and Çigdem Çelik. 2015. Turkey and the Southern Corridor, Harvard Business School case 715-042.

Abdelal, Rawi, Alexander Jorov, and Sogomon Tarontsi. 2008a. Gazprom (A): Energy and Strategy in Russian History, Harvard Business School case 709-008.

2008b. Gazprom (B): Energy and Strategy in a New Era, Harvard Business School case 709-009.

2008c. Gazprom (C): The Ukrainian Crisis and its Aftermath, Harvard Business School case 709-010.

Abdelal, Rawi and Jonathan Kirshner. 1999/2000. Strategy, Economic Relations, and the Definition of National Interests. *Security Studies* 9(1/2): 119–56.

Abdelal, Rawi, Leonardo Maugeri, and Sogomon Tarontsi. 2014. Europe, Russia, and the Age of Gas Revolution, Harvard Business School case 715-006.

Abdelal, Rawi, Morena Skalamera, and Sogomon Tarontsi. 2015. The Sino-Russian Rapprochement: Energy Relations in a New Era, Harvard Business School case 715-016.

Abdelal, Rawi and Sogomon Tarontsi. 2011a. Energy Security in Europe (A): Nord Stream, Harvard Business School case 711-026.

2011b. Energy Security in Europe (B): The Southern Corridor, Harvard Business School case 711-033.

2012. Russia and China: Energy Relations and International Politics, Harvard Business School case 713-045.

Abdelal, Rawi, Rafael Di Tella, and Sogomon Tarontsi. 2014. Ukraine: On the Border of Europe and Eurasia, Harvard Business School case 714-042.

Abizaid, John P. and Rosa Brooks. 2014. US Should Take Lead on Setting Global Norms for Drone Strikes, *The Washington Post*, June 26, available at: www.washingtonpost.com, last accessed February 13, 2015.

Abulude, Samuel. 2016. Nigeria: Army Wants Cooperation with Nollywood on Boko Haram War Movies, available at: http://allafrica.com/stories/2016021 70127.html, last accessed June 30, 2016.

Acheson, Keith and Christopher J. Maule. 1994. Understanding Hollywood's Organization and Continuing Success. *Journal of Cultural Economics* 18: 271–300.

Acland, Charles R. 2003. *Screen Traffic: Movies, Multiplexes, and Global Culture*. Durham, NC: Duke University Press.

Adas, Michael. 1989. *Machines as the Measure of Men*. Ithaca, NY: Cornell University Press.

Adler, Emanuel. 2008. The Spread of Security Communities: Communities of Practice, Self-Restraint, and Nato's Post-Cold War Transformation. *European Journal of International Relations* 14(2): 195–230.

Adler, Emanuel and Vincent Pouliot (eds.). 2011. *International Practices*. Cambridge University Press.

Adler-Nissen, Rebecca and Vincent Pouliot. 2014. Power in Practice: Negotiating the International Intervention in Libya. *European Journal of International Relations* 20(4): 893–96.

Admati, Anat and Martin Hellwig. 2013. *The Bankers' New Clothes: What's Wrong with Banking and What to Do about It*. Princeton University Press.

Agamben, Giorgio. 1999. *Potentialities*. Stanford University Press.

2014. What is a Destituent Power? *Environment and Planning D: Society and Space* 35: 65–74.

Ahlquist, John S. 2006. Economic Policy, Institutions, and Capital Flows: Portfolio and Direct Investment Flows in Developing Countries. *International Studies Quarterly* 50(3): 681–704.

Akerlof, George and Robert Shiller. 2009. *Animal Spirits: How Human Psychology Drives the Economy, and Why it Matters for Global Capitalism*. Princeton University Press.

Aksoy, Asu and Kevin Robins. 1992. Hollywood for the 21st Century: Global Competition for Critical Mass in Image Markets. *Cambridge Journal of Economics* (16): 1–22.

Al-Adnani, Abu Muhammad. 2015. Our People Respond to the Call of Allah, Site Intelligence Group.

Albahari, Maurizio. 2015. *Crimes of Peace: Mediterranean Migrations at the World's Deadliest Border*. Philadelphia, PA: University of Pennsylvania Press.

Al-Filistini, Abu Qatada. 2013. Radical Cleric Abu Qatada Advises Fighters in Syria to Reconcile, Site Intelligence Group.

Al-Gama'a al-Islamiya. 2004. The Strategy and Bombings of Al-Qa'ida: Errors and Perils, serialized in *Al-Sharq al-Awsat*.

Allen, Michael. 2003. *Contemporary US Cinema*. New York: Longman/Pearson.

Al-Maqdisi, Abu Muhammad. 2014. And Be Not Like Her Who Undoes the Thread Which She Has Spun, After It Has Become Strong, Pietervanostaeyen Blog, available at: http://pietervanostaeyen.com/2014/07/14/and-be-not-like-her-who-undoes-the-thread-which-she-has-spun-after-it-has-become-strong-by-shaykh-abu-muhammad-al-maqdisi.

Almond, Gabriel A. and Stephen J. Genco. 1977. Clouds, Clocks, and the Study of Politics. *World Politics* 29(4): 489–522.

Al-Qaeda in the Arabian Peninsula. 2010. *Inspire* 1, available at: http://jihadology.net/2010/06/30/al-qa%E2%80%99idah-in-the-arabian-peninsula-releases-it-first-english-language-magazine-inspire/.

Al-Sahab. 2007a. Interview with Aby Yahya al-Libi, Open Source Center.

2007b. The Will of the Martyr Uthman Who Carried Out a Suicide Operation, Open Source Center.

Al-Somali, Abu Salih. n.d. Terror Franchise: The Unstoppable Assassin – Techs Vital Role for its Success, available at: www.dni.gov/files/documents/ubl/english/Terror%20Franchise.pdf.

Alter, Karen J. and Sophie Meunier. 2009. The Politics of International Regime Complexity. *Perspectives on Politics* 7(1): 13–24.

Altman, Roger. 2016. The End of Economic Forecasting, *The Wall Street Journal*, June 23, A9.

Al-Zawahiri, Ayman. 2008. *The Exoneration*, available at: http://fas.org/irp/dni/osc/exoneration.pdf.

2013. General Guidelines for Jihad, Site Intelligence Group.

Anderson, Malcolm. 2000. The Transformation of Border Controls: A European Precedent, in Peter Andreas and Timothy Snyder (eds.), *The Wall Around the West: State Borders and Immigration Controls in North America and Europe*. Oxford: Rowman & Littlefield, 15–29.

Andreas, Peter. 2009. *Border Games: Policing the US–Mexico Divide*, 2nd edn. Ithaca, NY: Cornell University Press.

2013. *Smuggler Nation: How Illicit Trade Made America*. Oxford University Press.

Ang, Yuen Yuen. 2016. *How China Escaped the Poverty Trap*. Ithaca, NY: Cornell University Press.

Appiah, Kwame Anthony. 2005. *The Ethics of Identity*. Princeton University Press.

Arendt, Hannah. 1998. *The Human Condition*, 2nd edn. University of Chicago Press.

Arewa, Olufunmilayo. 2012. The Rise of Nollywood: Creators, Entrepreneurs, and Pirates, School of Law, University of California Irvine, Legal Studies Research Paper Series, No. 2012-11.

Aristotle. 1933. *Metaphysics*, vol. I: books 1–9, trans. Hugh Tredennick, Loeb Classical Library 271. Cambridge, MA: Harvard University Press.

2000. *Politics*, trans. Benjamin Jowett. Mineola, NY: Dover Publications.

Arnold, Martin. 2016. Big Banks Plan to Coin New Digital Currency, *Financial Times*, August 23, available at: www.ft.com/cms/s/0/1a962c16-6952-11e6-ae5b-a7cc5dd5a28c.html#axzz4lFOzurpn, last accessed August 23, 2016.

Axelrod, Robert and Michael D. Cohen. 1999. *Harnessing Complexity: Organizational Implications of a Scientific Frontier*. New York: Free Press.

Ayoub, Phillip M. 2014. With Arms Wide Shut: Threat Perception, Norm Reception, and Mobilized Resistance to LGBT Rights. *Journal of Human Rights* 13(3): 337–62.

2015. Contested Norms in New-Adopter States: International Determinants of LGBT Rights Legislation. *European Journal of International Relations* 21(2): 293–322.

Ayoub, Phillip M. and Agnes Chetaille. 2018. Movement/Countermovement Interaction and Instrumental Framing in a Multi-level World: Rooting Polish Lesbian and Gay Activism. *Social Movement Studies* 17(1).

Ayoub, Phillip M. and David Paternotte. 2014. Challenging Borders, Imagining Europe: Transnational LGBT Activism in a New Europe, in Jennifer Bickham-Mendez and Nancy Naples (eds.), *Border Politics, Social Movements and Globalization*. New York: New York University Press, 230–60.

Ayres, Ian and William Eskridge. 2014. The US Hypocrisy over Russia's Anti-Gay Laws, *The Washington Post*, Opinions section, January 31, available at: www.washingtonpost.com/opinions/us-hypocrisy-over-russias-anti-gay-laws/2014/01/31/3df0baf0-8548-11e3-9dd4-e7278db80d86_story.html, last accessed March 3, 2014.

Bachrach, Peter and Morton S. Baratz. 1962. Two Faces of Power. *American Political Science Review* 56(4): 947–52.

1963. Decisions and Nondecisions: An Analytical Framework. *American Political Science Review* 57(3): 632–42.

Baker, Peter. 2014. As World Boils, Fingers Point Obama's Way, *The New York Times*, August 15, A1, A9.

Baldwin, David A. 1985. *Economic Statecraft*. Princeton University Press.

1989. *Paradoxes of Power*. New York: Blackwell.

2013. Power and International Relations, in Walter E. Carlsnaess, Thomas Risse, and Beth Simmons (eds.), *Handbook of International Relations*. London: Sage, 273–97.

2016. *Power and International Relations: A Conceptual Approach*. Princeton University Press.

Bamman, David, Brendan O'Connor, and Noah A. Smith. 2013. Learning Latent Personas of Film Characters, ACL 2013, Sofia, Bulgaria, August.

Bank for International Settlements. 2016. *Quarterly Review: International Banking and Financial Market Developments*, December. Basel: Bank for International Settlements.

Barber, Benjamin R. 1992. Jihad vs McWorld, *Atlantic Monthly*, March, available at: www.theatlantic.com, last accessed June 26, 2015.

Barnes, Barry. 1988. *The Nature of Power*. Urbana, IL: University of Illinois Press.

Barnes, Brooks. 2013. Solving Equation of a Hit Film Script, with Data, *The New York Times*, May 6, available at: www.nytimes.com/2013/05/06/business/media/solving-equation-of-a-hit-film-script-with-data.html, last accessed September 7, 2017.

Barnett, Michael and Raymond Duvall. 2005. Power in Global Governance, in Michael Barnett and Raymond Duvall (eds.), *Power in Global Governance*. Cambridge University Press, 1–32.

Barnhart, Michael A. 1987. *Japan Prepares for Total War: The Search for Economic Security, 1919–1941*. Ithaca, NY: Cornell University Press.

Barrett, Devlin, Danny Yadron, and Daisuke Wakabayashi. 2014. Apple and Others Encrypt Phones, Fueling Government Standoff, *The Wall Street Journal*, November 18, available at: www.wsj.com/articles/apple-and-others-encrypt-ph ones-fueling-government-standoff-1416367801, last accessed September 6, 2017.

Barry, John, Amanda Bernard, Mark Dennis, Christopher Dickey, and Barbie Nadeau. 1999. Seeds of Carnage, *Newsweek International*, August 2, 28.

Bartel, Fritz. 2017. The Triumph of Broken: Oil, Finance, and the End of the Cold War, Ph D dissertation, Cornell University Promises.

Bateson, Ian. 2016. The "New Ukraine" is Failing Us, LGBT Activists Say, *The Guardian*, World news section, March 31, available at: www.theguardian.com/world/2016/mar/31/new-ukraine-government-lgbt-activists-gay-rights-zor yan-kis, last accessed July 13, 2016.

Bauman, Zygmunt. 2000. *Liquid Modernity*. Malden, MA: Blackwell.

2005. *Liquid Life*. Malden, MA: Polity Press.

Baumann, Martina. 2016. CRISPR/Cas9 Genome Editing: New and Old Ethical Issues Arising from a Revolutionary Technology. *NanoEthics* 10(2): 139–59.

Baumik, Kaushik. 2007. Lost in Translation: A Few Vagaries of the Alphabet Game Played between Bombay Cinema and Hollywood, in Paul Cooke (ed.), *World Cinema's "Dialogues" with Hollywood*. New York: Palgrave Macmillan, 201–17.

BBC News. 2015. Ukraine Passes Anti-Discrimination Law. November 12, available at: www.bbc.com/news/world-europe-34796835, last accessed December 5, 2015.

Beachy, Robert. 2014. *Gay Berlin: Birthplace of a Modern Identity*. New York: Knopf Doubleday.

Beck, Ulrich. 2005. *Power in the Global Age*. Malden, MA: Polity Press.

2007. *World at Risk*. Malden, MA: Polity Press.

Beckert, Jens. 2016. *Imagined Futures: Fictional Expectations and Capitalist Dynamics*. Cambridge, MA: Harvard University Press.

Beger, Nico J. 2004. *Tensions in the Struggle for Sexual Minority Rights in Europe: Que(e)rying Political Practices*. Manchester University Press.

Bennett, W. Lance. 2014. Response to Sidney Tarrow's Review. *Perspectives on Politics* 12(2): 470–71.

Bennett, W. Lance and Alexandra Segerberg. 2013. *The Logic of Connective Action: Digital Media and the Personalization of Contentious Politics*. Cambridge University Press.

Berenskoetter, Felix. 2007. Thinking About Power, in Felix Berenskoetter and M. J. Williams (eds.), *Power in World Politics*. New York: Routledge, 1–22.

2011. Reclaiming the Vision Thing: Constructivists as Students of the Future. *International Studies Quarterly* 55: 647–68.

Berger, J. M. and Jonathon Morgan. 2015. *The ISIS Twitter Census: Defining and Describing the Population of ISIS Supporters on Twitter*. Washington, DC: Brookings Institution.

Bernhard, William and David Leblang. 2006. *Democratic Processes and Financial Markets: Pricing Politics*. Cambridge University Press.

Bernhard, William, J. Lawrence Broz, and William Roberts Clark. 2002. The Political Economy of Monetary Institutions. *International Organization* 56(4): 693–723.

Bernstein, Peter. 1996. *Against the Gods: The Remarkable Story of Risk*. New York: John Wiley.

Bernstein, Steven, Richard Ned Lebow, Janice Gross Stein, and Steven Weber. 2000. God Gave Physics the Easy Problems: Adapting Social Science to an Unpredictable World. *European Journal of International Relations* 6(1): 43–76.

Berra, John. 2008. *Declarations of Independence: American Cinema and the Partiality of Independent Production*. Chicago, IL: Intellect.

Best, Jacqueline. 2008. Ambiguity, Uncertainty, and Risk: Rethinking Indeterminacy. *International Political Sociology* 2: 355–74.

Best, Jacqueline and William Walters. 2013. "Actor-Network Theory" and International Relationality: Lost (and Found) in Translation. *International Political Sociology* 7(3): 332–34.

Bially-Mattern, Janice 2005. Why "Soft Power" Isn't So Soft: Representational Force and the Sociolinguistic Construction of Attraction in World Politics. *Millennium – Journal of International Studies* 33(3): 583–612.

Biedroń, Robert and Marta Abramowicz. 2007. The Polish Educational System and the Promotion of Homophobia, in Marta Abramowicz (ed.), *The Situation of Bisexual and Homosexual Persons in Poland 2005 and 2006 Report*. Warsaw: Campaign Against Homophobia and Lambda Warsaw Association, 51–55.

Bigsby, C. W. E. 1975. Preface, in C. W. E. Bigsby (ed.), *Superculture: American Popular Culture and Europe*. Bowling Green, OH: Bowling Green University Popular Press, xi–xiii.

Bleiker, Roland. 2009. *Aesthetics and World Politics*. New York: Palgrave Macmillan.

Blodgett, Harold William. 1953. *The Best of Whitman*. New York: Ronald Press.

Blyth, Mark. 2002. *Great Transformations: Economic Ideas and Institutional Change in the Twentieth Century*. Cambridge University Press.

2006. Great Punctuations: Prediction, Randomness, and the Evolution of Comparative Political Science. *American Political Science Review* 100(4): 493–98.

Bob, Clifford. 2012. *The Global Right Wing and the Clash of World Politics*. Cambridge University Press.

Böhme, Rainer, Nicolas Christin, Benjamin Edelman, and Tyler Moore. 2015. Bitcoin: Economics, Technology, and Governance. *Journal of Economic Perspectives* 29(2): 213–38.

Bolton, Matthew and Thomas Nash. 2010. The Role of Middle Power–NGO Coalitions in Global Policy: The Case of the Cluster Munition Ban. *Global Policy* 1(2): 172–84.

Bookstaber, Richard. 2017. *The End of Theory: Financial Crises, the Failures of Economics, and the Sweep of Human Interaction.* Princeton University Press.

Borrie, John. 2009. *Unacceptable Harm: A History of How the Treaty to Ban Cluster Munitions Was Won.* Geneva: United Nations Publications.

Bouchard, Genevieve and Barbara Wake Carroll. 2002. Policy-making and Administrative Discretion: The Case of Immigration in Canada. *Canadian Public Administration* 45(2): 239–57.

Boulding, Kenneth E. 1962. *Conflict and Defense: A General Theory.* New York: Harper.

Bourne, Randolph. 1977. *The Radical Will: Selected Writings 1911–1918*, selection and Introduction Olaf Hansen. Berkeley, CA: University of California Press.

Bousquet, Antoine and Robert Geyer. 2011. Introduction: Complexity and the International Arena. *Cambridge Review of International Affairs* 24(1): 1–3.

Bower, Adam Stephen. 2012. Norm Development without the Great Powers: Assessing the Antipersonnel Mine Ban Treaty and the Rome Statute of the International Criminal Court, unpublished doctoral dissertation, University of British Columbia, Vancouver.

Boyd, Emily, Esteve Corbera, and Manuel Estrada. 2008. UNFCCC Negotiations (pre-Kyoto to COP-9): What the Process Says about the Politics of CDM-sinks. *International Environmental Agreements: Politics, Law and Economics* 8(2): 95–112.

Boykin, Scott A. 2010. Hayek on Spontaneous Order and Constitutional Design. *The Independent Review* 15(1): 19–34.

Breitegger, Alexander. 2012. *Cluster Munitions and International Law: Disarmament with a Human Face?* New York: Routledge.

Brigden, Noelle K. 2012. Like a War: The New Central American Refugee Crisis. *NACLA Report on the Americas* 45(4): 7–11.

2013. Uncertain Odysseys: Migrant Journeys and Transnational Routes, PhD dissertation, Cornell University.

2015. Transnational Journeys and the Limits of Hometown Resources: Salvadoran Migration in Uncertain Times. *Migration Studies* 3(2): 241–59.

2016. Improvised Transnationalism: Clandestine Migration at the Borders of International Relations and Anthropology. *International Studies Quarterly* 60 (2): 343–54.

Brigden, Noelle and Cetta Mainwaring. 2016. Matryoshka Journeys: (Im)mobility during Migration. *Geopolitics* 21(2): 407–34.

Brodie, Bernard. 1978. The Development of Nuclear Strategy. *International Security* 2(4): 65–83.

Brooks, Stephen G. and William C. Wohlforth. 2008. *World Out of Balance.* Princeton University Press.

Brown, Vahid. 2007. *Cracks in the Foundation: Leadership Schisms in al-Qa'ida from 1989–2006*. West Point, NY: Combating Terrorism Center.

Bryden, Alan. 2013. *International Law, Politics and Inhumane Weapons: The Effectiveness of Global Landmine Regimes*. New York: Routledge.

Buchanan, Paul G. 2010. Lilliputian in Fluid Times: New Zealand Foreign Policy after the Cold War. *Political Science Quarterly* 125(2): 255–79.

Buchheit, Lee C. and Jeremiah S. Pam. 2004. The *Pari Passu* Clause in Sovereign Debt Instruments. *Emory Law Journal* 53: 869–922.

Bunzel, Cole. 2016. "Come Back to Twitter": A Jihadi Warning Against Telegram, Jihadica Blog, available at: www.jihadica.com/come-back-to-twitter.

Burke, Edmund. 1908. On Conciliation with the Colonies, in *Speeches and Letters on American Affairs*. London: J. M. Dent, 76–141.

Butler, Judith. 1997. *The Psychic Life of Power: Theories in Subjection*. Stanford University Press.

2015. *Notes toward a Performative Theory of Assembly*. Cambridge, MA: Harvard University Press.

Buzan, Barry. 1991. New Patterns of Global Security in the Twenty-first Century. *International Affairs* 67(3): 431–51.

Byrne, David and Gillian Callaghan. 2013. *Complexity Theory and the Social Sciences: The State of the Art*. New York: Routledge.

Callimachi, Rukmini. 2015. ISIS and the Lonely Young American, *The New York Times*, June 27, available at: www.nytimes.com/2015/06/28/world/americas/isis-online-recruiting-american.html, last accessed September 6, 2017.

Callon, Michel. 1986. Some Elements of a Sociology of Translation: Domestication of the Scallops and Fishermen of St Brieuc Bay, in John Law (ed.), *Power, Action and Belief: A New Sociology of Knowledge?*. London: Routledge, 196–233.

Climate Action Network (CAN). 2006. Reducing Emissions from Tropical Deforestation, CAN International Briefing Paper, available at: www.climate network.org/sites/default/files/briefing_paper-reducing_deforestation_emiss ions_Final.pdf.

2007. Reducing Emissions from Deforestation in Developing Countries, 18 May, available at: http://climatenetwork.org/sites/default/files/CAN_I_inter vention_-_deforestation_SB24.pdf.

Carling, Jorgen. 2007. Migration Control and Migrant Fatalities at the Spanish–African Borders. *International Migration Review* 41(2): 316–43.

Caro, Mark. 2013. Nate Silver: In Hollywood, "Nobody Knows Anything," *Chicago Tribune*, May 15, available at: http://articles.chicagotribune.com/20 13–05-15/entertainment/ct-ent-0516-nate-silver-20130515_1_nate-silver-so-many-predictions-silver-linings-playbook, last accessed October 17, 2017.

Carpenter, Charli. 2011. Vetting the Advocacy Agenda: Network Centrality and the Paradox of Weapons Norms. *International Organization* 65(1): 69–102.

Carr, Matthew. 2016. *Fortress Europe: Dispatches from a Gated Continent*. New York: New Press.

Carruthers, Bruce G. 2015. Financialization and the Institutional Foundations of the New Capitalism. *Socio-Economic Review* 13(2): 379–98.

Cartwright, Nancy. 2007. *Hunting Causes and Using Them: Approaches in Philosophy and Economics.* Cambridge University Press.

Casillas, Rodolfo R. 2007. *Una Vida Discreta, Fugaz y Anonima: Los Centroamericanos Transmigrantes en Mexico.* Mexico City: CNDH.

Cassidy, John. 1997. Chaos in Hollywood: Can Science Explain Why a Movie is a Hit or a Flop? *The New Yorker,* March 31, 36–37, 41–44.

Castronova, Edward. 2014. *Wildcat Currency: How the Virtual Money Revolution is Transforming the Economy.* New Haven, CT: Yale University Press.

Castronova, Edward and Joshua A. T. Fairfield. 2014. The Digital Wallet Revolution, *The New York Times,* September 11, A23.

Chabot, Sean. 2002. Transnational Diffusion and the African-American Reinvention of the Ghandian Repertoire, in Jackie Smith and Hank Johnston (eds.), *Globalization and Resistance: Transnational Dimensions of Social Movements.* Oxford: Rowman & Littlefield, 97–114.

Chadi, Nicholas. 2017. When Doctors Know that They Don't Know, *The Boston Globe,* February 25.

Chafkin, Max. 2014. Sheriff of the Web. *Fastcompany,* 90–108.

Champagne, Phil. 2014. *The Book of Satoshi: The Collected Writings of Bitcoin Creator Satoshi Nakamoto.* USA: e53 Publishing.

Chan, Anita Say. 2013. *Networking Peripheries: Technological Futures, Information Contests and the Myth of Digital Universalism.* Cambridge, MA: MIT Press.

Chandler, David. 2013. Resilience and the Autotelic Subject: Toward a Critique of the Societalization of Security. *International Political Sociology* 7: 210–26.

2014. *Resilience: The Governance of Complexity.* New York: Routledge.

Chase, Kerry A. 2008. Moving Hollywood Abroad: Divided Labor Markets and the New Politics of Trade in Services. *International Organization* 62(4): 653–87.

Choi, Stephen J., Mitu Gulati, and Robert E. Scott. 2016. Contractual Arbitrage, in *Oxford Handbook of International Governance,* available at: https://papers.ss rn.com/sol3/papers.cfm?abstract_id=2795264.

Chong, Kimberly and David Tuckett. 2015. Constructing Conviction through Action and Narrative: How Money Managers Manage Uncertainty and the Consequence for Financial Market Functioning. *Socio-Economic Review* 13(2): 309–30.

Christopherson, Susan. 2011. Hard Jobs in Hollywood: How Concentration in Distribution Affects the Production Side of the Media Entertainment Industry, in Dwayne Winseck and Dal Yong Jin (eds.), *The Political Economies of Media: The Transformation of the Global Media Industries.* London: Bloomsbury Academic, 123–41.

2012. Hollywood in Decline? US Film and Television Producers Beyond the Era of Fiscal Crisis. *Cambridge Journal of Regions, Economics, and Society* 6(1): 141–57.

Christopherson, Susan and Michael Storper. 1989. The Effects of Flexible Specialization on Industrial Politics and the Labor Market: The Motion Picture Industry. *Industrial and Labor Relations Review* 42 (April): 331–47.

Clausewitz, Carl von. 1984. *On War*, ed. and trans. Michael Howard and Peter Paret. Princeton University Press.

Clegg, Stewart R. 1989. *Frameworks of Power*. London: Sage.

Clenfield, Jason and Pavel Alpeyev. 2014. The Other Bitcoin Power Struggle, *Bloomberg Businessweek*, April 24, available at: www.bloomberg.com/bw/arti cles/2014–04-24/bitcoin-miners-seek-cheap-electricity-to-eke-out-a-profit, last accessed March 18, 2015.

Clinton, Hillary. 2011. Hillary Clinton on Gay Rights Abroad: Secretary of State Delivers Historic LGBT Speech in Geneva, *Huffington Post*, Queer Voices section, December 6, available at: www.huffingtonpost.com/2011/12/06/hil lary-clinton-gay-rights-speech-geneva_n_1132392.html, last accessed November 12, 2016.

Cofnas, Abe. 2014. Bitcoin: Currency or Commodity? *Futures* 43(5): 10.

Cohen, Benjamin J. 2001. Electronic Money: New Day or False Dawn? *Review of International Political Economy* 8(2): 197–225.

2009. A Grave Case of Myopia. *International Interactions* 35(4): 436–44.

Collyer, Michael. 2010. Stranded Migrants and the Fragmented Journey. *Journal of Refugee Studies* 23(3): 273–93.

Connolly, William E. 2005. *Pluralism*. Durham, NC: Duke University Press.

2013. *The Fragility of Things: Self-Organizing Processes, Neoliberal Fantasies, and Democratic Activism*. Durham, NC: Duke University Press.

Cooke, Paul (ed.). 2007a. *World Cinema's "Dialogues" with Hollywood*. New York: Palgrave Macmillan.

2007b. From Caligari to Edward Scissorhands: The Continuing Meta-Cinematic Journey of German Expressionism, in Paul Cooke (ed.), *World Cinema's "Dialogues" with Hollywood*. New York: Palgrave Macmillan, 17–34.

Cooper, Andrew F. and Timothy M. Shaw. 2009. The Diplomacies of Small States at the Start of the Twenty-first Century: How Vulnerable? How Resilient? in Andrew F. Cooper and Timothy M. Shaw (eds.), *The Diplomacies of Small States: Between Vulnerability and Resilience*. Basingstoke: Palgrave Macmillan, 1–18.

Copeland, Dale. 2000. The Constructivist Challenge to Structural Realism: A Review Essay. *International Security* 25(2): 187–212.

Cornelius, Wayne. 2001. Death at the Border: Efficacy and Unintended Consequences of US Immigration Control Policy. *Population and Development Review* 27(4): 664–85.

Cottee, Simon. 2015. The Cyber Activists Who Want to Shut Down ISIS, *The Atlantic*, October 8, available at: www.theatlantic.com/international/archive/ 2015/10/anonymous-activists-isis-twitter/409312, last accessed September 6, 2017.

Cowen, Tyler. 2002. *Creative Destruction: How Globalization is Changing the World's Cultures*. Princeton University Press.

Culpepper, Pepper D. 2011. *Quiet Politics and Business Power: Corporate Control in Europe and Japan*. Cambridge University Press.

Culpepper, Pepper D. and Raphael Reinke. 2014. Structural Power and Bank Bailouts in the United Kingdom and the United States. *Politics and Society* 42(4): 427–54.

Currier, Ashley. 2012. *Out in Africa: LGBT Organizing in Namibia and South Africa*. Minneapolis, MN: University of Minnesota Press.

Curtin, Michael. 2007. *Playing to the World's Biggest Audience: The Globalization of Chinese Film and TV*. Berkeley, CA: University of California Press.

Curtin, Michael and Hemant Shah (eds.). 2010. *Reorienting Global Communication: Indian and Chinese Media Beyond Borders*. Champaign, IL: University of Illinois Press.

Dahl, Robert A. 1957. The Concept of Power. *Behavioral Science* 2(3): 201–15.

Dallas, Mark P. 2014. Cloth without a Weaver: Power, Emergence and Institutions across Global Value Chains. *Economy and Society* 43(3): 315–45.

Darby, Phillip. 2004. Pursuing the Political: A Postcolonial Rethinking of Relations International. *Millennium* 33(1): 1–32.

Davidson, Adam. 2015a. The Federal Reserve is Playing a Mind Game – but with Enormous Real-World Consequences, *The New York Times Sunday Magazine*, March 1, 20–23.

2015b. The Money Issue, *The New York Times Magazine*, May 3, 45–46.

Davies, Norman. 1996. *Europe: A History*. Oxford University Press.

de Grazia, Victoria. 1989. Mass Culture and Sovereignty: The American Challenge to European Cinemas, 1920–1960. *Journal of Modern History* 61: 51–87.

2005. *Irresistible Empire: America's Advance through Twentieth-Century Europe*. Cambridge, MA: Belknap at Harvard University Press.

De Vany, Arthur. 2004. *Hollywood Economics: How Extreme Uncertainty Shapes the Film Industry*. New York: Routledge.

Deacon, Robert T. and Paul Murphy. 1997. The Structure of an Environmental Transaction: The Debt-for-Nature Swap. *Land Economics* 73(1): 1–24.

Deal B%K. 2014. *The New York Times*, April 2.

Debrix, François and Alexander D. Barder. 2009. Nothing to Fear but Fear: Governmentality and the Biopolitical Production of Terror. *International Political Sociology* 3: 398–413.

Debs, Alexandre and Nuno P. Monteiro. 2014. Known Unknowns: Power Shifts, Uncertainty, and War. *International Organization* 68(1): 1–32.

Deleuze, Gilles. 1995. *Negotiations, 1972–1990*. New York: Columbia University Press.

Deleuze, Gilles and Félix Guattari. 1987. *A Thousand Plateaus: Capitalism and Schizophrenia*. Minneapolis, MN: University of Minnesota Press.

Dell, Paul F. 1986. In Defense of "Lineal Causality." *Family Process* 25: 513–21.

Dequech, David. 2003. Uncertainty and Economic Sociology: A Preliminary Discussion. *American Journal of Economics and Sociology* 62(3): 509–32.

Deutsch, Karl W. 1966. *Nerves of Government: Models of Political Communication*. New York: Free Press.

Dewast, Louise and Asthaa Chaturvedi. 2015. Refugee Crisis: Innovative Ways Germans are Welcoming Them, available at: abcnews.go.com/International/refugee-crisis-germans-welcoming/story?id=33589179, last accessed October 6, 2016.

Dewey, John. 1980. Conscience and Compulsion, in *The Middle Works, 1899–1924, vol. 10: 1916–17*, ed. Jo Ann Boydston. Carbondale, IL: Southern Illinois University Press, 244–51.

Diawara, Manthia. 1992. *African Cinema: Politics and Culture*. Bloomington, IN: Indiana University Press.

Diez, Thomas. 2013. Normative Power as Hegemony. *Cooperation and Conflict* 48 (2): 194–210.

Digeser, Peter. 1992. The Fourth Face of Power. *Journal of Politics* 54(4): 977–1007.

Docherty, Bonnie. 2009. Breaking New Ground: The Convention on Cluster Munitions and the Evolution of International Humanitarian Law. *Human Rights Quarterly* 31(4): 934–63.

Dominguez Villegas, Rodrigo and Victoria Rietig. 2015. Migrants Deported from the United States and Mexico to the Northern Triangle: A Statistical and Socioeconomic Profile, Regional Migration Study Group, Migration Policy Institute, Washington, DC.

Douglas, Mary. 1990. Risk as a Forensic Resource. *Daedalus* 119(4): 1–40.
1994. *Risk and Blame: Essays in Cultural Theory*. London: Routledge.

Dowd, Kevin. 2014. *New Private Monies: A Bit-Part Player?* London: Institute of Economic Affairs.

Dowd, Kevin and Martin Hutchinson. 2015. Bitcoin Will Bite the Dust. *Cato Journal* 35(2): 357–82.

Downs, Erica Streecker. 2000. *China's Quest for Energy Security*. Washington, DC: RAND.

Draper, G. I. A. D. 1977. The Emerging Law of Weapons Restraint. *Survival* 19(1): 9–15.

Dray, W. H. 1968. On How Explaining How-Possibly. *The Monist* 52(3): 390–407.

Duwe, Matthias. 2001. The Climate Action Network: A Glance behind the Curtains of a Transnational NGO Network. *Review of European Community and International Environment Law* 10(2): 177–89.

Dyson, Kenneth. 2014. *States, Debt, and Power: "Saints" and "Sinners" in European History and Integration*. Oxford University Press.

Earth Negotiations Bulletin. 2000. *ENB* 12, 139, 12 July, available at: www.iisd.ca/vol12/enb12139e.html.

Economist, The. 2007. Internet Jihad: A World Wide Web of Terror: Al-Qaeda's Most Famous Web Propagandist is Jailed, but the Internet Remains its Best Friend, July 12, available at: www.economist.com/node/9472498, last accessed September 6, 2017.
2010. Lights, Camera, Africa: Movies are Uniting a Disparate Continent and Dividing it Too, December 10, available at: www.economist.com/node/177 23124, last accessed October 17, 2017.
2013. Bitcoin Under Pressure, November 30, available at: www.economist.co m/news/technology-quarterly/21590766-virtual-currency-it-mathemati cally-elegant-increasingly-popular-and-highly, last accessed September 4, 2017.
2014. Converting the Preachers; The State and Islam, December 13, available at: www.economist.com/news/middle-east-and-africa/21636110-across-ara

b-world-rulers-tighten-their-grip-mosque-converting,   last   accessed September 6, 2017.

2015a. The Magic of Mining, January 10, available at: www.economist.com/ news/business/21638124-minting-digital-currency-has-become-big-ruth lessly-competitive-business-magic, last accessed March 18, 2015.

2015b. The Science of Swing, August 29, available at: www.economist.com/ news/obituary/21662492-howard-brody-physicist-tennis-died-august-11th-aged-83-science-swing, last accessed August 3, 2016.

2016a. Silver-Screen Playbook: How to Make a Hit Film, February 27, available at: www.economist.com/news/business/21693594-how-make-hit-film-silver-screen-playbook, last accessed September 7, 2017.

2016b. Lights, Camera, No Budget: Taking Shoe-string to Extremes, March 10, available at: www.economist.com/news/middle-east-and-africa/216939 38-taking-shoestring-extremes-lights-camera-no-budget,   last   accessed September 7, 2017.

2016c. Lights, Camera, Action Men: Pakistan's Army Gets into the Film Business, June 25, available at: www.economist.com/news/asia/21701127-paki stans-army-gets-film-business-lights-camera-action-men,   last   accessed September 7, 2017.

Eidinow, Ester. 2011. *Luck, Fate and Fortune: Antiquity and its Legacy*. Oxford University Press.

Elsaesser, T. P. 1994. German Postwar Cinema and Hollywood, in David W. Ellwood and Ron Kroes (eds.), *Hollywood in Europe: Experiences of a Cultural Hegemony*. Amsterdam: VU Press, 283–302.

Ember, Sydney. 2015. Data Security is Becoming the Sparkle in Bitcoin, *The New York Times*, March 1, B1, B4.

Epstein, Charlotte. 2011. Who Speaks? Discourse, the Subject and the Study of Identity in International Politics. *European Journal of International Relations* 17(2): 327–50.

Erickson, Jennifer L. 2015. *Dangerous Trade: Arms Exports, Human Rights, and International Reputation*. New York: Columbia University Press.

Eschbach, Karl et al. 1999. Death at the Border. *International Migration Review* 33 (2): 430–54.

Ettinger, Patrick. 2009. *Imaginary Lines: Border Enforcement and the Origins of Undocumented Immigration, 1882–1930*. Austin, TX: University of Texas Press.

European Values Study 1981–2008, 2011, Tilburg University, The Netherlands, available at: www.europeanvaluesstudy.eu, last accessed August 30, 2017.

Everson, Michelle and Ellen Vos. 2009. *Uncertain Risks Regulated*. New York: Routledge/Cavendish.

Fairfield, Tasha. 2015. Structural Power in Comparative Political Economy: Perspectives from Policy Formulation in Latin America. *Business and Politics* 17 (3): 411–41.

Falk, Marni J., Alan Decherney, and Jeffrey P. Kahn. 2016. Mitochondrial Replacement Techniques: Implications for the Clinical Community. *New England Journal of Medicine* 374(12): 1103–6.

Farrell, Henry. 2016. Bitcoin is Losing the Midas Touch, *Financial Times*, March 9, available at: www.ft.com/cms/s/0/12e155dc-e5e4-11e5-a09b-1f8b0d268 c39.html#axzz4CjfHghVZ, last accessed June 26, 2016.

Fay, Jennifer. 2008. *Theaters of Occupation: Hollywood and the Reeducation of Postwar Germany*. Minneapolis, MN: University of Minnesota Press.

Fearon, James D. 1995. Rationalist Explanations for War. *International Organization* 49(3): 379–414.

Fehrenbach, Heide. 1995. *Cinema in Democratizing Germany: Reconstructing National Identity after Hitler*. Chapel Hill, NC: University of North Carolina Press.

Ferguson, Niall. 2004. *Colossus: The Rise and Fall of the American Empire*. Harmondsworth: Penguin.

Financial Crisis Inquiry Commission (FCIC). 2011. *The Financial Crisis Inquiry Report*. New York: Public Affairs.

Fingar, Thomas. 2011. *Reducing Uncertainty: Intelligence Analysis and National Security*. Stanford University Press.

Finnemore, Martha. 2004. *The Purpose of Intervention: Changing Beliefs About the Use of Force*. Ithaca, NY: Cornell University Press.

2009. Legitimacy, Hypocrisy, and the Social Structure of Unipolarity. *World Politics* 61(1): 58–85.

Fioretos, Orfeo. 2011. Historical Institutionalism in International Relations. *International Organization* 65(2): 367–99.

Flandreau, Marc et al. 2010. The End of Gatekeeping: Underwriters and the Quality of Sovereign Debt Markets, 1815–2007, in Lucrezia Reichlin and Kenneth West (eds.), *NBER International Seminar on Macroeconomics, 2009*. University of Chicago Press, 53–92.

Flibbert, Andrew J. 2007 *Commerce in Culture: States and Markets in World Film Trade*. New York: Palgrave.

Fligstein, Neil and Doug McAdam. 2012. *A Theory of Fields*. Oxford University Press.

Fortna, Page. 2003. Scraps of Paper? Agreements and the Durability of Peace. *International Organization* 57(2): 337–72.

Foucault, Michel. 1977. *Discipline and Punish*. New York: Pantheon.

1980. *Power/Knowledge: Selected Interviews and Other Writings 1972–1977*. New York: Pantheon Books.

1981. Omnes Et Singulatim: Towards a Criticism of "Political Reason," in Sterling M. McMurrin (ed.), *The Tanner Lectures on Human Values II*. Salt Lake City, UT: University of Utah, 223–54.

1982. The Subject and Power. *Critical Inquiry* 8(4): 777–95.

2003. *"Society Must Be Defended": Lectures at the Collège de France, 1975–76*. New York: Palgrave.

2007. *Security, Territory, Population: Lectures at the Collège de France, 1977–78*. New York: Palgrave.

Fox, Annette Baker. 1969. The Small States in the International System, 1919–1969. *International Journal* 24(4): 751–64.

Fox, Justin. 2009. *The Myth of the Rational Market: A History of Risk, Reward, and Delusion on Wall Street*. New York: Harper Business.

Frank, Jill. 2005. *A Democracy of Distinction: Aristotle and the Work of Politics.* University of Chicago Press.

Frank, Robert. 2016. *Success and Luck: Good Fortune and the Myth of Meritocracy.* Princeton University Press.

Friedberg, Aaron L. 1993–94. Ripe for Rivalry: Prospects for Peace in a Multipolar Asia. *International Security* 18(3): 5–33.

Friedman, Thomas. 2005. *The World is Flat: A Brief History of the Twenty-First Century.* New York: Farrar, Straus & Giroux.

Fry, Ian. 2007. More Twists, Turns and Stumbles in the Jungle: A Further Exploration of the Evolution of Land Use, Land-Use Change and Forestry Decisions within the Kyoto Protocol. *Review of European, Comparative and International Environmental Law* 16(3): 341–55.

  2007. More Twists, Turns and Stumbles in the Jungle: A Further Exploration of Land Use, Land-Use Change and Forestry Decisions within the Kyoto Protocol. *Nature* 16(3): 341–55.

Funk, Russell J. and Daniel Hirschman. 2014. Derivatives and Deregulation: Financial Innovation and the Demise of Glass–Steagall. *Administrative Science Quarterly* 59(4): 669–704.

G20. 2009. Leaders' Statement at the Pittsburgh Summit, September 24–25, available at: https://g20.org/wp-content/uploads/2014/12/Pittsburgh_Decla ration_0.pdf.

Gaddis, John Lewis. 1986. The Long Peace: Elements of Stability in the Postwar International System. *International Security* 10(4): 99–142.

  1991. Toward the Post-Cold War World. *Foreign Affairs* 70(2): 102–22.

Garamone, Sam. 2016. Intelligence Chief Describes "Pervasive Uncertainty" of Worldwide Threats, US Department of Defense, available at: www.defense.go v/News/Article/Article/604190/intelligence-chief-describes-pervasive-uncer tainty-of-worldwide-threats, last accessed September 16, 2016.

Garcia, Denise. 2006. *Small Arms and Security: New Emerging International Norms.* New York: Routledge.

Gartzke, Erik. 1999. War is in the Error Term. *International Organization* 53(3): 567–87.

Gaventa, John. 1982. *Power and Powerlessness.* Champaign-Urbana, IL: University of Illinois Press.

Gelpern, Anna. 2016. Sovereign Debt: Now What? *Yale Journal of International Law* 41(2): 45–95.

Gerges, Fawaz. 2005. Buried in Amman's Rubble: Zarqawi's Support, *The Washington Post,* December 4, available at: www.washingtonpost.com/w p-dyn/content/article/2005/12/02/ar2005120202370.html, Last accessed September 6, 2017.

Gerring, John. 2012. Mere Description. *British Journal of Political Science* 42(4): 721–46.

Gerybadze, Alexander and Guido Reger. 1999. Globalization of R&D: Recent Changes in the Management of Innovation in Transnational Corporations. *Research Policy* 28(2): 251–74.

Giddens, Anthony. 1977. *Studies in Social and Political Theory.* New York: Basic Books.

Gilboy, Janet. 1991. Deciding Who Gets In: Decisionmaking by Immigration Inspectors. *Law & Society Review* 25(3): 571–600.

Gilpin, Robert. 1975. *US Power and the Multinational Corporation.* New York: Basic Books.

Goddard, Stacie E. 2010. *Indivisible Territory and the Politics of Legitimacy: Jerusalem and Northern Ireland.* Cambridge University Press.

Goddard, Stacie E. and Daniel H. Nexon. 2016. The Dynamics of Global Power Politics: A Framework for Analysis. *Journal of Global Security Studies* 1(1): 4–18.

Göhler, Gerhard. 2009. "Power To" and "Power Over," in Stewart R. Clegg and Mark Haugaard (eds.), *The Sage Handbook of Power.* Thousand Oaks, CA: Sage, 27–39.

Goldberg, Jeffrey. 2016. The Obama Doctrine: The US President Talks through His Hardest Decisions about America's Role in the World, *The Atlantic,* April, available at: www.theatlantic.com/magazine/archive/2016/04/the-oba ma-doctrine/471525, last accessed October 19, 2016.

Goldstein, Allie and Gloria Gonzalez. 2014. *Turning Over a New Leaf: The State of the Forest Carbon Markets 2014.* Washington, DC: Ecosystem Marketplace.

Gong, Gerrit W. 1984. *The "Standard of Civilization" in International Society.* Oxford: Clarendon.

Gordon, Colin. 1991. Governmental Rationality: An Introduction, in Colin Gordon, Graham Burchell, and Peter Miller (eds.), *The Foucault Effect: Studies in Governmentality.* University of Chicago Press, 1–51.

Gourevitch, Peter A. and James Shinn. 2005. *Political Power and Corporate Control: The New Global Politics of Corporate Governance.* Princeton University Press.

Graham, Erin R., Charles R. Shipan, and Craig Volden. 2014. The Communication of Ideas across Subfields in Political Science. *PS: Political Science and Politics* 47(2): 468–76.

Green, Jessica F. 2014. *Rethinking Private Authority: Agents and Entrepreneurs in Global Environmental Governance.* Princeton University Press.

  2017. Blurred Lines: Public–Private Interactions in Carbon Regulations. *International Interactions* 43(1): 103–28.

Greenblatt, Stephen. 1990. Culture, in Frank Lentricchia and Thomas McLaughlin (eds.), *Critical Terms for Literary Study.* University of Chicago Press, 225–32.

Greenspan, Alan. 2003. Corporate Governance. remarks by Mr. Alan Greenspan, Chairman of the Board of Governors of the US Federal Reserve System, at the 2003 Conference on Bank Structure and Competition, Chicago (via satellite), May 8.

Griffin, Andrew. 2015. Anonymous Vows to Take Down ISIS: How Twitter Has Become a Battleground for Propaganda, *The Independent,* February 11, available at: www.independent.co.uk/life-style/gadgets-and-tech/news/anon ymous-vows-to-take-down-isis-how-twitter-has-become-a-battleground-fo r-propaganda-10037989.html, last accessed September 6, 2017.

Griffin, Donovan. 2014. Bitcoin: No Trust Needed. *Information Today* 31(4): 31–33.

Grimes, William. 2015. Stanley Hoffmann, 86; Explored Foreign Policy, *The New York Times*, September 14, A19.

Grynaviski, Eric. 2014. *Constructive Illusions: Misperceiving the Origins of International Cooperation*. Ithaca, NY: Cornell University Press.

Guardian, The. 2015. "Inside Alphabet: Why Google Rebranded Itself and What Happens Next," August 11, available at: www.theguardian.com/technology/2015/aug/11/alphabet-google-rebranding-what-happens-next, last accessed August 12, 2015.

Gulati, Mitu and Robert E. Scott. 2013. *The Three and a Half Minute Transaction: Boilerplate and the Limits of Contract Design*. University of Chicago Press.

  2016. The Costs of Encrusted Contract Terms, unpublished paper, Duke University Law School and Columbia University Law School, January 25.

Gulbenkian Commission, The. 1996. *Open the Social Sciences: Report of the Gulbenkian Commission on the Restructuring of the Social Sciences*. Stanford University Press.

Gupta, Akhil. 1995. Blurred Boundaries: The Discourse of Corruption, the Culture of Politics, and the Imagined State. *American Ethnologist* 22(2): 375–402.

Guzzini, Stefano. 1993. Structural Power: The Limits of Neo-Realist Power Analysis. *International Organization* 47(3): 443–78.

  2010. Power Analysis: Encyclopedia Entries, DIIS Working Paper 34.

  2012. The Ambivalent "Diffusion of Power" in Global Governance, in Stefano Guzzini and Iver B. Neumann (eds.), *The Diffusion of Power in Global Governance: International Political Economy Meets Foucault*. Houndmills: Palgrave Macmillan, 1–37.

  2016a. Power and Cause. *Journal of International Relations and Development* (July): 1–23.

  2016b. Power: Three Conceptual Analyses of Power in International Relations, in Felix Berenskoetter (ed.), *Concepts in World Politics*. London: Sage, 23–40.

Guzzini, Stefano and Iver Neumann (eds.). 2012. *The Diffusion of Power in Political Governance: International Political Economy Meets Foucault*. Basingstoke: Palgrave.

Haas, Peter M. 2002. Constructing Environmental Conflicts from Resource Scarcity. *Global Environmental Politics* 2(1): 1–11.

Haass, Richard. 2014. A Closer Look at a World in Crisis, available at: www.npr.org/2014/07/26/335540268/a-closer-look-at-a-world-in-crisis?ft=1&f=, last accessed July 28, 2014.

  2017. *A World in Disarray*. New York: Penguin.

Hacking, Ian. 2004. Between Michel Foucault and Erving Goffman: Between Discourse in the Abstract and Face-to-Face Interaction. *Economy and Society* 33(3): 277–302.

Hagström, Linus. 2005. Ubiquity of "Power" and the Advantage of Terminological Pluralism: Japan's Foreign Policy Discourse. *Japanese Journal of Political Science* 6(2): 145–64.

Hagström, Linus and Björn Jerdén. 2014. East Asia's Power Shift: The Flaws and Hazards of the Debate and How to Avoid Them. *Asian Perspective* 38: 337–62.

Haldane, Andrew G. 2009. Why Banks Failed the Stress Test, speech by Mr. Andrew G. Haldane, Executive Director, Financial Stability, Bank of England, at the Marcus-Evans Conference on Stress-Testing, London, February 9–10.

Hamilton, Katherine, Milo Sjardin, Allison Shapiro, and Thomas Marcello. 2009. *Fortifying the Foundation: State of the Voluntary Carbon Market 2009.* New York: Ecosystem Marketplace and New Carbon Finance, available at: www.forest-trends.org/documents/files/doc_2343.pdf.

Hamilton, Katherine, Milo Sjardin, Molly Peters-Stanley, and Thomas Marcello. 2010. *Building Bridges: State of the Voluntary Carbon Markets 2010.* New York and Washington: Bloomberg New Energy Finance and Ecosystem Marketplace, available at: www.forest-trends.org/documents/files/do c_2434.pdf.

Hammerstad, Anne and Ingrid Boas. 2015. National Security Risks? Uncertainty, Austerity and Other Logics of Risk in the UK Government's National Security Strategy. *Cooperation and Conflict* 50(4): 475–91.

Hamrick, Kelley and Allie Goldstein. 2015. *Ahead of the Curve: State of the Voluntary Carbon Markets 2015.* Washington, DC: Ecosystem Marketplace.

Harding, Luke and Alec Luhn. 2016. Mh17: Buk Missile Finding Sets Russia and West at Loggerheads, *The Guardian*, September 28, available at: www.the guardian.com/world/2016/sep/28/flight-mh17-shot-down-by-missile-broug ht-in-from-russia-ukraine-malaysia-airlines, last accessed October 3, 2016.

Haugaard, Mark. 2010. Power: A "Family Resemblance" Concept. *European Journal of Cultural Studies* 13(4): 419–38.

Havel, Václav. 1990. Speech by Václav Havel, President of Czechoslovakia, to the Polish Sejm and Senate, available at: http://old.hrad.cz/president/Havel/spee ches/1990/2501_uk.html, last accessed June 27, 2009.

Hay, Colin. 2002. *Political Analysis.* New York: Palgrave.

Hayek, Friedrich A. 1945. The Use of Knowledge in Society. *American Economic Review* 35(4): 519–30.

    1960. *The Constitution of Liberty.* University of Chicago Press.

    1973. *Law, Legislation, and Liberty,* vol. 1: *Rules and Order.* University of Chicago Press.

    1976. *Choice in Currency: A Way to Stop Inflation.* London: Institute of Economic Affairs.

    1984a. The Origins and Effects of Our Morals: A Problem for Science, in Chiaki Nishiyama Leube and R. Kurt (eds.), *The Essence of Hayek.* Stanford, CA: Hoover Institution Press, 318–30.

    1984b. The Principles of a Liberal Social Order, in Chiaki Nishiyama Leube and R. Kurt (eds.), *The Essence of Hayek.* Stanford, CA: Hoover Institution Press, 363–81.

Hayward, Clarissa Rile. 1998. De-Facing Power. *Polity* 31(1): 1–22.

    2000. *De-Facing Power.* Cambridge University Press.

Hayward, Clarissa and Steven Lukes. 2008. Nobody to Shoot? Power, Structure, and Agency: A Dialogue. *Journal of Power* 1(1): 5–20.

Heal, Geoffrey and Antony Milner. 2013. Uncertainty and Decision in Climate Change Economics, Centre for Climate Change Economics and Policy Working Paper 128, Leeds and London.

Heclo, Hugh. 1974. *Modern Social Politics in Britain and Sweden.* New Haven, CT: Yale University Press.

Heidegger, Martin. (1977). *Basic Writings,* ed. David Farrell Krell. New York: Harper & Row.

Helleiner, Eric. 2003. *The Making of National Money: Territorial Currencies in Historical Perspective.* Ithaca, NY: Cornell University Press.

Helleiner, Eric and Stefano Pagliari. 2010. The End of Self-Regulation? Hedge Funds and Derivatives in Global Financial Governance, in Eric Helleiner et al. (eds.), *Global Finance in Crisis: The Politics of International Regulatory Change.* New York: Routledge, 74–90.

  2011. The End of an Era in International Financial Regulation? A Postcrisis Research Agenda. *International Organization* 65(1): 169–200.

Heller, Agnes. 1987. *Beyond Justice.* Oxford: Blackwell.

Hendricks, Darryll. 1994. Netting Agreements and the Credit Exposures of OTC Derivatives Portfolios. *Federal Reserve Bank of New York Quarterly Review* 19: 7.

Henn, Steve. 2014. Free Voice-Control Software Helps Tiny Start-Ups Build Big Ideas. *National Public Radio,* November 14, available at: www.npr.org/2014/11/14/364138291/free-voice-control-software-helps-tiny-start-ups-build-big-ideas, last accessed May 6, 2017.

Herrigel, Gary. 2005. Institutionalists at the Limits of Institutionalism: A Constructivist Critique of Two Edited Volumes from Wolfgang Streeck and Kozo Yamamura. *Socio-Economic Review* 3(3): 559–67.

  2010. *Manufacturing Possibilities: Creative Action and Industrial Recomposition in the United States, Germany, and Japan.* Oxford University Press.

Herrmann, Richard K. and Jong Kim Choi. 2007. From Prediction to Learning: Opening Experts' Minds to Unfolding History. *International Security* 31(4): 132–61.

Hertel, Shareen. 2006. *Unexpected Power: Conflict and Change among Transnational Activists.* Ithaca, NY: Cornell University Press.

Herthel, Major Thomas J. 2001. On the Chopping Block: Cluster Munitions and the Law of War. *The Air Force Law Review* 51: 229–69.

Hertle, Hans-Hermann. 1999. *Der Fall Der Mauer: Die Unbeabsichtigte Selbstauflösung des SED-Staates,* 2nd edn. Wiesbaden: VS Verlag für Sozialwissenschaften.

Heyman, Josiah M. 2009. Trust, Privilege, and Discretion in the Governance of US Borderlands with Mexico. *Canadian Journal of Law and Society* 24(3): 367–90.

Higham, Scott and Ellen Nakashima. 2015. Why the Islamic State Leaves Tech Companies Torn Between Free Speech and Security, *The Washington Post,* July 16.

Hindess, Barry. 1996. *Discourses of Power: From Hobbes to Foucault.* Oxford: Blackwell.

Hironaka, Ann. 2017. *Tokens of Power: Rethinking War*. New York: Cambridge University Press.

Hirschman, Albert O. [1945] 1980. *National Power and the Structure of Foreign Trade*. Berkeley, CA: University of California Press.

1967. The Principle of the Hiding Hand. *The Public Interest* 6 (Winter): 10–23.

Hirshleifer, Jack and John G. Riley. 1992. *The Analytics of Uncertainty and Information*. Cambridge University Press.

Ho, Karen. 2009. *Liquidated: An Ethnography of Wall Street*. Durham, NC: Duke University Press.

Hobbes, Thomas. 1996. *Leviathan*, ed. Richard Tuck. Cambridge University Press.

Hobson, John M. and Leonard Seabrooke. 2007. *Everyday Politics of the World Economy*. Cambridge University Press.

Hochstein, Marc. 2014. Why Bitcoin Matters for Bankers. *American Banker Magazine* 124(2): 19–26.

Hoffman, David E. 2009. *The Dead Hand: The Untold Story of the Cold War Arms Race and its Dangerous Legacy*. New York: Knopf Doubleday.

Hofmann, Bruce. 2006. *Inside Terrorism*. New York: Columbia University Press.

Högselius, Per. 2013. *Red Gas: Russia and the Origins of European Energy Dependence*. New York: Palgrave Macmillan.

Holzer, Boris and Yuval Millo. 2005. From Risks to Second-Order Dangers in Financial Markets: Unintended Consequences of Risk Management Systems. *New Political Economy* 10(2): 224–45.

Hopf, Ted. 1998. The Promise of Constructivism in International Relations Theory. *International Security* 23(1): 171–200.

2010. The Logic of Habit in International Relations. *European Journal of International Relations* 16(4): 539–61.

Hopf, Ted and John Lewis Gaddis. 1993. Getting the End of the Cold War Wrong. *International Security* 18(2): 202–10.

Howard, Marc Morjé and Meir R. Walters. 2014. Explaining the Unexpected: Political Science and the Surprises of 1989 and 2011. *Perspectives on Politics* 12(2): 394–408.

Hozic, Aida A. 2001. *Hollyworld: Space, Power, and Fantasy in the American Economy*. Ithaca, NY: Cornell University Press.

Hulme, Karen. 2009. The 2008 Cluster Munitions Convention: Stepping Outside the CCW Framework (Again). *International and Comparative Law Quarterly* 58(1): 219–27.

Human Rights Watch (HRW). 2015. Cluster Munitions Used in 5 Countries in 2015, September 3, available at: www.hrw.org, last accessed December 12, 2015.

Human Rights Watch (HRW) and the International Human Rights Clinic. 2015. Mind the Gap: The Lack of Accountability for Killer Robots, April, 978-1-6231-32408.

Huntington, Samuel P. 1993. The Clash of Civilizations? *Foreign Affairs* 72(3): 22–49.

Hyde-Price, Adrian G. V. 1991. *European Security beyond the Cold War*. London: Royal Institute of International Affairs.

Ingebritsen, Christine. 2006. *Scandinavia in World Politics*. Lanham, MD: Rowman & Littlefield.

Ingraham, Christopher. 2016. Toddlers Have Shot at Least 23 People This Year, *The Washington Post*, May 1.

Institute for Economics and Peace. 2015. *Global Terrorism Index 2014*, available at: http://economicsandpeace.org/wp-content/uploads/2015/06/Global-Ter rorism-Index-Report-2014.pdf.

Intergovernmental Panel on Climate Change (IPCC). 2007. *Climate Change 2007, Synthesis Report*. Geneva: Intergovernmental Panel on Climate Change.

International Committee of the Red Cross (ICRC). 1973. *Weapons that May Cause Unnecessary Suffering or Have Indiscriminate Effects: Report on the Work of Experts*. Geneva: ICRC.

2000. *Explosive Remnants of War: Cluster Bombs and Landmines in Kosovo*. Geneva: ICRC.

International Organization. 2017. The Behavioral Revolution and International Relations, vol. 71, S1 (Supplement).

International Organization for Migration (IOM). 2014. *Fatal Journeys: Tracking Lives Lost during Migration*. Geneva: IOM.

International Swaps and Derivatives Association (ISDA). 2015. ISDA Insight: A Survey of Issues and Trends for the Derivatives End-user Community, available at: www2.isda.org/functional-areas/research/surveys/end-user-surveys.

Iordanova, Dina, David Martin-Jones, and Belén Vidal (eds.). 2010. *Cinema at the Periphery*. Detroit, MI: Wayne State University Press.

Isaac, Jeffrey C. 1987. *Power and Marxist Theory: A Realist View*. Ithaca, NY: Cornell University Press.

Isaacson, Adam and Maureen Meyer. 2014. Mexico's Other Border: Security, Migration and the Humanitarian Crisis at the Line with Central America, Washington Office on Latin America, Washington, DC, available at: www.wol a.org/files/mxgt/report, last accessed October 19, 2015.

Islamic State. 2015a. The Extinction of the Grayzone, *Dabiq* 7, 54–66, available at: http://jihadology.net/2015/02/12/al-%E1%B8%A5ayat-media-center-pr esents-a-new-issue-of-the-islamic-states-magazine-dabiq-7.

2015b. *Dabiq* 9, available at: http://jihadology.net/2015/05/21/al-%E1%B8% A5ayat-media-center-presents-a-new-issue-of-the-islamic-states-magazine-dabiq-9.

Itçaina, Xabier, Antoine Roger, and Andy Smith. 2016. *Varietals of Capitalism: A Political Economy of the Changing Wine Industry*. Ithaca, NY: Cornell University Press.

Jäckel, Anne. 2003. *European Film Industries*. London: British Film Institute.

Jackson, Patrick Thaddeus. 2006. *Civilizing the Enemy: German Reconstruction and the Invention of the West*. Ann Arbor, MI: University of Michigan Press.

2011. *The Conduct of Inquiry in International Relations: Philosophy of Science and its Implications for the Study of World Politics*. New York: Routledge.

Jansen, Johannes. 1986. *The Neglected Duty: The Creed of Sadat's Assassins and Islamic Resurgence in the Middle East*. London: Macmillan.

Jentleson, Bruce W. 1986. *Pipeline Politics: The Complex Political Economy of East–West Energy Trade*. Ithaca, NY: Cornell University Press.

Jervis, Robert. 1997. *System Effects: Complexity in Political and Social Life*. Princeton University Press.

Jinnah, Sikina. 2011. Climate Change Bandwagoning: The Impacts of Strategic Linkages on Regime Design, Maintenance, and Death. *Global Environmental Politics* 11(3): 1–9.

Johal, Sukhdev, Michael Moran, and Karel Williams. 2014. Power, Politics and the City of London after the Great Financial Crisis. *Government and Opposition* 49(3): 400–25.

Johnson, Irving S. 1983. Human Insulin from Recombinant DNA Technology. *Science* 219(4585): 632–37.

Johnson, Simon and James Kwak. 2010. *13 Bankers: The Wall Street Takeover and the Next Financial Meltdown*. New York: Vintage.

Johnson, Tana. 2014. *Organizational Progeny: Why Governments are Losing Control over the Proliferating Structures of Global Governance*. Oxford University Press.

Jones, Huw D. 2015. Regulatory Uncertainty over Genome Editing. *Nature Plants*, available at: www.nature.com/articles/nplants201411, last accessed November 3, 2016.

Jones, Reece. 2012. Spaces of Refusal: Rethinking Sovereign Power and Resistance at the Border. *Annals of the Association of American Geographers* 102(3): 685–99.

Kagan, Robert. 2012. *The World America Made*. New York: Knopf.

Kaldor, Mary. 1999. *New and Old Wars: Organized Violence in a Global Era*. Stanford University Press.

Kalmadi, Kiran and Sukhna Dang. 2015. Virtual Currencies: Gold 2.0 or Mirage? *Global Finance* 29(3): 10–13.

Kaminska, Izabella. 2016. Bitcoin Bitfinex Exchange Hacked: The Unanswered Questions, *Financial Times*, August 4, available at: www.ft.com/cms/s/0/1ea8baf8-5a11-11e6-8d05-4eaa66292c32.htms#axzz4GNQ9gwan, last accessed August 4, 2016.

Kammen, Daniel M. and David M. Hassenzahl. 1999. *Should We Risk It? Exploring Environmental, Health, and Technological Problem Solving*. Princeton University Press.

Kaplan, Robert D. 1994. The Coming Anarchy, *Atlantic Monthly*, February, available at: www.theatlantic.com, last accessed June 19, 2015.

Kardon, Isaac. 2017. Rising Power, Creeping Jurisdiction: China's Law of the Sea, PhD dissertation, Cornell University.

Katzenstein, Peter J. 1985. *Small States in World Markets: Industrial Policy in Europe*. Ithaca, NY: Cornell University Press.

1996. *Cultural Norms and National Security: Police and Military in Postwar Japan*. Ithaca, NY: Cornell University Press.

2005. *A World of Regions: Asia and Europe in the American Imperium*. Ithaca, NY: Cornell University Press.

2014. Epilogue Power.1–4, or the Emperor's New Clothes, in Louis W. Pauly and Bruce W. Jentleson (eds.), *Power in a Complex Global System*. New York: Routledge, 209–21.

Katzenstein, Peter J. and Stephen C. Nelson. 2013a. Reading the Right Signals and Reading the Signals Right: IPE and the Financial Crisis of 2008. *Review of International Political Economy* 20(5): 1101–31.

2013b. Worlds in Collision: Risk and Uncertainty in Hard Times, in Miles Kahler and David Lake (eds.), *Politics in the New Hard Times: The Great Recession in Comparative Perspective*. Ithaca, NY: Cornell University Press, 233–52.

Katzenstein, Peter J. and Nicole Weygandt. 2017. Mapping Eurasia in an Open World: How the Insularity of Russia's Geopolitical and Civilizational Approaches Limit its Foreign Policies. *Perspectives on Politics* 15(2): 428–42.

Kavalski, Emilian. 2012. Waking up IR from its "Deep Newtonian Slumber." *Millennium – Journal of International Studies* 41(1): 137–50.

Keck, Margaret. 2016. Transnational America, Annual Meeting of the International Studies Association, Atlanta.

Keen, David. 1996. Organised Chaos: Not the New World We Ordered. *The World Today* 51(1): 14–17.

Keene, Edward. 2002. *Beyond the Anarchical Society*. Cambridge University Press.

Kelly, Brian. 2015. *The Bitcoin Big Bang: How Alternative Currencies are About to Change the World*. Hoboken, NJ: John Wiley.

Kenarov, Dimiter. 2015. Dashed Hopes in Gay Ukraine. *Foreign Policy*, available at: foreignpolicy.com/2015/01/19/dashed-hopes-in-gay-ukraine-maidan-rus sia, last accessed April 13, 2015.

Kennan, George. 1947. The Sources of Soviet Conduct. *Foreign Affairs* 25: 566–82.

Kessler, Oliver. 2012. Sleeping with the Enemy? On Hayek, Constructivist Thought, and the Current Economic Crisis. *Review of International Studies* 38: 275–99.

Keynes, John Maynard. 1937. The General Theory of Employment. *Quarterly Journal of Economics* 51: 209–23.

[1921] 1948. *Treatise on Probability*. New York: Macmillan.

Khatodia, Surender, Kirti Bhatotia, Nishat Passricha, S. M. P. Khurana, and Narendra Tuteja. 2016. The CRISPR/Cas Genome-Editing Tool: Application in Improvement of Crops. *Frontiers in Plant Science* 7: 506.

Kindem, Gorham (ed.). 2000a. *The International Movie Industry*. Carbondale, IL: Southern Illinois University Press.

2000b. Introduction, in Gorham Kindem (ed.), *The International Movie Industry*. Carbondale, IL: Southern Illinois University Press, 1–6.

Kindleberger, Charles. 1970. *Power and Money: The Politics of International Economics and the Economics of International Politics*. New York: Basic Books.

Kirshner, Jonathan. 2000. Rationalist Explanations for War? *Security Studies* 10 (1): 143–50.

2009. Keynes, Legacies, and Inquiry. *Theory and Society* 38(5): 527–41.

2012. *Hollywood's Last Golden Age: Politics, Society, and the Seventies Film in America*. Ithaca, NY: Cornell University Press.

2014. *American Power after the Financial Crisis*. Ithaca, NY: Cornell University Press.

2015. The Economic Sins of Modern IR Theory and the Classical Realist Alternative. *World Politics* 67(1): 155–83.

Klein Murillo, Helen. 2016. Are Hamas Attacks War or Terrorism? Hollywood Needs to Know, Lawfare Blog, June 29, available at: www.lawfareblog.com/ are-hamas-attacks-war-or-terrorism-hollywood-needs-know, Last accessed October 17, 2017.

Klein, Amanda A. and R. Barton Palmer. 2016. *Cycles, Sequels, Spin-Offs, Remakes, and Reboots: Multiplicities in Film and Television*. Austin, TX: University of Texas Press.

Knight, Frank H. 1921. *Risk, Uncertainty, and Profit*. New York: Houghton Mifflin.

Koh, Harold Hongju. 1997. Why Do Nations Obey International Law? *Yale Law Journal* 106: 2599–2659.

Kollman, Kelly. 2009. European Institutions, Transnational Networks and National Same-sex Unions Policy: When Soft Law Hits Harder. *Contemporary Politics* 15(1): 37–53.

2014. Deploying Europe: The Creation of Discursive Imperatives for Same-Sex Unions, in Phillip Ayoub and David Paternotte (eds.), *LGBT Activism and the Making of Europe: A Rainbow Europe*. Basingstoke: Palgrave Macmillan, 97–118.

Koremenos, Barbara. 2005. Contracting around International Uncertainty. *American Political Science Review* 99(4): 549–65.

Koremenos, Barbara, Charles Lipson, and Duncan Snidal. 2001. The Rational Design of International Institutions. *International Organization* 55(4): 761–99.

Koskenniemi, Martti. 1989. *From Apology to Utopia: The Structure of International Legal Argument*. Helsinki: Finnish Lawyers' Publishing.

2005. *From Apology to Utopia: The Structure of Legal Argument*. Cambridge University Press.

Krasner, Stephen D. 1978. *Defending the National Interest*. Princeton University Press.

1984. Approaches to the State: Alternative Conceptions and Historical Dynamics. *Comparative Politics* 16: 223–46.

1999. *Sovereignty: Organized Hypocrisy*. Princeton University Press.

2013. New Terrains: Sovereignty and Alternative Conceptions of Power, in Martha Finnemore and Judith Goldstein (eds.), *Back to Basics: State Power in a Contemporary World*. Oxford University Press, 339–58.

Krauthammer, Charles. 1990–91. The Unipolar Moment. *Foreign Affairs* 70(1): 23–33.

Krebs, Ron. 2015. *Narrative and the Making of US National Security*. Cambridge University Press.

Kremer, Jan-Frederik and Andrej Pustovitovskij. 2012. Structural Power and International Relations Analysis, paper delivered at International Studies Association Annual Convention, San Diego.

Kroenig, Matthew. 2013. Nuclear Superiority and the Balance of Resolve: Explaining Nuclear Crisis Outcomes. *International Organization* 67(1): 141–71.

Krugman, Paul. 2013. Gambling with Civilization, *The New York Review of Books*, November 7, available at: www.nybooks.com/articles/2013/11/07/climate-c hange-gambling-civilization, last accessed October 8, 2016.

Kunz, William. 2007. *Cultural Conglomerates: Consolidation in the Motion Picture and Television Industries*. Lanham, MD: Rowman & Littlefield.

Kupchan, Charles A. 1998. After Pax Americana: Benign Power, Regional Integration, and the Sources of a Stable Multipolarity. *International Security* 23(2): 40–79.

Kydd, Andrew H. and Barbara F. Walter. 2006. The Strategies of Terrorism. *International Security* 31(1): 49–80.

Kymlicka, Will and Magda Opalski. 2002. *Can Liberal Pluralism be Exported?: Western Political Theory and Ethnic Relations in Eastern Europe*. Oxford University Press.

Laffey, Mark and Jutta Weldes. 1997. Beyond Belief: Ideas and Symbolic Technologies in the Study of International Relations. *European Journal of International Relations* 3(2): 193–237.

Lake, David A. 2009a. Open Economy Politics: A Critical Review. *Review of International Organizations* 4(3): 219–44.

2009b. Trips across the Atlantic: Theory and Epistemology in IPE. *Review of International Political Economy* 16(1): 47–57.

Lake, David A. and Jeffrey A. Frieden. 1989. Crisis Politics: The Effects of Uncertainty and Shocks on Material Interests and Political Institutions, unpublished paper.

Lamont, Michele. 2012. Toward a Comparative Sociology of Valuation and Evaluation. *Annual Review of Sociology* 38: 201–21.

Larner, Wendy and William Walters. 2004. Globalization as Governmentality. *Alternatives* 29: 495–514.

Laruelle, Marléne. 2008. *Russian Eurasianism: An Ideology of Empire*. Washington, DC and Baltimore, MD: Woodrow Wilson Center Press and Johns Hopkins University Press.

Lasswell, Harold D. and Abraham Kaplan. 1950. *Power and Society: A Framework for Political Inquiry*. New Haven, CT: Yale University Press.

Latour, Bruno. 1986. The Powers of Association, in John Law (ed.), *Power, Action and Belief: A New Sociology of Knowledge?*. London: Routledge, 264–80.

Lavin, Cheryl. 2000. William Goldman Sticks by His Theory of Hollywood: "Nobody Knows Anything," *Chicago Tribune*, April 6, available at: http://articles.chicagotribune.com/2000–04-06/features/0004060115_1_butch-cassidy-mr-goldman-sundance-kid, last accessed October 17, 2017.

Layne, Christopher. 1993. The Unipolar Illusion: Why New Great Powers Will Rise. *International Security* 17(4): 5–51.

Leaver, Adam. 2010. A Different Take: Hollywood's Unresolved Business Model. *Review of International Political Economy* 17(3): 454–80.

Lecocq, Franck and Philippe Ambrosi. 2007. The Clean Development Mechanism: History, Status, and Prospects. *Review of Environmental Economics and Policy* 1(1): 134–51.

Ledford, Heidi. 2015a. Caution Urged over Editing DNA in Wildlife (Intentionally or Not). *Nature*, August 4, available at: www.nature.com/news/caution-urged-over-editing-dna-in-wildlife-intentionally-or-not-1.18123, last accessed November 3, 2016.

2015b. CRISPR, the Disruptor. *Nature*, June 8, available at: www.nature.com/news/crispr-the-disruptor-1.17673, last accessed November 3, 2016.

2016. Titanic Clash over CRISPR Patents Turns Ugly. *Nature*, September 21, available at: www.nature.com/news/titanic-clash-over-crispr-patents-turns-ugly-1.20631, last accessed October 26, 2016.

Lee, Ben. 2016. Maximizing Risk and Uncertainty in a Changing World: Notes on Volatility in Cultures of Finance, available at: www.publicseminar.org/2016/11/maximizing-risk-and-uncertainty-in-a-changing-world/#.WDii8 Dtu5PN, last accessed November 27, 2016.

Lee, Erika. 2003. *At America's Gates: Chinese Immigration during the Exclusion Era, 1882–1943*. Chapel Hill, NC: University of North Carolina Press.

Lee, Timothy B. 2013. The Switch: Twelve Questions About Bitcoin You Were Too Embarrassed to Ask, *The Washington Post*, November 19, available at: www.washingtonpost.com/blogs/the-switch/wp/2013/11/19/12-questions-you-were-too-embarrassed-to-ask-about-bitcoin, last accessed March 18, 2015.

Levi, Primo. 1988. *The Drowned and the Saved*. New York: Vintage.

Lévi-Strauss, Claude. 1968. *The Savage Mind*. University of Chicago Press.

Lia, Brynjar. 2007. *Architect of Global Jihad: The Life of Al-Qaida Strategist Abu Mus'ab Al-Suri*. London: Hurst.

Liebes, Tamar and Elihu Katz. 1990. *The Export of Meaning: Cross-Cultural Readings of "Dallas."* New York: Oxford University Press.

Lindblom, Charles E. 1959. The Science of "Muddling Through." *Public Administration Review* 19(2): 79–88.

1977. *Politics and Markets*. New York: Basic Books.

Linklater, Andrew (ed.). 2000. *Critical Concepts in Political Science*. London: Routledge.

Lipschutz, Ronnie D. 2007. On the Transformational Potential of Global Civil Society, in Felix Berenskoetter and M. J. Williams (eds.), *Power in World Politics*. New York: Routledge, 225–43.

Lipsky, Michael. [1989] 2010. *Street-Level Bureaucracy: Dilemmas of the Individual in Public Service*, 30th Anniversary Expanded Edition. New York: Russell Sage.

Litman, Barry. 1998. *The Motion Picture Mega-Industry*. Boston, MA: Allyn & Bacon.

Livingston, Alex. 2017. Between Means and Ends: Reconstructing Coercion in Dewey's Democratic Theory, unpublished paper, Government Department, Cornell University.

Lobato, Ramon. 2010. Creative Industries and Informal Economies: Lessons from Nollywood. *International Journal of Cultural Studies* 13(4): 337–54.

Lockwood, Erin. 2013. The Plague and Fortuna: Political Realism and the Politics of Uncertainty, unpublished paper, Northwestern University.

2015. Predicting the Unpredictable: Value-At-Risk, Performativity, and the Politics of Financial Uncertainty. *Review of International Political Economy* 22(4): 719–56.

Lohmuller, Michael. 2015. The Implications of Mexico's Rising Deportations, InSight Crime, available at: www.insightcrime.org/news-briefs/implications-mexico-rising-deportations, last accessed October 19, 2015.

Lovbrand, Eva. 2009. Revisiting the Politics of Expertise in Light of the Kyoto Negotiations on Land Use Change and Forestry. *Forest Policy and Economics* 11: 404–12.

Lukes, Steven. 2005. Power and the Battle for Hearts and Minds. *Millennium* 33 (3): 477–93.

2006a. *Power: A Radical View*, 2nd edn. New York: Palgrave.

2006b. Reply to Comments. *Political Studies Review* (4): 164–73.

Lumpe, Lora. 1999. Curbing the Proliferation of Small Arms and Light Weapons. *Security Dialogue* 30(2): 151–64.

Machiavelli, Niccolò. [1513/32] 1998. *The Prince*, trans. and with an Introduction by Harvey C. Mansfield, 2nd edn. University of Chicago Press.

MacKenzie, Donald. 2008. *An Engine, Not a Camera: How Financial Models Shape Markets*. Cambridge, MA: MIT Press.

Madsen, Kenneth D. 2007. Local Impacts of the Balloon Effect of Law Enforcement. *Geopolitics* 12(2): 280–98.

Mainwaring, Cetta. 2016. Migrant Agency: Negotiating Borders and Migration Controls. *Migration Studies* 4(3): 289–308.

Maney, Kevin. 2014. The Other Side of the Bitcoin, *Newsweek*, March 19, available at: www.newsweek.com/2014/03/28/other-side-bitcoin-248009.html, last accessed March 18, 2015.

Mann, Michael. 1986. *The Sources of Social Power*, vol. 1. Cambridge University Press.

Manners, Ian. 2013. Assessing the Decennial, Reassessing the Global: Understanding European Union Normative Power in Global Politics. *Cooperation and Conflict* 48(2): 304–29.

Maresca, Louis and Stuart Maslen. 2000. *The Banning of Anti-Personnel Landmines: The Legal Contribution of the International Committee of the Red Cross*. Cambridge University Press.

Marglin, Stephen A. 1990. Losing Touch: The Cultural Conditions of Worker Accommodation and Resistance, in Frederique Apffel and Stephen A. Marglin (eds.), *Dominating Knowledge: Development, Culture, and Resistance*. Oxford University Press, 217–82.

Markoff, John. 2015. Sorry Einstein, but "Spooky Action" Seems Real, *The New York Times*, October 21, A1, A15.

Marlin-Bennet, Renée. 2017. Power, Given Flow: Looking at Power from a Different Vantage Point, International Studies Association Annual Convention, Baltimore, MD.

Martinez, Oscar. 2011. The Border: Funneling Migrants to Their Doom. *North American Congress on Latin America* 44(5): 5.

Massumi, Brian. 2015. *The Power at the End of the Economy*. Durham, NC: Duke University Press.

Maugeri, Leonardo. 2012. Oil: The Next Revolution, Discussion Paper 2012-10, Belfer Center for Science and International Affairs, Harvard Kennedy School, Cambridge, MA.

Maurer, Tim. 2011. Cyber Norm Emergence at the United Nations: An Analysis of the UN's Activities Regarding Cyber-security?, Discussion Paper 2011-11,

Belfer Center for Science and International Affairs Harvard Kennedy School, Cambridge, MA.

Max, D. T. 2011. The Prince's Gambit: A Chess Star Emerges for the Post-Computer Age, *The New Yorker*, March 21, available at: www.newyorker.co m/magazine/2011/03/21/the-princes-gambit, last accessed April 2, 2017.

May, Christopher. 2000. Addendum: Fifty Years of International Affairs Analysis: An Annotated Bibliography of Susan Strange's Academic Publications, in Thomas C. Lawton, James N. Rosenau, and Amy C. Verdun (eds.), *Strange Power: Shaping the Parameters of International Relations and the International Political Economy*. Burlington, VT: Ashgate, 421–43.

Mazower, Mark. 2009. *No Enchanted Palace: The End of Empire and the Ideological Origins of the United Nations*. Princeton University Press.

McCall, John C. 2004. Nollywood Confidential: The Unlikely Rise of Nigerian Video Film. *Transition* 95: 98–109.

McCloskey, Donald N. 1991. History, Differential Equations, and the Problem of Narration. *History and Theory* 30: 21–36.

McCourt, David M. 2016. Practice Turn and Relationalism as the New Constructivism. *International Studies Quarterly* 60(3) (September): 475–85.

McCullough, K. B. 1992. America's Back Door: Indirect International Immigration via Mexico to the United States from 1875 to 1940, PhD dissertation, Texas A&M University.

McDermott, Rose. 1998. *Risk-Taking in International Politics: Prospect Theory in American Foreign Policy*. Ann Arbor, MI: University of Michigan Press.

McGrath, Rae. 2000. *Landmines and Unexploded Ordnance: A Resource Book*. London: Pluto Press.

McKeen-Edwards, Heather and Tony Porter. 2013. *Transnational Financial Associations and the Governance of Global Finance: Assembling Wealth and Power*. New York: Routledge.

McLannahan, Ben. 2015. Mt. Gox "Lost Coins" Long Before Collapse, *Financial Times*, April 19.

McNamara, Robert S. and Hans A. Bethe. 1985. Reducing the Risk of Nuclear War, *Atlantic Monthly*, July, 43–51.

McRae, Rob. 2001. International Relations and the New Diplomacy, in Rob McRae and Don Hubert (eds.), *Human Security and the New Diplomacy: Protecting People, Promoting Peace*. Montreal: McGill-Queen's University Press, 250–59.

Mearsheimer, John J. 1990. Why We Will Soon Miss the Cold War, *Atlantic Monthly*, August, 35–50.

Mekata, Motoko. 2000. Building Partnerships toward a Common Goal: Experiences of the International Campaign to Ban Landmines, in Ann M. Florini (ed.), *The Third Force: The Rise of Transnational Civil Society*. Washington, DC: Carnegie Endowment for International Peace, 143–76.

Mendelsohn, Barak. 2005. Sovereignty Under Attack: The al-Qaeda Network Meets the International Society. *Review of International Studies* 31(1): 45–68.

   2009. *Combating Jihadism: American Hegemony and Interstate Cooperation in the War on Terrorism*. University of Chicago Press.

Mercer, Jonathan. 2013. Emotion and Strategy in the Korean War. *International Organization* 67(2): 221–52.

Middlebrook, Stephen T. and Sarah Jane Hughes. 2015. *A Historical Analysis of Substitutes for Legal Tender and their Implications for the Regulation of Virtual Currency*, Legal Studies Research Paper Series No. 316. Bloomington: Maurer School of Law, Indiana University.

Migdal, Joel S. 2001. *The State in Society: How States and Societies Transform and Constitute One Another*. Cambridge University Press.

2004. Mental Maps and Virtual Checkpoints: Struggles to Construct and Maintain State and Social Boundaries, in Joel S. Migdal (ed.), *Boundaries and Belonging: States and Societies in the Struggle to Shape Identities and Local Practices*. Cambridge University Press, 3–23.

Miller, Greg and Scott Higham. 2015. In a Propaganda War against ISIS, the US Tried to Play by the Enemy's Rules, *The Washington Post*, May 8, available at: www.washingtonpost.com, last accessed September 6, 2017.

Miller, Peter, Liisa Kurunmäki, and Ted O'Leary. 2008. Accounting, Hybrids and the Management of Risk. *Accounting, Organizations and Society* 33: 942–67.

Miller, Toby, Nitin Govil, John McMurria, and Richard Maxwell. 2001. *Global Hollywood*. London: British Film Industry Publishing.

Mitrova, Tatiana, Vyacheslav Kulagin, and Anna Galkina. 2015. The Transformation of Russia's Gas Export Policy in Europe. Proceedings of the Institution of Civil Engineers – Energy 168(1): 30–40.

Mitzen, Jennifer and Randall Schweller. 2011. Knowing the Unknown Unknowns: Misplaced Certainty and the Onset of War. *Security Studies* 20(1): 2–35.

Miyazaki, Hirokazu. 2013. *Arbitraging Japan: Dreams of Capitalism at the End of Finance*. Berkeley, CA: University of California Press.

Moe, Terry M. 2005. Power and Political Institutions. *Perspectives on Politics* 3: 215–33.

Mole, Richard. 2016. Nationalism and Homophobia in Central and Eastern Europe, in Koen Slootmaeckers, Heleen Touquet, and Peter Vermeersch (eds.), *The EU Enlargement and Gay Politics*. Basingstoke: Palgrave Macmillan, 99–121.

Moran, Albert (ed.). 1996. *Film Policy: International, National, and Regional Perspectives*. London: Routledge.

Morgan, Glenn. 2016. New Actors and Old Solidarities: Institutional Change and Inequality under a Neo-Liberal International Order. *Socio-Economic Review* 14(1): 201–26.

Morley, Jefferson. 2014. US Formally Ends Landmine Production. *Arms Control Today* (July/Aug.): 33–34.

Morriss, Peter. 1987. *Power: A Philosophical Analysis*. Manchester University Press.

2002. *Power: A Philosophical Analysis*. 2nd edn. Manchester University Press.

Mosley, Layna. 2006. Constraints, Opportunities, and Information: Financial Market–Government Relations around the World, in Samuel Bowles, Pranab Bardhan, and Michael Wallerstein (eds.), *Globalization and Egalitarian Redistribution*. Princeton University Press, 87–119.

Moura-Costa, Pedro and Marc Stuart. 1998. Forestry-based Greenhouse Gas Mitigation: A Short Story of Market Evolution. *Commonwealth Forestry Review* 77: 191–202.

Mueller, John and Mark Stewart. 2016. *Chasing Ghosts: The Policing of Terrorism*. Oxford University Press.

Mull, Stephen D. 2008. US Cluster Munitions Policy, On-the-Record Briefing, May 21, US Department of State, Washington, DC, available at: http://2001–2009.state.gov/t/pm/rls/rm/105111.htm, last accessed December 23, 2015.

Munro, Rolland. 2009. Actor-Network Theory, in Stewart R. Clegg and Mark Haugaard (eds.), *The Sage Handbook of Power*. Thousand Oaks, CA: Sage, 125–39.

Naím, Moisés. 2013. *The End of Power*. New York: Basic Books.

Nakamoto, Satoshi. 2008. Bitcoin: A Peer-to-Peer Electronic Cash System, available at: https://bitcoin.org/bitcoin.pdf, last accessed March 18, 2015.

Nakashima, Ellen and Barton Gellman. 2015. As Encryption Spreads, US Grapples with Clash between Privacy, Security, *The Washington Post*, April 10, available at: www.washingtonpost.com, last accessed September 6, 2017.

Nature Conservancy, The. 2009. Noel Kempff Mercado Climate Action Project: A Case Study in Reducing Emissions from Deforestation and Degradation, available at: www.nature.org/ourinitiatives/urgentissues/glo bal-warming-climate-change/how-we-work/noel-kempff-case-study-final .pdf.

Nelson, Stephen C. 2016. Market Rules: Social Conventions, Legal Fictions, and the International Organization of Sovereign Debt Markets in the Long Twentieth Century, in Grégoire Mallard and Jérôme Sgard (eds.), *Contractual Knowledge*. Cambridge University Press, 118–50.

Nelson, Stephen C. and Peter J. Katzenstein. 2014. Uncertainty, Risk, and the Financial Crisis of 2008. *International Organization* 68(2): 361–92.

Nesvetailova, Anastasia. 2014. Innovations, Fragility, and Complexity: Understanding the Power of Finance. *Government and Opposition* 49(3): 542–68.

Neumann, Iver and Ole Jacob Sending. 2010. *Governing the Global Polity: Practice, Mentality, Rationality*. Ann Arbor, MI: University of Michigan Press.

Nowell-Smith, Geoffrey. 1998. Introduction, in Geoffrey Nowell-Smith and Steven Ricci (eds.), *Hollywood and Europe: Economics, Culture, National Identity: 1945–95*. London: British Film Industry Publishing, 1–16.

Nye, Joseph S. 2011. *The Future of Power*. New York: Public Affairs.

O'Malley, Pat. 2000. Uncertain Subjects: Risks, Liberalism and Contract. *Economy and Society* 29(4): 460–84.

2004. *Risk, Uncertainty and Government*. London: Glasshouse.

Oatley, Thomas. 2011. The Reductionist Gamble: Open Economy Politics in the Global Economy. *International Organization* 65(2): 311–41.

Obama, Barack. 2016. Transcript: President Obama's Democratic National Convention Speech, available at: www.latimes.com/politics/la-na-pol-obama-2016-convention-speech-transcript-20160727-snap-story.html, last accessed October 6, 2016.

Office of the Director of National Intelligence (ODNI). 2006. National Intelligence Estimate, *Trends in Global Terrorism: Implications for the United States*, available at: www.governmentattic.org/5docs/NIE-2006-02R.pdf.

Ogren, Cassandra. 2007. Migration and Human Rights on the Mexico–Guatemala Border. *International Migration* 45(4): 203–43.

Olopade, Dayo. 2014. *The Bright Continent: Breaking Rules and Making Change in Modern Africa*. Boston, MA: Houghton Mifflin.

Olson, Scott Robert. 1999. *Hollywood Planet: Global Media and the Competitive Advantage of Narrative Transparency*. Mahwah, NJ: Lawrence Erlbaum.

Onishi, Norimitsu. 2016. Nollywood is Letting Africans Put Themselves in the Picture, *The New York Times*, February 19, A1, A10.

Ostrom, Elinor. 2006. The 2005 James Madison Award Lecture: Converting Threats into Opportunities. PS: *Political Science and Politics* 39(1): 3–12.

2009. Polycentric Systems as One Approach to Solving Collective-Action Problems, in M. A. Mohamed Salih (ed.), *Climate Change and Sustainable Development*. Northampton, MA: Edward Elgar, 17–35.

2010a. Beyond Markets and States: Polycentric Governance of Complex Economic Systems. *American Economic Review* 100: 1–33.

2010b. Polycentric Systems for Coping with Collective Action and Global Environmental Change. *Global Environmental Change* 20: 550–57.

Ostrom, Vincent. 1961. The Organization of Government in Metropolitan Areas: A Theoretical Inquiry. *American Political Science Review* 55: 831–42.

Owen, Taylor. 2015. *Disruptive Power: The Crisis of the State in the Digital Age*. Oxford University Press.

Oxford Advanced Learner's Dictionary, available at: www.oxfordlearnersdictionaries.com/definition/english, last accessed June 8, 2016.

Padgett, John F. and Walter W. Powell. 2012. The Problem of Emergence, in John F. Padgett and Walter W. Powell (eds.), *The Emergence of Organizations and Markets*. Princeton University Press, 1–29.

Pan, Raj Kumar and Sitabhra Sinha. 2010. The Statistical Laws of Popularity: Universal Properties of the Box Office Dynamics of Motion Pictures. *New Journal of Physics* 12(11): 115004.

Panizza, Ugo, Federico Sturzenegger, and Jeromin Zettelmeyer. 2009. The Economics and Law of Sovereign Debt and Default. *Journal of Economic Literature* 47(3): 651–98.

Pansardi, Pamela. 2011. Power To and Power Over, in Keith Dowding (ed.), *Encyclopedia of Power*. Los Angeles: Sage, 521–25.

Pape, Robert. 2005. *Dying to Win: The Strategic Logic of Suicide Terrorism*. New York: Random House.

Parsons, Craig. 2015. Before Eclecticism: Competing Alternatives in Constructivist Research. *International Theory* (September): 1–38.

Parsons, Talcott. 1963. On the Concept of Political Power. *Proceedings of the American Philosophical Society* 107(3): 232–62.

Partnoy, Frank. 2006. How and Why Credit Rating Agencies are Not Like Other Gatekeepers, in Yasuyuki Fuchita and Robert E. Litan (eds.), *Financial Gatekeepers: Can They Protect Investors?* Washington, DC: Brookings Institution, 7–46.

Paster, Thomas. 2015. Bringing Power Back In: A Review of the Literature of Business in Welfare State Politics, MPfG Discussion Paper 15/3. Cologne: Max-Planck Institute for the Study of Societies.

Paternotte, David. 2012. Back into the Future: ILGA-Europe before 1996. *Destination Equality: Magazine of ILGA-Europe* 11(1): 5–8.

Payne, Nick. 2012. *Constellations*. New York: Faber & Faber.

Pelopidas, Benoît. 2015. A Bet Portrayed as a Certainty: Reassessing the Added Deterrent Value of Nuclear Weapons, in George P. Shultz and James E. Goodby (eds.), *The War That Must Never Be Fought*. Stanford, CA: Hoover Institution Press, 5–55.

2016. The Theorist Who Leaves Nothing to Chance: How Thomas Schelling and His Legacy Normalized the Practice of Nuclear Threats. Reppy Institute, Cornell University.

Penet, Pierre and Grégoire Mallard. 2014. From Risk Models to Loan Models: Austerity as the Continuation of Calculation by Other Means. *Journal of Critical Globalization Studies* 7: 4–47.

Petersen, Karen Lund. 2011. Risk Analysis: A Field within Security Studies? *European Journal of International Relations* 18(4): 693–717.

Petrova, Margarita H. 2007. *Small States and New Norms of Warfare*. Florence: European University Institute.

Picq, Manuela Lavinas and Markus Thiel (eds.). 2015. *Sexualities in World Politics: How LGBTQ Claims Shape International Relations*. New York: Routledge.

Pierre, Andrew J. 1982. *The Global Politics of Arms Sales*. Princeton University Press.

(ed.). 1997. *Cascade of Arms: Managing Conventional Weapons Proliferation*. Washington, DC: Brookings Institution.

Pierson, Paul. 2015. Power and Path Dependence, in James Mahoney and Kathleen Thelen (eds.), *Advances in Comparative Historical Analysis*. Cambridge University Press, 125–46.

Pieterse, Jan Nederveen. 2004. *Globalization and Culture: Global Mélange*. Lanham, MD: Rowman & Littlefield.

Plassaras, Nicholas A. 2013. Regulating Digital Currencies: Bringing Bitcoin within the Reach of the IMF. *Chicago Journal of International Law* 14(1): article 12.

Popper, Karl R. 1972. Of Clouds and Clocks, in Karl R. Popper (ed.), *Objective Knowledge: An Evolutionary Approach*. Oxford: Clarendon Press, 206–55.

Popper, Nathaniel. 2015a. *Digital Gold: Bitcoin and the Inside Story of the Misfits and Millionaires Trying to Reinvent Money*. New York: HarperCollins.

2015b. Decoding the Enigma of Bitcoin's Birth, *The New York Times*, May 17.

2015c. Bitcoin Technology Piques Interest on Wall St., *The New York Times*, August 31.

2015d. Quick Change. *The New York Times Magazine*, May 3, 48–53, 78, 80.

2016a. A Bitcoin Believer's Crisis of Faith, *The New York Times Sunday Business*, January 17, 1, 4.

2016b. The New Bitcoin Superpower, *The New York Times Sunday Business*, June 29, 1, 4.

2016c. Liking Bitcoin's Technology, if Not Bitcoin, *The New York Times*, October 14, B1, B4.

2017. Bitcoin Technology to Power Database Used by World's Largest Banks, *The New York Times*, January 10, B4.

Popper, Nathaniel and Steve Lohr. 2017. IBM Bets Big on the Arcane Idea Behind Bitcoin, *The New York Times Sunday Business*, March 5, 1, 4.

Porter, Patrick. 2016. Taking Uncertainty Seriously: Classical Realism and National Security. *European Journal of International Security* 1(2): 239–60.

Posen, Barry R. 1984. *The Sources of Military Doctrine: France, Britain, and Germany between the World Wars*. Ithaca, NY: Cornell University Press.

Press-Barnathan, Galia. 2013. Popular Culture (Pc) and International Conflicts: The Role of Popular Culture in Conflict Management and Conflict Resolution: A Preliminary Analytical Map, paper presented at the Annual Meeting of the International Studies Association, San Francisco, CA.

Price, Richard. 1998. Reversing the Gun Sights: Transnational Civil Society Targets Land Mines. *International Organization* 52(3): 613–44.

Prindle, David. 1993. *Risky Business: The Political Economy of Hollywood*. Boulder, CO: Westview.

Przeworski, Adam. 1991. *Democracy and the Market: Political and Economic Reforms in Eastern Europe and Latin America*. Cambridge University Press.

Pulver, Simone. 2002. Organising Business: Industry NGOs in the Climate Debates. *Greener Management International* 39 (Autumn): 55–67.

Puttnam, David and Neil Watson. 1998. *Movies and Money*. New York: Knopf

Rabasa, Angel et al. 2010. *Deradicalizing Islamic Extremists*. Santa Barbara, CA: Rand Corp.

Rappert, Brian and Richard Moyes. 2009. The Prohibition of Cluster Munitions: Setting International Precedents for Defining Inhumanity. *Nonproliferation Review* 16(2): 237–56.

Rathbun, Brian. 2007. Uncertainty about Uncertainty: Understanding the Multiple Meanings of a Crucial Concept in International Relations Theory. *International Studies Quarterly* 51(3): 533–57.

Raymaekers, Wim. 2015. Cryptocurrency Bitcoin: Disruption, Challenges and Opportunities. *Journal of Payments Strategy & Systems* 9(1): 30–40.

Reed, Isaac Arial. 2013. Power: Relational, Discursive, and Performative Dimensions. *Sociological Theory* 31(3): 193–218.

Renner, Michael. 1997. Small Arms, Big Impact: The Next Challenge of Disarmament, Worldwatch Paper No. 137. Washington, DC: Worldwatch Institute.

Rennison, Joe. 2014. LCH and CME have Enough Capital, says ISDA's O'Connor. *Risk Magazine*, 24 September, available at: www.risk.net/risk-management/2371886/lch-and-cme-have-enough-capital-says-isdas-oconnor.

Resor, James. 1997. Debt-for-Nature Swaps: A Decade of Experience and New Directions for the Future. *Unasylva* 48: 188, available at: www.fao.org/doc rep/w3247e/w3247e06.htm, last accessed September 11, 2017.

Reus-Smit, Christian. 1999. *The Moral Purpose of the State*. Princeton University Press.

2011. Struggles for Individual Rights and the Expansion of the International System. *International Organization* 65(2): 207–42.

2013. *Individual Rights and the Making of the International System*. Cambridge University Press.

Reuters. 2011. Kenyan Project Issues First REDD Credits-Point Carbon, February 9, available at: www.reuters.com/article/2011/02/09/ozabs-redd-point-carbon-idaFJOE7180DE20110209, last accessed September 11, 2017.

Reynolds, James Branson. 1909. Enforcement of the Chinese Exclusion Law. *Annals of the American Academy of Political Science* 34(2).

Rhodes, Edward. 1989. *Power and Madness: The Logic of Nuclear Coercion*. New York: Columbia University Press.

Rickli, Jean-Marc. 2008. European Small States' Military Policies after the Cold War: From Territorial to Niche Strategies. *Cambridge Review of International Affairs* 21(3): 307–25.

Riles, Annelise. 2010. Collateral Expertise: Legal Knowledge in the Global Financial Markets. *Current Anthropology* 51(6): 795–818.

2011. *Collateral Knowledge: Legal Reasoning in the Global Financial Markets*. University of Chicago Press.

Ringmar, Erik. 2007. Empowerment among Nations: A Sociological Perspective, in Felix Berenskoetter and M. J. Williams (eds.), *Power in World Politics*. New York: Routledge, 189–203.

Rogojanu, Angela and Liana Badea. 2014. The Issue of Competing Currencies: Case Study – Bitcoin. *Theoretical and Applied Economics* 21(1): 103–14.

Rose, Nikolas. 1999. *Powers of Freedom: Reframing Political Thought*. Cambridge University Press.

Rosenberg, S. A. and J. M. Barry. 1992. *The Transformed Cell: Unlocking the Mysteries of Cancer*. New York: Putnam.

Rosendorff, B. Peter and Helen V. Milner. 2001. The Optimal Design of International Trade Institutions: Uncertainty and Escape. *International Organization* 55(4): 829–57.

Rumsfeld, Donald. 2011. *Known and Unknown*. New York: Sentinel.

Rutherford, Kenneth R. 2000. The Evolving Arms Control Agenda: Implications of the Role of NGOs in Banning Antipersonnel Landmines. *World Politics* 53(1): 74–114.

2011. *Disarming States: The International Movement to Ban Landmines*. Santa Barbara, CA: Praeger.

Rutschman, Ana Santos. 2015. Weapons of Mass Construction: The Role of Intellectual Property in Nigeria's Film and Music Industries. *Emory International Law Review* 29: 673–704.

Sabel, Charles F. and David G. Victor. 2015. Governing Global Problems under Uncertainty: Making Bottom-Up Climate Policy Work. *Climatic Change* 144 (1): 15–27.

Sagan, Scott. 1993. *The Limits of Safety: Organizations, Accidents and Nuclear Weapons*. Princeton University Press.

Salter, Mark B. 2008. When the Exception Becomes the Rule: Borders, Sovereignty and Citizenship. *Citizenship Studies* 12(4): 365–80.

Sarotte, Mary Elise. 2014. *The Collapse: The Accidental Opening of the Berlin Wall.* New York: Basic Books.

Saxenian, Anna Lee. 2006. *The New Argonauts: Regional Advantage in a Global Economy.* Cambridge, MA: Harvard University Press.

Schedler, Andreas. 2013. *The Politics of Uncertainty: Sustaining and Subverting Electoral Authoritarianism.* Oxford University Press.

Schelling, Thomas C. 1963. *The Strategy of Conflict.* Oxford University Press.

Schelling, Thomas C. and Morton H. Halperin. 1961. *Strategy and Arms Control.* New York: Twentieth Century Fund.

Schmidt, Michael S. and Sewell Chan. 2016. NATO Will Send Ships to Aegean Sea to Deter Human Trafficking, *The New York Times*, February 11, available at: www.nytimes.com/2016/02/12/world/europe/nato-aegean-migrant-crisis.html?_r=0. last accessed July 31, 2016.

Schulman, Sarah. 2012. *Israel/Palestine and the Queer International.* Durham, NC: Duke University Press.

Schwartz, Vanessa R. 2007. *It's so French! Hollywood, Paris, and the Making of Cosmopolitan Film Culture.* University of Chicago Press.

Schweller, Randall L. 2014. *Maxwell's Demon and the Golden Apples: Global Discord in the New Millennium.* Baltimore, MD: Johns Hopkins University Press.

Scott, Allen J. 2005. *On Hollywood: The Place, the Industry.* Princeton University Press.

Scott, James C. 1985. *Weapons of the Weak: Everyday Forms of Peasant Resistance.* New Haven, CT: Yale University Press.

1990. *Domination and the Arts of Resistance: Hidden Transcripts.* New Haven, CT: Yale University Press.

1998. *Seeing Like a State: How Certain Schemes to Improve the Human Condition Have Failed.* New Haven, CT: Yale University Press.

Seabrooke, Leonard. 2006. *The Social Sources of Financial Power: Domestic Legitimacy and International Financial Orders.* Ithaca, NY: Cornell University Press.

2007. Varieties of Economic Constructivism in Political Economy: Uncertain Times Call for Disparate Measures. *Review of International Political Economy* 14(2): 371–85.

2010. Everyday Legitimacy and Institutional Change, in Andreas Gofas and Colin Hayes (eds.), *The Role of Ideas in Political Analysis: A Portrait of Contemporary Debates.* London: Routledge, 78–94.

Seckinelgin, Hakan. 2009. Global Activism and Sexualities in the Time of HIV/AIDS. *Contemporary Politics* 15(1): 103–18.

Segrave, Kerry. 1997. *American Films Abroad: Hollywood's Domination of the World's Movie Screens from the 1890s to the Present.* Jefferson, NC: McFarland.

Sending, Ole Jacob and Iver B. Neumann. 2006. Governance to Governmentality: Analyzing NGOs, States, and Power. *International Studies Quarterly* 50(3): 651–72.

Sengupta, Kim. 2016. Inside ISIS: How UK Spies Infiltrated Terrorist Leadership, *The Independent*, October 19, available at: www.independent.co.uk/news/world/middle-east/isis-uk-spies-mosul-attack-latest-fear-desertions-revenge-traitors-executions-a7370451.html, last accessed September 6, 2017.

Shambaugh, David. 2013. *China Goes Global: The Partial Power*. Oxford University Press.

Sheridan, Alan. 1980. *The Will to Truth*. London: Tavistock.

Shevtsova, Maryna. 2017. Exporting "European" Values: Europeanization and Promotion of LGBTI Rights in Third Countries, PhD dissertation, Humboldt University.

Shubik, Martin. 2014. Simecs, Ithaca Hours, Berkshares, Bitcoins and Walmarts, Cowles Foundation Discussion Paper No. 1947, Yale University.

Sidel, Robin. 2014. Hard Times for a Bitcoin Evangelist, *The Wall Street Journal*, February 6, C1.

Siener, William H. 2008. Through the Back Door: Evading the Chinese Exclusion Act along the Niagara Frontier, 1900–1924. *Journal of American Ethnic History* 27(4): 34–70.

Sil, Rudra and Peter J. Katzenstein (eds.). 2010. *Beyond Paradigms: Analytic Eclecticism in the Study of World Politics*. New York: Palgrave.

Silverman, Gary. 2016. NBA Moneyballer Sam Hinkie Misses the Hoop, *Financial Times*, April 8, available at: www.ft.com/cms/s/0/07e606a2-fda7-1 1e5-b3f6-11d5706b613b.html#ixzz45MOSHkgz, last accessed April 2, 2017.

Skalamera, Morena. 2014. Booming Synergies in Sino-Russian Natural Gas Partnership, White Paper. Cambridge, MA: Harvard Kennedy School.

2015. Sino-Russian Energy Relations Reversed: A New Little Brother. *Open Democracy*, December 22.

Slack, Jeremy et al. 2016. The Geography of Border Militarization: Violence, Death and Health in Mexico and the United States. *Journal of Latin American Geography* 15(1): 7–32.

Slaughter, Anne-Marie. 2017. *The Chessboard and the Web: Strategies of Connection in a Networked World*. New Haven, CT: Yale University Press.

Smith, Adam. 1853. *Theory of Moral Sentiments*. London: Henry G. Bohn.

Smith, David. 2014. Where is Bitcoin Growing Faster Than the Internet, *Benziga*, available at: www.benzinga.com/tech/14/07/4699359/where-is-bit coin-growing-faster-than-the-internet, last accessed September 29, 2014.

Sobel, Andrew C. 1999. *State Institutions, Private Incentives, Global Capital*. Ann Arbor, MI: University of Michigan Press.

Soble, Jonathan. 2015. Chief of Failed Exchange for Bitcoin is Arrested, *The New York Times*, August 2.

Solomon, Ty. 2014. The Affective Underpinnings of Soft Power. *European Journal of International Relations* 20(3): 720–41.

Solum, Lawrence B. 1987. On the Indeterminacy Crisis: Critiquing Critical Dogma. *University of Chicago Law Review* 54(2): 462–503.

Soros, George. 2009. General Theory of Reflexivity, *Financial Times*, October 26, available at: www.ft.com/intl/cms/s/2/0ca06172-bfe9-11de-aed2-00144fea b49a.html.

Spar, Debora L. 1994. *The Cooperative Edge: The Internal Politics of International Cartels*. Ithaca, NY: Cornell University Press.

Spener, David. 2009. *Clandestine Crossings: Migrants and Coyotes on the Texas–Mexico Border*. Ithaca, NY: Cornell University Press.

Ssebuyira, Martin and Risdel Kasasira. 2014. I'll Do Business with the Russians Instead, Museveni Tells Obama. *Africa Review*, available at: www.africare view.com/News/-/979180/2219142/-/bht82z/-/index.html, last accessed December 5, 2015.

Stafford, Philip. 2015. Banks and Exchanges Turn to Blockchain, *Financial Times*, June 30.

Steele, Brent J. 2010. *Defacing Power: The Aesthetics of Insecurity in Global Politics*. Ann Arbor, MI: University of Michigan Press.

Stern, Jessica and J. M. Berger. 2015. *ISIS: The State of Terror*. New York: HarperCollins.

Stern, Jonathan and Howard Rogers. 2012. The Transition to Hub-based Gas Pricing in Continental Europe, in Jonathan Stern (ed.), *The Pricing of Internationally Traded Gas*. Oxford University Press.

Stoppard, Tom. 1993. *Arcadia*. New York: Farrar, Straus & Giroux.

Storper, Michael 1993. Flexible Specialization in Hollywood: A Response to Aksoy and Robins. *Cambridge Journal of Economics* 17: 479–84.

Strange, Susan. 1988. *States and Markets: An Introduction to International Political Economy*. New York: Blackwell.

1996. *The Retreat of the State: The Diffusion of Power in the World Economy*. Cambridge University Press.

Strauss, Robert B. (ed.). 2008. *The Landmark Thucydides: A Comprehensive Guide to the Peloponnesian War*. New York: Free Press.

Streeck, Wolfgang. 2016. *How Will Capitalism End? Essays on a Failing System*. New York: Verso.

Streeck, Wolfgang and Kathleen Thelen. 2005. Introduction: Institutional Change in Advanced Political Economies, in Wolfgang Streeck and Kathleen Thelen (eds.), *Beyond Continuity: Institutional Change in Advanced Political Economies*. Oxford University Press, 1–39.

Suchman, Mark C. 1995. Managing Legitimacy: Strategic and Institutional Approaches. *Academy of Management Review* 20(1): 571–610.

Summers, Lawrence. 1991. The Scientific Illusion in Empirical Macroeconomics. *Scandinavian Journal of Economics* 93(2): 129–48.

Surowiecki, James. 2011. Cryptocurrency. *Technology Review* (Sept./Oct.): 106–7.

Susen, Simon. 2014. 15 Theses on Power. *Filozofija I Društvo* 25(3): 7–28.

Swann, Paul. 1994. The Little State Department: Washington and Hollywood's Rhetoric of the Postwar Audience, in David W. Ellwood and Ron Kroes (eds.), *Hollywood in Europe: Experiences of a Cultural Hegemony*. Amsterdam: VU University Press, 176–95.

Swiebel, Joke. 2009. Lesbian, Gay, Bisexual and Transgender Human Rights: The Search for an International Strategy. *Contemporary Politics* 15(1): 19–35.

Swimelar, Safia. 2016. The Struggle for Visibility and Equality: Bosnian LGBT Rights Developments, in Koen Slootmaeckers, Heleen Touquet, and Peter Vermeersch (eds.), *The EU Enlargement and Gay Politics*. Basingstoke: Palgrave Macmillan, 175–202.

Symons, Jonathan and Dennis Altman. 2015. International Norm Polarization: Sexuality as a Subject of Human Rights Protection. *International Theory* 7(1): 61–95.

Taleb, Nassim Nicholas. 2010. *The Black Swan.* New York: Random House.

Tannenwald, Nina. 2005. Ideas and Explanation: Advancing the Theoretical Agenda. *Journal of Cold War Studies* 7(2): 13–42.

Tapscott, Don. 2016. *Blockchain Revolution: How the Technology Behind Bitcoin is Changing Money, Business, and the World.* New York: Portfolio/Penguin.

Tarrow, Sidney. 1994. *Power in Movement: Social Movements and Contentious Politics.* Cambridge University Press.

Taylor, Lance. 2010. *Maynard's Revenge: The Collapse of Free Market Macroeconomics.* Cambridge, MA: Harvard University Press.

Taylor, Monique. 2014. *The Chinese State, Oil, and Energy Security.* New York: Palgrave Macmillan.

Tepe, Daniela. 2011. *The Myth about Global Civil Society: Domestic Politics to Ban Landmines.* New York: Palgrave Macmillan.

Tetlock, Philip E. 2005. *Expert Political Judgment: How Good is It? How Can We Know?* Princeton University Press.

Tetlock, Philip and Dan Gardner. 2015. *Superforecasting: The Art and Science of Prediction.* New York: Random House.

Tett, Gillian. 2009. *Fool's Gold: The Inside Story of J.P. Morgan and How Wall St. Greed Corrupted its Bold Dream and Created a Financial Catastrophe.* New York: Free Press.

Thomas, Mark. 2014. Everything You Need to Know About Bitcoin, *Money Management,* available at: www.moneymanagement.comau/analysis/invest ment/2014/everything-you-need-to-know-about-bitcoin, last accessed September 29, 2014.

Tilly, Charles. 2000. How Do Relations Store Histories? *Annual Review of Sociology* 26 (August): 721–23.

Tomz, Michael and Mark L. J. Wright. 2013. Empirical Research on Sovereign Debt and Default. *Annual Review of Economics* 5: 247–72.

Torgovnik, Jonathan. 2003. *Bollywood Dream: An Exploration of the Motion Picture Industry and its Culture in India.* London: Phaidon.

Toska, Silvana. 2017. Rebel Passions: How Emotions Fuel the Diffusion of Rebellion, PhD dissertation, Cornell University.

Trautman, Lawrence. 2014. Virtual Currencies; Bitcoin and What Now after Liberty Reserve, Silk Road, and Mt. Gox? *Richmond Journal of Law & Technology* 20(4): 1–108.

Trumbull, Gunnar. 2012. *Strength in Numbers: The Political Power of Weak Interests.* Ithaca, NY: Cornell University Press.

Tsika, Noah A. 2015. *Nollywood Stars: Media and Migration in West Africa and the Diaspora.* Bloomington, IN: Indiana University Press.

Tsingou, Eleni. 2006. The Governance of OTC Derivatives Markets, in Peter Mooslechner et al. (eds.), *The Political Economy of Financial Market Regulation.* Cheltenham: Edward Elgar, 89–114.

Turpin, Jonathan B. 2014. Bitcoin: The Economic Case for a Global, Virtual Currency Operating in an Unexplored Legal Framework. *Indiana Journal of Global Legal Studies* 21(1): 335–68.

United Nations Framework – Convention on Climate Change (UNFCCC). 2000. Mechanisms Pursuant to Articles 6, 12 and 17 of the Kyoto Protocol, FCCC/CP/2000/MISC.2.

2002. Modalities and Procedures for a Clean Development Mechanism, as Defined in Article 12 of the Kyoto Protocol, FCCC/CP/2001/13/Add.2, Decision 17/CP.7, available at: http://unfccc.int/resource/docs/cop7/13a0 2.pdf#page=20.

2005. Reducing Emissions from Deforestation in Developing Countries: Approaches to Stimulate Action, submissions from Parties, FCCC/CP/ 2005/MISC.1, available at: http://unfccc.int/resource/docs/2005/cop11/en g/misc01.pdf.

2007. Report of the Conference of the Parties on its thirteenth session, held in Bali, December 3–15, 2007, FCCC/CP/2007/6/Add.1.

2008a. Views on Outstanding Methodological Issues Related to Policy Approaches and Positive Incentives to Reduce Emissions from Deforestation and Forest Degradation in Developing Countries, available at: http://unfccc.int/resource/docs/2008/sbsta/eng/misc04.pdf.

2008b. Views Regarding the Work Programme of the Ad Hoc Working Group on Long-term Cooperative Action under the Convention, FCCC/ AWGLCA/2008/MISC.1.

United Nations General Assembly. 1952. The Rights of Peoples and Nations to Self-Determination, A/RES/637 (VII), December 16.

United Nations. 1949. *Yearbook of the United Nations 1948–49*. New York: UN Office of Public Information.

1951. *Yearbook of the United Nations 1951*. New York: UN Office of Public Information.

2006. *Report of the International Law Commission: Fifty-Eighth Session June– August 2006*. United Nations: United Nations Publications.

Vail, Kenneth III et al. 2010. A Terror Management Analysis of the Psychological Functions of Religion. *Personality and Social Psychology Review* 14(1): 84–94.

Varottil, Umakanth. 2011. Sovereign Debt Documentation and the Pari Passu Clause, in Robert W. Kolb (ed.), *Sovereign Debt: From Safety to Default*. Hoboken, NJ: John Wiley, 227–34.

Velde, François R. 2013. Bitcoin: A Primer. *Chicago Fed Letter* 317 (December).

Vernon, Raymond. 1971. *Sovereignty at Bay*. New York: Basic Books.

Vigna, Paul and Michael J. Casey. 2015. *The Age of Cryptocurrency: How Bitcoin and Digital Money are Challenging the Global Economic Order*. New York: St. Martin's Press.

Vogt, Wendy. 2013. Crossing Mexico: Structural Violence and the Commodification of Undocumented Central American Migrants. *American Ethnologist* 40: 764–80.

Wagner, Gernot and Richard Zeckhauser. 2016. Confronting Deep and Persistent Climate Uncertainty, Harvard Kennedy School, Faculty Research Working Paper Series, August, available at: http://gwagner.com/ wp-content/uploads/Wagner-Zeckhauser-Hks-2016-Deep-and-persistent-climate-uncertainty.pdf.

Wagnleitner, Reinhold. 1994. American Cultural Diplomacy, the Cinema, and the Cold War in Central Europe, in David W. Ellwood and Ron Kroes (eds.), *Hollywood in Europe: Experiences of a Cultural Hegemony*. Amsterdam: VU University Press, 196–210.

Wagnleitner, Reinhold and Elaine Tyler May. 2000. Here, There, and Everywhere: Introduction, in Reinhold Wagnleitner and Elaine Tyler May (eds.), *"Here, There and Everywhere": The Foreign Politics of American Popular Culture*. Hanover, NH: University Press of New England, 1–13.

Walker, Jeremy and Melinda Cooper. 2011. Genealogies of Resilience: From Systems Ecology to the Political Economy of Crisis Adaptation. *Security Dialogue* 42(2): 143–60.

Walters, William. 2012. *Governmentality: Critical Encounters*. London: Routledge.

Waltz, Kenneth N. 1964. The Stability of a Bipolar World. *Daedalus* 93(3): 881–909.

1993. The Emerging Structure of International Politics. *International Security* 18(2): 44–79.

Wasko, Janet. 1994. *Hollywood in the Information Age: Beyond the Silver Screen*. Austin, TX: University of Texas Press.

2003. *How Hollywood Works*. Thousand Oaks, CA: Sage.

2005. Critiquing Hollywood: The Political Economy of Motion Pictures, in Charles C. Moul (ed.), *A Concise Handbook of Movie Industry Economics*. Cambridge University Press, 5–31.

Waterman, David. 2005. *Hollywood's Road to Riches*. Cambridge, MA: Harvard University Press.

Watson, James D. 2003. *DNA: The Secret of Life*. New York: Knopf.

Watson, Robert T., Ian R. Noble, Bert Bolin, N. H. Ravindranath, David J. Verardo, and David J. Dokken (eds.). 2000. *Land Use, Land-Use Change, and Forestry: A Special Report of the Intergovernmental Panel on Climate Change*, 1st edn. Cambridge University Press.

Weaver, Warren. 1948. Science and Complexity. *American Scientist* 36(4): 536–44.

Weber, Beat. 2016. Bitcoin and the Legitimacy Crisis of Money. *Cambridge Journal of Economics* 40(1): 17–41.

Weber, Max. 1925. *Wirtschaft und Gesellschaft*, 2nd edn. Tübingen: J. C. B. Mohr (Paul Siebeck).

Weidemaier, W. Mark C. and Mitu Gulati. 2015. The Relevance of Law to Sovereign Debt. *Annual Review of Law and Social Science* 11: 395–408.

Weisberg, Jacob. 1998. Keeping the Boom from Busting. *The New York Times Sunday Magazine*, July 19, available at: www.nytimes.com/1998/07/19/magazine/keeping-the-boom-from-busting.html?pagewanted=all, last accessed January 29, 2016.

Weiss, Meredith L. and Michael J. Bosia. 2013. *Global Homophobia: States, Movements, and the Politics of Oppression*. Urbana-Champaign, IL: University of Illinois Press.

Wendt, Alexander. 1998. On Constitution and Causation in International Relations. *Review of International Studies* 24: 101–17.

2001. Driving with the Rearview Mirror: On the Rational Science of Institutional Design. *International Organization* 55(4): 1019–49.

2015. *Quantum Mind and Social Science: Unifying Physical and Social Ontology.* Cambridge University Press.

Werksman, Jacob. 1998. The Clean Development Mechanism: Unwrapping the Kyoto Surprise. *Review of European Community and International Environmental Law* 7(2): 147–58.

Weyland, Kurt. 2012. The Arab Spring: Why the Surprising Similarities with the Revolutionary Wave of 1848? *Perspectives on Politics* 10(4): 917–34.

Whitehouse, Tammy. 2014. Virtual Currencies Come with Real Accounting Concerns, *Compliance Week*, January 14.

Wike, Richard. 2015. Widespread Concerns About Extremism in Muslim Nations, and Little Support for It, PEW Research Center, available at: www.pewresearch.org/fact-tank/2015/02/05/extremism-in-muslim-nations.

Wildau, Gabriel. 2017. China Probes Bitcoin Exchanges amid Capital Flight Fears, *Financial Times*, January 10, available at: www.ft.com/content/bad16 a88-d6fd-11e6-944b-e7eb37a6aa8e, last accessed January 10, 2017.

Wilkinson, Cai. 2014. Putting "Traditional Values" into Practice: The Rise and Contestation of Anti-Homopropaganda Laws in Russia. *Journal of Human Rights* 13(3): 363–79.

Williams, Jody. 1997. Nobel Lecture, Oslo, Norway, available at: www.nobel prize.org/nobel_prizes/peace/laureates/1997/williams-lecture.html,   last accessed September 26, 2016.

Wilson, Angelia R. 2013. *Why Europe is Lesbian and Gay Friendly (and Why America Never Will Be)*. Albany, NY: SUNY Press.

Wohlleben, Peter. 2017. *The Hidden Life of Trees: What They Feel, How They Communicate – Discoveries from a Secret World.* Vancouver: Greystone.

Woll, Cornelia. 2014. *The Power of Inaction: Bank Bailouts in Comparison.* Ithaca, NY: Cornell University Press.

Wood, Elisabeth Jean. 2003. *Insurgent Collective Action and Civil War in El Salvador.* Cambridge University Press.

Wu, Chen Y. and Vivek K. Pandey. 2014. The Value of Bitcoin in Enhancing the Efficiency of an Investor's Portfolio. *Journal of Financial Planning* 27(9): 44–52.

Yermack, David. 2013. Is Bitcoin a Real Currency? An Economic Appraisal. Cambridge, MA: National Bureau of Economic Research.

Ylikoski, Petri. 2013. Causal and Constitutive Explanation Compared. *Erkenn* 78: 277–97.

Yoffie, David B. and Michael A. Cusumano. 2015. *Strategy Rules: Five Timeless Lessons from Bill Gates, Andy Grove, and Steve Jobs.* New York: HarperCollins.

Young, Margaret C. 2012. *Regime Interaction in International Law: Facing Fragmentation.* Cambridge University Press.

Young, Oran R., Frans Berkhout, Gilberto C. Gallopin, Marco A. Janssen, Elinor Ostrom, and Sander van der Leeuw. 2006. The Globalization of Socio-Ecological Systems: An Agenda for Scientific Research. *Global Environmental Change* 16(3): 304–16.

Zepeda, Rodrigo. 2014. *The ISDA Master Agreement: The Derivatives Risk Management Tool of the 21st Century?* Amazon Digital Services (Kindle book).

Zhao, Suisheng (ed.). 2014. *China's Search for Energy Security.* London: Routledge.

Ziliak, Stephen T. and Deirdre N. McCloskey. 2008. *The Cult of Statistical Significance: How Standard Error Costs Us Jobs, Justice, and Lives.* Ann Arbor, MI: University of Michigan Press.

Žižek, Slavoj. 1999. You May! *London Review of Books* 21(6): 3–6.

Zuckerman, Ezra. 1999. The Categorical Imperative: Securities Analysts and the Illegitimacy Discount. *American Journal of Sociology* 104(5): 1398–438.

　　2012. Construction, Concentration, and (Dis)Continuities in Social Valuations. *Annual Review of Sociology* 38: 223–45.

Index